United in Endeavour

A History of
Abbey United / CambridgeUnited
Football Club 1912-1988

Written and researched by

Paul M Daw

Published in 1988 by Dawn Publications (Bar Hill)
84 The Spinney, Bar Hill, Cambridge. CB3 8SU

© Dawn Publications (Bar Hill) 1988

ISBN 0-9514108-0-6

Designed and typeset by
Electronic Images
46 High Street
Milton
Cambridge
CB4 4DF

Printed by
Target Litho
Cottenham

RB : HB

Further copies of this book are obtainable from P M Daw, Dawn Publications (Bar Hill),
84 The Spinney, Bar Hill, Cambridge. CB3 8SU
Telephone (0954) 82647

© All rights reserved. No part of this publication may be reproduced, stored in a retrieval system, or transmitted in any form, or by any means, whether electronic, mechanical, photocopying, recording or otherwise, without prior permission of Dawn Publications (Bar Hill) except for brief passages in criticism or review.

Contents

Map of Cambridge	4
Acknowledgements	5
Introduction	7
Formative Years	9
The Twenties	13
The Thirties	29
The Forties	43
The Fifties	55
The Sixties	85
The Seventies	121
The Eighties	155
Statistics	183

Map of Cambridge

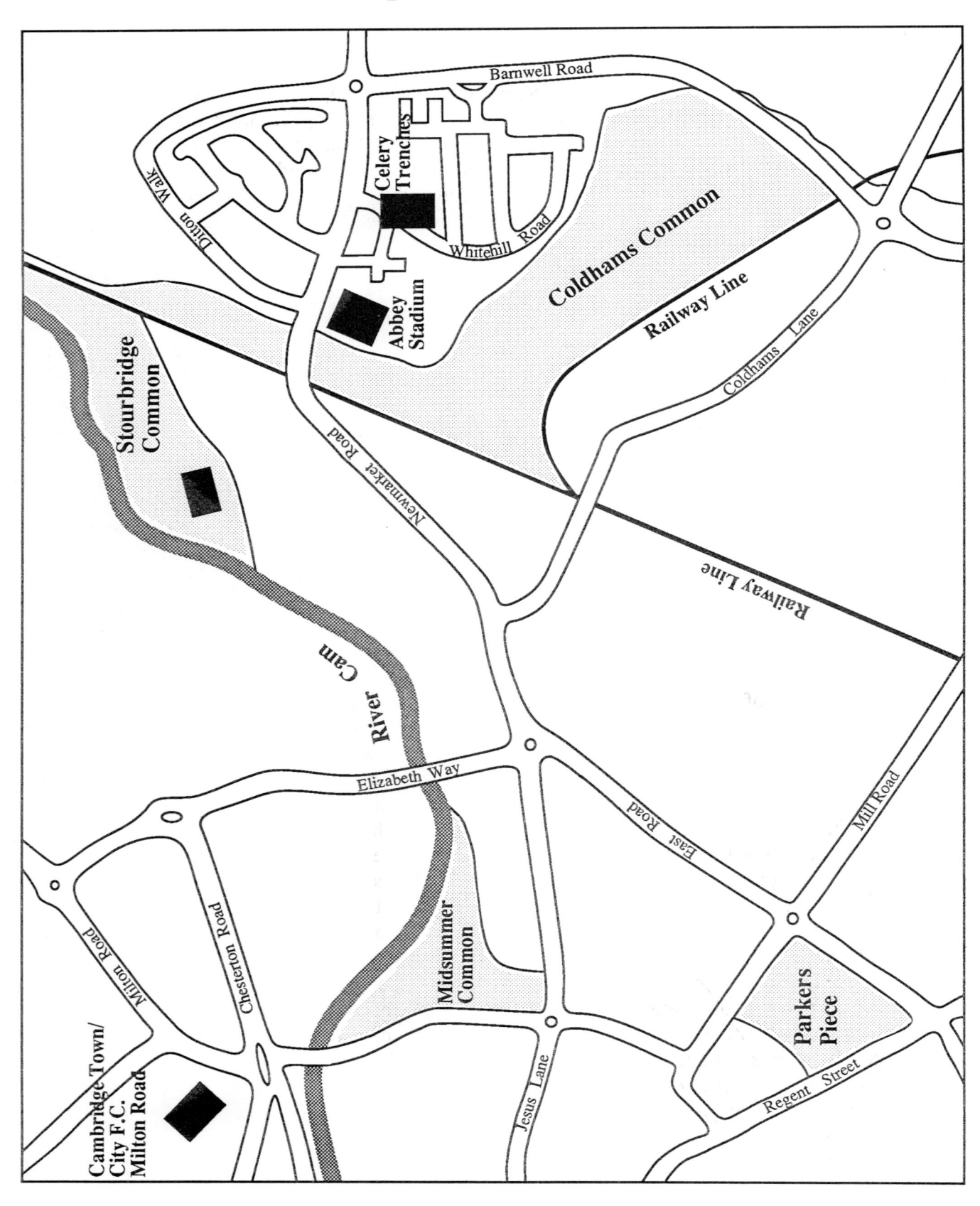

ACKNOWLEDGEMENTS

When I was appointed as Secretary of Cambridge United Football Club in April 1984, I was surprised to find that the Club had virtually no record of its history. Because there were frequent requests for information on the Club, mainly from children working on school projects, but sometimes from supporters in other countries, I decided to try and compile as complete a list as possible of the Club's final league tables and cup results.

Initial progress with my research was good, and with the help of the Club's meticulous Statistician, Colin Faiers, I was able to collect a substantial number of final tables and cup results for the first team, going back to the Club's Cambs League days as Abbey United. Much of this early research was typed up for me by Amanda Castle, to whom I owe a great debt, and offer my sincere thanks.

To fill in the missing gaps in my research I then started delving into the archives of the Cambridgeshire Collection on the Third Floor of the Lion Yard Library in Cambridge. I have nothing but the utmost admiration and praise for Mike Petty, Chris Jakes and the other members of their staff, who for over three years of reading through their extensive collection of local newspapers, have always been helpful, courteous and extremely efficient.

Undoubtedly, filling in the missing gaps has been the most pains-taking and time-consuming part of my research, and frustratingly some odd results and final league tables which were not reported in the press, have not been obtained, despite exhaustive efforts. I have visited the British Newspaper Library at Collindale, London, on numerous occasions to try and fill in some of these "gaps", and would like to express my gratitude, not only for their extensive collection of newspapers, but also for their co-operation.

This type of detective work is always interesting, but the most pleasurable part of my research has involved visiting former players and other members of the Club to reminisce and exchange information. Without exception I have received wonderful hospitality, and have had some very enjoyable evenings talking about the "good times". During these visits everyone has been very helpful and trusting, in loaning their treasured photographs to me so that I could have them copied. David Campbell has undertaken the task of copying over a hundred photographs for me, often managing to improve upon the quality of time-worn originals, and for his help I am extremely grateful.

The *Cambridge Evening News*, and their forerunners the *Cambridge Daily News*, and *Cambridge Independent Press*, have provided a most valuable photographic record of the Club's progress. Many of the photographs in this book emanate from their files, and I would like to take this opportunity of acknowledging Cedric Tarrant for his help in supplying these photographs and allowing me the use of them. I also wish to thank other members of the *Cambridge Evening News* staff who have helped with my research, particularly Randall Butt and Jonathan Lang.

As my research has progressed the project has tended to 'snowball' in size, to the stage where I have now tried to compile a complete list of the Club's past matches, including where possible dates, results, goalscorers and attendances. When this list is as complete as possible I intend to donate a copy to the Cambridgeshire Collection in the Lion Yard Library, together with a large presentation book including the complete collection of my photographs and other items of interest, for viewing by the general public.

I have been fortunate to obtain the willing help of Diane Ilott for proof reading the text and statistical information in the book. I am indebted to her thoroughness and attention to detail.

To all of the people who have helped in any way towards the publication of the book, who I have not mentioned, I extend a sincere thank you. Finally my biggest debt of gratitude must go to my wife and close family, who have put up with the inevitable disruption that such a project causes. To them I dedicate this book.

Paul M Daw

WE'RE TALKING FOOTBALL.

"Football is not a matter of life and death. It's much more important than that." BILL SHANKLY.

"Soccer is the biggest thing that's happened in creation, bigger than any 'ism' you can name".
ALAN BROWN,
Sunderland manager, 1968.

"And they were lucky to get nil".
LEN SHACKLETON,
after six goal debut for Newcastle in 13-0 defeat of Newport, 1946.

"It is our new tactics. We equalise before the others have scored".
DANNY BLANCHFLOWER, 1958.

SOURCE: THE BOOK OF FOOTBALL QUOTATIONS, PETER BALL AND PHIL SHAW (STANLEY PAUL. AN IMPRINT OF CENTURY HUTCHINSON LTD).

YOU'RE BETTER OFF TALKING TO BARCLAYS

INTRODUCTION

Cambridge has long been proud of its cricket tradition, particularly the fact that the legendary Jack Hobbs played his early cricket on Parker's Piece, but few people are aware that Cambridge figures prominently in the game of association football.

As early as 1575, Cambridge University students were forbidden to take part in "unlawful, hurtful pernicious, and unhonest games". This instruction was almost certainly the sequel to a violent football match at Chesterton, which ended in a 'great rumpus', after which the Vice-Chancellor prohibited the game, except in the colleges. Later on students were not allowed "to wear long or curled locks", and it was declared that "the hurtful and unscholarly like exercise of football and meetings tending to that end to from henceforth utterly cease".

Football in various forms has been played throughout the country for several centuries, and some of the traditional Shrove Tuesday games, which sometimes involve whole crowds of players, are still played to this day. The game of football as we know it today developed in schools and colleges, but as each school had its own rules there were often arguments about which rules were used.

The first set of rules which resemble the present Laws of the Game were written at Cambridge University around 1848, and these 'Cambridge Rules' were posted on Parker's Piece, two years after the earliest attempts to play organized football on the Piece. It was at Trinity College where a number of ex-public schoolboys, who had come to the University, decided to formulate a complete set of laws. As the students graduated and entered professions they took their ideas and enthusiasms with them and gradually their code was adopted.

One of the earliest sets of rules published was called 'The Simplest Game'. It consisted of ten rules which were modified with improvements, and became known as the Cambridge University Football Rules. It was these that formed the basis of the first Football Association Laws of the Game when the Association was formed in 1863.

In the north of the country many clubs adopted the 'Sheffield Rules' which were drawn up by Sheffield F.C., the oldest football club in the world. Other rules were also used in different parts of the country, including those compiled by Uppingham School in 1862, and Blackheath, who are now reputed for their rugby football.

At an early meeting of the Football Association the Cambridge group found themselves to be in disagreement with the officials representing Blackheath and a split took place. The main issue of contention was a clause preferred by the Cambridge group that "no player was to be held, and hacked at the same time".

The formation of the Football League in 1888 increased the popularity of the game which became more widespread, and by doing so helped to standardize the rules used throughout the country. The Football Association's Laws of the Game have been amended many times over the last century, but these have formed the basis of the game which is now the most popular in the world.

Today the rules are governed by F.I.F.A. (the Federation of International Football Associations), but the current Laws of the Game owe their origins to the enthusiasm of a band of Cambridge scholars.

Abbey United Football Club

(Founded 1912).

Affiliated to the Football Association and Cambs. League, Div. I.

Winners of Cambs. League, Div. III., 1921-22; Winners of Cambs. League, Div. II., 1922-23; Runners-up Cambs. League, Div. I., 1923-24; Holders Cambs. Challenge Cup, 1924-25; Holders Cottenham Nursing Cup, 1924-25; Holders Chatteris Works Cup, 1924-25; Joint Holders Creake Charity Shield, 1924-25; Winners Cambs. League, Div. I., 1925-26; Holders Creake Charity Shield, 1925-26; Runners-up Cambs. Challenge Cup, 1925-26.

President: H. C. FRANCIS, Esq.

Chairman:
F. MORTLOCK,
11, Garlic Row.

Hon. Sec.:
C. E. ELSDEN,
69, Stanley Road.

Hon. Treas.:
H. BOWMAN,
479, Newmarket Road.

Headquarters & Dressing Room:
Dog & Pheasant, Newmarket Road.

Colours:
Black & Amber.

Oct 8 1926

Balance Sheet Stearn's Benefit

	£	s	d
Tickets Sold 771	19	5	6
Old Chesterton F.C. 10/- Donation		10	0
A. E. Rogers — 4/- "		4	0
Abbey Un. v Railway (Gate)	1	9	3
Abbey Un. v R.A.F.	3	10	3
	£24	19	0

Cheque made out for £25. Twenty-Five Pounds.

Audited & found correct } E. Bridges
W. Harrison

Copy of Abbey United Football Club's letterheaded paper showing the statement of accounts in respect of Mr W Stearn's testimonial match and noting that the foundation date of the Club was in 1912.

Chapter One

THE FORMATIVE YEARS

A club known as Cambridge United was formed in 1909 and immediately staked a claim to be one of the most senior football clubs in the area by attracting the best players from other clubs in Cambridge and the surrounding towns. The Club quickly built up a strong fixture list and a good reputation, but after five years their brief history was brought to a close by the outbreak of the First World War, and the Club was not re-formed after the cessation of hostilities in 1918.

This early 'Cambridge United' was not connected in any way with the present Club, which was originally known as Abbey United until they changed their name in 1951. For some time it was believed that Abbey United F.C. was formed shortly after the 1914-18 World War, but my research has revealed that a club known as Abbey United was in existence before the First World War. A copy of the Club's letter-headed paper in 1926 clearly states that Abbey United F.C. was founded in 1912, and research in the local newspapers has revealed that Abbey United were playing football in the 1913-14 season. The Club had connections with the Abbey Rifle Shooting Club, which competed in an organized league of rifle shooting clubs in Cambridge at that time.

The football club's formation was so inauspicious that it is believed that the first match was arranged under a street lamp in the Stanley Road area of Cambridge. Not surprisingly no written records of an inaugural meeting of Abbey United F.C. exist, and indeed any friendly games that the Club did play in the 1912-13 season were not considered to be of sufficient importance to be reported in the local press.

The first mention of Abbey United in the newspapers occurred in the Saffron Walden edition of the *Cambridge Independent Press* on Friday 21st November 1913, which gave the following fixture:

Saturday 22nd November 1913
Friendly
On Midsummer Common.
Abbey United   v   M.J.Drew's XI

Unfortunately no result was given in the newspapers the following week, so it is not known whether the game was played or not. However, the following game was reported in the same newspaper two weeks later, and therefore has the distinction of being Abbey United's first recorded match:

Thursday 4th December 1913
Friendly
Abbey United   4,   0   St. Phillip's

This match was played on Midsummer Common on Thursday afternoon and resulted in a win for Abbey United as stated above. The scorers were: Blunt, Hancock, Coulson, and Maltby.
Abbey United: Pink; Golding, W.J. Howlett; Codling, Smith, Hancock; H. Smith, Deers, Maltby, Coulson, and Blunt.

That season the Club played five other matches, all on Midsummer Common, and finished the season with the satisfying record: Played 6, Won 5, Drawn 0, Lost 1, Goals for 23, Goals against 10.

The outbreak of hostilities in 1914 brought a sudden end to all football, by Government Order, but shortly after the end of the First World War a meeting of a number of young enthusiasts resident in the Abbey Ward of Cambridge was held to re-form the Abbey United Football Club. At the meeting the Reverend W.Carr, Curate of the nearby Abbey Church, was elected as the Club's President. Mr. S.J.Brown became Secretary of the Club and Mr. R.J.Wadsworth, who many years later became Chairman of the Board of Directors of Cambridge United Football Club Limited, began his long association with the Club by becoming a committee member.

Abbey United played their first game after the War at their new home ground on Stourbridge Common on Saturday 20th September 1919. The game resulted in a win for United by 6 goals to 3 against Ditton Rovers. In all seven games were played that season, five of them on Stourbridge Common, with the relatively successful record of: Played 7, Won 3, Drawn 3, Lost 1, Goals for 18, Goals against 9.

In 1920-21 Abbey United did not play any friendly matches, but they did enter a six-a-side football contest at Littleport F.C. with twenty other clubs on Whit Monday 15th May 1921 at which 1,350 persons paid for admission. The games were of 20 minutes' duration and 4 points were awarded for a goal, 2 points for a 'side goal', and 1 point for a corner. Abbey United beat Kerry Hill by 5 points to 2 in the Preliminary Round and then beat Cambridge Rovers 19 points to nil in the First Round. They then withdrew from the competition in the Second Round (Quarter-finals) presumably because the competition lasted over 8 hours and they had to get back to Cambridge before its conclusion.

A team from the March G.E.R. club eventually ran out winners of the competition, beating Chatteris Engineers in the Final.

1913-14 SEASON

Saturday 22nd November 1913
Friendly
On Midsummer Common.
Abbey United v M.J.Drew's XI

Thursday 4th December 1913
Friendly
Abbey United 4 0 St. Phillip's

"The match was played on Midsummer Common on Thursday afternoon and resulted in a win for Abbey United as stated above. The scorers were: Blunt, Hancock, Coulson, and Maltby.
Abbey United: Pink; Golding, W.J.Howlett; Codling, Smith, Hancock, H. Smith, Deers, Maltby, Coulson, and Blunt."

Thursday 8th January 1914
Friendly
Abbey United 7 1 Hallack & Bonns 2nd XI

"Played on Midsummer Common yesterday afternoon. Coulson (2); Deards (2); Codling, Golding and Maltby scored for the winners who played with ten men."

Saturday 24th January 1914
Friendly
Saint's Building Works 4 1 **Abbey United**

"Played on Midsummer Common on Saturday. Saint's were the first to become in evidence. Hume scored two goals for them, then Maltby did the needful for United, and at half-time Saint's were leading by 2 goals to 1. In the second half Hume and Barker scored for the Works, and then won by 4 goals to 1."

Saturday 14th February 1914
FRIENDLY
Abbey United 4 0 University Press 3rd XI

"Played on Midsummer Common on Saturday afternoon and ended in a victory for the United by 4 goals to nil. Thurston (2), Whybrow, and Smith were the scorers."

Thursday 12th March 1914
Friendly
Abbey United 5 1 People's Mission

Saturday 28th March 1914
Friendly
Abbey United 2 1 People's Mission

"These teams met in a friendly match on Saturday, and the game ended in a win for the United by 2 goals to 1. Thurston and Mathews scored for the winners, and Coe for the Mission."

1919-20 SEASON

Saturday 20th September 1919
Friendly
Abbey United 6 3 Ditton Rovers

"Played on Stourbridge Common on Saturday afternoon, and ended in a win for the United by 6 goals to 3."

Saturday 10th January 1920
Friendly
Abbey United 7 1 Star Rovers

"Played on Saturday on Stourbridge Common, Abbey United won the toss and the Stars played against a very strong wind. The Abbey had practically all the play in the first half. Towards full-time the Stars broke through the Abbey defence and Stevens scored. F.Stevens (3), J. Edwards (2), J. Livermore and Arnold scored for the Abbey."

Saturday 17th January 1920
Friendly
Abbey United 0 0 Cherry Hinton

"Played on Stourbridge Common on Saturday. The visitors, who won the toss and kicked-off with the wind in their favour, at once pressed, but the United goalkeeper brought off a splendid save. The visitors continued to press, but were unable to score. Half-time came with the score sheet blank.
The United began to press on the re-start, and bombarded the visitors' goal. The visitors' goalkeeper brought off some splendid saves, and the game ended without either side scoring."

Saturday 14th February 1920
Friendly
Abbey United 0 0 Chesterton Rovers

"These two unbeaten teams met on Stourbridge Common on Saturday. The United kicked-off, and at once attacked, but the Rovers soon transferred matters to the other end. Throughout the first-half this ding-dong struggle was kept up, and the interval came with no score.

After the interval the United again attacked strongly, but the Rovers defence gradually wore them down, the goalkeeper making splendid saves from Stearn, Stevens and Brown. During the last 20 minutes the Rovers attack played better than at any period of the game, the United goal having narrow escapes from shots by Camps, W. Taylor, Wild and Walker."

Saturday February 21st 1920
Friendly
Abbey United 2 4 Waterbeach

"Played last Saturday on Stourbridge Common, with the above result. The visitors kicked off with the wind in their favour. Play was very even during the first-half until ten minutes from the interval, when from a scrimmage in the United goal P. Saunders opened the scoring for the visitors. During the second-half both teams put in several good shots, and both goalies were called upon to save. The United equalised some little time after the resumption, but C.Holl put his side ahead again with a brilliant grounder. After this the United forced several corners without result until after about 20 minutes play, when the ball was played in the net. An appeal for offside was made and the referee decided to "bounce" the ball. Another scrimmage took place in the visitors' goal and after several attempts to clear, the ball was sent into the net. In the last few minutes of the game two more goals were scored through the work of Holl and Barker."

Saturday 6th March 1920
Friendly
Waterbeach 0 2 **Abbey United**

"Played at Waterbeach on Saturday. The United won the toss and kicked-off with the wind. United at once pressed, and after about a minute's play gained a corner, which was nicely placed. The home goalkeeper, however, brought off a splendid save. After some midfield play Stevens broke away and passed to Brown, who scored with a splendid shot. At half-time United were leading 1-0. On the resumption, Waterbeach pressed, and gained a corner which was put behind. The United had the best of the game, and from a good pass by Stevens, Devonport scored from about 25 yards out."

Saturday 13th March 1920
Friendly
Fulbourn Institute 1 1 **Abbey United**

"Played at Fulbourn on Saturday. The United won the toss, and at once began to press. The institute broke away, and became dangerous round the visitors' goal, Wombold eventually scoring. The United then had a turn of attacking, and after a smart bit of work on the right wing Longford equalised with a beautiful shot. There was no more scoring in the second-half, although United had the best of the game."

1920-21 SEASON

Whit-Monday
15th May 1921

"The Whit-Monday six-a-side football contests, promoted by the Littleport Football Club on Highfield, easily broke all previous records for both entries and attendance. Last year ten Clubs entered, and 816 persons paid for admission, whereas on Monday the gate returns showed 1,350 tickets sold and 21 Clubs competed. A team styling themselves the March Choir Boys (composed of members of the March G.E.R. Club) eventually ran out winners of an interesting contest, which lasted over eight hours, by beating Chatteris Magpies (actually engineers) by 16 points to 8. The games were of 20 minutes each way, and points were awarded as follows: Goal 4, Side Goal 2, and Corner 1.

Preliminary Round
Abbey United 5 2 Kerry Hill
First Round
Abbey United 19 0 Cambridge Rovers

NOTE: Abbey United did not play in the Second Round (Quarter-Finals) and Cambridge Rovers took their place, losing 4-13 to Ely Old Crocks."

Chapter Two

THE TWENTIES

1921-22 SEASON

Abbey United played their first season of competitive football in 1921-22 when they were accepted into Division Three of the Cambridgeshire Football League. They got off to a fine start, and won their first game 4-0 away to Cherry Hinton St. Andrews, with Wally Wilson scoring a hat-trick in the first half. Their first home game was played on Stourbridge Common a week later on Saturday 10th September 1921, and resulted in a 12-0 victory over Chesterton Rovers 2nd XI. It was a record day in more ways than one, with Wally Wilson scoring five times, and the Club recording their biggest victory.

Wally Wilson's scoring efforts did not go unnoticed, and during the season Cambridge Town signed him for some of their league games and F.A. Challenge Cup ties. He did return later in the season and notched up 24 goals in the league for the Abbey, but he could not prevent the Club losing their first ever cup match in the Second Round of the Cambs Minor Challenge Cup on Saturday 3rd December 1921. They lost by a goal to nil, to Girton United who were from a higher division.

In the league the Club went from strength to strength, and eventually won the division by nine clear points ahead of their nearest rivals, Burwell Rovers. Wally Wilson was the pick of the forwards, but the defence was also the best in the league and was ably led by George Alsop, a local player who went on to play for Chelsea F.C.

Local philanthropist Mr. Henry Clement Francis, a man with a special affection for the Abbey Ward of Cambridge, became the Club's President, although the running of the Club was left firmly in the hands of the committee. The Club's headquarters were at the Mission Hut in River Lane and on match days the goal posts and other appurtenances were carried alongside the river to the football ground on Stourbridge Common.

Cambs Minor Challenge Cup

First Round   Bye
Second Round
Girton United   1   0   **Abbey United**

Cambs League Division Three

	Pld	W	D	L	F	A	Pts
Abbey United	24	20	1	3	75	17	41
Burwell Rovers	24	15	2	7	74	25	32
Littleport Town	22	13	5	4	59	29	31
Cambridge Wanderers	18	13	3	2	57	18	29
Willingham	22	12	4	6	52	33	28
Histon Institute Res.	23	11	3	9	52	43	25
Romsey Rovers	23	9	6	8	33	48	24
Over Hotspurs	22	9	5	8	38	31	23
Cherry Hinton St. Andrews	24	9	2	13	39	52	20
Cambridge Swifts	23	7	2	14	41	45	16
Cottenham North End	23	4	2	17	39	69	10
New Chesterton Inst. Res.	23	3	4	16	26	90	10
Old Chesterton Rovers Res.	20	2	2	16	25	100	6

1922-23 SEASON

With the first team's promotion into the Second Division of the Cambs League, the Club formed a reserve team which took their place in Division Three (Section A). The reserves generally struggled, and on 30th December the Club asked the Cambs Football Association for permission to withdraw their reserve team from the league owing to a scarcity of players. The application was granted.

In their higher division the first team surpassed the achievements of the previous season and won the league by dropping only three points in 22 matches, scoring 80 goals and conceding only ten. Wally Wilson found a goalscoring ally in Albert "Twitter" Dring, who was the highest goalscorer for the season, and the team was strengthened during the year with the inclusion of several new players, among them a young Harvey Cornwell, who continued to play football into his late fifties, and who was to become the Club's longest serving player.

Abbey United achieved their first cup victory on 21st October 1922 when they beat Old Chesterton Rovers 3-0 at home in the First Round of the Cambs Minor Cup, the Club's sixth successive victory of the season. The Abbey were favoured with home draws and beat Over Hotspurs, Chatteris Town and Soham Comrades on the way to their first Final, against Cambridge G.E.R. Abbey United did not have to play outside Cambridge in any round as the Final was played on the Cambridge Town F.C. ground at Milton Road. Albert Dring scored in the first half but the teams were level after 90 minutes and in extra-time G.E.R. scored once more for a narrow victory. That defeat ended a run of eleven consecutive league and cup wins for Abbey United, although they won their remaining two league games to take the title by a margin of 7 points from Newnham Institute.

Cambs Minor Cup

First Round
Abbey United   3   0   Old Chesterton Rvrs

Second Round
Abbey United   5   1   Over Hotspurs

Third Round
Abbey United   3   0   Chatteris Town

Semi-final (at Cambridge Town F.C.)
Abbey United   3   2   Soham Comrades

Final (at Cambridge Town F.C.)
Cambridge G.E.R.   2   1   **Abbey United**

Cambs League Division Two

	Pld	W	D	L	F	A	Pts
Abbey United	22	20	1	1	80	10	41
Newnham Institute	23	16	2	5	67	37	34
United Cantabs	24	15	2	7	68	53	32
Romsey Old Boys	24	15	2	7	56	41	32
New Chesterton Institute	23	10	2	11	66	47	22
Old Chesterton Rovers	23	10	2	11	39	50	22
Cambridge G.E.R.	17	10	1	6	51	38	21
Sawston Institute	21	8	3	10	49	48	19
Cambridge Y.M.C.A.	23	8	3	12	31	49	19
Burwell	24	7	3	14	39	72	17
Romsey Athletic	22	7	2	13	33	58	16
Willingham	21	6	3	12	38	48	15
Chesterton Victoria	23	0	0	23	22	86	0

Cambs League Division Three (Section A)

	Pld	W	D	L	F	A	Pts
Coton Institute	14	13	0	1	52	8	26
Cottenham Res.	14	12	0	2	59	6	24
Histon Institute Res.	14	11	0	3	48	19	22
Over Hotspurs	14	7	0	7	30	32	14
Swavesey	14	5	0	9	24	37	10
Old Chesterton Rovers Res.	14	3	1	10	24	37	7
Cambridge Y.M.C.A.	14	2	1	11	12	50	5
New Chesterton Inst. Res.	14	2	0	12	15	53	4

NOTE: Abbey United Reserves withdrew from the league after Christmas, and their record was expunged.

1923-24 SEASON

The Summer of 1923 was a busy one for Abbey United as they prepared for their first season at the top level of Cambridgeshire football. The Club moved from their ground on Stourbridge Common to a new ground at Station Farm, Barnwell, just off Newmarket Road. The ground was hired from Mr.Bert Rayment and was known locally as the "Celery Trenches" because of the long furrows that ran the full length of the pitch. It later became part of Marshall's Aerodrome, and now forms part of the Whitehill Road housing estate, near the Co-op.

With the change of ground the headquarters of the Club were moved to a public house, the "Dog & Pheasant" in Newmarket Road. Visiting players in particular changed into their playing kit there, and the Club held their committee meetings there at regular intervals.

Before the start of the 1923-24 season, Abbey United applied to join Division One of the Cambs Thursday League, but they were not admitted as the Division had a full complement of ten clubs. The Club were invited to join Division Two, but they declined the offer.

The first match on the new ground was against Histon institute in the Cambs League Division One on Saturday 8th September 1923 and resulted in a 1-0 victory, with Albert Dring scoring the only goal. Although there was no covered accommodation of any kind at the new ground, the early matches attracted crowds in the order of 300 spectators.

Few people would have predicted that Abbey United could make a strong challenge for the Division One Championship in their first season, yet they did exactly that, and came within a whisker of winning the title. The Championship became a three-horse-race between Abbey United, Saffron Walden Town and St.Ives, and the fixtures were so arranged that the Abbey had to travel to both of their main challengers in the last three games. Three points from these two important games would have been enough to secure the League Championship for the Club, but as it turned out they drew both games 1-1 and lost the title to St.Ives by one point.

The Cambs Challenge Cup and Creake Charity Shield were both entered for the first time, but the Club, rather disappointingly, went out of each competition in the First Round against Chatteris Engineers and March G.E.R. United respectively.

Cambs Challenge Cup

Preliminary Round   Bye

First Round
Chatteris Engineers   2   0   **Abbey United**

Creake Charity Shield

First Round
Abbey United   1   1   March G.E.R. United

First Round Replay
March G.E.R. United   3   0   **Abbey United**

Cambs League Division One

	Pld	W	D	L	F	A	Pts
St.Ives	20	13	3	4	48	25	29
Abbey United	20	11	6	3	42	15	28
Saffron Walden Town	20	13	2	5	43	26	28
Histon Institute	20	8	7	5	35	27	23
Cottenham United	19	10	1	8	39	33	21
Ely City	20	7	6	7	43	39	20
R.A.F. Duxford	20	7	6	7	39	36	20
Royston Town	19	5	5	9	20	40	15
Girton United	19	4	5	10	33	51	13
Chatteris Engineers	18	4	4	10	24	37	12
Ely G.E.R.	19	2	1	16	13	51	5

1924-25 SEASON

By contrast to the previous season 1924-25 proved to be disappointing in the league, where the Club finished sixth out of eleven clubs, but highly successful in cup competitions, in which Abbey United remained unbeaten in fifteen matches.

The Club's league form was inconsistent, but did produce one fine result, a 5-1 thrashing of the eventual champions St.Ives. Wally Wilson was the Club's leading goalscorer with over twenty goals, which included four hat-tricks during the season.

Success in cup competitions meant that the last month of the season still left plenty to play for. The first Final was at Chatteris on Saturday 11th April 1925 in the Chatteris Engineering Works Cup against Cottenham, and drew gate receipts of £30, which represented a crowd of over 2,000 people. Over 300 supporters travelled by bus from Cambridge, on an outing which included a meal in Chatteris. Following a well deserved 5-0 victory, the Abbey captain, George Alsop, remarked that he was proud to receive the first cup that Abbey United had won. Harvey Cornwell scored four of the goals, all of which came in the second half.

Just two days later at Cottenham, the Abbey appeared in the Cottenham Nursing Cup Final, and goals from Wally Wilson and George Alsop were enough to beat Girton United 2-1 for their second trophy. The following Saturday, 18th April 1925, Abbey United were to meet Girton United once again in Cambridgeshire's premier cup competition, the Cambs Challenge Cup Final at Cambridge Town's ground in Milton Road. Girton finished above the Abbey in the league in third place, and a close game was anticipated, but a large crowd saw the Abbey take a 2-1 half-time lead. A penalty save by the Abbey goalkeeper, R.Wilson, just after the interval, provided the inspiration for his side to score four second half goals. Harvey Cornwell showed that he was developing into a fine player by scoring a hat-trick in the 6-1 victory. The Abbey United captain, George Alsop, was therefore able to receive his third trophy in seven days.

On Saturday 2nd May 1925 Abbey United played at Milton Road again in the Final of the Creake Charity Shield against United Cantabrians, but even after extra-time neither side could score a goal. The replay took place a week later, and after going a goal down in the first half George Alsop hit the bar twice before scoring an equalizer in the second half. A further period of extra-time could not separate the sides, and it was agreed that both clubs should share the trophy for the next twelve months.

A reserve team was entered in the Cambs League Division 3 (Section B) and finished in a respectable second place.

Cambs Challenge Cup

First Round
Royston Town 0 5 **Abbey United**

Second Round
Abbey United 4 2 Ely City

Semi-final (Trinity New Ground)
Abbey United 2 0 R.A.F. Duxford

Final (at Milton Road)
Abbey United 6 1 Girton United

Creake Charity Shield

First Round Bye

Second Round
Romsey Old Boys 2 9 **Abbey United**

3rd Round
Abbey United 5 1 March Town

Semi-final (Trinity New Ground)
Ely City 0 3 **Abbey United**

Final (at Milton Road)
United Cantabs 0 0 **Abbey United**

Final Replay (at Milton Road)
Abbey United 1 1 United Cantabs
(A.E.T.)
(The trophy was shared for a year by both clubs)

Chatteris Engineering Works Cup

First Round Bye

Second Round
Abbey United 3 2 United Cantabs

Semi-final (at Chatteris)
Abbey United 2 1 March Town

Final (at Chatteris)
Abbey United 5 0 Cottenham United

First Team 1924-25 Season

Back Row: F.Adams (Vice-President), F.Brown, C.Harrison, H.Bowman (Hon. Treasurer), H.F.Newman, C.E.Elsden.
Standing: Tom Bilton, Fred Mortlock (Hon. Secretary), Joe Livermore, W."Pimp" Stearn, R."Percy" Wilson, Jim Self, Harold "Darley" Watson, William Taverner, W.Harrison. **Sitting**: Bill Walker, Harvey Cornwell, Henry Clement Francis (President), George Alsop (Captain), Bob Patman, Charlie Taverner. **Front**: W."Fanny" Freeman Frank Luff.

DEVELOPING THROUGHOUT EAST ANGLIA

A RANGE OF LUXURY PROPERTIES
ONE BED BUNGALOWS TO SUPERIOR FIVE BED DETACHED HOUSES

Reason Homes build residential property using traditional materials in a wide variety of styles and prices, set in prestigious locations throughout East Anglia. The common factor throughout the range of bungalows and houses is based upon quality and variation in styling to suit particular requirements. Be it single bedroom flat, a small family home, or a luxurious five bedroom house, nothing is left to be desired. All properties are built to a high specification including luxury fitted kitchens, custom-built wardrobes, central heating and, in larger properties, deluxe fittings to satisfy the most discerning of purchasers.
Please may we send you a brochure?

For further details contact Head Office - CONSTRUCT REASON LTD., BEAVER HOUSE, NORTHERN ROAD, SUDBURY, SUFFOLK. TEL: (0787) 76241

REASON HOMES

Cottenham Nursing Cup

First Round   Bye

Second Round
Histon Institute Res.   0   5   **Abbey United**

Semi-final (at Cottenham)
Abbey United   8   0   Romsey Old Boys

Final (at Cottenham)
Abbey United   2   1   Girton United

Cambs League Division One

	Pld	W	D	L	F	A	Pts
St. Ives Town	19	14	1	4	43	22	29
Ely City	20	13	1	6	45	37	27
Girton	20	9	3	8	39	32	21
Cambridge Swifts	20	9	3	8	33	34	21
Histon Institute	20	9	2	9	40	33	20
Abbey United	18	8	3	7	35	29	19
Saffron Walden Town	17	8	1	8	42	32	17
Cottenham	17	6	5	6	41	43	17
United Cantabs	17	5	3	9	28	39	13
R.A.F. Duxford	15	5	2	8	30	29	12
Chatteris Engineers	19	2	2	15	17	57	6

Cambs Minor Cup

First Round
Abbey United Res.   5   1   Willingham

Second Round
Linton Granta   4   0   **Abbey United Res.**

Cambs League Division Three (Section B)

	Pld	W	D	L	F	A	Pts
Trumpington	10	9	0	1	40	9	18
Abbey United Res.	10	5	1	4	22	17	11
Cherry Hinton Liberals	10	4	3	3	22	20	11
Norfolk United	10	5	1	4	21	20	11
New Chesterton Inst.	10	3	0	7	7	25	6
Linton Granta	10	1	1	8	8	32	3

1925-26 SEASON

The Club got off to an excellent start to the season and did not experience defeat until after Christmas in their tenth game. On 12th December 1925 they came close to equalling their highest score when they beat Cambridge Swifts 11-1 in a league game. C.Greaves scored four of the goals and the Club's new captain, Harvey Cornwell, contributed with a hat-trick. Abbey United's unbeaten league run came to an end on Saturday 20th February with a 4-2 home defeat against Gamlingay which stayed in the memory of many for the wrong reasons. Hall, the visiting goalkeeper, came to blows with a spectator for coming over the line, near the end of the game. It was stated that Hall addressed an insulting remark to the spectator and struck him. The man returned the blow, and a free fight would have ensued had not the referee intervened. The men were parted with some difficulty and ordered off the ground by the Abbey officials. Followed by a large crowd, they met elsewhere to settle their differences.

The season built up to an exciting climax as the team progressed through to the finals of both the Cambs Challenge Cup and the Creake Charity Shield, but the Division One Cambs League Championship was the most treasured prize and with four games to go it became a straight battle with Girton United as both teams were level on points and had to play each other twice. In the first match at Girton on Tuesday 20th April the home side won by 2 goals to 1, the winning goal being scored with the last kick of the game. However, a 5-0 victory over March Town the following Saturday meant that Abbey United just needed to beat Girton in the return at the "Celery Trenches" on Tuesday 27th April to clinch the Championship. The biggest crowd of the season, expecting a close game, saw the Abbey storm into a 4-0 half-time lead, and with Harvey Cornwell completing his hat-trick in the second half, the Championship was won with a 5-1 victory.

Hopes of winning the 'triple crown' of the League, Challenge Cup and Creake Charity Shield were dashed on Saturday 1st May 1926 when they lost 3-1 to R.A.F. Duxford in the Final of the Cambs Challenge Cup on the Cambridge Town F.C. ground.

On the same pitch a week later both sides met again in the Final of the Creake Charity Shield. Four goals were scored in a five minute period in the first half. R.A.F. Duxford took the lead, and then the Abbey scored three times in three minutes through E.Fuller, G.Alsop, and H.Cornwell to take a 3-1 half-time lead. A 50th minute header from George Alsop completed the scoring and enabled the Club to retain the trophy.

Cambs Challenge Cup

First Round
Cambridge Town Res.   2   3   **Abbey United**

Second Round
Abbey United   6   1   United Cantabs

Semi-final (at Cambridge Town F.C.)
Abbey United   2   0   Ely City

Final (at Cambridge Town F.C.)
R.A.F. Duxford   3   1   **Abbey United**

Creake Charity Shield

First Round
Abbey United 9 1 Cambridge Inst. Co.

Second Round
Abbey United Walk Over Sawston Paper Mills

Third Round
Abbey United 7 0 Wisbech Town 'A'

Semi-final (at Cambridge Town F.C.)
Abbey United 2 0 United Cantabs

Final (at Cambridge Town F.C.)
Abbey United 4 1 R.A.F. Duxford

Cottenham Nursing Cup

First Round
Abbey United 1 5 Girton United

Chatteris Engineering Cup

First Round
Cottenham 2 3 **Abbey United**

Second Round
Abbey United Walk Over Godmanchester Town

Semi-final (at Chatteris)
March Town 2 0 **Abbey United**

Cambs League Division One

	Pld	W	D	L	F	A	Pts
Abbey United	26	20	3	3	103	26	43
Girton United	26	18	3	5	66	37	39
Cambridge Town Res.	26	17	2	7	82	48	36
Cottenham	26	15	4	7	70	47	34
St. Ives Town	25	14	1	10	56	47	29
Ely City	25	14	0	11	62	58	28
Chatteris Town	26	12	2	12	48	61	26
Histon Institute	25	10	3	12	59	67	23
United Cantabs	24	9	2	13	58	60	20
March Town	26	7	6	13	40	72	20
Cambridge Swifts	26	9	1	16	59	73	19
Gamlingay	25	6	7	12	54	73	19
Chatteris Engineers	26	7	3	16	45	73	17
Old Chesterton Rovers	26	1	3	22	28	87	5

Cambs Minor Cup

First Round
Abbey United Res. 1 7 Foxton

Cambs League Division Three (Section B)

	Pld	W	D	L	F	A	Pts
Fulbourn Institute	8	7	0	1	34	10	14
Norfolk United	8	5	1	2	21	12	11
Abbey United Res.	8	4	0	4	22	14	8
Cherry Hinton Liberals	8	2	0	6	12	28	4
Duxford United	8	1	1	6	6	31	3

1926-27 SEASON

Abbey United, who were nicknamed the "Wasps" during the 1920s because of their amber and black striped shirts, got off to another good start in the league, remaining unbeaten in the first six games. For one of these games against Duxford United on 25th September 1926 the Club decided to donate the proceeds of the match to "Pim" Stearn, a former player who had met with an accident. A good crowd saw the Abbey win 8-0, and with donations a total of £25 was raised.

The Club entered the F.A. Amateur Cup for the first time, but even with home advantage and a first half lead through a goal by Albert Mickle they could not hold out for victory and eventually lost a close game by 3 goals to 2 against Norwich Y.M.C.A. on Saturday 9th October.

In the league the Abbey made another strong challenge for the Championship, but unfortunately lost both of their games with their main contenders, Girton United, and had to be content with second place, seven points behind their old rivals.

The reserve team made sure that the Club maintained their record of always winning at least one trophy each season, when they remained undefeated in winning Division 3 (Section B) of the Cambs League by a margin of 4 points. However, they lost the Championship match with the (Section A) winners Littleport Town by 5 goals to 1.

In the Creake Charity Shield the Abbey lost their grip on the trophy in the Second Round when they lost 1-0 away to Cambridge Town Reserves. The Club entered the Scott-Gaty Cup for the first time and lost 5-0 in the Semi-final against Huntingtdon Town. They lost at the same stage of the Chatteris Nursing Cup, but in the Cambs Challenge Cup they once again progressed through to the final with excellent victories over Wisbech Town (4-1), Cambridge Town Reserves (4-1) and Chatteris Engineers (5-0). The Final was played at Milton Road on Saturday 7th May against Newmarket Town, and the Club's leading goalscorer for the second season in succession, Harvey Cornwell, put the Abbey ahead in the 26th minute. Newmarket equalized twelve minutes later, and thereafter no side could score again even with the addition of extra-time. The Abbey were without Harvey Cornwell for the replay, played the following Friday on the Cambridge Town ground, in what turned out to be a thoroughly entertaining game. Newmarket took a 2-1 interval lead, then went 3-1 up before being pegged back at 3-3. The trophy looked to be

First Team 1926-27 Season
Back Row: C.Morley, Bill Walker, Joe Livermore, Fred "Erstie" Clements, Harvey Cornwell, Harold "Darley" Watson.
Front Row: Dick Harris, Edward Fuller, George Alsop (Captain), C. Clements, Freddie Stevens.
Photograph by Scott and Wilkinson.

First Team 1927-28 Season
Back Row: Bill Walker, H.V. "Dick" Camps, Fred "Erstie" Clements, Joe Livermore.
Middle Row: Harold "Darley" Watson, Bob Patman, George Alsop, Wally Wilson, Jack Rayner.
Front Row: Harvey Cornwell, Fred Taverner.
Photograph by Scott and Wilkinson

theirs when they went into a 5-3 lead, but two goals in the last three minutes from C.Morley once again brought the Abbey level. Newmarket scored once more in extra-time, but when Dick Harris equalized to make it six goals each there was no further scoring and the trophy was shared by the two teams for the next year.

F.A. Amateur Cup

Preliminary Round Bye

First Qualifying Round
Abbey United 2 3 Norwich Y.M.C.A.

Cambs Challenge Cup

First Round Bye

Second Round
Abbey United 4 1 Wisbech Town

Third Round
Abbey United 4 1 Cambridge Town Res.

Semi-final (at Ely)
Abbey United 5 0 Chatteris Engineers

Final (at Milton Road Cambridge)
Abbey United 1 1 Newmarket Town
(A.E.T. 1-1 at full time)

Final Replay (at Cambridge Town F.C.)
Abbey United 6 6 Newmarket Town
(A.E.T. 5-5 at full time)
NOTE: Trophy shared jointly

Creake Charity Shield

First Round Bye

Second Round
Cambridge Town Res. 1 0 **Abbey United**

Scott-Gaty Cup

First Round
Godmanchester Town 1 4 **Abbey United**

Second Round
Brampton 0 2 **Abbey United**

Semi-final (at St. Ives)
Huntingdon Town 5 0 **Abbey United**

Chatteris Nursing Cup

First Round
Abbey United 8 1 Warboys Town

Second Round
Cottenham United 2 4 **Abbey United**

Semi-final
Chatteris Town 4 2 **Abbey United**

Cambs League Division One

	Pld	W	D	L	F	A	Pts
Girton United	24	18	2	4	75	36	38
Abbey United	24	14	3	7	76	39	31
Cambridge Swifts	23	14	3	6	77	46	31
Ely City	24	11	3	10	83	65	25
Cottenham United	22	12	1	9	46	51	25
Cambridge Town Res.	24	11	2	11	55	47	24
Chatteris Town	24	8	7	9	78	74	23
Soham Rangers	24	10	3	11	58	62	23
United Cantabs	22	10	2	10	61	58	22
Gamlingay	24	7	5	12	42	76	19
St. Ives Town	24	7	4	13	41	59	18
Histon Institute	23	6	4	13	50	96	16
March Town	24	4	3	17	40	76	11

Cambs Minor Cup

First Round Bye

Second Round
Foxton 2 1 Abbey Utd Res.

Cambs League Division Three (Section B)

	Pld	W	D	L	F	A	Pts
Abbey United Res.	12	10	2	0	49	7	22
R.A.F. Duxford Res.	12	8	2	2	37	19	18
Old Cherry Hinton	12	8	1	3	46	17	17
Sawston Institute	12	5	1	6	39	32	11
Dullingham	12	4	0	8	23	50	8
A.S.L.E. & F.	12	2	0	10	18	50	4
Fulbourn Reserves	12	2	0	10	7	44	4

Cambs League Division Three

Championship Match
Littleport Town 5 1 Abbey Utd Res.

1927-28 SEASON

Prior to the start of the season Abbey United decided to take their reserve side out of the Cambs League and enter a team in the Bury & District League instead. As it turned out the Bury & District League proved to be stronger than the Cambs League Division One, and on dates where the fixtures clashed for both leagues, the Club decided to field the first team in the Bury League, and the reserve team in the Cambs League match. Twice this happened, with the Abbey losing to Chatteris and St.Ives when they would have been expected to win with a full side. Such was the uproar in local football circles that the Cambs Football Association decided to fine Abbey United £5 and warned them not to field a weakened side in future.

On Saturday 3rd September 1927 the Club played their first ever F.A. Challenge Cup match away to Great Yarmouth Town in the Extra Preliminary Round. They were proud of the fact that they were watched by 3,000 spectators, but Harold "Darley" Watson's first half goal was not enough and Yarmouth ran out 3-1 winners.

A massive 11-1 victory was recorded over Great Shelford on Saturday 21st January 1928 in the Second Round of the Creake Charity Shield, with G.Alsop scoring four of the goals. However, three weeks later the Abbey broke their goalscoring record when they beat Godmanchester 14-1 in the Second Round of the Chatteris Engineering Works Cup. G.Chapman scored five of the goals, but amazingly the Abbey played for 75 minutes with only ten men when R.Camps retired from the field with the score at 1-0.

On ten occasions during the season Abbey United scored six goals or more in a match, but the extra fixtures caused by entering the Bury & District League took their toll and the team did not realize their full potential, finishing third in the Cambs League.

Three players scored more than twenty goals in the season: George Alsop, Harold Watson, and Harvey Cornwell, with Cornwell being the Club's highest goalscorer for the third season in succession.

The Club was knocked out of the Cambs Challenge Cup at the Semi-final stage by Histon Institute (2-1), but they did reach the Final of two other competitions, losing 2-0 to Cambridge Town Reserves in the Creake Charity Shield, but beating Romsey Town 3-0 in the Chatteris Engineering Works Cup on Saturday 5th May 1928, to win their only trophy of the season. That Final was played at Chatteris in the afternoon, and in the evening of the same day the team took to the field once more to play their last league game against Chatteris Town, but with weary legs they lost a thrilling game by 5 goals to 4.

F.A. Challenge Cup

Extra Preliminary Round
Great Yarmouth Town 3 1 Abbey United

Cambs Challenge Cup

Preliminary Round Bye
First Round
Abbey United 7 0 Cambridge Town Res.
Second Round
Ely City 2 8 Abbey United
Semi-final (at Cambridge Town F.C.)
Histon Institute 2 1 Abbey United

Creake Charity Shield

First Round
Abbey United 6 1 Coton Institute
Second Round
Abbey United 11 1 Great Shelford
Third Round
Abbey United 3 0 Soham Rangers
Semi-final (at Chatteris)
Abbey United 2 1 Cottenham United
Final (at Cambridge Town F.C.)
Cambridge Town Res. 2 0 Abbey United

Chatteris Engineering Works Cup

First Round Bye
Second Round
Abbey United 14 1 Godmanchester
Semi-final (at Chatteris)
Abbey United 2 1 Cottenham United
Final (at Chatteris)
Abbey United 3 0 Romsey Town

Cottenham Nursing Cup

Preliminary Round
Girton United 3 0 Abbey United

Cambs League Division One

	Pld	W	D	L	F	A	Pts
Cambridge Swifts	24	21	2	1	78	25	44
Soham Rangers	25	11	9	5	69	61	31
Abbey United	19	10	4	5	65	31	24
Ely City	24	12	0	12	68	62	24
Cambridge Town Res.	24	10	4	10	68	63	24
United Cantabs	24	10	4	10	63	67	24
Histon Institute	24	8	7	9	60	65	23
Chatteris Engineers	26	9	5	12	56	65	23
Chatteris Town	25	10	3	12	62	85	23
Cottenham United	24	10	2	12	44	52	22
St. Ives Town	22	8	4	10	52	59	20
Gamlingay	24	9	2	13	53	70	20
Girton United	20	8	1	11	47	46	17
Coton Institute	25	2	5	18	39	25	9

Bury & District League Division One

	Pld	W	D	L	F	A	Pts
Newmarket Town	12	8	2	2	37	18	18
Bury Town	11	6	4	1	30	19	16
Stowmarket	11	5	2	4	43	32	12
Long Melford	10	2	4	4	21	25	8
Thetford Town	10	2	2	6	29	43	6
Sudbury Town	11	2	1	8	18	43	5
Abbey United	5	2	1	2	17	15	3

Abbey United were deducted 2 points by League Council.

1928-29 SEASON

Without doubt the 1928-29 season was the most successful in the Club's history, with the first team winning five trophies and the reserves also winning one for good measure.

The first team lost their F.A.Challenge Cup Preliminary Round match 3-1 at Clacton, but a goal from R.Ding was sufficient to beat Soham Rangers 1-0 in the Preliminary Round of the F.A. Amateur Cup, the Club's first victory in a Football Association competition, on Saturday 22nd September 1928. They followed this up with a 2-1 victory over Thetford Town, before going out in the Second Round after a narrow 2-1 defeat at Kings Lynn.

At the start of the season Division One of the Cambs League was split into two regional sections. Abbey United were in the Southern Group, Section A, and they lost just two matches in the whole campaign. The title was clinched in front of one of the largest crowds ever seen at the "Celery Trenches" with a 3-2 victory over Cambridge Town Reserves on Thursday 18th April 1929.

Chatteris Town won Section B, and in the deciding Division One Championship match against them at Milton Road, an exciting game finished level at three goals each after 90 minutes. The Abbey lasted the pace longer, and with two extra-time goals from George Alsop managed to win the game 5-4, to lift the trophy for the second time in their history. That game was played in the evening of Saturday 11th May 1929 as earlier in the afternoon on the same ground Abbey United Reserves, who won Division Three (Section A) of the Cambs League, lost the deciding Championship match 3-0 to the Division Three (Section B) winners, Linton Granta. However, in winning their section of the league the reserve team set up as Club goalscoring record when they beat Haddenham Rovers Reserves 16-1 at home on Saturday 3rd November 1928.

Abbey United's first Final of the season was in the Cambs Challenge Cup, but for a change the game was not staged on Cambridge Town's ground and instead went north of the county at the March G.E.R ground on 6th April 1929. A close game saw the Abbey beat Chatteris Engineers by 4 goals to 3 with Harvey Cornwell scoring the winning goal in the second half. The next Final was away to Chatteris Town in the Chatteris Nursing Cup on Saturday 20th April. A high scoring game resulted in the Abbey just edging home again by 3 goals to 2.

On Friday 3rd May the Club reached the Final of the Bury & District Cup after beating Diss Town 2-0 in the Semi-final. The Final was played at Bury St. Edmunds and resulted in a comfortable 4-1 victory over Stowmarket. Not surprisingly when they had to travel to Chatteris the next day, near the end of a hectic season, with a mixed side, they lost 4-1 to Ramsey Town in the Chatteris Engineering Works Cup Semi-final replay, to end an unbeaten run of twenty three matches.

The Creake Charity Shield was won on Tuesday 7th May 1929 at Milton Road against Cambridge Town Reserves. Although there was no score at half-time, goals from Harvey Cornwell, Harold "Darley" Watson and Sid Hulyer in the second half secured a comfortable 3-0 victory. By winning the Cambs League, the Cambs Challenge Cup and the Creake Charity Shield, Abbey United became the first Club to achieve the 'triple-crown' in Cambridgeshire football.

F.A. Challenge Cup

Preliminary Round
Clacton Town 3 — 1 **Abbey United**

F.A. Amateur Cup

Preliminary Round
Abbey United 1 — 0 Soham Rangers

First Round
Abbey United 2 — 1 Thetford Town

Second Round
Kings Lynn 2 — 1 **Abbey United**

Cambs Challenge Cup

First Round Bye

Second Round
Abbey United 4 — 0 Cambridge Swifts

Third Round
Cottenham United 1 — 6 **Abbey United**

Semi-final (at Ely City F.C.)
Soham Rangers 3 — 3 **Abbey United**

Semi-final Replay (at Histon F.C.)
Abbey United 7 — 2 Soham Rangers

Final (at March G.E.R. F.C.)
Abbey United 4 — 3 Chatteris Engineers

Creake Charity Shield

First Round
St. Ives Town 2 — 3 **Abbey United**

Second Round
Abbey United 10 — 0 Steeple Morden

First Team 1928-29 Season
Back Row: H.Bowman (Treasurer), Jack Rayner, Bill Walker, Fred "Erstie" Clements, H. "Darley" Watson, G.Chapman (Secretary), Tom Bilton (Trainer). **Middle Row**: Cyril Haylock, Richard "Dick" Harris, George Alsop (Captain), H.C.Francis (President), Harvey Cornwell, Bob Patman. **Front Row**: Sid Hulyer, Tommy James.
Winners of the Bury & District Cup, Cambs Challenge Cup, Creake Charity Shield, Cambs League Division One Championship, and the Chatteris Nursing Cup.

Saturday 22nd September 1928. F.A. Amateur Cup. Preliminary Round. Abbey United 1, Soham Rangers 0.
Wing-half R.Ding scores Abbey United's winning goal with a 20 yard shot in the 65th minute on the Club's home ground at the "Celery Trenches". In the next round the Abbey also beat Thetford Town 2-1 at home, before losing 2-1 at King's Lynn in the Second Round.
Photograph by courtesy of Cambridge Evening News.

Third Round
Sawston Institute	1	7	**Abbey United**

Semi-final (at Chatteris)
Abbey United	7	0	Whittlesey Amateurs

Final (at Cambridge Town F.C.)
Cambridge Town Res.	0	3	**Abbey United**

Bury & District Cup

First Round — Bye

Semi-final (at Bury Town F.C.)
Diss Town	1	1	**Abbey United**

Semi-final Replay
Abbey United	2	0	Diss Town

Final (at Bury Town F.C.)
Abbey United	4	1	Stowmarket

Chatteris Engineering Works Cup

First Round
Cottenham United	3	9	**Abbey United**

Second Round
St. Ives Town	2	2	**Abbey United**

Second Round Replay
Abbey United	4	1	St. Ives Town

Semi-final (at Chatteris)
Abbey United	0	0	Ramsey Town

Semi-final Replay (at Chatteris)
Ramsey Town	4	1	**Abbey United**

Chatteris Nursing Cup

Semi-final (at Chatteris Engineers F.C.)
Abbey United	4	2	Histon Institute

Final (at Chatteris)
Chatteris Town	2	3	**Abbey United**

Cambs League Division One (Section A)

	Pld	W	D	L	F	A	Pts
Abbey United	17	14	1	2	77	24	29
Cambridge Swifts	18	12	1	5	41	35	25
Cambridge Town Res.	18	10	3	5	62	40	23
Gamlingay	18	8	3	7	58	52	19
Histon Institute	18	8	1	9	48	52	19
Soham Rangers	17	7	1	9	47	40	15
Cottenham United	18	6	2	10	40	62	14
United Cantabs	18	5	3	10	43	60	13
Sawston Paper Mills	18	6	1	11	40	77	13
Ely City	18	4	2	12	34	50	10

Division One Championship Match
(at Cambridge Town F.C.)

Abbey United	5	4	Chatteris Town

(A.E.T. 3-3 at full time)

Cambs Minor Cup

First Round
Rattee & Kett	2	5	**Abbey United Res.**

Second Round
Old Cherry Hinton	0	6	**Abbey United Res.**

Third Round
Abbey United Res.	2	5	Coton Institute

Cambs League Division Three (Section A)

	Pld	W	D	L	F	A	Pts
Abbey United Res.	19	16	0	3	86	29	32
Wilburton	18	11	3	4	58	45	25
Newnham Institute	20	9	5	6	58	45	23
Histon Institute Reserves	20	10	2	8	70	50	22
Coton Institute Reserves	17	9	3	5	54	39	21
Milton	19	10	1	8	64	60	21
Corporation Staff	20	8	2	10	53	54	18
Ely City Reserves	16	5	3	8	34	43	13
Haddenham Rovers Res.	18	4	2	12	36	90	10
Cottenham United Res.	17	3	3	11	33	59	9
Swavesey	18	2	4	12	27	61	8

Division Three Championship Match
(at Cambridge Town F.C.)

Linton Granta	3	0	**Abbey United Res.**

1929-30 SEASON

Hopes that Abbey United might emulate the triumphs of the previous season seemed to be well founded when they won their first three games of the new campaign. They started the season on Saturday 7th September 1929 by winning their first ever F.A. Challenge Cup match by 2 goals to 1 away to Newmarket Town in the Extra Preliminary Round. Wally Wilson and Harvey Cornwell were the goalscorers. This was followed by an even better win in the Preliminary Round when the Abbey scored four times without reply away to the much fancied Wisbech Town. An enthusiastic crowd of 1,200 spectators turned up for the First Qualifying Round match at the "Celery Trenches" hoping that the Abbey could produce another shock result against Crittall's Athletic from Braintree. However, the Spartan League outfit, who were one of the strongest teams in East Anglia, put on an impressive display and ran out comfortable 5-0 winners.

Thereafter the Club suffered a crippling injury crisis, and after several defeats, there was a loss of confidence as a host of new players were introduced to the side. The Club's league form was poor, and only three victories in the last three games helped the Abbey to finish third from bottom in the Cambs

League Division One Section A. The reserve team also struggled all season and finished bottom of the Cambs League Division Two.

The first team's cup form was generally much better than their league form and they reached the Semi-final of the Chatteris Nursing Cup before losing 2-1 against March Town at Chatteris. The Semi-final of the Cambs Challenge Cup was also reached, but after impressive victories over March Town and the University Press in the earlier rounds, the Club lost 3-1 to Chatteris Engineers on the March G.E.R. ground.

The one moment of glory occurred in the Creake Charity Shield, when a string of impressive performances earned a place in the Final against Soham Rangers at the Cambridge Town F.C. ground on Thursday 8th May 1930. Two goals from "Dick" Harris gave the "Wasps" a 2-0 interval lead, and further goals from George Alsop and Harvey Cornwell secured a 4-0 victory for Abbey United and ensured that the Club maintained its record of having won at least one trophy per season since it started playing competitive football.

F.A. Challenge Cup

Extra Preliminary Round
Abbey United 2 1 Newmarket Town

Preliminary Round
Wisbech Town 0 4 **Abbey United**

First Qualifying Round
Abbey United 0 5 Crittall's Athletic (Braintree)

F.A. Amateur Cup

First Qualifying Round Bye

Second Qualifying Round
St. Ives Town 4 1 **Abbey United**

Cambs Challenge Cup

First Round Bye

Second Round
Abbey United 3 2 March Town

Third Round
Abbey United 5 0 University Press

Semi-final (at March G.E.R. F.C.)
Chatteris Engineers 3 1 **Abbey United**

Creake Charity Shield

First Round
Cambridge Swifts 1 5 **Abbey United**

Second Round

Abbey United 7 2 Haddenham Rovers

Third Round
Abbey United 6 2 Littleport Town

Semi-final (at Histon F.C.)
Abbey United 2 1 Cambridge Town Res.

Final (at Cambridge Town F.C.)
Abbey United 4 0 Soham Rangers

Hinchingbrooke Cup

First Round
Godmanchester 0 1 **Abbey United**

Second Round
Abbey United 1 3 Queen's Park Rangers (Bedford)

Chatteris Nursing Cup

First Round Bye

Second Round
Abbey United 8 2 Histon Institute

Semi-final (at Chatteris)
March Town 2 1 **Abbey United**

Cambs League Division One (Section A)

	Pld	W	D	L	F	A	Pts
Gamlingay	18	12	3	3	76	37	27
Cambridge Swifts	18	12	1	5	63	37	25
Histon Institute	18	10	5	3	57	40	25
University Press	18	7	5	6	39	47	19
United Cantabs	18	8	2	8	51	44	18
R.A.F. Duxford	18	6	4	8	43	37	16
Sawston Paper Mills	18	6	4	8	46	51	16
Abbey United	17	6	2	9	38	46	14
Sawston Institute	18	6	2	10	35	60	14
Cottenham United	17	1	2	14	24	73	4

Cambs Minor Cup

Preliminary Round
Abbey United Res. Milton United
(NOTE: Abbey United Res. lost, but result not known)

Cambs League Division Two

	Pld	W	D	L	F	A	Pts
Chesterton Victoria	15	11	1	3	47	24	23
Coton Institute	14	10	2	2	46	26	22
Linton Granta	15	6	4	5	41	31	16
Girton United	16	5	6	5	27	31	16
Fulbourn Athletic	13	4	5	4	27	29	13
Grantchester	13	4	4	5	20	24	12
Trumpington	16	4	3	9	41	48	11
Willingham	16	2	7	7	17	26	11
Abbey United Res.	12	3	0	9	14	38	6

Cambridge United

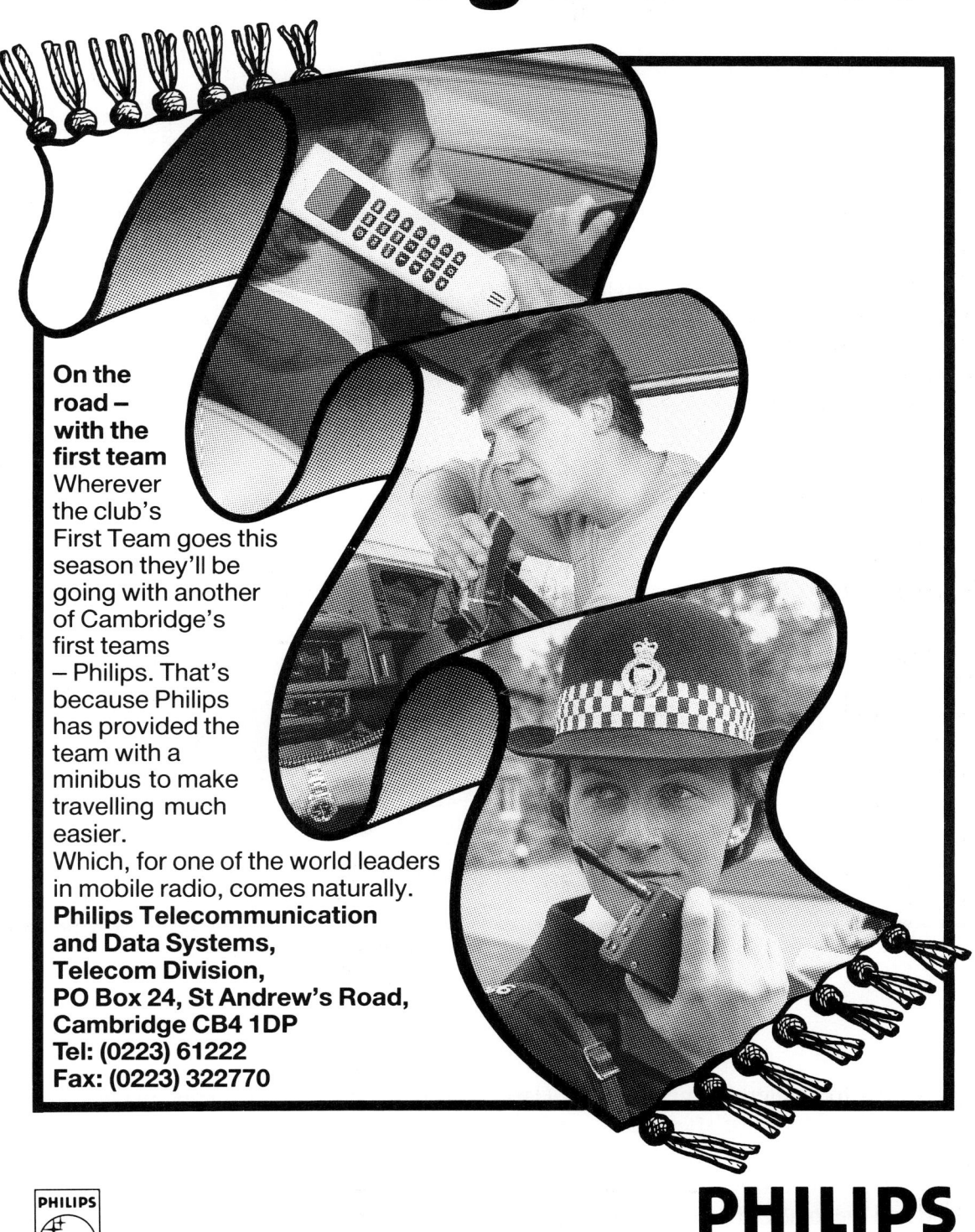

On the road – with the first team
Wherever the club's First Team goes this season they'll be going with another of Cambridge's first teams – Philips. That's because Philips has provided the team with a minibus to make travelling much easier.
Which, for one of the world leaders in mobile radio, comes naturally.
**Philips Telecommunication and Data Systems,
Telecom Division,
PO Box 24, St Andrew's Road,
Cambridge CB4 1DP
Tel: (0223) 61222
Fax: (0223) 322770**

PHILIPS

Harvey Cornwell

Abbey United's star footballer was undoubtedly Harvey Cornwell Senior who started playing for the Club in 1922, and continued until just after the Second World War, with only a few breaks. He is known to have scored 185 goals for the Club in League and Cup matches, more than any other player, but this figure is almost certainly higher because of unaccounted goals. A tough, wiry forward Harvey was a formidable opponent, and had the knack of scoring goals at the right time, on the big occasion when trophies were at stake. Although a keen competitor he always upheld true sportsmanship values and became known as the "Grand Old Master" of Cambridge football.

His three sons Harvey Junior, Jack and Sam, all represented the Abbey at some time, and all regularly played for the Cambridge Thursday Wanderers. Always keen to play a game Harvey Senior continued to play football until he was sixty years of age. He was indeed a remarkable character.

Chapter Three

THE THIRTIES

1930-31 SEASON

The "Celery Trenches" ground, which had been the Club's home for seven years, was considered to be unsuitable for Division One Cambs. League football because of its uneven surface and lack of facilities. After playing only one home game the Club decided not to use the pitch, and from November onwards the remainder of Abbey United's home games that season were played on Parker's Piece.

A number of the Club's best players left, some of them to play for Cambridge Town, and as a consequence the Abbey lost their first five games of the season. In fact they could only manage to win one of their first eighteen fixtures, that being a 3-2 win over Haddenham Rovers in the Cambs. Challenge Cup First Round. The first league win did not arrive until Saturday 7th March 1931, a narrow 3-2 home victory over R.A.F. Duxford, which was followed a week later by a 5-1 win in the important relegation battle against Chesterton Victoria. A surprise 4-3 away win over Coton Institute on Saturday 11th April virtually ended Coton's hopes of winning the league title, and caused bad feeling between the two rival sets of supporters. The Club finished second from bottom in the Cambs. League Division One Section A with 9 points from 19 games, and were somewhat fortunate to gain a place in the Premier Division for the 1931-32 season. Two of the clubs who finished above the Abbey, the University Press and Sawston Institute, were not given a place in the new Premier Division.

The reserves who were entered in Division Two of the Cambs. League, also had a miserable time, and they were given permission to pull out of the league at Christmas, with their record being expunged.

In the F.A. Challenge Cup the Club lost 4-3 at Thetford Town in the Extra Preliminary Round, and Second Round exits were made in the Creake Charity Shield and Cambs. Challenge Cup competitions against Cambridge Swifts and Histon Institute respectively.

Some consolation was gained at the end of the season when Abbey United beat Ely City 1-0 in the Semi-final of the Chatteris Nursing Cup, having received a bye and a walk-over in the first two rounds. In the Final at Chatteris on Friday 1st May 1931 the Club drew 2-2 with Soham Rangers, and the trophy was shared over the next twelve months. Fred Taverner and "Dick" Harris scored the goals for the Abbey.

F.A. Challenge Cup

Extra Preliminary Round
Thetford Town 4 3 **Abbey United**

Cambs Challenge Cup

First Round
Abbey United 3 2 Haddenham Rovers

Second Round
Abbey United 2 4 Histon Institute

Creake Charity Shield

First Round Bye

Second Round
Abbey United 3 5 Cambridge Swifts

Chatteris Nursing Cup

First Round Bye

Second Round
Abbey United Walk Over Littleport Town

Semi-final (at Chatteris)
Abbey United 1 0 Ely City

Final (at Chatteris)
Soham Rangers 2 2 **Abbey United**
(Trophy shared for six months each)

Cambs League Division One (Section A)

	Pld	W	D	L	F	A	Pts
Cambridge Swifts	20	14	1	5	61	43	29
Gamlingay	20	13	2	5	70	35	28
United Cantabs	20	11	4	5	49	40	26
Coton Institute	20	11	3	6	60	43	25
Sawston Paper Mills	20	10	5	5	48	36	25
R.A.F. Duxford	20	11	2	7	56	50	24
Histon Institute	20	8	3	9	41	52	19
University Press	20	6	4	10	43	52	16
Sawston Institute	20	3	6	11	36	60	12
Abbey United	19	3	3	13	39	65	9
Chesterton Victoria	19	0	5	14	27	78	5

Cambs Minor Cup

Preliminary Round Bye

First Round
Bottisham **Abbey United Res.**
(NOTE: Match Drawn, but score not known)

First Round Replay
Bottisham 0 3 **Abbey United Res.**

Second Round
Cherry Hinton 5 1 **Abbey United Res.**

Cambs League Division Two

	Pld	W	D	L	F	A	Pts
Royston Town	20	16	2	2	85	30	34
Linton Granta	20	15	1	4	61	38	31
Fulbourn	19	11	1	7	56	34	23
Grantchester	19	11	0	8	52	47	22
Cottenham United	18	6	7	5	49	43	19
Haddenham Rovers	20	8	3	9	49	57	19
Sawston Paper Mills Res.	19	7	3	9	50	63	17
Girton United	20	8	0	12	43	48	16
Barnwell United	20	5	3	12	39	59	13
Trumpington	20	4	3	13	43	72	11
Willingham	19	3	3	13	36	67	9

NOTE: Abbey United Reserves withdrew from the league at Christmas, and their record was expunged from the league table.

1931-32 SEASON

There is no doubt that having to play their home games on Parker's Piece proved to be a handicap to Abbey United's financial welfare and general progress.

It came as a pleasant surprise when during the Summer of 1931 Henry Clement Francis, President of the Club since its entry into the Cambs. League, summoned the Officers of the Club to meet him on a piece of land he had acquired at the back of Mr.Sindall's old works (now Corona's). At the meeting Mr.Francis made two offers to the Club. They could either accept the whole of the land that he had acquired, or they could accept a smaller parcel of land for a new ground, on which he would erect a grandstand for between 300 and 400 spectators as well as a fence. The Officers of the Club took little time to decide on the second option. Mr.R.J.Wadsworth, who was appointed as the Club's Vice-President at the Annual General Meeting that year, was responsible for the erection of the dressing rooms on the other side of the pitch a year later.

While the new pitch was being levelled and seeded, the Club returned to playing on the "Celery Trenches" for just one more season. Bearing in mind the prevailing circumstances, the Abbey found it difficult to attract better quality players, and the Club's first game of the season in the Preliminary Round of the F.A.Amateur Cup resulted in an inglorious defeat at the hands of St.Ives Town. The Abbey also made a First Round exit in the Cambs. Challenge Cup when they lost 3-2 at home to Cambridge Swifts.

The Club's league form improved after Christmas and six successive victories in an unbeaten run of eleven games enabled them to move up into sixth place in the Cambs. League Premier Division with 21 points from 21 games. The reserve team finished third in Division Two Section A of the league, but were granted one of the promotion places at the end of the season.

The Creake Charity Shield was the only competition in which the Club had any form of success, providing some interest in an otherwise disappointing season. Following victories over Chesterton Victoria, Sawston Paper Mills and Coton Institute, the Club met March G.E.R. United in the Semi-final at Chatteris on Saturday 9th April. Two goals from Harvey Cornwell and A. Edwards gave Abbey United an impressive 2-0 win. The Final was played in Cambridge on the Railway Social Club ground against Linton Granta. After 90 minutes the scores were level at one goal each with Harvey Cornwell being the Abbey's goalscorer. A further goal in extra-time by Jackie Bond looked to have given Abbey United the trophy, but Linton Granta hit back by scoring twice to give them the large shield. For the first time in Abbey United's history the Club failed to win a trophy during a season.

F.A. Amateur Cup

Preliminary Round
St. Ives Town 5 0 **Abbey United**

Cambs Challenge Cup

First Round
Abbey United 2 3 Cambridge Swifts

Creake Charity Shield

First Round
Abbey United 3 2 Chesterton Victoria

Second Round
Sawston Paper Mills 2 5 **Abbey United**

Third Round
Coton Institute 1 2 **Abbey United**

Semi-final (at Chatteris)
Abbey United 2 0 March G.E.R. United

Final (at Railway Social Club, Cambridge)
Linton Granta 3 2 **Abbey United**
(A.E.T. 1-1 at full time)

Cambs League Premier Division

	Pld	W	D	L	F	A	Pts
Chatteris Town	21	16	1	4	94	34	33
Soham Rangers	22	16	0	6	79	55	32
Royston Town	22	12	3	7	59	47	27
Gamlingay	22	13	1	8	70	56	27
R.A.F. Duxford	22	12	2	8	56	49	26
Abbey United	21	8	5	8	52	50	21
Histon Institute	22	9	3	10	65	72	21
Cambridge Swifts	19	7	4	8	52	68	18
United Cantabs	22	7	2	13	46	58	16
Ely City	21	7	1	13	48	62	15
Coton Institute	22	5	3	14	49	79	13
Sawston Paper Mills	20	3	1	16	35	76	7

Cambs Minor Cup

Preliminary Round
Abbey United Res. 7 2 Wilburton

First Round
Fulbourn 6 2 **Abbey United Res.**

Cambs League Division Two (Section A)

	Pld	W	D	L	F	A	Pts
Royston Town Reserves	18	11	4	3	53	25	26
Histon Institute Reserves	18	10	4	4	61	34	24
Abbey United Res.	18	10	4	4	57	51	24
Prims	18	10	2	6	68	34	22
Over	18	7	4	7	53	49	18
Camden United Reserves	18	8	0	10	38	47	16
Cottenham United Res.	18	7	2	9	44	54	16
Swavesey	18	7	1	10	47	51	15
Coton Institute Reserves	18	5	4	9	43	65	14
Horningsea	18	2	1	15	21	76	5

1932-33 SEASON

Abbey United's new ground was officially opened on Wednesday evening 31st August 1932 with a friendly match against the University Press. The Abbey were decidedly superior, and Jackie Bond scored both goals in a 2-0 victory. Situated in Newmarket Road, close to the former pitch, the opening ceremony was performed by Mr. R.J. Wadsworth, the senior Vice-President, accompanied by Mrs. K.R.J. Saxon, daughter of the Club's President, Mr. Francis, and wife of a Rugby and Athletic Blue and Cambs. County Cricketer. Mr. Francis and Mr. Saxon were unable to attend the ceremony owing to their absence from the town on business.

Having acquired their new ground, Abbey United re-entered the F.A. Challenge Cup, but in their first competitive game on their new ground on Saturday 3rd September 1932 they lost a high scoring game by 5 goals to 4 against Histon Institute in the Extra Preliminary Round. Harvey Cornwell scored the first two goals for the Abbey and "Herby" Bailey scored the other two in a thrilling local derby.

After that reverse on the opening day of the season, the first team went five games without defeat. So it came as quite a shock when the Club suffered their heaviest ever defeat away to Wisbech Town, by eleven goals to four, on Saturday 22nd October 1932 in the Second Qualifying Round of the F.A. Amateur Cup (after receiving a bye in the First Round). The Club played in just two other cup competitions that season, the Cambs. Challenge Cup and the Creake Charity Shield, going out of both at the first attempt, 3-2 against Pye Radio and 4-2 against Chatteris Engineers respectively. This meant that the first team had a relatively small programme of only twenty four fixtures during the season, eleven of them at home, which was a blessing in disguise, enabling the young grass on the pitch to get established.

Although never in contention for the Cambs. League Premier Division Championship, the first team did manage to finish in third place with 27 points from 20 games. The reserve team struggled in Division One Section A, without a win in ten league games, and through lack of interest from their players they withdrew from the competition in February.

F.A. Challenge Cup

Extra Preliminary Round
Abbey United 4 5 Histon Institute

F.A. Amateur Cup

First Qualifying Round Bye

Second Qualifying Round
Wisbech Town 11 4 **Abbey United**

Cambs Challenge Cup

First Round Bye

Second Round
Pye Radio 3 2 **Abbey United**

Creake Charity Shield

First Round Bye

Second Round
Chatteris Engineers 4 2 **Abbey United**

Cambs League Premier Division

	Pld	W	D	L	F	A	Pts
Gamlingay	19	16	2	1	85	26	34
Linton Granta	20	13	5	2	73	23	31
Abbey United	20	11	5	4	60	26	27
Histon Institute	19	9	3	7	50	42	21
University Press	20	7	4	9	50	53	18
Royston Town	19	8	1	10	54	51	17
R.A.F. Duxford	20	5	7	8	40	53	17
Ely City	20	7	2	11	36	55	16
Soham Rangers	19	6	3	10	46	66	15
United Cantabs	20	5	2	13	37	77	12
Sawston Paper Mills	20	4	2	14	42	97	10

Cambs Minor Cup

Preliminary Round
Abbey United Res. 7 1 Girton United

First Round
Kings United 10 0 **Abbey United Res.**

Cambs League Division One (Section A)

	Pld	W	D	L	F	A	Pts
Coton Institute	17	13	2	2	90	27	28
Orwell	15	10	3	2	56	17	23
Cottenham United	16	8	3	5	56	44	19
Sawston Institute	17	8	2	7	45	47	18
Fulbourn	18	7	3	8	53	55	17
Grantchester	18	7	3	8	42	44	17
Royston Town Reserves	16	6	2	8	40	33	14
Girton United	17	6	2	9	30	58	14
Newnham Institute	17	4	1	12	24	62	9
Sawston Paper Mills Res	15	2	1	12	42	94	5

NOTE: Abbey United Reserves withdrew from the league in February, and their record was expunged from the league table.

1933-34 SEASON

After two years without winning a trophy the 1933-34 season brought a welcome return to winning ways for Abbey United, and they finished their season winners of one trophy and runners-up in two other competitions.

For the first time in the Club's history Abbey United were drawn to play against Cambridge Town's first team in the First Qualifying Round of the F.A. Amateur Cup on Saturday 1st October 1933. There was plenty of bad feeling between the two clubs as the Town consistently stole the Abbey's better players by being able to offer the players jobs at a time of high unemployment. Although keen to put on a good performance the Abbey were no match for their Southern Amateur League hosts and suffered a 9-1 thrashing.

Four weeks later Abbey United recorded a 10-1 victory over Ely City in the Cambs. League, their fourth consecutive league win, but the game will be remembered for the fact that three players, Bill Asplin, Jackie Bond and W.R.Reeve each scored hat-tricks.

In the F.A. Challenge Cup the Abbey overcame Chatteris Town in the Extra Preliminary Round after a replay, but went out of the competition in the next round by 3 goals to 1 away to Newmarket Town. The Club must have dreaded the prospect of playing at Wisbech when they were drawn against them in the Second Round of the Cambs. Challenge Cup, following their 11-4 defeat the previous season. This time the game was another high scoring affair, but the "Wasps" fared a little better in losing by 8 goals to 4.

Coton Institute were Abbey United's main contenders for the Cambs. League Premier Division Championship, yet on 10th February 1934 the Abbey thrashed them 7-2 in the Third Round of the Creake Charity Shield. Three weeks later when the two clubs met again on Coton's ground, in what was the Abbey's penultimate league match, the "Wasps" had to win to have a chance of winning the league. With fifteen minutes left to play the Abbey were 2-1 ahead, and on course for the title, when the ball appeared to accidentaly strike the hand of the Abbey defender Bill Asplin. A penalty was rather harshly awarded against the Abbey and Coton scored to secure the point which clinched the league title. Had they failed to score the Championship would have been Abbey United's, as they beat Linton Granta 4-1 in the last game and therefore had a marginally better goal average.

In the Final of the Cottenham Nursing Cup at Cottenham on Saturday 30th April 1934, Abbey United took a two goal lead over Chatteris Engineers, but their opponents fought back strongly and eventually ran out 5-2 winners.

A 7-0 victory over Cottenham in the Creake Charity Shield Semi-final gave the Abbey some hope of winning at least one trophy. In the Final at Milton Road a crowd of over 1,000 saw Abbey United and Pye Radio finish level after 90 minutes and go into extra-time. Two goals from Harvey Cornwell and one from "Darley" Watson were just enough to allow Abbey United to win the trophy for the fifth time with a narrow 3-2 victory.

1933-34 Season First Team
Back Row: Charlie Taverner, Bob Brown, Harry Wilsher, Harvey Cornwell, William Asplin, Fred Taverner.
Front Row: Fred Bowles, Harold "Darley" Watson, Wally Wilson (Captain), Herbert Bailey, Jackie Bond. Winners of the Creake Charity Shield after beating Pye Radio 3-2 in the Final at Milton Road. Photograph by courtesy of Cambridge Evening News.

The Club's new wooden grandstand nears completion as workers apply the finishing touches. The stand was opened on Saturday 10th March 1934 when Abbey United celebrated the occasion by beating Gamlingay 1-0 in the Cambs League Premier Division. Photograph by courtesy of Cambridge Evening News.

F.A. Challenge Cup

Extra Preliminary Round
Chatteris Town 2 2 **Abbey United**

Extra Preliminary Round Replay
Abbey United 3 2 Chatteris Town

Preliminary Round
Newmarket Town 3 1 **Abbey United**

F.A. Amateur Cup

First Qualifying Round
Cambridge Town 9 1 **Abbey United**

Cambs Challenge Cup

First Round Bye

Second Round
Wisbech Town 8 4 **Abbey United**

Creake Charity Shield

First Round Bye

Second Round
Abbey United 3 2 Ely City

Third Round
Abbey United 7 2 Coton Institute

Semi-final (at Histon)
Abbey United 7 0 Cottenham

Final (at Cambridge Town F.C.)
Abbey United 3 2 Pye Radio
(A.E.T. 1-1 at full-time)

Cottenham Nursing Cup

First Round
Abbey United 6 0 Gamlingay

Semi-final
R.A.F. Duxford 2 4 **Abbey United**

Final (at Cottenham)
Abbey United 2 5 Chatteris Engineers

Cambs League Premier Division

	Pld	W	D	L	F	A	Pts
Coton Institute	22	15	5	2	68	34	35
Abbey United	22	15	3	4	67	33	33
Linton Granta	22	11	5	6	71	48	27
Histon Institute	22	10	6	6	62	45	26
Bottisham	22	10	4	8	51	53	24
University Press	22	6	8	8	51	47	20
Gamlingay	22	9	2	11	46	53	20
Soham Rangers	22	8	3	11	45	56	19
Ely City	22	8	3	11	41	63	19
R.A.F. Duxford	22	6	6	10	50	65	18
Royston Town	22	5	4	13	27	41	14
United Cantabs	22	4	1	17	40	81	9

Cambs Minor Cup

Preliminary Round
Abbey United Res. 1 1 Pye Radion Reserves

Preliminary Round Replay
Pye Radio Reserves 0 4 **Abbey United Res.**

First Round
Fordham 1 1 **Abbey United Res.**

First Round Replay
Abbey United Res. 2 0 Fordham

Second Round
Fulbourn 6 1 **Abbey United Res.**

Cambs League Division Two (Section A)

	Pld	W	D	L	F	A	Pts
Coton Institute Reserves	13	10	1	2	62	32	21
Cottenham United Res.	14	9	1	4	44	39	19
Over	13	7	2	4	48	25	16
Abbey United Res.	13	7	2	4	48	27	16
Horningsea	13	7	0	6	54	33	14
Swavesey	13	6	1	6	34	26	13
Hildersham	12	2	0	10	15	73	4
Sawston Paper Mills Res.	13	0	1	12	18	68	1

1934-35 SEASON

Abbey United got off to a good start in the league with two wins and a draw, but a dispute cost them the services of one of their star players. Harvey Cornwell's son, Harvey junior, had joined the Club at the start of the season and played several first team games, but when the selection committee could not guarantee him a place Harvey senior decided to get a transfer to United Cantabs.

Ironically Abbey United were drawn to play at home to the United Cantabs shortly afterwards in the Second Round of the Cambs. Challenge Cup. They progressed comfortably through to the Semi-finals by 3 goals to 1. However, in the Semi-final Histon Institute reversed the score-line when they beat the Abbey by 3 goals to 1 at Histon. Earlier in the season Histon also knocked the Abbey out of the F.A.Challenge Cup in the First Qualifying Round. In the first game at Histon the Abbey gained a very creditable 1-1 draw, but in the replay at Newmarket Road, Histon repeated their success of two years earlier, with an identical 5-4 victory, although this time the tension continued into extra-time.

There was no success in other cup competitions. The Abbey went out of the F.A.Amateur Cup in the Second Qualifying Round, 2-1 away to St.Neots & District, and made an exit from the Cottenham Nursing Cup at the Second Round stage, losing 2-1 away to the University Press. At that game on Saturday 9th February 1935 the Abbey's centre-half, Wally Wilson, was sent off in the last few minutes of the game after being alleged to have "had words" with the referee. He was the first Abbey player to be sent off from the field of play.

A run of nine consecutive league wins, which started just before Christmas, put Abbey United in with an excellent chance of winning the Cambs. League Premier Division, especially when they beat their main challengers, the University Press, by 2 goals to 1 with just three games to go. Inexplicably Abbey United, who had averaged four goals a game in their previous seventeen league games, failed to score a goal in their last three games, and they had to be content with the runners-up spot, three points behind the University Press.

The reserve team once again withdrew from their league in February owing to difficulties in raising a side.

F.A. Challenge Cup

First Qualifying Round
Histon Institute 1 1 **Abbey United**

First Qualifying Round Replay
Abbey United 4 5 Histon Institute
A.E.T. (3-3 at full-time)

F.A. Amateur Cup

First Qualifying Round
Abbey United 2 1 Ely City

Second Qualifying Round
St. Neots & District 2 1 **Abbey United**

Cambs Challenge Cup

Preliminary Round Bye

First Round
University Press 2 2 **Abbey United**

First Round Replay
Abbey United 7 2 University Press

Second Round
Abbey United 3 1 United Cantabs

Semi-final
Histon Institute 3 1 **Abbey United**

Creake Charity Shield

First Round Bye

Second Round
Histon Institute 4 2 **Abbey United**

Cottenham Nursing Cup

First Round
Chatteris Engineers Walk Over **Abbey United**

Second Round
University Press 2 1 **Abbey United**

Cambs League Premier Division

	Pld	W	D	L	F	A	Pts
University Press	19	14	3	2	60	31	31
Abbey United	20	13	2	5	62	29	28
Soham Rangers	19	13	1	5	67	30	27
Histon Institute	19	9	3	7	49	41	21
Coton Institute	17	9	1	7	57	45	19
Bottisham	20	9	1	10	45	66	19
R.A.F. Duxford	19	6	4	9	51	51	16
Gamlingay	19	6	3	10	39	62	15
Ely City	20	6	2	12	50	58	14
Linton Granta	20	6	2	12	46	62	14
Sawston Church Institute	20	2	4	14	33	83	8

Cambs Minor Cup

First Round
Abbey United Res. Rampton
(NOTE: Abbey United Reserves won, but score not known)

Second Round
Grantchester 9 1 **Abbey United Res.**

Cambs League Division Two (Section A)

	Pld	W	D	L	F	A	Pts
Over	24	21	1	2	106	28	43
St. Philip's	23	18	1	4	117	27	37
Fordham	25	18	1	6	93	41	37
Central Old Boys	24	16	4	4	85	34	36
Cambridge Town 'A'	23	15	2	6	83	35	32
Dale's Brewery	24	14	2	8	90	38	30
Swavesey	24	13	3	8	75	56	29
Wilburton	25	11	2	12	72	70	24
Sawston Institute Reserves	22	6	3	13	43	88	15
Cottenham United Reserves	20	5	2	13	41	90	12
Electric Supply Company	23	5	1	17	31	144	11
Horningsea	23	5	0	18	41	72	10
Sawston Paper Mills Res.	24	4	1	19	42	113	9
New Chesterton Institute	24	2	1	21	27	107	5

NOTE: Abbey United Reserves withdrew from the league in February, and their record was expunged from the league table.

1935-36 SEASON

Abbey United commenced their season on Saturday 14th September 1935 with a massive 13-0 home victory over Gamlingay in the Cambs. League Premier Division. Monty Bull scored five of the goals.

In the First Qualifying Round of the F.A. Challenge Cup Abbey United and Chatteris

First Team. 1935-36 Season
Back Row: Harry Wilsher, Wally Wilson, Reg Kimberley, S."Fred" Sewell, Jim Langford, Len Johnson.
Front Row: Harvey Cornwell, Basil Saunders, William Asplen, Fred Taverner, Ernie Wilsher.
Photograph by courtesy of Cambridge Evening News.

Engineers played for 300 minutes before the Chatteris team won 3-1 in the second replay. Extra-time was also required as the Abbey beat Histon Institute 2-1 in the First Qualifying Round of the F.A.Amateur Cup, but in the next round the Abbey surprisingly lost 2-1 at home to Ely City.

The Club made steady progress through to the Final of both the major Cambridgeshire cup competitions. The first of these was at Chatteris on Saturday 11th April 1936, against March G.E.R. United in the Cambs. Challenge Cup. Although the Abbey had the better of the game, they could not score and the game ended goal-less.

On Wednesday 22nd April at Cambridge Town F.C.'s ground, the Abbey played Coton Institute in the Final of the Creake Charity Shield. Len Johnson put the Abbey ahead after half an hour, but within five minutes Coton drew level. Ten minutes before the close the Abbey took the lead again with a controversial goal that would not have been allowed today. S.Sewell and B.Saunders hit the Coton goalkeeper together and knocked the ball out of his grasp for Len Johnson to net the winner. The goalkeeper had to receive attention before play could resume.

Five days later a crowd of over 2,000 spectators gathered at Cottenham to witness the Semi-final of the Cottenham Nursing Cup between Haddenham Rovers and Abbey United. The reason for such great interest was due to the fact that Haddenham had won all of their nineteen league games that season in Division One Section B, and an upset was anticipated. An exciting game finished level at 3-3 at full-time, but in extra-time Haddenham scored two more goals without reply to preserve their unbeaten record for the season.

Despite a congested fixture list at the end of the season, the Abbey finished in fourth place in the Cambs League Premier Division, having dropped just two more points than the League Champions, Linton Granta.

The season was completed on Saturday 9th May 1936 with the Cambs Challenge Cup Final replay held on Cambridge Town F.C.'s ground against March G.E.R. United. The Abbey were ahead at half-time through a goal from Len Johnson, but March equalized after 55 minutes, and scored the winner from a penalty two minutes from time.

One consolation for the Club was that they found a consistent goalscorer in S. Sewell, who netted 34 first team goals throughout the season.

F.A. Challenge Cup

First Qualifying Round
Abbey United 1 1 Chatteris Engineers

First Qualifying Round Replay
Chatteris Engineers 3 3 **Abbey United**
A.E.T. (3-3 at full-time)

First Qualifying Round Second Replay (at St. Ives F.C.)
Chatteris Engineers 3 1 **Abbey United**

F.A. Amateur Cup

First Qualifying Round
Abbey United 2 1 Histon Institute

Second Qualifying Round
Abbey United 1 2 Ely City

Cambs Challenge Cup

First Round
Gamlingay 0 4 **Abbey United**

Second Round (at Pye Radio F.C.)
Cambridge Town Res. 2 2 **Abbey United**

Second Round Replay
Abbey United 0 0 Cambridge Town Res.
(Match abandoned after 66 minutes owing to fog)

Second Round Replay
Cambridge Town Res. 1 3 **Abbey United**

Semi-final (at Cambridge Town F.C.)
Abbey United 3 1 Histon Institute

Final (at Chatteris Engineers F.C.)
Abbey United 0 0 Histon Institute

Final Replay (at Cambridge United F.C.)
Abbey United 1 2 March G.E.R. United

Creake Charity Shield

First Round
Abbey United 3 0 Soham Town

Second Round
Soham Rangers 2 4 **Abbey United**

Third Round
Isleham 2 9 **Abbey United**

Semi-final (at Cambridge Town F.C.)
Abbey United 4 0 Sawston Church Inst.

Final (at Cambridge Town F.C.)
Abbey United 2 1 Coton Institute

Cottenham Nursing Cup

First Round
Abbey United 3 1 Pye Radio

Second Round
Abbey United 11 1 Soham Town

Semi-final (at Cottenham United F.C.)
Haddenham Rovers 5 3 **Abbey United**
A.E.T. (3-3 at full-time)

Cambs League Premier Division

	Pld	W	D	L	F	A	Pts
Linton Granta	24	16	5	3	90	33	37
Histon Institute	24	16	3	5	82	39	35
University Press	23	15	3	5	72	34	33
Abbey United	22	14	3	5	84	30	31
Bottisham	24	13	2	9	64	65	28
Ely City	22	11	3	8	59	67	25
Coton Institute	23	10	3	10	70	68	23
Pye Radio	24	10	1	13	51	39	21
Soham Rangers	20	9	2	9	76	58	20
Camden United	23	8	4	11	50	53	20
United Cantabs	23	4	6	13	42	86	14
R.A.F. Duxford	24	2	3	19	33	88	7
Gamlingay	22	0	2	20	20	116	2

Cambs Minor Cup

Preliminary Round
Fen Ditton 1 7 **Abbey United Res.**

First Round
Great Shelford Inst. 3 2 **Abbey United Res.**

Cambs League Division Two (Section A)

	Pld	W	D	L	F	A	Pts
Landbeach	23	17	5	1	94	30	39
Swavesey	23	17	4	2	108	36	38
Willingham	22	16	2	4	79	33	34
Dale's Brewery	23	15	2	6	109	43	32
Abbey United Res.	23	13	2	8	93	52	28
Oakington	23	10	3	10	64	56	23
Lode	21	8	3	10	55	73	19
Wilburton	23	7	4	12	47	70	18
Whittlesford	21	7	3	11	44	55	17
Cambridge Town 'A'	23	5	6	12	37	84	16
Sawston Paper Mills Res.	22	6	1	15	36	111	13
Duxford	23	3	3	17	47	95	9
Sawston Church Inst. Res.	20	1	3	16	24	100	5

1936-37 SEASON

The first five games of the new season were all away, and after opening with two defeats the Club recovered to record five wins in the next six games. However, with the loss of several established players at the beginning of the season, the Club lacked depth in quality, and the results soon took a turn for the worse.

An early exit was made in the F.A. Challenge Cup with a 2-0 defeat away to March G.E.R

United. In the F.A. Amateur Cup, although the Abbey were able to beat United Cantabs 2-1 away from home in the Preliminary Round, they were no match for Histon Institute in the next round, and went down by 4 goals to 1.

Abbey United were able to turn the tables on Histon Institute in the First Round of the Cambs. Challenge Cup three weeks later, as Len Johnson scored both goals in a 2-1 victory. A 5-2 victory over United Cantabs in the next round gave the Abbey some hope of success, but in the Third Round against University Press, in a match which also counted for league points, the "Wasps" were on the receiving end of a 5-2 thrashing.

Club spirit reached an all time low when only ten men played throughout the Abbey's home match against Camden United in the Second Round of the Creake Charity Shield. Not surprisingly the Club suffered its heaviest defeat at home by 8 goals to 0.

As in the previous season, Abbey United met Haddenham Rovers in the Semi-final of the Cottenham Nursing Cup. With newly promoted Haddenham occupying second place in the Cambs. League Premier Division, and the Abbey finishing fourth from bottom, it was Haddenham this time who went into the match as favourites. Another good crowd saw Haddenham justify their optimism by winning a place in the Final with a 2-1 victory.

The season was equally disappointing for the reserve team, who finished second from bottom in Division Two Section A of the Cambs. League.

F.A. Challenge Cup

Preliminary Round
March G.E.R. United   2   0   **Abbey United**

F.A. Amateur Cup

Preliminary Round
United Cantabs   1   2   **Abbey United**

First Round
Histon Institute   4   1   **Abbey United**

Cambs Challenge Cup

First Round
Abbey United   2   1   Histon Institute

Second Round
United Cantabs   2   5   **Abbey United**

Third Round (at Cambridge Town F.C.)
University Press   5   2   **Abbey United**

Creake Charity Shield

First Round   Bye

Second Round
Abbey United   0   8   Camden United

Cottenham Nursing Cup

First Round   Bye

Second Round
Histon Institute   1   3   **Abbey United**

Semi-final
Haddenham Rovers   2   1   **Abbey United**

Cambs League Premier Division

	Pld	W	D	L	F	A	Pts
Linton Granta	24	19	2	3	99	28	40
Haddenham Rovers	24	16	2	6	93	51	34
Histon Institute	23	15	2	6	74	40	32
Camden United	21	11	4	6	62	35	26
Coton Institute	20	11	3	6	67	54	25
University Press	24	9	5	10	62	65	23
Cottenham United	24	10	2	12	55	67	22
United Cantabs	23	8	2	13	56	80	18
Soham Rangers	20	7	3	10	46	50	17
Abbey United	22	6	5	11	46	60	17
Pye Radio	24	7	2	15	43	79	16
Ely City	23	6	2	15	38	64	14
R.A.F. Duxford	24	6	2	16	41	106	14

Cambs Minor Cup

Preliminary Round
Cambridge Inst. Co.   3   0   **Abbey United Res.**

Cambs League Division Two (Section A)

	Pld	W	D	L	F	A	Pts
Chatteris Eng. Res.	24	18	3	3	101	46	39
Cambridge Town 'A'	24	17	2	5	105	39	36
Wilburton	24	17	1	6	121	47	35
Burwell	24	16	1	7	100	66	33
Lode	23	13	5	5	96	49	31
Waterbeach	23	9	5	9	62	70	23
Dale's Brewery	22	10	3	9	48	55	23
Cambridge Inst. Co.	23	6	5	12	49	91	17
Cherry Hinton	21	5	6	10	42	67	16
Railway Social	23	6	2	15	57	83	14
Oakington	22	6	1	15	37	77	13
Abbey United Res.	18	3	1	14	27	86	7
Over Reserves	22	2	1	19	27	106	5

1937-38 SEASON

The Abbey lost their first three games of the 1937-38 season and in the process went out of the F.A. Challenge Cup in the Preliminary Round by 3 goals to 1 away to March G.E.R. United. However, the "Wasps" embarked on their best run in the F.A. Amateur Cup, overwhelming Histon Institute

5-1 and Ramsey Town 3-1, before losing narrowly by 2 goals to 1 at home to Newmarket Town in the Third Qualifying Round.

Any euphoria gained from the F.A. Amateur Cup run was dispelled when the Abbey lost at home to Histon Institute by 2 goals to 1 in the Preliminary Round of the Cambs. Challenge Cup.

In the Creake Charity Shield the Abbey made an early exit in the Second Round, when they lost 5-1 to the eventual runaway Champions of the Cambs. League Premier Division, Linton Granta. It was the Club's only defeat in fifteen games, a run of results which coincided with the return of Harvey Cornwell to the forward line.

Success in Cambs. county cup competitions was left to the reserve team who won their way through four rounds of the Cambs. Minor Cup before losing 3-1 to Soham Town in the Semi-final at Soham Rangers F.C.'s ground. Their league form was not so impressive, and they finished fourth from bottom in the Cambs. League Division Two Section A.

After Christmas the first team lost only three games, two of them against Linton Granta, and as a result they moved up the league table to finish in a creditable fourth place in the Cambs. League Premier Division. There was also a little bit of success when the Club won the Soham Nursing Cup by beating Camden United 3-1 in the Final, although there was only a small entry for the competition. Leading goalscorer for the Club was Fred Mansfield who scored 22 first team goals during the season.

F.A. Challenge Cup

Preliminary Round
March G.E.R. United 3 1 **Abbey United**

F.A. Amateur Cup

First Qualifying Round
Abbey United 5 1 Histon Institute

Second Qualifying Round
Abbey United 3 1 Ramsey Town

Third Qualifying Round
Abbey United 1 2 Newmarket Town

Cambs Challenge Cup

Preliminary Round
Abbey United 1 2 Histon Institute

Creake Charity Shield

First Round
Abbey United 2 2 United Cantabs

First Round Replay
United Cantabs 1 5 **Abbey United**

Second Round
Linton Granta 5 1 **Abbey United**

Soham Nursing Cup

Semi-final
Abbey United 5 0 Soham Town

Final (at Soham)
Abbey United 3 1 Camden United

Cambs League Premier Division

	Pld	W	D	L	F	A	Pts
Linton Granta	24	22	1	1	113	26	45
University Press	21	15	0	6	66	43	30
Haddenham Rovers	20	12	3	5	65	34	27
Abbey United	20	11	4	5	49	36	26
Cottenham United	24	11	1	12	71	57	23
Camden United	21	10	2	9	63	44	22
Histon Institute	20	10	2	8	49	41	22
Chatteris Town	22	7	3	12	57	63	17
Coton Institute	18	7	3	8	46	53	17
Soham Rangers	24	7	2	15	45	97	16
Pye Radio	20	6	3	11	42	64	15
Girton United	21	4	2	15	36	82	10
United Cantabs	21	2	2	17	40	102	6

Cambs Minor Cup

Preliminary Round
Lode 2 4 **Abbey United Res.**

First Round
Abbey United Res. 7 1 Pye Radio Reserves

Second Round
Abbey United Res. 3 2 Littleport Town

Third Round
Abbey United Res. 4 0 Newnham Institute

Semi-final (at Soham Rangers F.C.)
Soham Town 3 1 **Abbey United Res.**

Cambs League Division Two (Section A)

	Pld	W	D	L	F	A	Pts
Manea	21	16	4	1	86	26	36
Wilburton	21	17	0	4	91	27	34
Cambridge Town 'A'	21	13	2	6	63	44	28
Dale's Brewery	21	10	4	7	53	43	24
Burwell	20	11	0	9	75	47	22
Waterbeach	21	10	0	11	63	55	20
Lode	19	9	1	9	62	45	19
Haddenham Reserves	18	8	2	8	49	46	18
Abbey United Res.	18	8	0	10	51	56	16
Fen Ditton	21	5	2	14	33	104	12
Over Reserves	21	3	3	15	29	107	9
Cottenham United Res.	22	2	2	18	34	90	6

1938-39 SEASON

A season which ended with the Abbey returning as a force in Cambridgeshire football did not start at all well. On the first day of the season the "Wasps" beat their old rivals, Histon Institute, 2-1 in the Preliminary Round of the F.A. Challenge Cup, in the first of five meetings between the two clubs that season. However, in the next round the Abbey lost as expected away to Cambridge Town by 3 goals to 0, a considerable improvement on the first meeting five years earlier. That defeat began a sequence of five consecutive losses, including a 5-1 reverse away to Histon in the F.A. Amateur Cup and a 3-1 home defeat against the University Press in the First Round of the Cambs. Challenge Cup, in which the Abbey played well with only ten men.

Following a 7-0 home defeat in the league on 26th November 1938 against lowly Coton Institute, the Abbey bounced back with a shock 1-0 victory over the previously unbeaten league leaders, Linton Granta, a week later.

Shortly afterwards at a Cambs. F.A. meeting, two Abbey United reserve team players, Smart and Mason, were banned from playing football for a month for their conduct after a Cambs. Minor Cup game against Landbeach. Immediately after his ban Smart was promoted to the first team and he scored goals as frequently as he did in the reserves, quickly establishing his place in the side. A run of eighteen matches, in which the Abbey suffered just one defeat, saw them move up into strong contention for the league championship, particularly after winning 2-1 away to Linton Granta, who suffered their first home defeat for four years.

Despite winning ten and drawing one of their last twelve league matches, it was a 3-1 home defeat against Histon Institute in the last week of the season which ended the Abbey's challenge for the league title. They had to be content with the runners-up spot, two points behind the winners Linton Granta and one point ahead of Histon.

The Creake Charity Shield provided a thirteen goal thriller against Haddenham Rovers in the Semi-final staged at Ely on Saturday 25th March 1939. At one stage in the second half, Abbey United led by 7 goals to 2. Then Haddenham missed a penalty and their injured goalkeeper left his goal to play on the field. With his help they staged a remarkable four goal fight back to narrowly lose 7-6.

Approximately 1,200 spectators watched the Final between Abbey United and Histon Institute at Milton Road on Thursday 11th May 1939. H.Smart gave the Abbey a first half lead. In the second half the Abbey's right half Joe Richardson and A.Carter the Histon goalkeeper were sent off following an incident after Carter had saved the Abbey player's penalty shot. Hero of the Abbey team was centre-forward H.Smart, who, despite an injured arm received in a tackle which resulted in the penalty, scored the winning goal in the 87th minute, less than a minute after Todd had put the teams on level terms. After such a tense struggle the Abbey United supporters returned across the river in jubilant mood.

In 1939 the Club's President for twenty years, Mr.Henry Clement Francis, died. The Officers of the Club were called to his solicitors to be told that the football ground had been left in trust to the Mayor of Cambridge, the Vicar of Fen Ditton and the District Nursing Association, to be used for grazing and football by the Abbey United Football Club at a nominal rent of half-a-crown per year. Very few football pitches at that time were cut by mechanical means, and it was normal practice for sheep to be left on the pitch to graze all day Friday. Then on Saturday morning the Committee members would undertake the task of clearing the droppings before play could commence.

F.A. Challenge Cup

Preliminary Round
Abbey United   2   1   Histon Institute

First Qualifying Round
Cambridge Town   3   0   **Abbey United**

F.A. Amateur Cup

First Qualifying Round
Histon Institute   5   1   **Abbey United**

Cambs Challenge Cup

First Round
Abbey United   1   3   University Press

Creake Charity Shield

First Round   Bye

Second Round
Abbey United   1   0   University Press

Third Round
Royston Town   1   3   **Abbey United**

Semi-final (at Ely City F.C.)
Haddenham Rovers   6   7   **Abbey United**

Final (at Cambridge Town F.C.)
Abbey United   2   1   Histon Institute

Soham Nursing Cup

First Round
University Press 2 – 2 **Abbey United**

First Round Replay
Abbey United 5 – 1 University Press

Second Round
Sawston Paper Mills v **Abbey United**
(Abbey United withdrew from competition after First Round)

Cambs League Premier Division

	Pld	W	D	L	F	A	Pts
Linton Granta	24	17	4	3	88	29	38
Abbey United	24	17	2	5	71	41	36
Histon Institute	24	16	3	5	66	41	35
Soham Town	24	13	5	6	65	50	31
Royston Town	24	14	2	8	45	42	30
Pye Radio	23	10	8	5	68	45	28
Haddenham Rovers	24	12	3	9	90	76	27
Camden United	24	7	6	11	55	62	20
University Press	20	6	5	9	48	52	17
Coton Institute	22	7	3	12	69	75	17
Cottenham United	23	6	1	16	41	66	13
Chatteris Town	22	2	3	17	29	71	7
Soham Rangers	24	1	1	22	28	110	3

Cambs Minor Cup

Preliminary Round Bye

First Round
Pye Radio Reserves 1 – 4 **Abbey United Res.**

Second Round
Landbeach 3 – 2 **Abbey United Res.**

Willingham Nursing Cup

Preliminary Round Bye

First Round
Abbey United Res. 4 – 1 Longstanton

Second Round
Sawston Paper Mills 7 – 3 **Abbey United Res.**

Cambs League Division Two (Section A)

	Pld	W	D	L	F	A	Pts
Burwell	16	12	2	2	77	36	26
Abbey United Res.	16	10	3	3	70	44	23
Cambridge Town 'A'	16	9	3	4	69	41	21
Lode	16	10	1	5	85	51	21
Stretham	15	7	2	6	42	48	16
Camden United Reserves	16	7	1	8	53	55	15
Waterbeach	16	6	1	9	56	76	13
Haddenham Rovers Res.	15	2	1	12	46	65	5
Cottenham United Res.	14	0	0	14	13	95	0

First Team 1938-39 Season
Back Row: Herbert Smart, Reg Kimberley, A. "Buck" Arnold, Ron Sanderson, Ernie Caston, Reg Wilson.
Front Row: Fred Mansfield, Monty Bull, Wally Wilson, Bob Brown, Joe Richardson, Jim Langford.
Winners of the Creake Charity Shield.

Chapter 4

THE FORTIES

THE WAR YEARS

When Great Britain declared war on Germany early in September 1939, the following statement was made in the national and local press: "Sports gatherings which involve large numbers congregating together are prohibited until further notice".

The ban was only in force for a couple of weeks, but it was not until Saturday 14th October 1939 that Abbey United played their first competitive game of the season in the First Round of the Cottenham Nursing Cup, which resulted in a convincing 5-0 victory over Willingham. A week later the Club progressed through the First Round of the Willingham Nursing Cup when they beat Orwell 6-4.

The Cambs. Challenge Cup and Creake Charity Shield competitions were suspended for the season, but the Cambs. F.A. Emergency League was formed, and started at the end of October with two divisions of ten clubs each. During the season Willingham, Swavesey and the University Press had to withdraw because of difficulty in raising a team, and their records were deleted.

A weakened Abbey United, which included several new players, finished fifth out of nine teams in Section A with 8 points from 8 games. The Cambs. F.A. closed the league on 11th May 1940, and the clubs with the most points on that day were adjudged the winners of the divisions. Camden United won Section A, and they easily defeated Section B winners R.A.F. 'A' 3-0 in the Final to win the Charity Shield.

After beating Littleport Town 4-0 in the Second Round of the Cottenham Nursing Cup, Abbey United lost 2-0 away to Camden United in the Semi-final. However, the Willingham Nursing Cup was suspended at the Semi-final stage, after Abbey United had beaten Bottisham 4-1 in the Second Round.

It was important that the Club's ground was kept open during the War, because if football matches were not regularly played the ground would have been requisitioned by the Government for military use. As the War continued, the Club had Frank Pettit to thank for keeping football going, because he undertook the duties of Secretary and Treasurer throughout the duration of hostilities. It was his responsibility to arrange friendly matches with the sports officers of R.A.F. and Army Units stationed nearby. Petrol was in short supply, but with plenty of determination, and often by hook or by crook, scratch teams managed to travel to the Club's ground in Newmarket Road for their game of football.

The scores of the matches were largely irrelevant. What mattered was the maintenance of moral, with the provision of competitive, entertaining football matches. There were scores of top class players who played on the ground, including the famous Dixie Dean and Alex James.

The ground was once borrowed by the service units to stage one of their finals. One of the units was from the Birmingham area, and had moved into the locality, and all of their players had previously been with Aston Villa. Realising that the game would attract a large crowd, the Club asked if they could charge a 'gate', but permission was refused as it was thought that the soldiers would tear the place to pieces if they were asked to pay to watch the game.

On one occasion during the War when all R.A.F. matches were cancelled, Abbey United hastily arranged a game against Cambridge Town, who also managed to keep their ground open. The match was played at Milton Road and resulted in the Abbey's first victory over them by 7 goals to 2.

The Abbey's matches were reported in the local newspapers, but details of the teams could not be revealed because the Government did not want the enemy to know that there were a large number of R.A.F. Units stationed near Cambridge. Nor were the Club allowed to report that the games were abandoned because of fog, in case the information got into the wrong hands.

The longer the War went on the poorer the Club became, mainly due to the Ground Tax which had to be paid over to the Government. In 1944 Herby Spicer, a railway engine driver from Ditton Fields, came up with an idea that would either save the Club or break it. Frank Pettit was asked to scrape together every penny the Club had, and with the money, about £38, Herby Spicer hired a band and the Beaconsfield Hall in Gwydir Street and held a dance there. Fortunately the gamble paid off, and a profit of £80 was made on the evening. Similar functions enabled the Club to have a bit of money in hand when the War came to an end.

Cottenham Nursing Cup

First Round
Abbey United   5   0   Willingham

Second Round
Littleport Town   0   4   **Abbey United**

Semi-final
Camden United   2   0   **Abbey United**

Willingham Nursing Cup

First Round
Abbey United   6   4   Orwell

Second Round
Abbey United   4   1   Bottisham

NOTE: The competition was suspended at the Semi-final stage.

Cambs Emergency League Section A

	Pld	W	D	L	F	A	Pts
Camden United	9	6	3	0	53	15	15
Bottisham	11	6	3	2	26	19	15
Cottenham United	11	6	1	4	27	23	13
Histon Institute	10	5	0	5	26	37	10
Abbey United	8	4	0	4	25	19	8
Landbeach	8	4	0	4	18	23	8
Cambridge Town Reserves	10	3	0	7	28	27	6
Post Office Telephones	9	0	1	8	12	44	1

NOTE: Swavesey, Univesity Press and Willingham all withdrew from the league during the season, owing to difficulties in raising a team, and their records were expunged from the league table.

Cambs Emergency League Section B

	Pld	W	D	L	F	A	Pts
R.A.F. 'A'	10	8	1	1	40	12	17
Atlas Sports (Meldreth)	10	6	3	1	34	21	15
Royston Town	10	5	3	2	33	15	13
Orwell	8	6	1	1	28	19	13
R.A.F. 'C'	9	6	0	3	34	16	12
Bassingbourn	13	4	2	7	26	37	10
Foxton	14	3	1	10	27	45	7
R.A.F. 'B'	8	1	0	7	11	30	2
Barrington	7	0	1	6	7	43	1

Final (at Cambridge Town F.C.)
Camden United   3   0   R.A.F. 'A'

1945-46 SEASON

Organized football began again, to a limited extent, at the start of the 1945-46 season, and Abbey United re-joined the Cambs. League, which consisted of just two regionalized divisions. The Southern Division (Section A) initially had nine clubs, but during the season R.A.F Quy withdrew, and the Abbey's two victories against them were deleted from the records.

At the end of the season Abbey United finished in fourth place out of eight clubs with eleven points from eleven games, but they had quite a bearing on the Championship. In their last game on Thursday 2nd May 1946, the Abbey were leading 3-2 when Histon scored a last minute equalizer to take the Section A title on goal difference over R.A.F. Bassingbourn. R.A.F. Waterbeach were not able to play their last game against Abbey United, and consequently lost their chance of taking the league title. Histon beat the Northern Section winners, Ely City, by 6 goals to 1 to win the Cambs. League Championship.

Abbey United's first cup game of the season was at home to Cambridge Town in the First Qualifying Round of the F.A.Challenge Cup, but as in previous encounters against their more senior hosts the match resulted in heavy defeat by 8 goals to 0. The Club received byes in the F.A.Amateur Cup into the Third Qualifying Round, and progressed further by beating Newmarket Town 2-0 at home. When their opponents in the Fourth Qualifying Round, Lowestoft Town, withdrew, the Abbey obtained a passage into the First Round Proper for the first time. They were favoured with a home draw against Hitchin Town on Saturday 19th January 1946, but a plucky performance could not prevent them losing by 5 goals to 3, with J.Connelly, Reg Kimberley and Sid High scoring the Abbey's goals.

For the first time in the Club's history, an entry was made in the East Anglian Cup, but after two drawn matches against Histon Institute, Abbey United collapsed in the second replay and lost 7-0. The two teams met again in the Southern Final of the Creake Charity Shield at Cambridge Town F.C.'s ground on Saturday 23rd March 1946, but Histon again won comfortably by 6 goals to 1.

The Club's last chance of glory that season was in the Cambs. Challenge Cup. By scoring 22 goals in the first three rounds, the Abbey reached the Southern Final against R.A.F. Bassingbourn at the Cambridge Town F.C. ground on Saturday 13th April. However, having lost 4-3 at home to R.A.F. Bassingbourn in the league a week earlier, the Abbey's prospects of victory were not too good. At half-time the R.A.F. men led 1-0, then a.Bailey missed a penalty for the Abbey before A.Pauley hit a post prior to scoring the equalizer. With the tide turning in their favour the Abbey pressed for victory, but it was not to be, and the R.A.F. scored near the end to reach the County Final.

F.A. Challenge Cup

First Qualifying Round
Abbey United 0 – 8 Cambridge Town

F.A. Amateur Cup

First Qualifying Round Bye

Second Qualifying Round Bye

Third Qualifying Round
Abbey United 2 – 0 Newmarket Town

Fourth Qualifying Round
Abbey United Walkover Lowestoft Town

First Round Proper
Abbey United 3 – 5 Hitchin Town

East Anglian Cup

First Round
Abbey United 1 – 1 Histon Institute

First Round Replay
Histon Institute 2 – 2 **Abbey United**

First Round Second Replay
Histon Institute 7 – 0 **Abbey United**

Cambs Challenge Cup

First Round
Abbey United 7 – 1 Sawston Paper Mills

Second Round
Abbey United 7 – 2 Saxons

Southern Semi-final (at Histon)
Abbey United 8 – 2 Cambridge Town Res.

Southern Final (at Cambridge Town F.C.)
Abbey United 1 – 2 R.A.F. Bassingbourn

Creake Charity Shield

Preliminary Round
Orwell 0 – 3 **Abbey United**

First Round
Abbey United 3 – 3 Saxons
(Match abandoned after 86 minutes - fog)

First Round Replay
Abbey United 5 – 4 Saxons

Southern Semi-final (at Ely City F.C.)
Abbey United 6 – 1 Soham Town

Southern Final (at Cambridge Town F.C.)
Abbey United 1 – 6 Histon Institute

Cottenham Nursing Cup

Semi-final
Cottenham United 4 – 3 **Abbey United**

Cambs League (Section A)

	Pld	W	D	L	F	A	Pts
Histon Institute	14	10	2	2	75	23	22
R.A.F. Bassingbourn	14	10	2	2	55	27	22
R.A.F. Waterbeach	13	10	1	2	45	23	21
Abbey United	11	3	5	3	35	26	11
Cambridge Town Res.	14	4	2	8	31	36	10
Camden United	14	4	2	8	29	59	10
Cottenham United	13	1	4	8	18	50	6
Royston Town	13	1	2	10	14	58	4

1946-47 SEASON

The Club decided not to enter the F.A. Challenge Cup for the 1946-47 season, and interest in the F.A. Amateur Cup was short-lived when they went out of the competition in the First Qualifying Round, losing 6-1 at home to Ely City.

Steady progress was made in the Cambs. Challenge Cup and Creake Charity Shield, until at the end of January two months of the season was lost owing to the very severe weather. At the point when football was frozen out, the Abbey had gained just five points from seven games in the Cambs. League Premier Division. When football did resume after the thaw the Abbey lost only one game out of their remaining eleven matches to move up into a respectable fourth place in the final table.

On Easter Monday, 7th April 1947, the Abbey beat Haddenham Rovers 4-2 in the Semi-final of the Cambs. Challenge Cup at Histon, but in the Semi-final of the Creake Charity Shield at the same ground on Saturday 19th April the "Wasps" lost 2-0 to Camden United, the club that had dominated Cambs. football that season.

A crowd of over 1,000 spectators watched the Final of the Cambs. Challenge Cup on the Cambridge Town F.C. ground in which Abbey United took on Camden United for the fifth time during the season, having lost all four of the previous encounters. This time the Abbey gave the best account of themselves, but one goal from Camden proved to be enough to give them the cup.

Because of the backlog of matches, the season turned out to be the longest on record, and the Abbey's last game was played against Ely City in the league on 5th June.

At the end of the season, Mr. Wadsworth, who had been the Club's Senior Vice-President since 1931, and the Club's President since the start of the War, was succeeded as President by Mr. W. McLaren-Francis. Frank Pettit, who had been

Chairman, Secretary and Treasurer throughout the War, reverted back to his post as Treasurer, while Bill Taverner became Chairman, and Lew Sylvester took over the position of Club Secretary.

F.A. Amateur Cup

First Qualifying Round
Abbey United   1   6   Ely City

Cambs Challenge Cup

First Round
Cottenham United   2   2   **Abbey United**

First Round Replay
Abbey United   6   2   Cottenham United

Second Round
Abbey United   2   0   Saxons

Semi-final (at Histon Institute F.C.)
Abbey United   4   2   Haddenham Rovers

Final (at Cambridge Town F.C.)
Abbey United   0   1   Camden United

Creake Charity Shield

Preliminary Round
Royston Town   1   1   **Abbey United**

Preliminary Round Replay
Abbey United   2   1   Royston Town

First Round
Wisbech Canners   2   3   **Abbey United**

Second Round
Abbey United   4   4   Sawston United

Second Round Replay
Sawston United   0   2   **Abbey United**

Semi-final (at Histon Institute F.C.)
Abbey United   0   2   Camden United

Cambs League Premier Division

	Pld	W	D	L	F	A	Pts
Camden United	22	17	4	1	98	38	38
Saxons	21	14	5	2	94	55	33
Histon Institute	21	12	4	5	70	53	28
Abbey United	18	9	4	5	42	44	22
Haddenham Rovers	20	8	5	7	79	66	21
Linton Granta	19	8	4	7	38	29	20
Royston Town	19	5	7	7	45	57	17
Sawston United	21	6	5	10	53	72	17
Soham Town Rangers	22	3	7	12	46	66	13
Ely City	20	5	3	12	43	63	13
Cottenham United	21	4	5	12	47	82	13
Coton Institute	20	1	6	13	42	82	8

1947-48 SEASON

An unofficial and tentative invitation to join the United Counties League was made to the Club at the end of the 1946-47 season. A formal invitation had been made to Cambridge Town F.C. to join the league, but they turned it down, preferring to stay amateur. Frank Pettit raised the matter at the Club's next meeting in their new headquarters, the "Ancient Druids" in Fitzroy Street, and despite the fact that the league consisted of professional and semi-professional clubs the committee decided to take a gamble, and made an application to join the league.

The Annual General Meeting of the United Counties League was held at the "Red Bull" in Stamford, and when the new applications to join the league were considered, some clubs had not even heard of Abbey United. In fact the Club's officials were even facetiously asked if the team consisted of monks. However, when the Club pointed out that before the War they had beaten Wisbech on their own ground, and only lost by the odd goal at King's Lynn in the F.A.Cup, as well as having an enclosed ground where they could charge gate money, the league decided to accept their application.

The Club's Secretary, Lew Sylvester, offered to guarantee that any outstanding bills would be settled if the move was unsuccessful, but as it turned out he need not have bothered. A large crowd gathered to watch the Club's first game in the new league at home to Rushden Town on Saturday 23rd August 1947, in which J.Gaunt put the Abbey ahead before the visitors fought back to narrowly win 2-1. But club officials were happy, as they took more 'gate' money from that game than they did from all their home games in the previous season. During the season crowds of over one thousand spectators were commonplace, and for the visit of the eventual Champions, Wisbech Town, on 18th October 1947, over two thousand people were present at the ground.

A meeting was held at the Corner House, on the corner of Newmarket Road and River Lane, on Thursday 2nd October 1947 to form the Abbey United Supporters Club, and to elect the officers and a committee. Over forty people attended the meeting, at which Mr.Habbin was elected President, Mr.Wakefield Vice-President, Mr.W.L.Selmes Chairman, and Mr.H.E.Bowman Secretary and Treasurer. It was a move designed to harness the increased support at the Club's home matches.

First Team 1947-48 Season
Back Row: Reg Barker (Trainer), Ted Humphreys, Bob Bishop, Albert George, S. "Pop" Ballard, Brian Holmes, R. Jones, Mr. W. Taverner (Chairman).
Front Row: Russell Crane, Roy Taylor, Joe Richardson, Reg Marsh, Cyril Kirby. Mascot: Peter Morgan

First Team 1948-49 Season
Back Row: Reg Barker (Trainer), Albert "Lofty" Adams, Brian Holmes, Tony Gallego, Albert George, Neville Chambers, Ernie Humphries.
Front Row: Terry McGrath, Roy Taylor, Derek King, Russell Crane, Cyril Kirby.

Shortly afterwards, in December, a start was made on banking the ground behind the Newmarket Road goal near the entrance to the ground.

All of the players within the Club remained amateur, but with the 'gates' picking up enormously, the Club were able to pay for taking some players to away matches by taxi, often picking them up as soon as they finished at work.

The Club were reasonably happy with their first season in the higher grade of football. They managed to win ten and draw four of their thirty four league matches, although finishing third from bottom in the league.

Elimination in the Preliminary Round of the F.A. Challenge Cup, by 6 goals to 4 against Histon Institute, was particularly disappointing, but this was more than compensated for by the Club's best ever run in the F.A. Amateur Cup. Four straight wins in the Qualifying Rounds over Ely City, St. Ives Town, St. Neots & District and Achilles earned the Abbey a home draw against Cambridge Town in the First Round Proper on Saturday 17th January 1948. A record crowd of over 5,000 people squeezed into the Newmarket Road ground expecting a close game, and they were not disappointed. The Abbey United team, led by Joe Richardson, fought bravely, but the more experienced Town emerged victorious by the narrow margin of a goal to nil.

The reserve team continued to play in the Cambs. League Division Two (Section A), where they finished fifth. They took the first team's place in the Cambs. Challenge Cup and Creake Charity Shield, but lost in the First Round in each instance.

F.A. Challenge Cup

Preliminary Round
Histon Institute 6 4 **Abbey United**

F.A. Amateur Cup

First Qualifying Round
Ely City 0 4 **Abbey United**

Second Qualifying Round
Abbey United 1 0 St. Ives Town

Third Qualifying Round
St. Neots & District 0 4 **Abbey United**

Fourth Qualifying Round
Abbey United 4 3 Achilles

First Round Proper
Abbey United 0 1 Cambridge Town

United Counties League

	Pld	W	D	L	F	A	Pts
Wisbech Town	34	30	2	2	143	42	62
Brush Sports	34	22	6	6	133	60	50
Spalding United	34	22	5	7	92	50	49
Stamford Town	34	18	6	10	88	72	42
S. & L. (Corby)	34	16	6	12	77	72	38
Leicester City	34	17	3	14	87	77	37
Bourne Town	34	15	7	12	72	82	37
Kettering Reserves	34	14	8	12	102	73	36
Desborough Town	34	14	7	13	60	62	35
Boston Reserves	34	12	5	17	92	99	29
King's Lynn	34	10	8	16	63	77	28
Holbeach	34	13	2	19	73	102	28
Wellingborough Town	34	9	9	16	55	88	27
Peterborough United Res.	34	10	6	18	62	98	26
Rushden Town	34	8	9	15	62	81	25
Abbey United	34	10	4	20	59	83	24
Symingtons (Market Harborough)	34	8	6	20	83	114	22
Eynesbury Rovers	34	7	3	24	50	121	17

Cambs Challenge Cup

First Round
Coton Institute 1 0 **Abbey United Res.**

Cambs Junior Cup

Preliminary Round
Soham Town Rngrs Res. 4 2 **Abbey United Res.**

Creake Charity Shield

First Round
Abbey United Res. 2 5 New Chesterton Inst.

Cambs League Division Two (Section A)

	Pld	W	D	L	F	A	Pts
Camden United Res.	24	22	1	1	125	23	45
Histon Institute Res.	24	15	4	5	90	41	34
Oakington	24	15	4	5	67	35	34
Meldreth	23	12	3	8	64	58	27
Abbey United Res.	23	11	4	8	86	59	26
New Town	24	12	2	10	80	56	26
Willingham Reserves	23	9	4	10	54	60	22
Cambs Mental Hospital	24	8	2	14	47	78	18
Cottenham United Res.	22	8	1	15	59	108	17
Sawston United Res.	22	6	4	12	53	77	16
Haslingfield	24	6	4	14	35	76	16
Saxons Reserves	22	6	3	13	52	63	15
Coton Institute Res.	23	4	0	19	40	118	8

1948-49 SEASON

Several ground improvements were made during the close-season, in preparation for a season in which the United Counties League were to appoint neutral linesmen for the first time. Previously clubs had to supply one linesman each. The Club were badly in need of two sets of shirts for the start of the season, and coupons were issued to raise sufficient funds for the new kit.

On Saturday 20th September 1948 Abbey United were drawn at home to the United Counties League Champions, Wisbech Town, in the Preliminary Round of the F.A.Challenge Cup, with the knowledge that should they win they would be at home to Cambridge Town in the next round. Two and a half thousand people saw the Abbey earn a creditable 1-1 draw, but in the replay at Fenland Park a week later they were overwhelmed by the "Fenmen" and lost 8-0 in front of 3,500 spectators. Amazingly all eight goals were scored in the second half. Two weeks later the Club's centre-half, Albert Adams, broke a leg against Ramsey in the F.A.Amateur Cup First Qualifying Round, but following a 3-3 draw, the Abbey won through by 4 goals to 1 in the replay.

A.E.Target, a left back who had previously played for Southampton, Millwall and Dundee, was appointed by Abbey United as a player-coach on 19th October 1948, but he was unable to play in the Club's F.A.Amateur Cup Second Qualifying Round match at home to Histon Institute four days later, and he could only watch as his team-mates were thrashed by 5 goals to 0.

Full back Ernie Humphries, who had been with the Club for sixteen years, had to retire from the game through injury in November. Yet despite these setbacks the Club managed to strengthen their side, and continued their steady progress by finishing twelfth out of twenty clubs in the United Counties League. Part of the team's improvement in form could be attributed to the appointment of Len Hartley as player-coach in January 1949, as he brought several new players to the Club.

The reserve team also improved in strength and reached the Fourth Round of the Cambs. Junior Cup, as well as finishing in the runners-up position in the Cambs. League Division Two (Section A). In an effort to continue raising the playing standards of the Club, the committee decided to withdraw their reserve team from the Cambs. League at the end of the season and instead enter them in the Premier Division of the Peterborough & District League, in addition to forming an 'A' team for the first time.

First Team 1949-50 Season

Back Row: Percy King, Herbert Crane, W. "Taffy" Edwards, Jack Rayner, Eric Brown, Tony Gallego, Derek King, Len Hartley (Player/Manager), Reg Barker (Trainer), Ray Bradley, Len Selmes.
Front Row: Roy Taylor, David Robson, Albert George, Russell Crane, Cyril Kirby.

During the season Russell Crane set a new Club goalscoring record by scoring 43 first team goals, and he was ably assisted by another local player, Albert George, who netted 20 goals. Altogether the Club scored 101 goals in the United Counties League, only the second time that Abbey United had managed to score more than a hundred goals in a season.

Shortly after the end of the playing season a General Meeting was called at the Brunswick School on the 16th May 1949. At the meeting it was decided to form a limited company to "provide funds to purchase the football ground, and to provide better football in Cambridge". The freehold of the ground and grandstand had been offered to the Club for £700, and at the meeting guarantees amounting to £1,000 were received. Mr.Wadsworth felt that the ground was left in trust to the Club, but the decision was taken to obtain the freehold. A limited company with a share capital of £2,500 was formed, and there were to be two kinds of shares valued at £10 or ten shillings each. The Club had been impressed with the set-up at Wisbech Town F.C., who had turned professional while in the United Counties League, and they decided to run a company on similar lines.

F.A. Challenge Cup

Preliminary Round
Abbey United 1 1 Wisbech Town

Preliminary Round Replay
Wisbech Town 8 0 **Abbey United**

F.A. Amateur Cup

First Qualifying Round
Ramsey Town 3 3 **Abbey United**
A.E.T. (1-1 at full-time)

First Qualifying Round Replay
Abbey United 4 1 Ramsey Town

Second Qualifying Round
Abbey United 0 5 Histon Institute

United Counties League

	Pld	W	D	L	F	A	Pts
Desborough Town	38	25	5	8	118	55	55
Wisbech Town	38	25	4	9	148	71	54
Stamford Town	38	24	5	9	130	83	53
Rushden Town	38	22	7	9	114	63	51
Spalding United	38	21	4	13	112	86	46
Kettering Reserves	38	20	5	13	84	61	45
Wellingborough Town	38	20	4	14	88	77	44
Rugby Town	38	20	2	16	91	77	42
Brush Sports Reserves	38	15	10	13	95	88	40
Symingtons	38	15	6	17	100	93	36
Corby Town	38	16	4	18	89	91	36
Abbey United	38	14	7	17	101	100	35
Grantham Reserves	38	15	5	18	86	110	35
Holbeach United	38	14	6	18	83	100	34
Eynesbury Rovers	38	14	4	20	98	120	32
Peterborough Reserves	38	12	8	18	74	97	32
March Town United	38	9	9	20	75	96	27
Boston Reserves	38	11	4	23	80	140	26
Bourne Town	38	8	3	27	58	138	19
Northampton 'A'	38	8	2	28	61	139	18

Cambs Challenge Cup

Preliminary Round
Parson Drove United 4 0 **Abbey United Res.**

C. & F.L. PROCTOR BUILDERS LIMITED

"Oatlands", Somersham Road
Colne, Cambs PE17 3NG
Tel: (0487) 842777

Wish Cambridge United F.C. every success on their 75th anniversary.

Cambs Junior Cup

First Round
Cottenham United Res.　0　1　**Abbey United Res.**

Second Round
Abbey United Res.　3　1　Over Sports

Third Round
Abbey United Res.　2　1　Waterbeach

Fourth Round
Abbey United Res.　3　4　**Histon Institute Res.**

Creake Charity Shield

Preliminary Round
Histon Institute Res.　5　3　Abbey United Res.

Cottenham Charity Cup

First Round
Abbey United Res.　1　4　**Cottenham United**

Cambs League Division Two (Section A)

	Pld	W	D	L	F	A	Pts
New Chesterton Inst.	20	18	2	0	132	13	38
Abbey United Res.	18	13	3	2	71	31	29
Oakington	19	10	4	5	57	40	24
Cottenham United Reserves	19	12	0	7	48	57	24
Linton Granta Reserves	20	10	2	8	64	39	22
Sawston United Reserves	19	9	2	8	47	35	20
New Town	19	6	3	10	41	59	15
Willingham Reserves	17	4	2	11	41	60	10
Meldreth	18	4	2	12	29	60	10
Haslingfield	19	4	0	15	19	77	8
Coton Institute Reserves	16	1	2	13	21	99	4

1949-50 SEASON

With Abbey United bringing professional football to Cambridge for the first time, by signing players under contract, the Club did not enter the F.A. Amateur Cup for the 1949-50 Season. The F.A. Challenge Cup was entered, and in the Preliminary Round the Abbey were drawn at home to the formidable Wisbech Town on Saturday 17th September. Work had already been progressing well on building some concrete terracing behind the Newmarket Road goal, but as over 1,500 supporters were expected to travel from Wisbech for the game, strenuous efforts were made in the preceding week to improve the banking around the ground. Jack Branch was largely responsible for co-ordinating the work. The effort was worthwhile, for goals from J. Lewis and Arthur George gave Abbey United an excellent 2-1 victory. However, in the next round, the Abbey lost 1-0 away to Newmarket Town on 1st October despite being favourites to win. The match created much interest, and attracted a record crowd for the "Jockeys" of 2,701 spectators.

The East Anglian Cup was entered again, after a break, but in the First Round on Wednesday 21st September the Abbey lost a keen struggle away to Harwich & Parkeston by 4 goals to 2 after extra-time.

On 17th December J. Summersgill and D. Smith both scored on their debuts as the Club held on to their unbeaten home record for the season with a 2-2 draw against Spalding United. Abbey United's home form was certainly impressive, and they did not lose on their own ground until Saturday 25th March 1950, ending a run of eighteen games with a surprising 1-0 defeat against mid-table Symingtons from Market Harborough. It was the Club's only home defeat of the season. With the defence showing an improvement, Abbey United finished the season in a highly respectable seventh place in the United Counties League, despite the first team scoring 24 fewer goals than in the previous season. Russell Crane once again finished as the first team's leading goalscorer with 17 goals, one ahead of Albert George and two ahead of Stan Thurston.

A week before the first team lost their unbeaten home record, the reserves lost their first home match in the Peterborough & District League Premier Division by 2 goals to 0 against Downham Town. However, the decision to join the new league was entirely vindicated when they finished the season in fourth place. The reserve team also came close to winning the Club's first trophy since the War when they reached the Final of the Peterborough & District Hospital Cup, and narrowly lost 1-0 to Spalding United Reserves on Peterborough United F.C.'s ground. A measure of their progress was shown when they reached the Semi-final of the Cambs. Challenge Cup and only lost to Histon Institute's first team by 2 goals to 1 in a replay, after drawing the first match 2-2.

The Club's first ever Board Meeting was held on 26th April 1950 at the "Globe", with Messrs. Brown, Harris, Starr, Swainland and Thulbourn as original members, and Mr.W.McLaren Francis appointed as Chairman. On his retirement a short time later, Mr.R.J.Wadsworth was appointed Chairman, and Mr.G.C.Proctor as Vice-Chairman. Mr.F.T.Ward was appointed as Club Secretary having previously been Assistant Secretary. The season was concluded with a Club Dinner at the Co-op Hall, Burleigh Street, on Saturday 6th May 1950, costing 10 shillings and 6 pence per head.

F.A. Challenge Cup

Preliminary Round
Abbey United 2 1 Wisbech Town

First Qualifying Round
Newmarket Town 1 0 **Abbey United**

East Anglian Cup

First Round
Harwich & Parkeston 4 2 **Abbey United**
(A.E.T. 2-2 at full-time)

United Counties League

	Pld	W	D	L	F	A	Pts
Wisbech Town	40	26	6	8	109	56	58
Rushden Town	40	24	8	8	103	56	56
Corby Town	40	24	6	10	100	56	54
Desborough Town	40	21	10	9	89	72	52
Kettering Town Reserves	40	22	6	12	91	75	50
Wellingborough Town	40	18	10	12	82	70	46
Abbey United	40	17	8	15	77	72	42
Spalding United	40	18	6	16	80	88	42
Rugby Town	40	16	7	17	100	96	39
March Town United	40	16	7	17	79	88	39
Eynesbury Rovers	40	14	9	17	84	87	37
Boston Reserves	40	12	13	15	87	94	37
Symingtons	40	16	5	19	84	96	37
Peterborough United Res.	40	14	9	17	65	80	37
Holbeach United	40	14	8	18	70	78	36
Stamford	40	13	9	18	93	89	35
Brush Sports Reserves	40	13	6	21	74	110	32
Coventry City 'A'	40	12	5	23	73	91	29
Northampton Town 'A'	40	10	9	21	69	103	29
Bourne Town	40	11	5	24	78	105	27
Grantham Reserves	40	8	10	22	68	93	26

Cambs Challenge Cup

First Round
Willingham 1 4 **Abbey United Res.**

Second Round
Abbey United Res. 1 1 Linton Granta

Second Round Replay
Linton Granta 1 4 **Abbey United Res.**

Semi-final (at Ely City F.C.)
Abbey United Res. 2 2 Histon Institute

Semi-final Replay (at Cambridge Town F.C.)
Abbey United Res. 1 2 Histon Institute

Peterborough Senior Cup

First Round Bye

Second Round
Abbey United Res. 2 0 Crowland Town

Third Round
Parson Drove United 2 0 **Abbey United Res.**

Peterborough Hospital Cup

First Round
Abbey United Res. 3 2 Wimblington Old Boys

Semi-final
King's Lynn Reserves 1 1 **Abbey United Res.**

Semi-final Replay
Abbey United Res. 2 0 King's Lynn Reserves

Final (at Peterborough United F.C.)
Abbey United Res. 0 1 Spalding United Res.

Peterborough & District League Premier Division

	Pld	W	D	L	F	A	Pts
Parson Drove	30	22	3	5	131	50	47
Spalding Reserves	30	21	3	6	104	55	45
Wisbech Town Reserves	30	19	2	9	91	56	40
Abbey United Res.	30	17	4	9	79	42	38
Holbeach United Reserves	30	18	2	10	103	68	38
King Lynn Reserves	30	17	4	9	104	78	38
Crowland	30	14	3	13	79	78	31
Chatteris Town	30	13	4	13	78	82	30
Peterborough United 'A'	29	9	7	13	48	89	25
Phorpes Sports	30	9	6	15	47	60	24
March Town Reserves	30	10	2	18	61	77	22
Downham Town	29	9	4	16	56	71	22
Wimblington Old Boys	28	8	5	15	64	85	21
Stamford Reserves	30	8	4	18	57	101	20
Long Sutton	28	9	1	18	74	102	19
Bourne Reserves	24	3	2	19	38	120	8

Cambs Junior Cup

Preliminary Round
Abbey United 'A' 1 1 Stretham Hotspur

Preliminary Round Replay
Stretham Hotspur 3 0 **Abbey United 'A'**

Cambs League Division Four (Section B)

	Pld	W	D	L	F	A	Pts
Newmarket Town 'A'	24	22	0	2	132	19	44
Sparta	24	21	1	2	154	24	43
Little Downham Swifts	24	17	1	6	108	24	35
Trumpington Rovers	24	16	1	7	88	44	33
Abbey United 'A'	24	15	1	8	90	55	31
Balsham	24	15	0	9	88	53	30
Swavesey Institute Reserves	23	11	0	12	70	71	22
Simplex	24	8	0	16	51	86	16
Pest Control	23	7	2	14	68	117	16
Milton Reserves	24	7	1	16	42	95	15
Marshalls Sports	24	7	0	17	33	81	14
Teversham Reserves	24	3	0	21	19	118	6
Swaffham Prior Reserves	24	2	1	21	21	178	5

First Team 1950-51 Season

Back Row: Stan Thurston, Percy Anderson, Albert George, Tony Gallego, Eddie Connelly, Ray Ruffett, Fred Mansfield.
Front Row: Neville Haylock, Harry Bullen, Russell Crane, Mourice Hipkin.

CHATERS
CERTIFIED ACCOUNTANTS

We have been pleased to support
Abbey United/Cambridge United F.C.
in their success over the years

9 Clifton Court, CAMBRIDGE CB1 4BN (0223) 243345
and at 27 High Street, SAFFRON WALDEN, ESSEX (0799) 22535
68 Boxworth End, SWAVESEY, CAMBRIDGE (0954) 30686

Chapter Five

THE FIFTIES

1950-51 SEASON

For the first time in their four years in the United Counties League, the Club were able to make a serious challenge for the league championship. The forward line formed a prolific goalscoring attack and Russell Crane was once again leading first team goalscorer with 29 goals, closely followed by Ken Coates with 25 goals, Neville Rose 19 and Stan Thurston 17.

In the First Qualifying Round of the F.A.Challenge Cup the Club did very well to earn a 2-2 draw at King's Lynn, but were unable to perform so well in the replay at Newmarket Road, and went down by a goal to nil before a crowd of 4,256 spectators.

However, in the Second Round of the United Counties League Cup the first team had a fantastic 5-0 victory over Spalding United, who were previously unbeaten, and eventually finished second in the league. The Abbey progressed through to the Final of the competition, with a 4-3 away victory against March Town, and by beating Stamford. In the game at March, Abbey United were two goals in arrears with ten minutes to go when Eddie Connelly crashed the ball home, closely followed by a Russell Crane goal which levelled the scores. With barely a minute left "Dolly" Pierson, playing in the "Black and Amber" for the first time, forced his way through a crowd of players to plant the winning shot into the net. On the same day, the 31st March 1951, the Club reached another milestone when they heard that they had been accepted into the Eastern Counties League at the third attempt.

The Club also had a successful run in the East Anglian Cup, and managed to beat two Eastern Counties League teams, Wisbech Town and Colchester United Reserves, on their way to the Semi-final. Ipswich Town Reserves were the visitors for the Semi-final on the 10th March 1951, and a large crowd saw a most memorable game. At half-time Abbey United were 3-0 down, but a tremendous fight back saw the Club draw level at 4-4 by the end of 90 minutes, and two more goals in extra-time clinched a famous 6-4 win and a place in the Final for the first time.

Three league defeats in succession ruined any Championship hopes, and by the end of the season the Club finished in their highest position of fifth. Abbey United had to play six games in the last twelve days of the season, and they had a distinct disadvantage in the Final of the East Anglian Cup when they had to travel away to another Eastern Counties League club, Great Yarmouth Town, for an evening kick-off on Thursday 10th May 1951. It was not surprising that United were unable to lift the trophy, and they went down by 3 goals to 1.

Just before the end of the season the Cambs Football Association gave Cambridge Town F.C. permission to change their name to Cambridge City F.C. and Abbey United F.C. permission to change their name to Cambridge United F.C. Cambridge Town changed their name straight away, whereas Abbey United decided to wait until the start of the next season. The decision to change the name from Abbey to Cambridge United was taken purely on commercial grounds, as the progressive minded Directors felt that few people would know where Abbey United came from, if they were to become nationally known.

The reserve team finished seventh in the Peterborough & District League Premier Division, and for the second season in succession they reached the Final of the Peterborough & District Hospital Cup. This time they drew 1-1 with King's Lynn Reserves at Peterborough United F.C.'s ground, and shared the trophy for six months each. They did suffer one shock though in the First Round of the Cambs Challenge Cup when they lost 12-1 away to Atlas Sports of Meldreth on 25th November 1950.

With the Semi-final of the United Counties League Cup against Stamford not being concluded until the 12th May 1951, the Final of the competition had to be held over to the start of the following season. A crowd of 2,750 people were attracted to the Newmarket Road ground on Thursday 23rd August 1951 to see the Club win their first trophy under their new name. A hat-trick from Russell Crane, supported by two goals from Albert George and one from Stan Thurston, gave the Club a most convincing 6-0 victory over Symingtons of Market Harborough in a one-sided Final.

F.A. Challenge Cup

First Qualifying Round
King's Lynn   2   2   **Abbey United**

First Qualifying Round Replay
Abbey United   0   1   King's Lynn

United Counties League Cup

First Round.   Bye

Second Round
Abbey United   5   0   Spalding United

Third Round
March Town   3   4   **Abbey United**

Semi-final
Abbey United   1   1   Stamford

Semi-final Replay
Stamford   2   3   **Abbey United**
(A.E.T. 1-1 at full-time)

Final
Cambridge United   6   0   Symingtons
(NOTE: Match played during 1951-52 Season)

East Anglian Cup.

First Round   Bye

Second Round
Abbey United   2   1   Wisbech Town

Third Round.
Abbey United   3   2   Colchester United Res.

Semi-final
Abbey United   6   4   Ipswich Town Res.

Final
Gt. Yarmouth Town   3   1   Abbey United

United Counties League.

	Pld	W	D	L	F	A	Pts
Corby Town	34	26	4	4	123	34	56
Spalding United	34	25	5	4	101	48	55
Kettering Town Reserves	34	19	7	8	85	73	43
Rushden Town	34	17	7	10	87	55	41
Abbey United	34	15	11	8	88	61	41
Stamford	34	17	7	10	77	71	41
Eynesbury Rovers	34	15	7	12	77	70	37
Holbeach United	34	16	3	15	71	70	35
Peterborough United Res.	34	13	7	14	74	75	33
Wellingborough Town	34	15	3	16	50	78	33
March Town United	34	15	2	17	72	68	32
Coventry 'A'	34	12	6	16	62	65	30
Desborough Town	34	14	2	18	60	72	30
Boston Reserves	34	10	5	19	59	77	25
Symingtons	34	10	2	22	57	89	22
Bourne Town	34	8	6	20	55	92	22
Grantham Reserves	34	6	5	23	57	98	17
Northampton Town 'A'	34	5	7	22	24	93	17

Cambs Challenge Cup

First Round
Atlas Sports   12   1   Abbey United Res.

Peterborough Senior Cup

First Round
Abbey United Res.   2   2   Chatteris Town

First Round Replay
Chatteris Town   2   1   Abbey United Res.

Peterborough Hospital Cup

Semi-final
March Town Reserves   0   1   **Abbey United Res.**

Final. (at Peterborough)
Abbey United Res.   1   1   King's Lynn Reserves
NOTE: Trophy shared for six months each.

Peterborough & District League Premier Division

	Pld	W	D	L	F	A	Pts
King's Lynn Reserves	30	26	1	3	118	39	53
March Town Reserves	30	18	6	6	97	46	42
Spalding United Reserves	29	18	5	6	87	46	41
Holbeach United Reserves	30	18	5	7	85	46	41
Parson Drove United	30	17	4	9	97	62	38
Wisbech Town Reserves	30	16	5	9	87	59	37
Abbey United Res.	30	10	7	13	60	74	27
Wimblington Old Boys	29	12	3	14	69	101	27
Long Sutton	30	11	4	15	57	90	26
Chatteris Town	30	10	5	15	75	75	25
Stamford Reserves	30	10	3	17	69	93	23
Crowland Town	30	9	4	17	60	84	22
Downham Town	30	8	6	16	69	100	22
South Lynn	30	9	4	17	55	91	22
Phorpes Sports	30	7	3	20	59	85	17
Deeping Town Athletic	30	6	3	21	55	108	15

Cambs Lower Junior Cup.

Preliminary Round
Abbey United 'A'   7   1   Fulbourn Reserves

First Round
Abbey United 'A'   6   2   Guilden Morden

Second Round
Abbey United 'A'   0   1   **Barrington**

Cambs League Division Three (Section B)

	Pld	W	D	L	F	A	Pts
Little Downham	26	21	4	1	131	36	46
Sparta	24	21	0	3	145	22	42
Balsham	24	16	3	5	63	36	35
Newmarket Town 'A'	25	16	2	7	134	45	34
Histon Institute 'A'	21	12	2	7	67	51	26
Trumpington	26	11	3	12	78	64	25
Abbey United 'A'	25	12	0	13	82	85	24
Girton United Reserves	23	9	3	11	71	75	21
Coulson's Sports	25	9	3	13	48	89	21
Bottisham Reserves	24	8	2	14	44	114	18
Over Reserves	26	7	1	18	61	95	15
Swavesey Reserves	21	5	3	13	39	85	13
Quy	24	4	1	19	55	138	9
Wilbraham Reserves	24	4	1	19	32	115	9

1951-52 SEASON

1951 was a time of great change for the Club, but it was a year that marked a prominent landmark in their history. Not only did the Club change their name but they appointed their first full-time manager, Bill Whittaker, after advertising for the position. He was a former England schoolboy international, and as a professional footballer won an F.A.Challenge Cup winners medal for Charlton Athletic in 1947-48 against Burnley. He joined Cambridge United from Huddersfield Town and took up a player-manager's role, where his experience at right half considerably helped the team.

Another important landmark was the completion of the Supporters Club canteen and clubhouse for the start of the season. Under the guidance of G.C.Proctor, a real 'live-wire', the new building was constructed by a keen band of voluntary helpers at a cost of £3,000.

After the clubhouse was completed, volunteers also carried concrete slabs from the Atlas works in Coldhams Lane to the ground to help improve the terracing, as the Club's crowds kept growing in size. Facilities were improved even further with the construction of a bridge over the stream to give access to the ground for supporters coming from the Coldhams Lane direction.

Ironically, Cambridge United's first game in the Eastern Counties League, on Saturday 18th August 1951, was at home to Great Yarmouth Town, the team who beat them in the previous season's East Anglian Cup Final. This time, watched by an enthusiastic crowd of 3,300 people, United beat them by 3 goals to 0, and they got off to an excellent start in their new league by winning their first three games without conceding a goal. In fact Cambridge United remained unbeaten in their first ten league games, and by mid-November had moved to the top of the table.

Success was not forthcoming in the major cup competitions, and in three cups the Club made an early exit in the First Round. The most surprising was in the F.A.Challenge Cup when, after drawing 1-1 away to March Town United, the Club let a 2-0 lead slip at home and eventually lost 4-3. A 3-2 defeat away to Gorleston in the Eastern Counties League Cup was not entirely unexpected, nor was the 3-1 defeat at King's Lynn in the East Anglian Cup, which attracted 6,879 spectators on Wednesday 5th September 1951, the largest crowd yet to see the Club play.

The first defeat in the league was at home to Chelsea 'A' on 17th November by 2 goals to 1, and was due mainly to an injury to the Club captain, Harry Bullen, who carried on bravely, but was a 'passenger' for three quarters of the match. This reverse started a run of five consecutive league defeats, four of them by the odd goal, and was only halted by the inclusion of a few players from the successful reserve side.

At the turn of the year the reserves were unbeaten in their last ten league matches, and were still unbeaten in all cup competitions. On 23rd February 1952 they beat Long Sutton 11-1 to go top of the Peterborough & District League for the first time. Daylight saving did not start until 20th April, and the Peterborough & District League closed their fixtures just six days later, which caused the reserves to have a congested end of season with five matches in nine days. Yet despite this the reserves won the Premier Division Championship by two clear points over Wisbech Town Reserves, and were also able to complete the 'double' by winning 3-2 away to Ely City in the Final of the Peterborough Senior Cup. The only blemish on their season was a 2-1 defeat away to Ely City in the Third Round of the Cambs Challenge Cup. Much to the Club's annoyance, they were only allowed to use amateur players in this competition, and therefore had to call on several 'A' team players.

The Semi-final of the Peterborough & District Hospital Cup was held over to the following season, and when the game was played the reserve team registered a 3-0 win against Ely City to reach the Final for the third year in succession. Victory over Crowland Town in the Final by 4 goals to 2 on Saturday 22nd November 1952, watched by 1,074 spectators at Newmarket Road, gave the reserves their third trophy for the 1951-52 season. Attendances of up to a thousand were not uncommon for reserve team games, and against King's Lynn Reserves on Saturday 15th March 1952, 2,494 people turned up at the "Walks", King's Lynn, to see the clubs draw a league game 1-1.

After Christmas the first team returned to winning ways in the league, and eventually finished in fourth place, just two points away from the runners-up spot. At the end of the season the Club played in the Cambs. Invitation Cup for the first time, having not been invited in the previous inaugural season of the competition. A 2-1 victory over March Town United in the Semi-final at Milton Road gave the Cambridge United supporters a long awaited opportunity to beat their main rivals Cambridge City in a competitive match. They were not disappointed, for although Cambridge City had

First Team 1951-52 Season
Back Row: Albert George, Bill Whittaker (Player-Manager), Harry Bullen, John Percival, Tony Gallego, Bob Bishop, Jack Thomas, Reg Barker (Trainer).
Front Row: Stan Thurston, Russell Crane, Ray Ruffett, Len Crowe, Joe Gallego.

Reserve Team 1951-52 Season
Back Row: Charlie Barker, W. "Sonny" Northfield (Manager), Reg Wallis, Derek King, Arthur Morgan, Roy Dunkley, Ron Simpson, Morris Flack, Frank George, Bert Stallan.
Front Row: Fred Mansfield, Taffy Edwards, Eric Brown, Albert George, Neville Rose.
Winners of the Peterborough Senior Cup and Winners of the Peterborough & District League Premier Division Championship.

home advantage, it was United who won by 2 goals to 0 in front of 9,814 spectators on 1st May 1952 to take the trophy. Russell Crane scored both goals.

Before the end of the season Cambridge United reached the Final of the Hunts. Premier Cup with victories over Biggleswade and Histon, but in the Final away to Bedford Town they were no match for the very strong Southern League side and lost by 4 goals to 1.

F.A. Challenge Cup

First Qualifying Round
March Town 1 1 **Cambridge United**

First Qualifying Round Replay
Cambridge United 3 4 March Town

Eastern Counties League Cup

First Round
Gorleston 3 2 Cambridge United

East Anglian Cup

First Round
King's Lynn 3 1 Cambridge United

Cambs Invitation Cup

Semi-final (at Cambridge City F.C.)
Cambridge United 2 1 March Town

Final (at Cambridge City F.C.)
Cambridge United 2 0 Cambridge City

Hunts Premier Cup

First Round
Biggleswade 1 4 **Cambridge United**

Semi-final (at Cambridge City F.C.)
Cambridge United 1 0 Histon

Final
Bedford Town 4 1 Cambridge United

Cambs Challenge Cup

First Round
Cambridge Utd Res. 6 1 Bassingbourn

Second Round
Cambridge Utd Res. 4 1 Parsons Drove United

Third Round
Ely City 2 1 Cambridge Utd Res.

Peterborough Senior Cup

First Round
Lynn United 0 1 **Cambridge Utd Res.**

Second Round
Cambridge Utd Res. 3 0 Brotherhoods

Third Round
Crowland Town 0 1 **Cambridge Utd Res.**

Semi-final
Cambridge Utd Res. 1 0 King's Lynn Reserves

Final (at Ely)
Ely City 2 3 **Cambridge Utd Res.**

Eastern Counties League

	Pld	W	D	L	F	A	Pts
Gillingham Reserves	34	22	9	3	84	31	53
Colchester Utd Reserves	34	19	7	8	70	41	45
Gorleston	34	18	8	8	90	47	44
Cambridge United	34	20	3	11	72	41	43
Arsenal 'A'	34	17	8	9	72	46	42
King's Lynn	34	19	3	12	103	61	41
Chelmsford City Reserves	34	15	10	9	67	52	40
West Ham United 'A'	34	18	3	13	69	57	39
Harwich & Parkeston	34	17	4	13	76	72	38
Tottenham Hotspur 'A'	34	15	3	16	67	50	33
Lowestoft Town	34	13	6	15	65	63	32
Bury Town	34	13	4	17	69	78	30
Chelsea 'A'	34	11	7	16	54	64	29
Wisbech Town	34	12	5	17	56	68	29
Clacton Town	34	12	4	18	58	68	28
Great Yarmouth Town	34	11	4	19	51	80	26
Norwich City 'A'	34	9	2	23	44	96	20
Newmarket Town	34	0	0	34	19	171	0

SHARP & SONS

CLEANING SERVICES

Upholstery and Carpet Cleaning by Steam Vacuum Extraction

Car Valeting

Industrial and domestic floor contractors. Free estimates.

10 TUKES WAY, SAFFRON WALDEN, ESSEX CB11 3ES

Tel: Saffron Walden 22538

Peterborough Hospital Cup

First Round   Bye

Second Round
Cambridge Utd Res. 4   1   Spalding Reserves

Semi-final
Cambridge Utd Res. 3   0   Ely City

Final
Cambridge Utd Res. 2   4   Crowland Town

Peterborough & District League Premier Division

	Pld	W	D	L	F	A	Pts
Cambridge United Res.	30	21	5	4	107	35	47
Wisbech Reserves	30	21	3	6	89	47	45
King's Lynn Reserves	30	19	5	6	118	59	43
Crowland	30	20	2	8	96	59	42
Holbeach Reserves	30	17	3	10	91	77	37
Chatteris Town	30	13	9	8	87	67	35
Upwell	30	15	2	13	93	97	32
Downham Town	30	11	8	11	79	74	30
Ely City	30	12	5	13	93	72	29
Spalding Reserves	30	12	2	16	67	78	26
Wimblington Old Boys	30	10	5	15	54	90	25
Long Sutton	29	7	9	13	58	83	23
Stamford Town Reserves	30	9	2	19	74	106	20
March Town Reserves	30	8	2	20	52	106	18
Peterborough 'A'	30	7	3	20	50	85	17
Lynn United	29	4	1	24	38	111	9

Peterborough & District League Championship Match

Cambridge Utd Res. 3   7   The Rest of Peterborough & D.L.

Cambs Lower Junior Cup

First Round
Weston Colville   0   4   **Cambridge Utd 'A'**

Second Round
Lode Reserves   1   7   **Cambridge Utd 'A'**

Third Round
Cambridge Utd 'A'   3   7   R.A.F. Waterbeach

Cambs League Division Three (Section B)

	Pld	W	D	L	F	A	Pts
R.A.F. Waterbeach	18	17	0	1	126	11	34
Milton Reserves	18	12	4	2	62	33	28
Pest Control	18	11	2	5	63	43	24
Cambridge United 'A'	17	10	3	4	57	25	23
Elsworth	17	8	3	6	43	45	19
Trumpington	18	7	2	9	54	45	16
Lode Reserves	18	6	1	11	34	94	13
Coulson's Sports	18	4	4	10	41	65	12
Quy	18	2	2	14	24	85	6
Wilbraham Reserves	18	1	1	16	21	83	3

1952-53 SEASON

Volunteers were busy once again during the summer of 1952 levelling and draining the pitch, as well as making further improvements to the terracing around the ground.

A new centre-forward, Jack Thomas, was signed at the start of the season, and he made the best possible debut scoring four goals in a 6-2 home win over Gorleston. Again the Club made a good start in the league, but they lost 3-2 at home to Chelmsford City Reserves in the First Round of the Eastern Counties League Cup, and went out of the East Anglian Cup at the First Round stage in a replay at Gorleston, losing 4-1 on Monday 29th September.

The Club had a good run in the F.A. Challenge Cup though, and eliminated Chatteris Town and March Town United, before drawing 0-0 at home to Wisbech Town. In the replay at Fenland Park, Cambridge United were twice quickly pegged back after taking the lead, and with the score at 2-2 the game went into extra-time. Just when it seemed that another replay would be required, Stan Thurston scored a last minute winner to give United a home match against King's Lynn in the Third Qualifying Round. A ground record crowd of 7,344 people saw United miss several excellent scoring opportunities, and the game ended with no goals being scored. King's Lynn made no mistake in the replay and won convincingly by 4 goals to 0.

A 5-1 victory over the previous year's Champions, Gillingham Reserves, put Cambridge United on top of the table early in November, and they held on to that position until Christmas when their 'bogey' side, Eynesbury Rovers, beat them twice over the holiday period.

The reserve team remained unbeaten for just over twelve months until they lost 4-2 away to Downham Town at the end of October. At that time they were top of the Premier Division of the Peterborough & District League, a position they held for the rest of the season to retain the Championship by a margin of eight points. The reserves continued their remarkable run of success by winning the Isle of Ely Senior Cup with a 3-2 victory over Wimblington Old Boys in the Final at March on Tuesday 28th April 1953. Once again end of season congestion caused the reserves to play seven games in the last twelve days of the season.

After Christmas the first team's league form was inconsistent, but there were more good results than bad, including a fine 4-1 away victory against

King's Lynn who finished in the runners-up spot. Eventually United finished fourth, but they would have occupied third place barring a piece of bad luck. They were leading 2-0 away to Gorleston when fog caused the postponement of the match in the second half, and when the match was re-played against the eventual champions, Gorleston took both points with a 1-0 victory.

In the Hunts. Premier Cup, Cambridge United avenged their defeat earlier in the season by beating Eynesbury Rovers 3-1 on their ground in the First Round. Against Ronnie Rooke's Bedford Town the Club gained a very worthy 1-1 draw at home in the Semi-final, and after an equally close contest in the replay, the Southern League outfit emerged as narrow 2-1 winners. Hopes of retaining the Cambs. Invitation Cup were dashed with a disappointing 4-1 defeat away to Wisbech Town.

As the Club's 'gate' receipts were insufficient to meet the rising cost of increased wages, taxes, rates and other expenses, the Supporters Club Management Committee decided to form an organization known as the Cambridge and District Sportsmen's Guild, whose purpose was to raise funds for Cambridge United Football Club in an effort to improve their status and amenities for players and supporters. It was a wise move for the Guild still exists today, and in its earlier years particularly made a significant contribution to the successful development of the Club.

F.A. Challenge Cup

Preliminary Round
Chatteris Town 0 4 **Cambridge United**

First Qualifying Round
Cambridge United 3 1 March Town

Second Qualifying Round
Cambridge United 0 0 Wisbech Town

Second Qualifying Round Replay
Wisbech Town 2 3 **Cambridge United**
(After extra-time)

Third Qualifying Round
Cambridge United 0 0 King's Lynn

Third Qualifying Round Replay
King's Lynn 4 0 **Cambridge United**

Eastern Counties League Cup

First Round
Cambridge United 2 3 Chelmsford City Res.

East Anglian Cup

First Round
Cambridge United 1 1 Gorleston

First Round Replay
Gorleston 4 1 **Cambridge United**

Cambs Invitation Cup

Semi-final
Wisbech Town 4 1 **Cambridge United**

Eastern Counties League

	Pld	W	D	L	F	A	Pts
Gorleston	36	23	6	7	114	47	52
King's Lynn	36	22	5	9	94	51	49
Arsenal 'A'	36	21	5	10	78	48	47
Cambridge United	36	19	8	9	80	49	46
Gt. Yarmouth Town	36	18	8	10	70	44	44
Tottenham Hostpur 'A'	36	13	16	7	61	43	42
Eynesbury Rovers	36	18	5	13	100	80	41
Gillingham Reserves	36	17	7	12	70	63	41
West Ham United 'A'	36	16	7	13	63	68	39
Norwich City 'A'	36	13	9	14	71	71	35
Colchester United Reserves	36	14	7	15	59	62	35
Harwich & Parkeston	36	11	13	12	71	82	35
Bury Town	36	12	8	16	61	77	32
Clacton Town	36	12	7	17	55	82	31
Lowestoft Town	36	11	5	20	34	79	27
Crittall Athletic	36	9	8	19	52	81	26
Stowmarket	36	9	7	20	55	86	25
Chelmsford City	36	8	6	22	42	79	22
Chelsea 'A'	36	5	5	26	45	82	15

Hunts Premier Cup

First Round
Eynesbury Rovers 1 3 **Cambridge United**

Semi-final
Cambridge United 1 1 Bedford Town

Semi-final Replay
Bedford Town 2 1 **Cambridge United**
(After extra time)

Peterborough Senior Cup

First Round
Cambridge Utd Res. 4 4 Wimblington Old Boys

First Round Replay
Wimblington Old Boys 1 5 **Cambridge Utd Res.**

Second Round
Ely City 1 1 **Cambridge Utd Res.**

Second Round Replay
Cambridge Utd Res. 3 0 Ely City

Third Round
Cambridge Utd Res. 3 3 Morton (Lincs)

Third Round Replay
Morton (Lincs) 3 1 **Cambridge Utd Res.**

Isle of Ely Senior Cup

First Round
Manea United 0 5 **Cambridge Utd Res.**

Second Round
Phorpes Sports 2 3 **Cambridge Utd Res.**

Semi-final
March Town Reserves 0 0 **Cambridge Utd Res.**

Semi-final Replay
Cambridge Utd Res. 2 0 March Town Reserves
(Match abandoned during extra-time)

Semi-final Replay
Cambridge Utd Res. 1 0 March Town Reserves

Final (Played at March)
Cambridge Utd Res. 3 2 Wimblington Old Boys

Peterborough Hospital Cup

First Round
Cambridge Utd Res. 3 0 Holbeach United Res.

Semi-final
Cambridge Utd Res. 2 0 Stamford Reserves

Final (at Milton Road)
Cambridge Utd Res. 4 2 Exning United

Peterborough District League Premier Division

	Pld	W	D	L	F	A	Pts
Cambridge United Res.	30	24	3	3	112	40	51
King's Lynn Reserves	30	19	5	6	111	65	43
Downham Town	30	17	5	8	86	61	39
March Town Reserves	30	15	3	12	82	58	33
Ely City	30	14	5	11	79	67	33
Crowland	30	15	2	13	76	60	32
Exning	30	11	10	9	90	75	32
Chatteris Town	30	12	8	10	78	75	32
Stamford Town Reserves	30	13	4	13	96	78	30
Bourne Town Reserves	30	11	7	12	77	90	29
Holbeach Reserves	30	11	5	14	67	73	27
Long Sutton	30	9	7	14	69	76	25
Upwell	30	8	8	14	67	96	24
Ramsey	30	7	5	18	52	84	19
St. Ives	30	7	4	19	55	115	18
Wimblington Old Boys	30	5	3	22	72	156	13

Cambs Lower Junior Cup

First Round
Cambridge Utd 'A' 3 1 Burwell Reserves

Second Round
Fen Ditton Reserves 0 2 **Cambridge Utd 'A'**

Third Round
Stetchworth 2 0 Cambridge Utd 'A'

Cambs League Division Three (Section B)

	Pld	W	D	L	F	A	Pts
Soham United	19	18	0	1	115	25	36
Stetchworth	20	13	3	4	63	25	29
Pest Control	20	14	0	6	77	40	28
Rooke's Sports	20	13	1	6	77	45	27
Cambridge United 'A'	20	11	2	7	74	44	24
Burwell Reserves	20	10	2	8	59	64	22
Trumpington	20	7	4	9	60	61	18
Elsworth	19	6	3	10	41	47	15
Lode Reserves	20	4	1	15	34	97	9
Fordham Reserves	20	3	2	15	32	87	8
Quy	20	1	0	19	23	120	2

1953-54 SEASON

Cambridge United made a strong bid for the Eastern Counties League Championship when they started the campaign with an unbeaten run of ten matches, before tasting defeat for the first time at the hands of Gorleston on the 28th November 1953. The Club's only other defeat before that was against King's Lynn, when they were unlucky to draw them in the First Round of the Eastern Counties League Cup.

Victory by 3 goals to 0 against St.Neots & District saw the Club embark on their most successful F.A.Challenge Cup run. An amazing crowd of 11,908 spectators watched Cambridge United and Cambridge City battle it out in the Second Qualifying Round at Milton Road, as cup fever gripped the city. Two goals from Albert George, and a penalty from Bill Whittaker, were enough to enable United to progress through to the next round with a 3-1 victory. 6,600 people saw Albert George score the only goal of the game in the next round against Wisbech Town two weeks later on Saturday 24th October 1953. It was almost an anti-climax when the Club were drawn away to Stowmarket in the Fourth Qualifying Round. Over 3,000 people packed into the Suffolk club's tiny ground, but Cambridge United made no mistake and made certain of a place in the First Round Proper for the first time in their history with a 5-0 thrashing of the home team.

Excitement reached fever pitch when the Club were drawn to play at home to Newport County on Saturday 21st November 1953, their first ever game against a Football League club. A marvellous match watched by a crowd of 7,500 saw United draw 2-2 with goals from Les Stevens and Len Crowe. The Club travelled to Monmouthshire the following Thursday thinking that their best chance had gone, but United surprised the football world when Len Saward and Les Stevens scored the goals in a remarkable 2-1 victory.

The attendance record at the Club's Newmarket Road ground was shattered when 10,000 people saw Cambridge United take on Bradford Park Avenue in the Second Round Proper on Saturday 12th December 1953. Another keen struggle ended in brave defeat for Cambridge United, with Bill Whittaker's penalty not being enough to cancel out the Football League Division Three North side's two goals.

The week before the Bradford game, Cambridge went out of the East Anglian Cup, losing 3-0 away to Great Yarmouth Town, and later in the season they surprisingly lost 1-0 at home to March Town United in the First Round of the Hunts. Premier Cup.

Crowds for the Club's home league games averaged 2,678 as the Club kept in contention for the Championship right up until the end of the season. Defeat in three of their last four games cost Cambridge United the title, and they had to settle for third place after losing 2-0 at Clacton in the last game.

The Club reached the Final of the Cambs. Invitation Cup when they beat Cambridge City 2-1 in the Semi-final on a neutral ground at Grange Road, Cambridge. A capacity 5,000 crowd watched that game on Saturday 20th March 1954, and Jack Thomas notched both goals. The Final was played at Milton Road and attracted a crowd of 5,645 spectators to see United take on Histon. United were hit by injury problems for this game, with John Percival ruled out and Bill Whittaker playing only after having pain killing injections for a leg

Saturday 21st November 1953. F.A. Challenge Cup. First Round Proper.
Cambridge United 2, Newport County 2. Cambridge United's leading goalscorer Albert George can only watch as his shot strikes the outside of the post. However, the crowd of 7,500 were delighted when Les Stevens and Len Crowe scored later in the game to earn a 2-2 draw against their Football League opponents. The following Thursday United travelled down to Wales and surprised the 7,434 crowd and the rest of the football world when they won by 2 goals to 1.
Photograph by courtesy of *Cambridge Evening News*.

injury. Then within a few minutes of the start they were effectively reduced to ten men when Jack Thomas strained a leg muscle and was a 'passenger' for the rest of the game. Histon had several chances to win the cup, and United were awarded a penalty for handball in the 75th minute, only for Bill Whittaker to miss from the spot for the first time in the season. There was still no score at the end of extra-time, and a replay had to be held over to the next season. When the Final was re-played on the Cambridge City ground, another crowd of over 5,000 spectators saw Cambridge United lift the trophy for the second time with a 3-1 victory.

It was not such a successful season for the reserve team who could only finish seventh in the Premier Division of the Peterborough & District League. They did not enter the Peterborough & District Hospital Cup, in which they had been finalists for the past four seasons, and went out early in the other cup competitions although they did register an 11-0 win over East Ward United in the Peterborough Senior Cup First Round on 17th October 1953.

During the season Mr R.J.Wadsworth retired from the Board of Directors, thus severing his long association with the Club extending over a period of 22 years. He was succeeded as Chairman by Mr.G.C.Proctor, with Mr.J.Woolley as Vice-Chairman.

At the end of the season the Club's application for full membership of the Football Association was supported by the Cambs. F.A. and later granted by the Football Association.

First Team 1953-54 Season.
Back Row: Reg Barker (Trainer), Pat Kearney, Bob Bishop, Arthur Morgan, Johnnie Percival, Len Saward, Len Crowe.
Front Row: "Teddy" Bowd, Albert George, Bill Whittaker (Player/Manager), Russell Crane, Les Stevens.
Photograph taken at Newmarket Road on Saturday 12th December 1953 before the F.A. Challenge Cup Second Round Proper match against Bradford Park Avenue in which the Football League Club won by 2 goals to 1 before a ground record crowd of 10,000 people. Photograph by courtesy of *Cambridge Evening News*.

F.A. Challenge Cup

First Qualifying Round
St. Neots 0 3 **Cambridge United**

Second Qualifying Round
Cambridge City 1 3 **Cambridge United**

Third Qualifying Round
Cambridge United 1 0 Wisbech Town

Fourth Qualifying Round
Stowmarket 0 5 **Cambridge United**

First Round Proper
Cambridge United 2 2 Newport County

First Round Proper Replay
Newport County 1 2 **Cambridge United**

Second Round Proper
Cambridge United 1 2 Bradford Park Avenue

Eastern Counties League Cup

First Round
Cambridge United 2 4 King's Lynn

East Anglian Cup

First Round Bye

Second Round
Gt. Yarmouth Town 3 0 **Cambridge United**

Hunts Premier Cup

First Round
Cambridge United 0 1 March Town

Cambs Invitation Cup

First Round
Cambridge United 6 1 March Town

Semi-final (at Grange Rd)
Cambridge United 2 1 Cambridge City

Final (at Cambridge City F.C.)
Histon 0 0 **Cambridge United**

Final Replay (at Cambridge City F.C.)
Cambridge United 3 1 Histon
(NOTE: Match played during 1954-55 season).

**Saturday 20th March 1954. Cambs Invitation Cup. Semi-final.
Cambridge United 2, Cambridge City 0.**
Jack Thomas (Right) and Albert George (No. 9) put the Cambridge City defence under pressure, but this time the ball is cleared. Jack Thomas did manage to find the net twice for United in the local 'derby' played on the neutral Grange Road Ground, Cambridge, before a capacity 5,000 crowd, to earn them a place in the final against Histon.
Photograph by courtesy of *Cambridge Evening News*.

66

Eastern Counties League

	Pld	W	D	L	F	A	Pts
King's Lynn	34	22	8	4	108	41	52
Clacton Town	34	20	9	5	62	28	49
Cambridge United	34	18	10	6	88	44	46
Eynesbury Rovers	34	18	6	10	86	53	42
Gt. Yarmouth Town	34	18	6	10	58	46	42
Gorleston	34	15	11	8	70	41	41
Lowestoft Town	34	14	7	13	64	59	35
Tottenham Hotspurs 'A'	34	11	11	12	49	47	33
Gillingham Reserves	34	12	9	13	56	58	33
Colchester Utd Reserves	34	13	7	14	60	69	33
West Ham Utd 'A'	34	13	7	14	56	75	33
Arsenal 'A'	34	11	9	14	44	57	31
Chelmsford City Reserves	34	12	6	16	51	66	30
Stowmarket	34	9	10	15	42	61	28
Harwich & Parkeston	34	8	7	19	49	73	23
Crittal Athletic	34	9	5	20	48	87	23
Norwich City 'A'	34	7	7	20	43	91	21
Bury Town	34	5	7	22	31	64	17

Peterborough Senior Cup

First Round
Cambridge Utd Res. 11   0   East Ward United

Second Round
Cambridge Utd Res. 3   5   Upwell Town

Isle of Ely Senior Cup

First Round
Parson Drove   2   1   **Cambridge Utd Res.**

Peterborough and District League Premier Division

	Pld	W	D	L	F	A	Pts
King's Lynn Reserves	29	22	4	3	148	43	48
Stamford Reserves	30	19	8	3	93	63	41
Chatteris Town	30	18	3	9	94	80	39
Ely City	30	14	8	8	85	73	36
Downham Town	30	15	5	10	87	66	35
Whittlesey	30	16	2	12	101	112	34
Cambridge Utd Res.	30	15	3	12	86	61	33
March Town	30	15	3	12	72	62	33
Somersham	30	15	3	12	85	80	33
Sutton Bridge	30	14	4	12	85	62	32
Crowland	30	13	3	14	73	71	29
Exning	30	10	2	18	83	94	22
Holbeach Reserves	30	9	2	19	63	104	20
Upwell Town	28	7	3	18	72	113	17
Bourne Reserves	28	5	4	19	49	94	14
Ramsey	29	3	2	24	29	127	8

Cambs Lower Junior Cup

First Round
Simplex   2   2   **Cambridge Utd 'A'**

First Round Replay
Cambridge Utd 'A'   0   1   Simplex

Cambs League Division Three (Section B)

	Pld	W	D	L	F	A	Pts
Simplex	26	23	3	0	153	23	49
Cambridge Y.M.C.A	24	21	2	1	159	26	44
Cambridge City 'B'	26	17	2	7	104	49	36
Cambridge United 'A'	25	16	0	9	80	57	32
R.A.F. Duxford	22	15	1	6	122	38	31
Wicken Amateurs	26	10	5	11	69	69	25
Elsworth	24	9	3	12	73	64	21
Littleport Reserves	25	10	1	14	70	88	21
Rooke's Sports	24	9	2	13	49	93	20
Trumpington	22	9	1	12	50	70	19
Burwell Reserves	25	9	1	15	68	115	19
Lode Reserves	24	5	4	15	47	116	14
Fordham Reserves	25	2	6	17	29	127	10
Weston Colville	26	0	3	23	36	174	3

1954-55 SEASON

The efforts of enthusiastic volunteers were again much in evidence during the summer of 1954. Having built the Supporters Club canteen at the Coldhams Lane end of the ground the previous year, they further improved that end of the ground by building more terracing and an end wall. A wall was also built behind the Newmarket Road stand in preparation for a roof which was erected by contractors during October 1954.

In a pre-season friendly the reserve team beat Camden United 12-2, but not to be outdone the first team travelled to Fakenham for a friendly on Tuesday 7th September 1954 and registered a 14-3 victory with Peter Dobson scoring 6 goals and Percy Anderson 5.

The Club made another good start in the Eastern Counties League and quickly moved to the top of the table after remaining unbeaten in the first five games. There was then a loss of form which coincided with a three week ankle injury to player-manager Bill Whittaker.

For the first time the Club got through the First Round of the Eastern Counties League Cup with a 2-0 win against Tottenham Hotspur 'A'. A further 2-0 victory at Crittall Athletic put them into the Semi-final with an away tie against Lowestoft Town. Cambridge United had already completed a league 'double' over them, but on this occasion the scores were level after 90 minutes, and the home side scored twice in extra-time to take the match.

Owing to their excellent F.A. Challenge Cup run the previous season, the Club were exempt until the Fourth Qualifying Round this time, and passed safely through with a 3-1 success against Eynesbury Rovers. The luck of the draw gave Cambridge

United a difficult away match in the First Round Proper against Torquay United on 20th November 1954, and as expected the Football League club were comfortable winners by 4 goals to 0 before a crowd of 8,224 spectators.

Despite problems with injuries, the first team managed to stay in the championship race, thanks largely to the sterling work of Peter Dobson who dominated the goalscoring with 32 league and cup goals. However, all events on the field were overshadowed by the sudden departure of the player-manager, Bill Whittaker, at the end of March, leaving the Club managerless for the rest of the season.

Shortly afterwards Cambridge United lost 3-0 at home to March Town in the Hunts. Premier Cup. That was the third defeat against the 'Hares' that season, but it was not to be the last, because after United had beaten Histon 2-1 in the Semi-final of the Cambs. Invitation Cup, the clubs met again in the Final at Milton Road on Thursday 21st April. Crowds of over 5,000 people watched both the Semi-final and Final of this popular competition, but goals from Teddy Bowd and Len Saward could not prevent March Town lifting the trophy with a 3-2 victory.

As the season came to a close, the first team still had a chance of finishing in the runners-up spot in the league, but they could only manage one point from their last two games away from home against lowly opposition when they needed three points. The Club finished in fourth place, another successful effort, vindicated by the fact that home attendances for league matches increased to an average of 3,013 per game. A Benefit Match for the popular former first team captain, Harry Bullen, on 2nd May attracted a crowd of over 1,000 spectators as the Club drew 1-1 with a Combined XI.

It was left to the reserve team to win the Club's only trophy of the season. They had another successful year in the Peterborough & District League Premier Division, and won the Championship in an exciting finish by one point over Bourne Town Reserves.

F.A. Challenge Cup

Fourth Qualifying Round
Cambridge United 3 1 Eynesbury Rovers

First Round Proper
Torquay United 4 0 **Cambridge United**

Eastern Counties League Cup

First Round Bye

Second Round
Cambridge United 2 0 Tottenham Hotspur 'A'

Third Round
Crittall Athletic 0 2 **Cambridge United**

Semi-final
Lowestoft Town 2 0 **Cambridge United**
(After extra-time)

East Anglian Cup

First Round Bye

Second Round
March Town United 2 1 **Cambridge United**

Cambs Invitation Cup

First Round Bye

Semi-final (at Cambridge City F.C.)
Cambridge United 2 1 Histon

Final (at Cambridge City F.C.)
Cambridge United 2 3 March Town United

Hunts Premier Cup

Cambridge United 0 3 March Town United

Eastern Counties League

	Pld	W	D	L	F	A	Pts
Arsenal 'A'	34	19	10	5	68	38	48
Colchester United Res.	34	18	7	9	72	45	43
March Town United	34	19	4	11	80	45	42
Cambridge United	34	17	7	10	80	58	41
Eynesbury Rovers	34	16	9	9	66	58	41
Crittall Athletic	34	18	4	12	61	60	40
Clacton Town	34	17	5	12	61	48	39
Peterborough United Res.	34	16	6	12	65	52	38
Gorleston	34	14	10	10	60	54	38
Tottenham Hotspur 'A'	34	15	6	13	60	48	36
Gt. Yarmouth Town	34	15	5	14	55	52	35
Lowestoft Town	34	13	6	15	56	61	32
West Ham United 'A'	34	11	8	15	50	57	30
Chelmsford City Reserves	34	8	10	16	63	68	26
Stowmarket	34	10	6	18	48	78	26
Bury Town	34	9	6	19	45	76	24
Norwich City 'A'	34	8	4	22	36	75	20
Harwich & Parkeston	34	2	9	23	24	77	13

Peterborough Senior Cup

First Round
Wisbech Town 'A' 1 7 **Cambridge Utd Res.**

Second Round
Cambridge Utd Res. 4 0 Hemingford United Res.

Third Round
Cambridge Utd Res. 1 2 Stamford Reserves

First Team 1954-55 Season
W."Sonny" Northfield, Jim Swainland, Arthur Vince, Ken Gilbert (Director), Ron Thulbourn (Director), Arthur Morgan, John Percival, Reg Barker (Trainer), Russell Crane, Bob Bishop, Len Crowe, Geoffrey Proctor (Chairman), Jack Thomas, Harry Bullen, Percy Anderson, A.E. Milner (Chairman Torquay United F.C.), F.T. Ward (Secretary), Les Stevens, Ray Ruffett, Eric Webber (Player/Manager Torquay United F.C.), "Teddy" Bowd, Peter Dobson, Bill Whittaker (Manager).

'A' Team 1955-56 Season
Back Row: Brian Short, Jimmy Tarrant, Albert Simpson, Mervyn Miller, Richard "Buster" Dunn, Eric Mansfield, Malcolm Watkinson, Neville Rose ('A' Team Manager).
Front Row: John Simpson, David Chapman, Dickie Turpin, Alan Hawkins, David "Dilly" Windmill, Richard Turpin.
Photograph by courtesy of *Cambridge Evening News*.

69

Peterborough & District League. Premier Division

	Pld	W	D	L	F	A	Pts
Cambridge United Res.	26	16	4	6	72	35	36
Bourne Town Reserves	26	17	1	8	93	57	35
Chatteris Town	26	15	4	7	85	53	34
Sutton Bridge	26	15	4	7	78	49	34
Downham Town	26	14	3	9	91	57	31
Ely City	26	14	3	9	67	57	31
Stamford Reserves	26	11	5	10	73	75	27
Somersham	25	11	4	10	81	67	26
Holbeach United Reserves	26	11	3	12	67	64	25
March Town Reserves	26	9	6	11	72	75	24
Exning United	26	10	3	13	72	83	23
Crowland Town	26	6	7	13	42	81	19
Upwell Town	25	5	3	17	58	99	13
Phorpes Sports	26	1	2	23	28	127	4

Cambs Lower Junior Cup

Preliminary Round
Pest Control Reserves 0 5 **Cambridge Utd 'A'**

First Round
Cambridge Utd 'A' 1 0 Swaffham United

Second Round
Cambridge YMCA Res. 5 0 **Cambridge Utd 'A'**

Cambs League Division Three (Section B)

	Pld	W	D	L	F	A	Pts
Wilburton	21	18	1	2	126	27	37
Prickwillow	22	15	1	6	107	58	31
Cambridge United 'A'	22	12	4	6	71	45	28
Soham United Reserves	22	13	2	7	74	49	28
Wicken Amateurs	21	11	3	7	63	48	25
St. Andrew's	21	9	3	9	75	53	21
Rooke's Sports	21	9	1	11	46	55	19
Elsworth	19	6	5	8	64	61	17
Littleport Reserves	21	8	1	12	59	79	17
Burwell Reserves	22	5	5	12	50	96	15
Weston Colville	20	3	3	14	54	121	9
Fordham Reserves	22	2	3	17	32	129	7

1955-56 SEASON

Gerald Evan Williams was appointed as player-manager for the 1955-56 season. He was a former Welsh schoolboy international, and had played for Blackpool, Birmingham, Accrington Stanley and Bolton. Several new signings were made, but his efforts to sign "The Golden Boy of Football", Wilf Mannion, became a major talking point, not only locally but in all the national newspapers. Mannion, who was capped by England 17 times and had been transferred from Middlesbrough to Hull City, was suspended for life from playing in the Football League because of certain statements he had made in the National Press about "under the counter payment to football stars". Despite the intense speculation the 'capture' did not materialize.

The league season got off to a spectacular start when Len Saward scored within half a minute of the kick-off at home to Lowestoft on Saturday 20th August 1955. He went on to score a hat-trick as United went on to win by 3 goals to 1. The sensational start to the season continued when Gerald Williams was dismissed less than two months after his appointment following a nightmare 2-1 defeat at Chatteris in the First Qualifying Round of the F.A.Challenge Cup on 10th September. Amazingly, at that time, the Club were unbeaten after five league games and were on top of the Eastern Counties League table. However, the Board of Directors decided that Williams had been given his chance, but did not fit the bill, and the football management was temporarily taken over by the Chairman (G.C.Proctor), the Vice-Chairman (J.E.Woolley) and the Football Director (A.E.Harris). The Board also decided to suspend Len Saward for a month for failing to be: "In a fit state to give of his best in the interest of the Club on the field".

The temporary managerial arrangement lasted for a period of ten matches, and was quite successful with the team winning six and drawing two of the games. The Board eventually appointed Bert Johnson as player-manager on 5th November 1955. He was a former England international and Charlton Athletic player who appeared at Wembley in both the 1946 and 1947 F.A.Challenge Cup Finals. He was keen on youth players, and had made quite a name with his managership of Bexleyheath & Welling F.C., the only non-league club allowed in the South-East Counties League.

Shortly after his arrival the Club played their first ever game under floodlights away to Bury Town in the Third Round of the East Anglian Cup on Tuesday 6th December 1955, and emerged victorious by 3 goals to 0. In the first two rounds the Club had beaten Norwich City 'A' and Norwich C.E.Y.M.S., and in the Semi-final they were drawn at home to Romford from the Isthmian League, who were the current holders of the cup and four times winners of the competition. In front of their own supporters Cambridge United gained a very creditable 2-2 draw, but in the replay on their own ground Romford were comfortable winners by 5 goals to 1.

Four defeats in December effectively killed off any hopes Cambridge United had of winning the league Championship, although on Boxing Day the Club managed to record their biggest win in the Eastern Counties League by 9 goals to 3 over Eynesbury Rovers. The very next day, however, when the two sides met in the return at Eynesbury, the match resulted in a 2-2 draw. The Club's form after Christmas did not match up to that of previous years, and at the end of the season they finished in their lowest position in the Eastern Counties League, a mid-table tenth place.

It was a similar season for the reserves who also finished in tenth place in the Peterborough & District League Premier Division, and went out of the Peterborough Senior Cup after their first match, a disappointing 7-0 defeat away to Ely City.

As Peterborough United Reserves won the Eastern Counties League, it was not surprising that their first team beat Cambridge United 5-1 on their own ground in the First Round of the Hunts. Premier Cup on Thursday 22nd March 1956. In the Semi-final of the Cambs. Invitation Cup the Club drew 1-1 against Wisbech Town on March Town F.C.'s ground, but when the replay was played on Cambridge City's ground United lost 3-1, and finished the season without a trophy.

It was left to the 'A' team to provide the Club with some silverware, and they capped a most successful season under the leadership of former first team player Neville Rose, by winning the Cambs. League Division Three Championship. They also won the Cambs. Lower Junior Cup when they beat Soham United Reserves 3-0 in the Final on 7th May 1956, with Dunn scoring two goals, and Simpson one.

F.A. Challenge Cup

First Qualifying Round
Chatteris Town   2   1   **Cambridge United**

Eastern Counties League Cup

First Round
Cambridge United   0   2   Tottenham Hotspur 'A'

East Anglian Cup

First Round
Cambridge United   2   0   Norwich City 'A'

Second Round
Cambridge United   4   1   Norwich C.E.Y.M.S.

Third Round
Bury Town   0   3   **Cambridge United**
(NOTE: Cambridge United's first ever game under floodlights - 6th December, 1955)

Semi-final
Cambridge United   2   2   Romford

Semi-final replay
Romford   5   1   **Cambridge United**

Cambs Invitation Cup

Semi-final (at March Town F.C.)
Wisbech Town   1   1   **Cambridge United**

Semi-final replay (at Cambridge City F.C.)
Cambridge United   1   3   Wisbech Town

Hunts Premier Cup

First Round
Cambridge United   1   5   Peterborough United

Eastern Counties League

	Pld	W	D	L	F	A	Pts
Peterborough United Res.	38	27	7	4	115	33	61
March Town United	38	28	3	7	90	42	59
Spalding United	38	24	7	7	90	57	55
Colchester United Reserves	38	22	5	11	118	61	49
Clacton Town	38	23	2	13	90	55	48
Sudbury Town	38	20	4	14	85	76	44
Tottenham Hotspur 'A'	38	18	7	13	64	48	43
Lowestoft Town	38	20	3	15	99	82	43
Gt. Yarmouth Town	38	18	6	14	65	57	42
Cambridge United	38	16	9	13	71	67	41
Holbeach United	38	18	4	16	74	70	40
Gorleston	38	17	3	18	68	69	37
Stowmarket	38	15	5	18	68	77	35
Bury Town	38	11	7	20	66	89	29
Harwich & Parkeston	38	9	10	19	57	79	28
West Ham United 'A'	38	10	6	22	49	85	26
Biggleswade	38	9	7	22	75	124	25
Eynesbury Rovers	38	8	6	24	49	117	22
Norwich City 'A'	38	4	10	24	46	93	18
Chelmsford City Reserves	38	4	7	27	48	106	15

Peterborough Senior Cup

First Round   Bye

Second Round
Ely City   7   0   **Cambridge Utd Res.**

Chatteris Engineering Cup

First Round   Bye

Second Round
Cambridge Utd Res.   5   0   Eynesbury Rovers Res.

Semi-final
Cambridge Utd Res.   2   1   Wisbech Town Res.

Final
Cambridge Utd Res.   2   3   March Town Utd Res.

Peterborough & District League. Premier Division

	Pld	W	D	L	F	A	Pts
Ely City	28	21	3	4	93	33	45
King's Lynn Reserves	28	18	5	5	108	43	41
Wisbech Town Reserves	28	16	5	7	109	52	37
March Town Reserves	27	16	4	7	99	63	36
Peterborough United 'A'	28	14	7	7	85	58	35
Bourne Town Reserves	28	15	5	8	81	60	35
Holbeach United Reserves	28	12	5	11	87	68	29
Sutton Bridge	28	13	2	13	73	68	28
Chatteris Town	28	11	5	12	70	88	27
Cambridge United Res.	27	8	7	12	78	72	23
Downham Town	28	8	6	14	71	99	22
Somersham Town	28	8	5	15	61	97	21
Exning United	27	7	5	15	64	97	19
Upwell Town	28	4	3	21	59	145	11
Stamford Reserves	27	1	5	21	47	142	7

Cambs Lower Junior Cup

Preliminary Round Bye

First Round
Cambridge Utd 'A' 6 0 Sawston United 'A'

Second Round
Cambridge Utd 'A' 11 0 Weston Colville

Third Round
Burwell Reserves 0 8 **Cambridge Utd 'A'**

Semi-final
Cambridge Utd 'A'   Elsworth
(NOTE: Result not known)

Final
Cambridge Utd 'A' 3 0 Soham United Res.

Cambs League Division Three (Section B)

	Pld	W	D	L	F	A	Pts
Cambridge United 'A'	26	22	2	2	110	35	46
Moulton	26	20	3	3	114	48	43
Camden United 'A'	26	20	2	4	103	36	42
Wicken Amateurs	25	16	2	7	84	40	34
Swaffham United	26	13	5	8	72	51	31
Long Sutton	26	13	2	11	92	79	28
Soham United Reserves	23	13	1	9	91	47	27
Burwell Reserves	26	11	2	13	74	67	24
Isleham Reserves	23	8	3	12	48	84	19
Albion Reserves	24	6	4	14	72	87	16
Willingham Reserves	24	7	2	15	43	88	16
Littleport Reserves	23	5	3	15	40	93	13
Fordham Reserves	24	2	1	21	39	134	5
Weston Colville	26	2	0	24	40	133	4

Cambs League Division Three Championship Match (at Histon F.C.)

Cambridge United 'A' 4 1 Eastern Gas Board

1956-57 SEASON

In the summer of 1956 the pitch at the Newmarket Road ground was widened to give a playing area of 110 x 76 yards. The treasured signing of Wilf Mannion also took place, and with several other new signings optimism was high for a successful season. However, things did not turn out quite as well as expected, and the Club made their worst start since joining the Eastern Counties League.

Holbeach United were overcome in the First Qualifying Round of the F.A.Challenge Cup after a replay, but with Wilf Mannion out following a knee injury, the Club suffered another disaster when they lost 5-2 at home to Ely City in the next round. A month later United's reserves drew 3-3 away to Ely City in the First Round of the Peterborough Senior Cup, and in fact progressed into the next round when Ely withdrew from the competition because of their continued involvement in the F.A.Challenge Cup and F.A. Amateur Cup. The first team went out of the East Anglian Cup in the First Round following a 2-1 home defeat against Stowmarket, and the gloom worsened as the Club lost 3-0 away to Spalding United in the Second Round of the Eastern Counties League Cup.

Several changes took place, with V. Chapman replacing W.E.F. Silk as Secretary. The arrival of Bernard Moore, formerly of Luton Town and Bedford Town, in November coincided with an improvement in the results, which was much needed as the Club had slipped into the lower reaches of the league table. A month later the forward line was strengthened even further with the unexpected signing of Brian Moore from West Ham United's first team. It was a stroke of good fortune for Cambridge United, as Brian Moore had been compensated for an eye injury which had seemed to end his playing career, but when it suddenly cleared up he was unable to return to the Football League because of their regulations.

Cambridge United's revival continued as the experienced forward line started scoring with greater regularity, and the Club climbed in the league table up to their final place of sixth at the end of the season.

Following a 1-1 draw at home to Wisbech Town in the First Round of the Cambs. Invitation Cup, the Club recorded an excellent 2-1 win at Fenland Park in the replay. The new spirit was typified by the fact that Brian Moore flew back from Belfast specially for the game. Victory in front of 6,372 spectators over Pegasus, the Combined University side, in the Semi-final by 3 goals to 2 gave United the prospect of an exciting Final against Cambridge City. The match was played on the Milton Road ground, on Easter Monday 22nd April 1957, and United overcame the loss of home advantage to win the cup for the third time with a 1-0 victory. Brian Moore scored the only goal of the game before another large, excited crowds of 9,668 spectators.

A 3-2 victory over Eynesbury Rovers earned Cambridge United a Semi-final place against Bedford Town in the Hunts. Premier Cup, but because of lack of time, the game had to be held over to the following season, and when played United put up a brave fight before going down by 4 goals to 3.

The reserve team had another disappointing season in the Premier Division of the Peterborough & District League, finishing in 13th place, but they did reach the Third Round of the Peterborough Senior Cup before losing to Wisbech Town Reserves 4-2 in a replay.

For the first time the F.A. Youth Challenge Cup was entered, and in the First Qualifying Round Sawston Village College Y.C. were beaten 4-1, but R.A.F. Apprentices (Halton) proved to be too strong in the Second Qualifying Round, and won 5-1. A youth team was also entered in the Anglian Youth Cup, where the Cambridge United Youth team ran up a record score of 20 goals to 0, against Cherry Hinton Youth, before losing 3-1 to Eynesbury Rovers Juniors in the Semi-final.

Not long before the end of the season the Football League announced that they were to lift the life-ban on Wilf Mannion, but fortunately for the Club he decided to continue playing for Cambridge United. Leading goalscorer for the season for the first team was Kevin Barry with 22 goals, while Bernard and Brian Moore scored 15 goals each. Wilf Mannion netted 11 goals in his first full campaign.

During the season Keith Payne and Vic Phillips shared the distinction of having played in the first team at the age of 15 years.

F.A. Challenge Cup

First Qualifying Round
Holbeach United 2 2 **Cambridge United**

First Qualifying Round Replay
Cambridge United 5 0 Holbeach United

Second Qualifying Round
Cambridge United 2 5 Ely City

Eastern Counties League Cup

First Round
Cambridge United 2 1 Sudbury Town

Second Round
Spalding United 3 0 **Cambridge United**

East Anglian Cup

First Round
Cambridge United 1 2 Stowmarket

Cambs Invitation Cup

First Round
Cambridge United 1 1 Wisbech Town

First Round Replay
Wisbech Town 1 2 **Cambridge United**

Semi-final (at Cambridge City F.C.)
Cambridge United 3 2 Pegasus

Final (at Cambridge City F.C.)
Cambridge City 0 1 **Cambridge United**

Hunts Premier Cup

First Round
Cambridge United 3 2 Eynesbury Rovers

Semi-final
Bedford Town 4 3 **Cambridge United**

Eastern Counties League

	Pld	W	D	L	F	A	Pts
Colchester United Reserves	36	25	2	9	119	54	52
Gt. Yarmouth Town	36	24	3	9	82	53	51
Clacton Town	36	21	7	8	74	43	49
Peterborough United Res.	36	21	5	10	92	55	47
Tottenham Hotspur 'A'	36	20	6	10	86	46	46
Cambridge United	36	19	7	10	76	56	45
Holbeach United	36	20	4	12	70	55	44
Sudbury Town	36	19	5	11	76	56	43
Spalding United	36	19	4	13	76	60	42
Stowmarket	36	15	1	20	85	74	31
Harwich & Parkeston	36	13	5	18	54	75	31
March Town United	36	12	6	18	84	86	30
Lowestoft Town	36	11	8	17	66	82	30
Chelmsford City	36	11	7	18	61	84	29
Bury Town	36	10	7	19	59	94	27
Eynesbury Rovers	36	8	9	19	54	98	25
Biggleswade Town	36	9	5	22	50	87	23
Norwich City 'A'	36	7	8	21	41	90	22
Gorleston	36	5	7	24	36	93	17

First Team 1956-57 Season
Back Row: Len Saward, Bernard J. Moore, Colin Senior, Ted Culver, Harry Chapman, Jock Kyle, Bob Bishop (Coach).
Front Row: Russell Crane, Brian Moore, Ron Murchinson, Wilf Mannion, Kevin Barry. Mascot: John Dunne
Photograph taken at Milton Road, Cambridge, after the 1-0 victory over Cambridge City in the Final of the Cambs Invitation Cup on Easter Monday 22nd April 1957. Attendance: 9,668. Photograph by courtesy of *Cambridge Evening News*.

Wednesday 19th March 1958. Wilf Mannion Benefit Match. Cambridge United 4, International XI 3.
Back Row: S.J. Dent (Linesman), Jack Howe (Derby County), Ted Ditchburn (Tottenham Hotspur & England), Len Saward, Ron Murchinson, Neville Haylock, Neil Franklin (ex England centre-half), Joe Mercer (Arsenal & England), Brian Moore, Taffy Jones, Russell Crane, Harry Chapman, Peter Bye (Linesman), Kevin Barry, Jack Cooke (Referee).
Front Row: Frank Lock, Jock McKinley, Lawrie Scott (Arsenal & England), Jimmy Hagan (Sheffield United & England), Henry Cockburn (Manchester United), Wilf Mannion, Stanley Mortenson (Blackpool & England) Johnny Morris (Derby County & England), Bobby Langton (Bolton & England), D. Tapscott (Arsenal). Mascot: John Dunne. Attendance: 9,500
Photograph by courtesy of *Cambridge Evening News*.

Peterborough Senior Cup

First Round
Ely City 3 3 **Cambridge Utd. Res.**

First Round Replay
Cambridge Utd. Res. v Ely City (Ely withdrew)

Second Round
Cambridge Utd. Res. 4 1 Sutton Bridge

Third Round
Cambridge Utd. Res. 1 1 Wisbech Town Reserves

Third Round Replay
Wisbech Town Res. 4 2 **Cambridge Utd. Res.**

Chatteris Engineering Cup

First Round Bye

Second Round
Cambridge Utd. Res. 1 2 Eynesbury Rovers Res.

Peterborough & District League. Premier Division

	Pld	W	D	L	F	A	Pts
King's Lynn Res.	34	27	4	3	197	40	58
Ely City	34	24	2	8	124	55	50
Holbeach Utd. Res.	34	21	6	7	103	64	48
Bourne Town	33	20	3	10	123	80	43
Wisbech Town Res.	34	18	5	11	97	60	41
Somersham Town	34	17	6	11	105	86	40
Chatteris Town	34	17	4	13	101	95	38
Soham Town	33	15	6	12	113	94	36
March Town Res.	34	17	2	15	92	88	36
Sutton Bridge	34	15	6	13	92	89	36
Exning United	34	14	5	15	107	110	33
Peterborough United 'A'	34	15	1	18	82	100	31
Cambridge Utd. Res.	34	12	7	15	76	85	31
Downham Town	34	13	4	17	107	104	30
Warboys Town	34	10	4	20	78	108	24
Newmarket Town	34	6	8	20	60	108	20
Stamford Rovers	34	4	4	26	51	159	12
Upwell Town	34	1	1	32	32	255	3

Cambs Junior Cup

Preliminary Round
Simplex 1 1 **Cambridge Utd 'A'**

Preliminary Round Replay
Cambridge Utd 'A' 4 1 Simplex

First Round
St. Andrew's 1 6 **Cambridge Utd 'A'**

Second Round
Cambridge Utd 'A' 2 4 Willingham

Waterbeach Cup

First Round
Cambridge Utd. 'A' 5 3 Waterbeach

Second Round
Cambridge Utd 'A' 0 2 Camden United Reserves

Cambs League Division Two (Section B)

	Pld	W	D	L	F	A	Pts
Willingham	26	23	0	3	150	42	46
Pye's	25	21	2	2	120	26	44
Bottisham	25	15	3	7	78	58	33
Wilbraham	25	14	5	6	79	63	33
Prickwillow	26	12	6	8	80	74	30
Soham Town Res.	25	14	1	10	120	83	29
Balsham	26	13	2	11	88	71	28
Cambridge Utd 'A'	24	11	2	11	71	58	24
Fisons Pest Control	25	9	1	15	65	80	19
Moulton	24	7	3	14	62	80	17
Haddenham Rovers Res.	22	6	0	16	43	89	12
Over	24	4	3	17	54	103	11
Cottenham Reserves	23	5	1	17	59	129	11
Milton Reserves	24	3	1	20	34	147	7

F.A. Youth Challenge Cup

First Qualifying Round
Cambridge Utd. Yth 4 2 Sawston Village College Y.C.

Second Qualifying Round
R.A.F. App (Halton) 5 1 **Cambridge Utd Yth**

Anglia Youth Cup

First Round Bye

Second Round
Cambridge Utd Yth 4 3 Sawston Village College Colts

Third Round
Cambridge Utd Yth 20 0 Cherry Hinton Youth

Semi-final
Eynesbury Rovers Jnrs 3 1 **Cambridge Utd Yth**

1957-58 SEASON

Brian Moore opened the season in fine goalscoring style by registering eleven goals in the first eight games, but the first team defence was also conceding goals at an alarming rate, and only six points were gained from the first seven league matches.

St. Neots Town were beaten 6-2 in the First Qualifying Round of the F.A. Challenge Cup, but a 4-1 defeat was suffered away to March Town in the next round. On Saturday 19th October 1957, 4,900 people saw Cambridge United beat Cambridge City 4-1 in the First Round of the Cambs. Invitation Cup. Two days later the Club staged their first ever floodlit match, using floodlights attached to telegraph poles, with a combined power of 32,000 watts. The match, a First Round replay in the East Anglian Cup, resulted in a successful 3-0 win over Great Yarmouth Town.

A week later Len Saward was granted a Benefit Match under the floodlights, having played for the Club for five years. His brother, Pat Saward, an Aston Villa player, took part in the Benefit Match. Len generously contributed £400 from his testimonial fund towards the cost of the rather primitive set of floodlights. On 4th November the floodlights were used again as the Club beat Stowmarket 5-0 in the Second Round of the East Anglian Cup, but later that evening severe gales caused extensive damage to the Newmarket Road Stand roof, putting extra demand on the voluntary labour that helped to complete the new dressing rooms, office and board room, which were opened a few weeks later.

All three of the Club's teams had a tremendous run of success in November and December. Brian Moore scored 30 goals by Christmas to help the team into third place in the Eastern Counties League table. A string of good results put the reserve team top of the Peterborough & District League by mid-December, and the 'A' team received the *Cambridge Daily News* Merit Shield for December 1957 after achieving consecutive wins of 10-1, 11-0, 12-1 and 10-1.

In the New Year the first team started an unbeaten run of thirteen consecutive league games, including seven successive victories. The Club also remained unbeaten in the last eight league games to finish in the runners-up position in the Eastern Counties League with 51 points from 36 games. For the first time the Club scored over a hundred Eastern Counties League goals in a season, finishing with 108.

March Town United were beaten 2-0 in the Semi-final of the Cambs. Invitation Cup, and for the Final a crowd of 8,422 turned up at the Cambridge City ground to see Cambridge United take on Wisbech Town on Monday 7th April 1958. Brian Moore's penalty goal brought his tally to 60 for the Club that season and earned the Club a 2-2 draw. The replay was played at Fenland Park two weeks later, and United came off second best, losing by 3 goals to 1.

In the East Anglian Cup the Club lost 3-2 at home to a strengthened Norwich City Reserve team in the Third Round, but in the Eastern Counties League Cup the Final was reached for the first time, following impressive victories over Tottenham Hotspur 'A', Stowmarket and Spalding. The Final, played over two legs, proved to be a great disappointment to the supporters, as United conceded five goals in each match to lose 10-1 on aggregate to Colchester United Reserves, and for the third time that season they finished as runners-up in a competition.

For the third time the reserve team reached the Final of the Peterborough Senior Cup, although it was achieved in unsatisfactory circumstances when King's Lynn Reserves withdrew from the competition after a 1-1 draw in the Semi-final. As it turned out the Final was held over to the following season because of fixture congestion, and when it was played the reserves beat Warboys Town by 5 goals to 2 after a replay. The reserves slipped to a final place of fifth in the Peterborough & District League Premier Division, but the 'A' team completed a successful season by winning the Cambs. League Division Two (Section B), as well as the Division Two Championship match against St.Andrews by 2 goals to 1.

Much fuss was made in the national newspapers when Wilf Mannion was not granted a testimonial with his first club Middlesbrough, but shortly before he left Cambridge United a Benefit Match was played on his behalf against an International XI on Wednesday 19th March 1958. The Club's biggest crowd of the season, 9,500 spectators, saw a feast of good football, and some of the star footballers of the era took part. Goals came at regular intervals during the match, with Stan Mortenson opening the scoring, but United then took the lead with goals from Ron Murchinson and Brian Moore, before Jim Hagan scored an equalizer. Fittingly, Wilf Mannion scored to give United the lead once more, but Hagan again equalized. The game was finally won by United when Russell Crane scored in the dying minutes to make the score 4-3. The teams for that match were:

Cambridge United: G.Jones, H.Chapman, F.Lock, R.Murchinson, N.Haylock, J.McKinley, L.Saward, W.Mannion, R.Crane, Brian Moore, K.Barry.

International XI: E.Ditchburn, L.Scott, J.Howe, H.Cockburn, N.Franklin, J.Mercer, D.Tapscott, J.Hagan, S.Mortenson, J.Morris, R.Langton.

If that was not a big enough treat for the Cambridge United fans, then on Monday 14th April 1958 an All Stars XI came to the Newmarket Road ground fielding ten full international players from the Home Countries. Surprisingly, only 1,800 spectators turned up to see the 1-1 draw against the following line-up of players:

All Stars XI: Sam Bartram (Charlton & England), Wally Barnes (Arsenal & Wales), Alf Sherwood

(Cardiff & Wales), Bill Shankly (Preston & Scotland), Eddie Boot (Huddersfield), Willie Watson (Sunderland & England football and cricket international), Willie Moir (Bolton & Scotland), Bill Lucas (Swansea & Wales), Jimmy Hagan (Sheffield United & England), Peter Doherty (Derby & England), Charlie Mitten (Manchester United & England).

F.A. Challenge Cup

First Qualifying Round
Cambridge United 6 2 St. Neots Town

Second Qualifying Round
March Town 4 1 **Cambridge United**

Eastern Counties League Cup

First Round   Bye

Second Round
Cambridge United 3 1 Tottenham Hotspur 'A'

Third Round
Cambridge United 4 1 Stowmarket

Semi-final
Cambridge United 4 2 Spalding

Final - First Leg
Cambridge United 0 5 Colchester United Res.

Final - Second Leg
Colchester Utd. Res. 5 1 **Cambridge United**
(Colchester won 10-1 on aggregate)

East Anglian Cup

First Round
Great Yarmouth 1 1 **Cambridge United**

First Round Replay
Cambridge United 3 0 Great Yarmouth Town
(NOTE: Cambridge United's first game under their new floodlights)

Second Round
Cambridge United 5 0 Stowmarket

Third Round
Cambridge United 2 3 Norwich City Res.

Cambs Invitation Cup

First Round
Cambridge United 4 1 Cambridge City

Semi-final
Cambridge United 2 0 March Town

Final (at Cambridge City F.C.)
Cambridge United 2 2 Wisbech Town

Final Replay
Wisbech Town 3 1 **Cambridge United**

Coan Cup

Final
Clacton Town 5 2 Cambridge United
(After extra-time)

Eastern Counties League

	Pld	W	D	L	F	A	Pts
Tottenham Hotspur 'A'	36	29	3	4	129	49	61
Cambridge United	36	21	9	6	108	59	51
Spalding United	36	23	3	10	113	62	49
Peterborough Utd. Res.	36	19	5	12	82	54	43
Clacton Town	36	17	9	10	84	60	43
Colchester Utd. Res.	36	18	6	12	88	59	42
Holbeach United	36	15	11	10	94	62	41
Lowestoft Town	36	15	8	13	80	67	38
Chelmsford City	36	15	7	14	72	70	37
Harwich & Parkeston	36	13	10	13	69	69	36
Gt. Yarmouth Town	36	15	5	16	80	80	35
Sudbury Town	36	14	6	16	87	84	34
March Town United	36	13	7	15	87	89	33
Stowmarket	36	12	6	18	67	86	30
Gorleston	36	12	5	19	72	99	29
Norwich City 'A'	36	10	5	21	63	92	25
Biggleswade Town	36	8	6	22	64	122	22
Eynesbury Rovers	36	8	3	25	44	134	19
Bury Town	36	5	6	25	51	137	16

Peterborough Senior Cup

First Round   Bye

Second Round
Cambridge Utd Res. 0 0 March Town Utd Res.

Second Round Replay
March Town Utd Res. 0 0 **Cambridge Utd Res.**

Second Round Second Replay
Cambridge Utd Res. 5 2 March Town Utd Res.

Third Round
Warmington 1 1 **Cambridge Utd Res.**

Third Round Replay
Cambridge Utd Res. 2 0 Warmington

Semi-final
King's Lynn Res. 1 1 **Cambridge Utd Res.**
(NOTE: King's Lynn Reserves withdrew from the competition)

Final
Cambridge Utd Res. 1 1 Warboys Town

Final Replay
Warboys Town 2 5 **Cambridge Utd Res.**

Chatteris Engineering Cup

Semi-final
Cambridge Utd Res. 2 0 Eynesbury Rovers Res

Final
Cambridge Utd Res. 5 2 Downham Town

Peterborough & District League. Premier Division

	Pld	W	D	L	F	A	Pts
Newmarket Town	28	21	4	3	72	26	46
Ely City	28	20	5	3	89	28	45
Soham Town Rangers	28	17	6	5	90	57	40
Chatteris Town	28	15	5	8	87	63	35
Cambridge Utd Res.	28	14	5	9	75	44	33
Peterborough Utd 'A'	28	13	5	10	84	50	31
Warboys Town	28	14	3	11	76	71	31
Exning United	28	9	10	9	67	58	28
Bourne Town	28	13	2	13	74	68	28
March Town Utd Res.	28	9	6	13	65	63	24
Downham Town	28	10	3	15	56	91	23
Somersham Town	27	9	2	16	58	73	20
Sutton Bridge	27	7	3	17	54	87	17
Sawston United	28	5	3	20	36	95	13
Stamford Rovers	28	1	2	25	35	144	4

Cambs Junior Cup

Preliminary Round
Girton Rovers 0 3 **Cambridge Utd 'A'**

First Round
Cottenham 4 1 **Cambridge Utd 'A'**

Cambs League Division Two (Section B)

	Pld	W	D	L	F	A	Pts
Cambridge Utd 'A'	26	22	2	2	166	27	46
Soham Utd Res.	25	20	3	2	95	32	43
Soham Town Res.	26	18	2	6	109	45	38
Balsham	26	14	3	9	73	53	31
Longstanton	26	14	1	11	97	70	29
Bottisham	26	12	4	10	81	79	28
Over	26	12	1	13	74	73	25
Fisons Pest Control	25	11	3	11	58	74	25
Wilbraham	26	7	9	10	55	73	23
Haddenham Rovers Res.	25	10	1	14	77	93	21
Prickwillow	26	7	4	15	44	91	18
Stetchworth	25	5	4	16	48	89	14
Cottenham Res.	25	5	2	18	42	121	12
Fen Ditton	25	2	1	22	38	137	5

Cambs League Division Two Championship Match

(At Histon F.C.)
Cambridge Utd 'A' 2 1 St.Andrew's

1958-59 SEASON

Largely as a result of the ground improvements carried out during the previous season, the Club's application to join the Southern League was accepted, and for the first time in their history the Club were to play in the same league as their neighbours, Cambridge City, in the South-East Section. Because of cup matches, the two sides were to meet on no less than six occasions during the season, with honours even, as both teams won two games each and the other two were drawn.

The first meeting was in the First Qualifying Round of the F.A.Challenge Cup, and a crowd of 6,789 saw United proceed into the next round with a 2-1 home win. The Second Qualifying Round was a complete anti-climax, and resulted in a very disappointing 2-1 home defeat against Holbeach United. After beating Kettering Town 6-2 on aggregate in the First Round of the Southern League Cup, United were drawn at home to Cambridge City in the next round, but this time City took the honours with a 2-1 win.

Sandwiched between these two games Cambridge United were given another home tie against Cambridge City in the Semi-final of the Cambs. Professional Cup, which was being held for the first time. The match ended in a 1-1 draw, but when the replay at Milton Road was played later in the season, a crowd of 8,214 people watched Cambridge United register another excellent 2-1 victory.

Manager Bert Johnson's Charlton Athletic connection was very much in evidence in a team which included eight new players from the previous season. Jock Campbell, Frank Lock, Eddie Robinson and Kevin Barry had all previously played for Charlton Athletic. In the early part of the season the Club managed to pick up a point a game from the first ten games, but then they hit a bad patch, and started to slip into the bottom half of the table. It was a situation the Club could not afford to be in, because in October the Southern League management announced that at the end of the season the top eleven clubs in each regional division would be placed in the new Premier Division, with the remaining clubs being placed in Division One.

For much of the season the Club hovered close to the danger zone in the league, yet in the Inter-Zone Competition, which was held for one season only to supplement the league fixtures, their results were much better. They eventually won the five-team group on goal difference over the eventual league champions Bedford Town and the strong Chelmsford City. However, the Club went out of the competition at the next stage.

In the East Anglian Cup the entire reserve team represented the Club in the First Round away to Sudbury Town from the Eastern Counties League, and they returned home having secured a marvellous 1-0 victory. The reserve team enjoyed another successful season in the Peterborough & District

First Team 1958-59 Season
Back Row: Frank Lock, Jimmy Campbell, Fred Howell, Glanville "Taffy" Jones, Malcolm Handscombe, Jock McKinlay.
Front Row: Clive Chattin, Allan Bull, Brian Moore, Eddie Robinson, Kevin Barry.

Reserve Team 1958-59 Season
Back Row: Ron Simpson (Trainer), Keith Payne, Stan Thurston, Vic Phillips, Michael Bell, Glanville "Taffy" Jones, Reg Tailby, W. "Sonny" Northfield.
Front Row: Johnnie Coteman, Jock Kyle, Tony Copping (Captain), David Johnson, Ray Hamblett.
Photograph by courtesy of *Cambridge Evening News*.

League Premier Division, eventually winning the Championship for the fourth time by a margin of three points over Soham Town Rangers. In addition they won the Peterborough Senior Cup Final, which was held over from the previous season.

Near the end of the season the reserve team drew with March Town United's Eastern Counties League team to share the Doddington Hospital Cup, and this performance did their reputation no harm at all in their application to join the Eastern Counties League the following season, which was accepted at the League's Annual General Meeting in the summer of 1959.

Norwich City were the visitors for the Second Round of the East Anglian Cup, but unluckily the match was abandoned owing to fog at a time when Cambridge United were leading 1-0. When the match was re-played later in the season Norwich were more than comfortable winners by 5 goals to 1.

The Final of the Cambs. Professional Cup was played on a 'home and away' basis, and for the third year in succession Cambridge United met Wisbech Town in the Cambs. F.A.'s premier cup tournament. The first match was played at Fenland Park, and Cambridge United made virtually certain of winning the cup with an emphatic 6-2 victory that saw Phil Hayes score four goals. The second leg attracted only 2,006 spectators to Newmarket Road, but United tidied up the formalities with a 2-1 win.

Of more pressing importance was the Club's battle to finish in the top eleven places, to earn a place in the Premier Division of the Southern League for the following season. Six wins in eight games, including an impressive 2-1 victory over highly placed Yeovil Town in their penultimate game, meant that Cambridge United were level on points with Tonbridge but with an inferior goal difference, and needing to overhaul them in their last game to gain a Premier Division place. As it turned out United could only draw 3-3 away to Chelmsford City, while Tonbridge beat bottom placed Yiewsley by 5 goals to 3. Cambridge United therefore missed out by just one place, one point behind three teams on 31 points, one of whom was Cambridge City.

The youth team had a magnificent season, losing only one game, 1-0 away to Icknield of Hitchin in the Second Qualifying Round of the F.A. Youth Challenge Cup. They won every Cambs. Youth League match, including a 21-1 victory away to Sutton Athletic on the 25th October 1958. During the season the youth team scored over 300 goals,

and they also won the Cambs. F.A. Youth Cup 6-0 against Cambridge Y.M.C.A.

F.A. Challenge Cup

First Qualifying Round
Cambridge United 2 1 Cambridge City

Second Qualifying Round
Cambridge United 1 2 Holbeach United

Southern League Cup

First Round - First Leg
Kettering 1 5 **Cambridge United**

First Round - Second Leg
Cambridge United 1 1 Kettering

Second Round
Cambridge United 1 2 Cambridge City

East Anglian Cup

First Round
Sudbury Town 0 1 **Cambridge United**

Second Round
Cambridge United 1 0 Norwich City
(match abandoned owing to fog)

Second Round Replay
Cambridge United 1 5 Norwich City

Cambs Professional Cup

Semi-final
Cambridge United 1 1 Cambridge City

Semi-final Replay
Cambridge City 1 2 **Cambridge United**

Final - First Leg
Wisbech Town 2 6 **Cambridge United**

Final - Second Leg
Cambridge United 2 1 Wisbech Town

Southern League South East Section

	Pld	W	D	L	F	A	Pts
Bedford Town	32	21	6	5	90	41	48
Gravesend & Northfleet	32	21	2	9	79	54	44
Dartford	32	20	3	9	77	41	43
Yeovil Town	32	17	8	7	60	41	42
Weymouth	32	13	11	8	41	43	37
Chelmsford City	32	12	12	8	74	53	36
King's Lynn	32	14	5	13	70	63	33
Poole Town	32	12	8	12	60	65	32
Cambridge City	32	12	7	13	61	54	31
Hastings United	32	13	5	14	60	49	31
Tonbridge	32	14	3	15	51	59	31
Cambridge United	32	11	8	13	55	77	30
Trowbridge Town	32	12	4	16	52	75	28
Exeter City Res.	32	7	12	13	47	71	26
Guildford City	32	7	6	19	45	67	20
Clacton Town	32	6	7	19	44	81	19
Yiewsley	32	3	7	22	36	78	13

Southern League Inter Zone Competition

	Pld	W	D	L	F	A	Pts
Cambridge United	8	5	0	3	25	17	10
Bedford Town	8	3	4	1	22	17	10
Chelmsford City	8	3	4	1	16	14	10
Kettering Town	8	2	2	4	13	21	6
Clacton Town	8	1	2	5	13	20	4

Peterborough Senior Cup

First Round
Bourne Town 0 5 **Cambridge Utd Res.**

Second Round
Exning United 3 3 **Cambridge Utd Res.**

Second Round Replay
Cambridge Utd Res. 6 1 Exning United

Third Round
Cambridge Utd Res. 2 3 Chatteris Town

Chatteris Engineering Cup

First Round
Cambridge Utd Res. 5 1 Somersham Town

Second Round
Cambridge Utd Res. 1 1 Warboys Town

Second Round Replay
Warboys Town v **Cambridge Utd Res.**
(NOTE: Cambridge United Reserves withdrew from the competition)

Peterborough & District League Championship Match

Cambridge Utd. Res. 0 1 The Rest of the Peterborough & D.L.

Doddington Hospital Cup Final

March Town 4 4 **Cambridge Utd Res.**

Peterborough & District League Premier Division.

	Pld	W	D	L	F	A	Pts
Cambridge Utd Res.	30	22	4	4	86	45	48
Soham Town Rangers	30	19	7	4	109	43	45
Newmarket Town	30	17	6	7	83	42	40
Soham United	30	18	4	8	99	68	40
Chatteris Town	30	17	3	10	88	58	37
Sawston United	30	14	6	10	68	71	34
Exning United	30	14	5	11	81	67	33
Peterborough Utd. 'A'	30	13	5	12	96	61	31
Downham Town	30	12	5	13	64	92	29
March Town Res.	30	10	6	14	69	72	26
Warboys Town	30	8	8	14	64	71	24
Somersham	30	8	6	16	55	93	22
Pinchbeck	30	8	5	17	50	76	21
Sutton Bridge	30	5	10	15	52	90	20
Ely City Res.	30	8	4	18	65	84	20
Long Sutton	30	4	2	24	38	134	10

Creake Charity Shield

Preliminary Round
Cambridge Utd 'A' 1 3 Linton Granta

Cambs. Junior Cup

Preliminary Round Bye

First Round
Cambridge Utd. 3 4 Longstanton

Cambs League Division One (Section B)

	Pld	W	D	L	F	A	Pts
Willingham	22	21	0	1	134	37	42
Newmarket Town Res.	20	12	2	6	63	40	26
Cambridge Y.M.C.A	24	12	2	10	72	75	26
Lode	23	10	5	8	86	78	25
Littleport	22	11	3	8	67	63	25
Pye's	23	12	0	11	53	64	24
Cambridge United 'A'	22	8	7	7	73	60	23
Soham United Res.	23	9	4	10	69	67	22
Burwell	23	9	1	13	64	64	19
Histon 'A'	23	7	5	11	50	58	19
Isleham	23	7	3	13	61	93	17
Waterbeach	20	6	1	13	48	97	13
Little Downham	24	5	1	18	55	99	11

F.A. Youth Challenge Cup

Preliminary Round Bye

First Round
Cambridge Utd. Yth 0 0 Cambridge City Yth

First Round Replay
Cambridge City Youth 0 5 **Cambridge Utd Yth**

Second Round
Icknield Youth (Hitchin) 1 0 Cambridge Utd Yth

Cambs F.A. Youth Cup

Preliminary Round Bye

First Round
Cambridge Utd Yth 5 1 Cambridge City Yth

Second Round
Cambridge Utd Yth 11 1 Exning Youth

Semi-final
(NOTE: Result not known)

Final
Cambridge Utd Yth 6 0 Cambridge Y.M.C.A.

Cambs Youth League (Northern Section)

	Pld	W	D	L	F	A	Pts
Cambridge Utd Youth	13	13	0	0	106	8	26
Cambridge City Youth	14	12	0	2	100	21	24
Ely City Youth	14	7	1	6	44	76	15
Newmarket Town Youth	13	6	1	6	58	46	13
Littleport Youth	14	5	2	7	41	49	12
Soham Town Youth	13	4	1	8	37	62	9
Burwell Youth	12	3	1	8	31	82	7
Soham United Youth	13	0	0	13	10	83	0

Cambs Youth League (Southern Section)

	Pld	W	D	L	F	A	Pts
Cambridge Utd Youth	16	16	0	0	127	10	32
Cambridge City Youth	16	11	3	2	96	25	25
Cambridge Y.M.C.A. Yth	16	11	2	3	91	34	24
St. Andrew's Youth	15	7	2	6	53	42	16
Histon Youth	14	6	2	6	54	44	14
Cambridge Eagles Youth	16	7	0	9	46	88	14
Camden United Youth	16	4	2	10	31	109	10
Ickleton Youth	16	1	1	14	21	121	3
Willingham Youth	15	1	0	14	28	74	2

1959-60 SEASON

Bill Craig replaced Bert Johnson as player-manager for the Club's campaign in the First Division of the Southern League. Early season crowds averaging over 3,000 soon dropped to below 2,500 as a mixed set of results saw the team drop out of promotion contention by occupying a mid-table position in the league.

In the First Round of the Southern League Cup the Club were unlucky enough to be drawn against Premier Division Bedford Town, but in the 1st Leg United played well to earn a 1-1 draw at Newmarket Road. However, the forwards were well on top in the 2nd Leg, as the "Eagles" won an entertaining game by 6 goals to 4.

Two 3-0 victories over Ely City and Holbeach United gave Cambridge United a home tie against Cambridge City in the Third Qualifying Round of the F.A.Challenge Cup, but the Premier Division side scored the only goal of the game to proceed further in the competition. It took United just nine days to get their revenge with a 1-0 victory at Milton Road in the Semi-final of the Cambs. Professional Cup, with Fred Howell getting the important goal. Both matches attracted crowds of over 6,500, but that figure was exceeded when 8,325 saw the clubs meet again at Milton Road in the Third Round of the East Anglian Cup on Tuesday 15th March 1960. United went into the game confident after three successive wins and a 1-1 draw away to second in the table Romford, but it was Cambridge City who won the 'decider' by 2 goals to 0.

On their way to the Third Round of the East Anglian Cup, the first team beat Sudbury Town 6-1. The reserve team also met Sudbury Town at home in the First Round of the Eastern Counties League Cup, and beat them 4-2, before losing 6-1 against Peterborough United Reserves in the next round. On Tuesday 25th August 1959 the Eastern Counties League clash between Cambridge City Reserves and Cambridge United Reserves attracted a crowd of 2,086 spectators, but the Milton Road outfit won comfortably by 5 goals to 0. Generally Cambridge United reserve team struggled in the higher grade of football, and for much of the season occupied the bottom place in the league table, eventually finishing in that position with 16 points from 38 games.

The youth team, under the guidance of John Munns, continued their unbeaten run which lasted for eleven months until 1st October 1959 when they lost 4-2 away to Headington United Colts in the Preliminary Round replay of the F.A.Youth Challenge Cup. Throughout that unbeaten run the youth team won 36 games and drew just one match, scoring 242 goals and conceding only 25. They went on to win the Chiltern Youth League Championship as well as the Cambs. Youth League on goal average over Ely City Youth, who had scored 14 more goals, but conceded an extra 6 goals. The Club also took the decision to run an under 16 youth team for the following season, in addition to the under 18s.

In November 1959 work started on the popular side of the ground next to Coldham's Common, replacing the terracing formed of railway sleepers with new concrete terracing. The work was carried out with voluntary labour from supporters and players alike, and took many months to complete. The group of volunteers gave themselves the name of the 'Oughta Club', amusingly derived from the fact that they were often telling each other: "You oughta do this and you oughta do that". In the New Year builders erected new pay boxes and entrances on that side of the ground.

League results were disappointing in the first third of the season, and on 8th December 1959 the Board of Directors appointed Alan Moore, formerly of Sunderland and Nottingham Forest, as player-coach. Bill Craig continued to play in the side, but took a declining role in its management, and Alan Moore was appointed as player-manager in February. Strengthening the side with new players was difficult at that stage of the season, but there was a significant improvement in the Club's results.

On Thursday 17th March 1960 Wisbech Town were once again the opponents in the Final of the Cambs. Professional Cup. The 1st Leg at Cambridge attracted a disappointingly low crowd of only 1,500 spectators, as United built up a narrow 2-1 lead, but in the 2nd Leg they had an excellent 3-1 away win at Fenland Park to secure the Cup by 5 goals to 2 on aggregate.

Another excellent performance away to Peterborough United's first team in the Semi-final of the Hunts. Premier Cup earned Cambridge United a 1-1 draw, and an attractive home tie in the replay, yet only 2,600 people turned up to see Alan Moore's revitalized side secure a 2-0 victory. The Final away to Bedford Town was held over to the following season, but the "Eagles" from the Southern League Premier Division were too strong and won by 3 goals to 1.

F.A. Challenge Cup

First Qualifying Round
Ely City 0 3 **Cambridge United**

Second Qualifying Round
Cambridge United 3 0 Holbeach United

Third Qualifying Round
Cambridge United 0 1 Cambridge City

Southern League Cup

First Round - First Leg
Cambridge United 1 1 Bedford Town

First Round - Second Leg
Bedford Town 6 4 **Cambridge United**

East Anglian Cup

First Round
Cambridge United 1 0 Norwich C.E.Y.M.S.

Second Round
Cambridge United 6 1 Sudbury Town

Third Round
Cambridge City 2 0 **Cambridge United**

Cambs Professional Cup

Semi-Final
Cambridge City 0 1 **Cambridge United**

Final - First Leg
Cambridge United 2 1 Wisbech Town

Final - Second Leg
Wisbech Town 1 3 **Cambridge United**

Hunts. Premier Cup

Semi-final
Peterborough Utd. 1 1 **Cambridge United**

Semi-final Replay
Cambridge United 2 0 Peterborough United

Final
Bedford Town 3 1 **Cambridge United**

Southern League Division I

	Pld	W	D	L	F	A	Pts
Clacton Town	42	27	5	10	106	69	59
Romford	42	21	11	10	64	40	53
Folkestone Town	42	23	5	14	93	71	51
Exeter City Res.	42	23	3	16	85	62	49
Guildford City	42	19	9	14	74	55	47
Sittingbourne	42	20	7	15	66	55	47
Margate	42	20	6	16	88	77	46
Trowbridge	42	18	9	15	90	78	45
Cambridge United	42	18	9	15	71	72	45
Yiewsley	42	17	10	15	83	69	44
Bexleyheath & Welling	42	16	11	15	85	77	43
Merthyr Tydfil	42	16	10	16	63	65	42
Ramsgate Athletic	42	16	8	18	83	84	40
Ashford Town	42	14	12	16	61	70	40
Tunbridge Wells	42	16	5	21	75	76	37
Hinchley Athletic	42	14	8	20	62	75	36
Gloucester City	42	13	9	20	56	84	35
Burton Albion	42	12	10	20	54	77	34
Dover	42	14	6	22	59	85	34
Kidderminster Harriers	42	14	6	22	59	97	34
Corby Town	42	15	3	24	75	91	33
Rugby Town	42	10	11	21	67	91	31

Eastern Counties League

	Pld	W	D	L	F	A	Pts
Tottenham Hotspur 'A'	38	27	5	6	86	32	59
Chelmsford City Res.	38	24	6	8	114	59	54
Bury Town	38	23	3	12	94	49	49
March Town Utd	38	22	5	11	103	64	49
Holbeach Utd	38	21	6	11	91	49	48
Peterborough Utd Res.	38	21	4	13	101	68	46
Sudbury Town	38	18	9	11	63	44	45
Gt. Yarmouth Town	38	18	5	15	82	84	41
Stowmarket	38	18	5	15	67	77	41
Cambridge City Res.	38	14	11	13	63	63	39
Harwich & Parkeston	38	15	9	14	66	68	39
King's Lynn Res.	38	13	11	14	72	60	37
Romford Res.	38	12	11	15	75	75	35
Newmarket Town	38	12	7	19	71	88	31
Lowestoft Town	38	12	6	20	61	86	30
Biggleswade Town	38	11	7	20	60	97	29
Spalding Utd	38	12	3	23	64	101	27
Eynesbury Rovers	38	10	5	23	58	91	25
Gorleston	38	7	6	25	45	106	20
Cambridge Utd Res.	38	6	4	28	50	125	16

Eastern Counties League Cup

First Round
Cambridge Utd Res. 4 2 Sudbury Town

Second Round
Peterborough Utd Res. 6 1 **Cambridge Utd Res**

Cambs Junior Cup

Preliminary Round
Cambridge Utd 'A' 7 0 Sawston 'A'

First Round
Cambridge Utd 'A' 3 1 Cherry Hinton Reserves

Second Round
Fulbourn 3 2 **Cambridge Utd 'A'**

Cambs League Division One (Section B)

	Pld	W	D	L	F	A	Pts
Soham Town Res.	24	19	3	2	106	26	41
Lode	24	18	4	2	123	63	40
Littleport	24	17	1	6	92	60	35
Cambridge Y.M.C.A.	24	15	2	7	83	64	32
Cambridge United 'A'	24	10	7	7	69	61	27
Isleham	24	10	5	9	93	73	25
Balsham	24	10	3	11	57	67	23
Soham Utd. Res.	24	9	1	14	65	71	19
Pye's	24	8	3	13	66	78	19
Waterbeach	24	7	3	14	57	83	17
Histon 'A'	24	6	3	15	45	97	15
Burwell	24	4	2	18	55	102	10
Little Downham	24	4	1	19	41	107	9

F.A. Youth Challenge Cup

Preliminary Round
Cambridge Utd. Yth 3 — 3 Headington Utd Colts

Preliminary Round Replay
Headington Utd. Colts 4 — 2 **Cambridge Utd Yth**

Cambs Youth Cup

First Round
Cambridge Y.M.C.A. Youth 0 — 11 **Cambridge Utd Yth**

Second Round
Cambridge Utd Yth 13 — 0 Ely City Colts

Semi-final (at Pye's F.C.)
Cambridge Utd Yth 7 — 3 Cambridge Eagles Yth

Final. (at Histon F.C.)
Cambridge Utd. Youth 7 — 1 Camden United Youth

Chiltern United Youth League

First Round
Vauxhall Motors Youth 1 — 4 **Cambridge Utd Yth**

Second Round
Stotfold Colts 1 — 2 **Cambridge Ytd Yth**

Semi-final
Icknield Youth (Hitchin) 2 — 2 **Cambridge Utd Yth**

Semi-final Replay
Cambridge Utd Yth 5 — 0 Icknield Yth (Hitchin)

Final. (at Stotfold F.C.)
Cambridge Utd Yth 3 — 0 Redhearts (Luton)

Chiltern Youth League Championship Match

Cambridge Utd. Yth 5 — 3 The Rest of the Chiltern Youth League

Cambs Youth League

	Pld	W	D	L	F	A	Pts
Cambridge Utd Yth	18	16	0	2	90	23	32
Ely City Colts	18	16	0	2	104	29	32
Littleport Juniors	18	10	3	5	87	41	23
Soham Town Rangers Yth	18	11	1	6	90	49	23
St. Andrews Youth	18	11	1	6	79	44	23
Camden United Youth	18	6	4	8	57	71	16
Cambridge Eagles Youth	18	5	2	11	58	65	12
Cambridge Y.M.C.A. Yth	18	4	0	14	31	105	8
Histon Youth	18	3	1	14	23	95	7
Wilburton Youth	18	2	0	16	31	128	4

Chiltern Youth League (Under 18s)

	Pld	W	D	L	F	A	Pts
Cambridge Utd Yth	24	21	2	1	156	20	44
Redhearts (Luton) Youth	24	19	2	3	128	24	40
Icknield (Hitchin) Youth	24	17	2	5	102	35	36
Biscot Mill (Luton) Youth	24	15	2	7	111	47	32
Stotfold Colts	24	15	2	7	88	70	32
Pioneer Boys Club (Dunstable)	24	14	2	8	90	50	30
Vauxhall Motors Youth	24	12	4	8	96	56	28
Skefco (Luton) Youth	24	6	5	13	50	57	17
Royston Town Youth	24	5	3	16	46	117	13
Stockwood Pk (Luton) Yth	24	6	0	18	58	133	12
Letchworth Boys Brigade	24	5	0	19	39	96	10
Sundon Park (Luton) Youth	24	4	0	20	48	148	8
Luton Boys Club	24	4	0	20	32	144	8

STOPSHOP

TEAM CHECK ✓

1. Campkin Road (Convenience store) 7 days a week
2. Green End Road (Convenience store) 7 days a week
3. Carlton Way (Convenience store) 7 days a week
4. Waterbeach (Convenience store) 7 days a week
5. Histon (Newsagent)
6. Barnwell Road (Newsagent)
7. Cherry Hinton (Newsagent)
8. Chesterton 1/190 (Newsagent)
9. Chesterton II (Newsagent)
10. Impington (Newsagent)
11. Willingham (Newsagent)

Star signing
DITTON LANE
Soon to be appearing
HILLS ROAD ON TRANSFER LIST

Subs Bench
12. Milton (Beginning development)
13. Barnwell Spar (Soon to be developed)

SPONSORS TO THE CAMBRIDGE PREMIER LEAGUE

Chapter Six

THE SIXTIES

1960-61 SEASON

In order for the Club to make a strong bid for promotion, player-manager Alan Moore decided to make all of the first team players full-time professionals, as opposed to only five full professionals the previous season. The team had a new look with the acquisition of seven new players, and after the trial matches the team was reported to be strong, fit and full of talent. However, their potential was not fully realised early on, and by the end of October they were in a mid-table position, 9 points behind the league leaders Rugby Town, and at the turn of the year they looked doomed for another season in Division One. Only player-manager Alan Moore was adamant that promotion could be achieved.

The new concrete terracing on the Coldham's Common side of the ground was complete for the start of the season, but because of delays in planning approval, the construction of a roof on the first central bay of that stand was held up until the end of the season. The money for the roof was provided from the Supporters' Club's successful jackpot tickets and tombola promotions.

On 30th August 1960 a crowd of 8,918 turned up at Milton Road to see Cambridge City beat Cambridge United 2-0 in the 1st Leg of the Southern League Cup First Round. It was the first of eight meetings between the two clubs during the season, which attracted a total of 49,679 spectators at an average of 6,210 per game. Cambridge United won the 2nd Leg 2-0, but a replay was not necessary as both clubs progressed through to the next round, under the peculiar rules of the competition. In the Second Round United travelled to Corby Town, and lost disappointingly by 3 goals to 1 to go out of the competition.

Of greater disappointment was the Club's surprise 2-1 home defeat against Bury Town from the Eastern Counties League in the First Round of the East Anglian Cup. No mistake was made in the F.A. Challenge Cup against Eastern Counties League opposition as progress was made into the Third Qualifying Round with victories over Newmarket Town (5-1) and March Town United (7-3). Cambridge City were the visitors for the Third Round tie, and a tremendous struggle ended with the scores level at 1-1. Against the odds Cambridge United managed another 1-1 draw in the replay after extra-time, with the previous season's highest goalscorer, Phil Hayes, again scoring the only goal for United. The toss of a coin meant that the second replay was again played at Milton Road, but goals from Sam McCrory and Phil Hayes gave United a marvellous 2-1 victory over their Premier Division hosts. In the Fourth Qualifying Round, Phil Hayes maintained his record of scoring in all of United's six F.A. Cup matches, but it was not enough to stop newly promoted Clacton Town winning 2-1 on their own ground, in a match which was postponed until the afternoon of Wednesday 26th October 1960.

The first team's fortunes changed dramatically during one week in January when they won a league match 2-1 away to Corby Town, beat Wisbech Town 6-1 at home in the Semi-final replay of the Cambs Professional Cup in midweek, then thrashed Tunbridge Wells 9-0 in another league match. It was the start of a sequence of seven consecutive league wins, which saw the Club move from mid-table to the top of the league by the end of March.

A 2-1 home defeat against Kettering Town dented the Club's promotion hopes, especially as five of the last seven matches were away from home, but Alan Moore's men held their nerve well and clinched promotion with a 3-1 win away to Burton Albion on Saturday 22nd April. The following Saturday was a big day for the Club, as 2,000 supporters travelled to Kettering hoping their side would get the victory they needed to secure the Southern League Division One Championship. It was not to be, and Kettering won the trophy with an emphatic 3-0 victory. Back at Newmarket Road, the reserve team made it a great day by winning two trophies within a few hours. At the start of the season they had moved back to the Premier Division of the Peterborough & District League, and with a young side picked up only 3 points from their first five games, but the team was moulded into a winning combination, and they clinched the Championship on the afternoon of Saturday 29th April 1961 with a 7-1 win against Sutton Bridge. In the evening they beat Stamford Rovers 7-1 in the Final of the Peterborough Senior Cup to complete the 'double' which they had previously achieved in 1952.

In the Final of the Cambs Professional Cup Cambridge City won the 1st Leg at Milton Road 1-0. Not even the goalscoring exploits of Phil Hayes, who finished the season as the first team's highest goalscorer once more with 42 goals, could retrieve the situation, and City lifted the Cup for the first time, winning 2-0 on aggregate.

The youth section had another marvellous season, winning the Cambs Youth Cup and the Chiltern Youth League (Under 18 Section). On 4th February 1961 the under 18 team won by a record 27-2 away to Silvaron Rangers of Luton in a league game. Alan Carter, one of the Club's ground staff, scored 14 of the goals. The under 16 team just missed out on winning their section of the Chiltern Youth League.

F.A. Challenge Cup

First Qualifying Round
Cambridge United 5 1 Newmarket Town

Second Qualifying Round
Cambridge United 7 3 March Town

Third Qualifying Round
Cambridge United 1 1 Cambridge City

Third Qualifying Round Replay
Cambridge City 1 1 **Cambridge United**

Third Qualifying Round Second Replay
Cambridge City 1 2 **Cambridge United**

Fourth Qualifying Round
Clacton Town 2 1 **Cambridge United**

Southern League Cup

First Round First Leg
Cambridge City 2 0 **Cambridge United**

First Round Second Leg
Cambridge United 2 0 Cambridge City

Second Round
Corby Town 3 1 **Cambridge United**

East Anglian Cup

First Round
Cambridge United 1 2 Bury Town

Cambs Professional Cup

Semi-final
Wisbech Town 4 4 **Cambridge United**

Semi-final Replay
Cambridge United 6 1 Wisbech Town

Final First Leg
Cambridge City 1 0 **Cambridge United**

Final Second Leg
Cambridge United 0 1 Cambridge City

Peterborough Challenge Cup

Final
Cambridge United 1 0 Wisbech Town

Hunts Premier Cup

Semi-final
Cambridge United 3 2 St. Neots Town

Final
Not played, competition abandoned

Southern League First Division

	Pld	W	D	L	F	A	Pts
Kettering Town	40	26	7	7	100	55	59
Cambridge United	40	25	5	10	100	53	55
Bexleyheath & Welling	40	22	8	10	93	46	52
Merthyr Tydfil	40	23	6	11	88	65	52
Sittingbourne	40	21	10	9	77	63	52
Hinkley Athletic	40	17	13	10	74	59	47
Ramsgate Athletic	40	19	7	14	79	54	45
Rugby Town	40	18	9	13	89	71	45
Corby Town	40	16	10	14	82	73	42
Poole Town	40	18	5	17	69	65	41
Barry Town	40	16	9	15	65	74	41
Yiewsley	40	17	7	16	65	76	41
Trowbridge	40	14	10	16	71	73	38
Ashford Town	40	14	8	18	61	67	36
Margate	40	11	12	17	62	75	34
Dover	40	12	7	21	66	74	31
Canterbury Town	40	10	10	20	52	75	30
Nuneaton Borough	40	11	7	22	69	91	29
Burton Albion	40	12	4	24	63	85	28
Gloucester City	40	7	7	26	40	102	21
Tunbridge Wells	40	8	5	27	56	115	21

Peterborough Senior Cup

First Round
Cambridge Utd Res 3 0 Warboys Town

Second Round
March Town Reserves 2 2 **Cambridge Utd Res**

Second Round Replay
Cambridge Utd Res 3 2 March Town Reserves

Third Round
Cambridge Utd Res 7 0 Chatteris Town

Semi-final
Cambridge Utd Res 3 1 Soham Town Rangers

Final
Cambridge Utd Res 7 1 Stamford Rovers

Exning Charity Cup

Final
Exning United 3 4 **Cambridge Utd Res**

First Team 1960-61 Season
Back Row: Alan Moore (Manager), Peter Rapley, Alan Gammie, Ray Chandler, Fred Howell, David Deacon, Ron Simpson (Trainer).
Front Row: Dennis Woods, Sam McCrory, Roy Kirk, Phil Hayes, Billy Welsh, Brian Bastad.
Mascot: Keith Moore. Photograph by courtesy of *Cambridge Evening News*.

Reserve Team 1960-61 Season
Back Row: Gerald Butler, Vic Phillips, Tony Willson, David Wisbey, Richard Wilson, Neville Rose.
Front Row: John Hoskins, Brian Page, Paddy Graffin, Frank Allen, Peter Foster, Graham Ward.

Peterborough & District League

	Pld	W	D	L	F	A	Pts
Cambridge United Res	34	24	6	4	126	46	54
Exning United	34	25	3	6	110	58	53
Peterborough United 'A'	34	24	4	6	104	51	52
Warboys Town	34	22	6	6	103	49	50
Downham Town	34	16	7	11	69	60	39
Soham Town Rangers	34	15	7	12	85	68	37
Chatteris Town	34	17	3	14	113	85	37
Soham United	34	16	4	14	96	87	36
Parson Drove United	34	13	7	14	73	81	33
Wisbech Town Reserves	34	12	7	15	75	71	31
Haddenham Rovers	34	12	5	17	77	90	29
Pinchbeck United	34	12	4	18	63	70	28
Sutton Bridge	34	10	6	18	55	82	26
March Town Reserves	34	11	4	19	53	89	26
Sawston United	34	9	7	18	76	110	25
Somersham Town	34	8	6	20	67	123	22
Ely City Reserves	34	7	6	21	42	99	20
Newmarket Town Reserves	34	6	2	26	52	120	14

F.A. Youth Challenge Cup

First Round Proper
Cambridge Utd Yth 10　3 Eynesbury Rovers Youth

Second Round Proper
Watford Colts　4　1　**Cambridge Utd Yth**

Cambs Youth Cup

First Round　Bye

Second Round
Histon Youth　0　5　**Cambridge Utd Yth**

Semi-final
Cambridge Utd Yth 3　0　Ely City

Final
Cambridge Utd Yth 2　1　St. Andrew's

Chiltern Youth League Cup (Under 18s)

First Round
Stotfold Youth　0　6　**Cambridge Utd Yth**

Second Round
Redhearts (Luton) Youth　3　0　**Cambridge Utd Yth**

Chiltern Youth League (Under 18s)

	Pld	W	D	L	F	A	Pts
Cambridge Utd Yth	26	24	0	2	170	22	48
Redhearts (Luton) Youth	26	23	2	1	145	20	48
Limbury Old Boys Youth	26	16	3	7	101	76	35
Biscot Mill (Luton) Youth	26	14	4	8	126	69	32
Pioneer Boys Club	26	13	4	9	88	64	30
Icknield (Hitchin) Youth	26	13	3	10	93	60	29
East Park Youth	26	13	1	12	81	91	27
Vauxhall Motors Youth	26	12	1	13	67	103	25
Skefco (Luton) Youth	26	10	4	12	62	81	24
Luton Boys Club	26	9	3	14	76	83	21
Stotfold Youth	26	8	5	13	72	66	21
Harpenden Town Youth	26	6	1	19	68	111	13
Sundon Park (Luton) Yth	26	3	0	23	55	174	6
Silvaron Rangers Youth	26	2	1	23	49	222	5

Chiltern Youth League Under 18s Championship Play-off
(at Stotfold)

Cambridge Utd Yth 2　1　Redhearts (Luton) Youth

Chiltern Youth League (Under 16s)
Latest table available

	Pld	W	D	L	F	A	Pts
East Park (Luton) Youth	21	18	2	1	193	22	38
Cambridge Utd Yth	21	19	0	2	186	26	38
Stockwood Park Youth	22	18	1	3	170	41	37
Limbury Old Boys Youth	22	13	3	6	145	62	29
Icknield (Hitchin) Youth	22	13	2	7	144	43	28
Luton Boys Club	21	8	8	5	128	69	24
Beech Hill (Luton) Youth	22	8	2	12	78	114	18
Toddington Rovers Youth	22	6	1	15	51	93	13
Pioneer Boys Club	21	6	1	14	60	128	13
Harpenden Town Youth	20	6	0	14	52	118	12
Offley United Youth	22	2	0	20	29	198	4
Highfield B.C. (Harpenden)	22	1	0	21	22	331	2

Chiltern Youth League Cup (Under 16s)

First Round
Highfield Boys Club　　**Cambridge Utd Yth**
(Harpenden)
NOTE: Result not known, but Cambridge United Youth won

Second Round
Offley United Youth　0　15　**Cambridge Utd Yth**

Semi-final
Cambridge Utd Yth 2　1　Stockwood Park Youth

Final (at Stotfold)
East Park (Luton) Youth 4　4　**Cambridge Utd Yth**
(After extra-time, Trophy shared for six months each)

1961-62 SEASON

Mr.H.Habbin, who had been President of the Supporters Club since its formation in 1947, was succeeded by W.A.Nunn for the start of the new season. In recognition of the great service he gave to the Club, the covered stand on the Coldham's Common side of the ground was later named after him, when a commemorative plaque was placed over the central entrance to the stand on the 16th September 1967.

Dudley Arliss was appointed to run the "Lucky Number Pools" for the Club at the beginning of the season, starting a twenty-two year association with Cambridge United in a fund-raising capacity. Under his guidance, and with an enthusiastic band of helpers, the lottery was very successful, and put Cambridge United in a strong financial position by the end of the season.

During the close-season the Club signed a 20 year old centre-forward, Jimmy Gibson, from Newcastle United. He finished the season as the highest first team goalscorer with 35 goals, and was to play an important part in Cambridge United's progress over the next few years.

The first team got off to a good start in their first season in the Premier Division of the Southern League, and lost only two of their opening sixteen matches of the season. One of these defeats, by 2 goals to 0 away to Kettering Town, was in the Preliminary Round Second Leg of the Southern League Cup, and although Cambridge United won 2-1 in the First Leg, it meant that they lost 3-2 on aggregate. Fortunately the rules of the competition allowed Cambridge United to pass through to the First Round, as one of the narrowest losers, and few would have believed then that they could have gone on to win the cup. In the First Round Cambridge United won 2-1 away to Wisbech Town, and then followed that up with an excellent 2-1 away win against Chelmsford City to reach the Quarter-finals for the first time.

At the end of October the first team suffered a loss of form, and went seven league games without a victory. It was therefore somewhat fortunate that the Third Round of the League Cup was not played until 1st March 1962, when the Club had returned to winning ways. A home tie against First Division Yiewsley produced a comfortable 5-1 victory, and in the Semi-final United excelled when they beat highly placed Yeovil Town by 3 goals to 1 at home. Yeovil had taken the lead, then missed a penalty before Cambridge United scored three times in the last 27 minutes to win. Cambridge started as favourites in the Final against Margate from the First Division, but they made the job difficult for themselves when they could only draw 2-2 at home in the First Leg before 2,553 spectators. The Second Leg at Margate a week later on Saturday 14th April 1962 produced another close, exciting encounter. Margate took the lead in the 15th minute, but Mike Dixon levelled matters 3 minutes later, and an own goal from Margate's Peter Smith in the 60th minute gave Cambridge United a 4-3 aggregate win, and their most senior trophy in the Club's history.

Victories over Chatteris Town (5-1), Sudbury Town (5-1) and Bury Town (3-2) gave United a Fourth Qualifying Round tie away to Romford in the F.A.Challenge Cup. Cambridge took the lead in the first half and played well throughout, but they eventually lost 2-1 to a disputed goal and a penalty in what was described as their unluckiest defeat of the season.

Persistent intimidation of the match officials after home games, by a section of the Cambridge United supporters, caused the Club particular concern during the season. After the turn of the year the Club was threatened with closure of its ground by the Football Association, when notices in the programme and posters around the ground had little effect. Only when the trouble-makers were threatened with a life-ban from the ground did the misconduct subside.

Of particular delight to the Club was the continued success of the youth team during the season. The youth section was run by Wally Warren, formerly of Cambridge Eagles, and Messrs L.Smith, G.Farrington, and P.Reeve, and under their management they had their best ever run in the F.A.Youth Challenge Cup. In the First Round they won 6-3 away to Pressed Steel of Oxford, then had a splendid 2-1 home victory against Luton Town Youth in the Second Round. Following a 1-1 draw in the next round, United's Youth needed a replay to beat Wycombe Wanderers Youth 4-0 at home, to earn a place in the last sixteen of the competition. The Fourth Round tie created a great deal of interest, and was watched by a home crowd of 1,909 on 10th February 1962, but United's plucky youngsters were no match for the Chelsea Youth team, and lost by 3 goals to 0. However, as compensation the United Youth team won the Cambs F.A. Youth Cup again, beating Little Downham Youth 3-0 in the Final, and scoring 24 goals without reply in their four matches in the competition.

The Club's existing floodlights were not suitable for Southern League matches, and in order to avoid fixture backlogs the Supporters Club decided to form a "Floodlight Fund" in December, so that new pylons and floodlights could be installed. On matchdays a collecting bucket was paraded around the ground during the half-time interval, and this swelled the size of the fund considerably. The ground was referred to as the Abbey Stadium for the first time in "The New Abbey Stadium Project", included in which were plans to construct another 40 yards of cover for the terrace on the Coldham's Common side of the pitch. So successful were the Club's fund-raising promotions that the money was available for the new section of the stand roof to be constructed immediately after the end of the season in May.

The Club had a successful run in the East Anglian Cup, beating Histon (4-0) and Norwich C.E.Y.M.S. (7-2) under their sub-standard floodlights, before gaining an excellent 3-2 away win against Norwich City in the Third Round. An emphatic 4-1 home victory against Spalding United in the Semi-final gave Cambridge United a place in the Final for the second time, the previous occasion in 1951 being unsuccessful. The Final had to be squeezed in at the end of the congested season and was staged at Cambridge City's ground on Wednesday 25th April 1962, with Hitchin Town providing the opposition. It was a close match, but the United supporters went home happy when Graham Ward scored the winning goal four minutes from time to make the final score 2-1.

Despite their success in cup competitions, the first team were not absolutely safe from relegation as they entered the last month of the season. Thirteen games were played in April, and at one stage six games were played in nine days, but the Club picked up enough points to finish in 12th place. The first meeting of the season with Cambridge City did not take place until the 16th April, and in the space of three weeks the two clubs met on four occasions. Because of the congestion of fixtures, it was not surprising that United lost 3-0 away to City in the First Leg of the Cambs Professional Cup Final on Easter Monday 23rd April. The season was extended beyond the F.A.Cup Final to enable the Second Leg to take place, and United made a bold attempt to regain the Cup, but could only win by 2 goals to 0 on their own ground.

F.A. Challenge Cup

First Qualifying Round
Chatteris Town 1 5 **Cambridge United**

Second Qualifying Round
Cambridge United 5 1 Sudbury Town

Third Qualifying Round
Cambridge United 3 2 Bury Town

Fourth Qualifying Round
Romford 2 1 **Cambridge United**

Southern League Cup

Preliminary Round-First Leg
Cambridge United 2 1 Kettering Town

Preliminary Round Second Leg
Kettering Town 2 0 **Cambridge United**

First Round
Wisbech Town 1 2 **Cambridge United**

Second Round
Chelmsford City 1 2 **Cambridge United**

Third Round
Cambridge United 5 1 Yiewsley

Semi-final
Cambridge United 3 1 Yeovil Town

Final First Leg
Cambridge United 2 2 Margate

Final Second Leg
Margate 1 2 **Cambridge United**

East Anglian Cup

First Round
Cambridge United 4 0 Histon

Second Round
Cambridge United 7 2 Norwich C.E.Y.M.S.

Third Round
Norwich City 2 3 **Cambridge United**

Semi-final
Cambridge United 4 1 Spalding United

Final (at Cambridge City F.C.)
Cambridge United 2 1 Hitchin Town

Cambs Professional Cup

Semi-final
March Town 1 3 **Cambridge United**

Final First Leg
Cambridge City 3 0 **Cambridge United**

Final Second Leg
Cambridge United 2 0 Cambridge City

Southern League Premier Division

	Pld	W	D	L	F	A	Pts
Oxford United	42	28	5	9	118	46	61
Bath City	42	25	7	10	101	69	57
Guildford City	42	24	8	10	79	49	56
Yeovil Town	42	23	8	11	97	59	54
Chelmsford City	42	19	12	11	74	60	50
Weymouth	42	20	7	15	80	64	47
Kettering Town	42	21	5	16	90	84	47
Hereford United	42	21	2	19	81	68	44
Cambridge City	42	18	8	16	70	71	44
Bexleyheath & Welling	42	19	5	18	69	75	43
Romford	42	15	9	18	62	69	39
Cambridge United	42	13	12	17	76	78	38
Wellington Town	42	14	10	18	75	78	38
Gravesend & Northfleet	42	17	4	21	59	92	38
Bedford Town	42	16	5	21	73	79	37
Worcester City	42	15	7	20	51	64	37
Merthyr Tydfil	42	13	11	18	62	80	37
Clacton Town	42	13	10	19	74	91	36
Tonbridge	42	10	14	18	75	78	34
King's Lynn	42	12	8	22	59	74	32
Folkestone Town	42	12	6	24	64	103	30
Cheltenham Town	42	9	7	26	48	86	25

Peterborough Senior Cup

First Round
Cambridge Utd Res   2   1   Exning United

Second Round
Cambridge Utd Res   6   0   Haddenham Rovers

Third Round
Cambridge City Res   4   0   **Cambridge Utd Res**

Exning Charity Cup

Semi-final (at Exning)
Fordham   1   0   **Cambridge Utd Res**

Peterborough & District League
Premier Division

	Pld	W	D	L	F	A	Pts
Soham Town Rangers	32	24	5	3	96	42	53
Warboys Town	32	22	6	4	108	44	50
Downham Town	32	18	6	8	106	73	42
Cambridge Utd Res.	32	19	2	11	78	57	40
Peterborough United 'A'	32	16	7	9	72	53	39
Pinchbeck United	32	15	8	9	67	61	38
Parson Drove United	32	15	5	12	81	71	35
Haddenham Rovers	32	12	10	10	69	64	34
Chatteris Town	32	14	5	13	95	59	33
Somersham Town	32	14	4	14	80	85	32
Exning United	32	11	5	16	73	81	27
Ely City Reserves	32	11	5	16	58	77	27
Soham United	32	11	3	18	60	88	25
March Town United Res.	32	6	10	16	52	76	22
Sawston United	32	9	4	19	63	116	22
Newmarket Town Reserves	32	5	6	21	36	83	16
Sutton Bridge	32	2	5	25	45	119	9

F.A. Youth Challenge Cup

First Round Proper
Pressed Steel (Oxford) Youth   3   6   **Cambridge Utd Yth**

Second Round Proper
Cambridge Utd Yth   2   1   Luton Town Youth

Third Round Proper
Wycombe Wanderers Yth.   1   1   Cambridge Utd Yth

Third Round Replay
Cambridge Utd Yth   4   0   Wycombe Wndrrs Yth

Fourth Round Proper
Cambridge Utd Yth   0   3   Chelsea Youth

Cambs Junior Cup

Preliminary Round
Stapleford   1   5   **Cambridge Utd Yth**

First Round
Cherry Hinton Reserves   1   10   **Cambridge Utd Yth**

Second Round
Cambridge Utd Yth   5   2   Burwell

Third Round
Cambridge Eagles   5   0   **Cambridge Utd Yth**

Cambs F.A. Youth Cup

First Round
Cambridge Utd Yth   6   0   Ely City Youth

Second Round
Cambridge Utd Yth   9   0   St. Andrew's Youth

Semi-final (at Cambridge City F.C.)
Histon Youth   0   6   **Cambridge Utd Yth**

Final (at Histon F.C.)
Cambridge Utd Yth   3   0   Little Downham Youth

Chiltern Youth League Cup
(Under 18 years)

First Round
Skefco Athletic Youth   1   4   **Cambridge Utd Yth**

Second Round
Limbury O.B. (Luton) Yth   1   6   **Cambridge Utd Yth**

Semi-final
Pioneer B. Club (Luton)   0   13   **Cambridge Utd Yth**

Final (at Baldock)
Icknield (Hitchin) Youth   3   1   **Cambridge Utd Yth**

Chiltern Youth League (Under 18)

Latest table available

	Pld	W	D	L	F	A	Pts
Cambridge Utd Yth	23	19	1	3	118	27	39
Limbury O.B. (Luton) Yth	23	18	1	4	127	34	37
Icknield (Hitchin) Youth	22	17	1	4	125	25	35
Parkside (Luton) Youth	23	16	0	7	131	30	32
Vauxhall Motors Youth	21	14	0	7	90	43	28
Stockwood Park (Luton) Yth	22	13	1	8	77	44	27
Skefco Athletic Youth	21	11	0	10	82	65	22
Luton Boys Club	24	10	2	12	74	67	22
Stotfold Youth	23	9	1	13	52	79	19
Pioneer Boys Club	19	5	0	14	26	116	10
Harpenden Town Youth	23	4	1	18	28	86	9
Offley United Youth	22	3	0	19	27	151	6
Stockwood Athletic Yth	22	3	0	19	15	178	6

Chiltern Youth League Cup
(Under 16 years)

First Round
Stockwood Park (Luton) Youth   1   5   **Cambridge Utd Yth**

Second Round
Crusaders (Luton) Youth   4   4   **Cambridge Utd Yth**

Second Round Replay
Cambridge Utd Yth   5   1   Crusaders (Luton) Yth

Semi-final
Harpenden Town Youth   5   0   **Cambridge Utd Yth**

Chiltern Youth League (Under 16)
Latest table available

	Pld	W	D	L	F	A	Pts
Limbury O.B. (Luton) Yth	21	19	1	1	169	16	39
Beech Hill (Luton) Yth	22	19	0	3	175	50	38
Harpenden Town Youth	21	16	1	4	144	43	33
Cambridge Utd Yth	21	13	3	5	131	34	29
Icknield (Hitchin) Youth	20	12	2	6	161	53	26
Crusaders (Luton) Youth	21	11	1	9	94	79	23
Stockwood Park Youth 'A'	19	10	0	9	74	99	20
Dynamos Boys Club	22	9	1	12	121	110	19
Runfold United	21	5	2	14	41	136	12
Biscot Mill (Luton) Youth	22	5	1	16	64	146	11
Luton Boys Club	21	2	0	19	17	212	4
Stockwood Park (Youth) 'B'	22	0	0	22	21	219	0

1962-63 SEASON

The second stage of the Habbin Stand roof was completed in time for the new season, which saw early success for the first team when they were invited to play in the Culey Cup with King's Lynn, and managed to win the trophy against their Southern League Division One opponents by 3 goals to 2 on aggregate. However, as holders of the East Anglian Cup the Club made a disappointing exit in the First Round when they lost 1-0 at home to Norwich City on Tuesday 21st August 1962.

The Club made a good start in the Southern League Premier Division. They proceeded into the Second Round of the Southern League Challenge Cup after losing 4-2 at home to Bedford in the First Leg, and surprisingly winning 3-1 away from home in the Second Leg of the First Round.

With both Cambridge United and Cambridge City making a good start to their campaigns, the first league encounter of the season, on Saturday 29th September at the Abbey Stadium, was keenly awaited and attracted a crowd of 6,892 spectators. United were optimistic that they could capture both points as they were unbeaten in their previous six games, but City proved to be the stronger on the day, and won a closely fought game by 2 goals to 1. The two clubs met again just ten days later at Milton Road, in the Semi-final of the Cambs Professional Cup, and Cambridge City went through to the Final much easier than expected with a 5-1 victory. A week later on Tuesday 16th October, United redeemed themselves before another big crowd of over 7,600 people at Milton Road with a creditable 1-1 draw in the Second Round of the Southern League Cup. The replay on Thursday 1st November attracted only 2,323 spectators to the Abbey Stadium, because of the 3 o'clock kick-off time, but City once again emphasized their superiority with another 2-1 win.

After beating Bury Town (2-0), Sudbury Town (6-0) and Lowestoft Town (4-0), the Club reached the First Round Proper of the F.A. Challenge Cup for the first time in eight years. They were drawn away to Bedford Town, and had a considerable number of supporters in the crowd of 6,772, but this time they could not repeat their success at Bedford earlier in the season, and were somewhat unlucky to lose by 2 goals to 1.

Cambridge United's successful youth team disposed of Icknield of Hitchin in the First Round Proper of the F.A. Youth Challenge Cup, and then produced a memorable performance in the next round at the Abbey Stadium to beat Charlton Athletic's youth team by 2 goals to 1. By coincidence they were drawn against Chelsea again in the Third Round Proper, but without home advantage it was always going to be a difficult cup tie, and so it turned out as the Londoners won by 4 goals to 0.

Ground improvements continued as the Club placed an order with Mackay's for the steelwork to complete the last phase of the roof for the Habbin Stand. The handing over of a cheque for £4,000 by the Floodlight Committee to the Club's Directors prompted an order to be placed for the new floodlights. The scheme was going to cost £13,500 and included four new steel pylons and floodlights, which were to be erected in each corner of the ground. One of the fund-raising ideas for the Floodlight Fund was the sale of "Floodlight Badges" for £1 each, which proved to be a popular innovation. The 'old faithful' wooden tea hut in the corner of the ground was demolished by the Supporters Club and rebuilt with a brick structure to further improve the Club's facilities.

On Saturday 5th January 1963 history was due to be made when Cambridge United's home Southern League match with Bedford Town was to become the first ever match between non-Football League clubs to be shown on Anglia Television as their "Match of the Week", but the game had to be postponed because of heavy snowfalls. When the game was re-arranged for 11th March 1963, it made history in another way by being the first match under the new floodlights. Unfortunately though, the crowd of 5,847 did not see a goal to crown the occasion, although both goalkeepers, Rodney Slack and Jock Wallace, played brilliantly.

The "Big Freeze" put a stop to virtually all football for nearly three months, but Cambridge United were lucky enough to squeeze in a few games on frozen pitches, and finding the conditions to their liking, they picked up enough points to put them on top of the table by the end of March. In fact United put together an unbeaten run of eight league matches before losing 2-1 at home to Bath City on Saturday 23rd March.

Squeezed into the inevitable end of season congestion was the Southern League Challenge match between the previous year's League Champions, Oxford United, and the League Cup holders, Cambridge United, on Wednesday 6th March. With home advantage, the new Football League members, Oxford, won by 2 goals to 0, but shortly after the match Cambridge United were able to secure the transfer of Graham Atkinson, a forward from Oxford United, to help with their challenge for the Southern League Championship.

A record crowd of 11,574 people turned up at Milton Road on Thursday 4th April 1963 to see the vital Southern League 'derby' match between City and United. With the Championship possibly hinging on the result, it was Cambridge City who gained the vital points from a tense encounter with a narrow 2-1 victory.

Cambridge United's Championship chances seemed to have all but disappeared over the Easter holiday period when they lost both matches to Chelmsford City and only picked up one point from a possible six. However, an excellent recovery which saw them gain nine points from the next five games meant that the Southern League Premier Division Championship had to come to Cambridge with the outcome being decided in the final matches. The odds were in Cambridge City's favour as their last match was at home to mid-table Bexleyheath on Tuesday 7th May, whereas United faced a difficult trip away to sixth placed Wellington on Monday 6th May. United were also one point behind City, but with a better goal average, needing to get a point more than City in the last game. As it turned out the Championship was decided in the first 23 minutes of the match when Wellington stormed into a sensational 5-0 lead. United, minus leading goalscorer Jimmy Gibson who was nursing a broken thumb, did manage to pull one goal back to make the final score 5-1, but Cambridge City delighted a crowd of 5,791 spectators to clinch the title with an impressive 4-1 win over Bexleyheath. To rub salt into the wounds, Cambridge City's centre-forward, Alan Banks, just pipped Jimmy Gibson by one goal to become the highest goalscorer in the Southern League with 31 goals.

The reserve team finished as runners-up to Downham Town in the Premier Division of the Peterborough & District League, the same side that beat them 3-2 away in the Third Round of the Peterborough Senior Cup. The youth team continued playing until 25th May, when they won the Cambs F.A. Youth Cup for the fifth successive year with a 5-0 win over St.Andrew's Athletic Youth.

F.A. Challenge Cup

Second Qualifying Round
Bury Town 0 2 **Cambridge United**

Third Qualifying Round
Cambridge United 6 0 Sudbury Town

Fourth Qualifying Round
Cambridge United 4 0 Lowestoft Town

First Round Proper
Bedford Town 2 1 **Cambridge United**

Southern League Cup

First Round First Leg
Cambridge United 2 4 Bedford Town

First Round Second Leg
Bedford Town 1 3 **Cambridge United**

Second Round
Cambridge City 1 1 **Cambridge United**

Second Round Replay
Cambridge United 1 2 Cambridge City

East Anglian Cup

First Round
Cambridge United 0 1 Norwich City

Cambs Professional Cup

Semi-final
Cambridge City 5 1 **Cambridge United**

Culey Festival Cup

Final First Leg
King's Lynn 2 1 **Cambridge United**

Final Second Leg
Cambridge United 2 0 King's Lynn

Saturday 29th September 1962. Southern League. Premier Division
Cambridge United 1, Cambridge City 2. Watched by a large 'derby' crowd of 6,892 spectators, Matt McVittie scores for Cambridge United, but Cambridge City, who went on to win the League by three points from United at the end of the season, hit back to take both points with a 2-1 victory. Photograph by courtesy of *Cambridge Evening News*.

First Team 1962-63 Season
Back Row: Roy Kirk (Assistant Manager), Len Vallard, Rodney Slack, Billy Welsh, Norman Bleanch, Jim Sharkey, Jimmy Gibson, Alan Moore (Manager).
Front Row: Fred Bunce, Matt McVittie, Brian Boggis, Fred Howell, Dai Jones.

Southern League Premier Division

	Pld	W	D	L	F	A	Pts
Cambridge City	40	25	6	9	99	64	56
Cambridge United	40	23	7	10	74	50	53
Weymouth	40	20	11	9	82	43	51
Guildford City	40	20	11	9	70	50	51
Kettering Town	40	22	7	11	66	49	51
Wellington Town	40	19	9	12	71	49	47
Dartford	40	19	9	12	61	54	47
Chelmsford City	40	18	10	12	63	50	46
Bedford Town	40	18	8	14	61	45	44
Bath City	40	18	6	16	58	56	42
Yeovil Town	40	15	10	15	64	54	40
Romford	40	14	11	15	73	68	39
Bexleyheath	40	13	11	16	55	63	37
Hereford United	40	14	7	19	56	66	35
Merthyr Tydfil	40	15	4	21	54	71	34
Rugby Town	40	14	5	21	65	76	33
Wisbech Town	40	15	3	22	64	84	33
Worcester City	40	12	9	19	47	65	33
Poole Town	40	10	12	18	54	66	32
Gravesend	40	10	3	27	62	91	23
Clacton Town	40	3	7	30	50	135	13

Southern League Championship Match (1961-62 Season)

Oxford United 2 0 Cambridge United

Peterborough Senior Cup

First Round
Exning United 1 3 **Cambridge Utd Res**

Second Round
Haddenham Rovers 1 1 **Cambridge Utd Res**

Second Round Replay
Cambridge Utd Res 2 1 Haddenham Rovers
(A.E.T. 0-0 at full-time)

Third Round
Downham Town 3 2 **Cambridge Utd Res**

Peterborough & District League Premier Division

	Pld	W	D	L	F	A	Pts
Downham Town	32	25	2	5	148	65	52
Cambridge Utd Res	32	20	6	6	91	61	46
Soham Town Rangers	32	17	7	8	82	65	41
Warboys Town	32	17	6	9	81	51	40
Peterborough United 'A'	32	20	0	12	86	64	40
Haddenham Rovers	32	18	4	10	78	65	40
Chatteris Town	32	15	7	10	78	47	37
Somersham Town	32	13	8	11	84	63	34
March Town Utd. Res.	32	14	3	15	68	74	31
Pinchbeck United	32	13	3	16	59	63	29
Ely City Reserves	32	12	4	16	58	82	28
Exning United	32	8	9	15	65	92	25
Newmarket Town Res.	32	11	1	20	59	88	23
Sawston United	32	9	5	18	82	89	23
Sutton Bridge	32	8	4	20	64	93	20
Soham United	32	7	5	20	59	109	19
Parson Drove United	32	7	2	23	49	120	16

F.A. Youth Challenge Cup

First Round Proper
Icknield Youth (Hitchin) 2 5 **Cambridge Utd Yth**

Second Round Proper
Cambridge Utd Yth 2 1 Charlton Athletic Youth

Third Round Proper
Chelsea Youth 4 0 **Cambridge Utd Yth**

Cambs F.A. Youth Cup

First Round Bye

Second Round
Cambridge Utd Yth 7 0 Soham Town Rngrs Yth

Semi-final (at Milton F.C.)
Cambridge Utd Yth 3 2 Histon Youth

Final (at Cambridge City F.C.)
St. Andrew's Ath. Yth 0 5 **Cambridge Utd Yth**

1963-64 SEASON

Manager Alan Moore introduced several new players into the side, hopeful that they would strengthen the team sufficiently to improve on the previous season, but instead a poor start was made in the league and the first three games all resulted in defeats.

The players were given an interesting diversion from their league disappointments when a friendly match was arranged against Hapoel of Tel Aviv at the Abbey Stadium on Thursday 5th September 1963. The visitors were runners-up in Israel's First Division and their team included seven Israeli international players. An impressive performance by Cambridge United saw them draw 3-3, with two goals being scored by Norman Bleach and one by Jim Sharkey.

A 5-2 aggregate win over King's Lynn in the First Round of the Southern League Cup began a return to form, and was consolidated by a couple of convincing victories in the league. Despite this improvement nobody expected the 5-0 thrashing which United inflicted on Cambridge City in the First Leg of the Cambs Professional Cup Final at the Abbey Stadium on Monday 23rd September in front of 6,402 amazed spectators.

On 1st October 1963 Alan Moore resigned as Manager, but no successor was immediately appointed. Trainer-coach Roy Kirk took over the management of the team in a caretaker capacity, and the position was made permanent in February.

The Club were invited to play against Wisbech Town in the Bancroft Cup, but after a 5-1 defeat at Fenland Park in the First Leg they could not make up the deficit, and lost 6-3 on aggregate. However, in the East Anglian Cup, Roy Kirk's team made clear their intentions to try and retain the trophy when they beat Histon 3-0 at home in the Preliminary Round, and then recorded their highest score since changing their name to Cambridge United in an 11-4 romp against Crittall Athletic on Monday 4th November, in which Jimmy Gibson and Jimmy Dunne both scored hat-tricks. In the Second Round United were drawn at home again on Monday 16th December 1963 against Cambridge City, and created history once more when all five forwards (Colin Flatt, Matt McVittie, Graham Lawrence, Johnny Haasz and Jimmy Gibson) scored in another substantial 5-0 victory. The Third Round was not played until March, but despite home advantage, United could not overcome Norwich City, and lost by the odd goal in five.

Following their good F.A. Challenge Cup run the previous season, Cambridge United were given exemption until the Fourth Qualifying Round this time, and had no difficulty beating Hitchin Town 4-1. A home draw against Chelmsford City seemed to give United a good chance of progressing into the Second Round Proper, but cheered on by a large contingent in the crowd of 7,536 spectators, Chelmsford City won a good cup tie by a goal to nil.

The Club made its debut in the Midland Floodlit League Cup with a disastrous 7-2 away defeat at the hands of Peterborough United Reserves, but thereafter remained unbeaten in the remaining five matches played on a league basis. After winning 2-0 away to Worcester City in the final game on Wednesday 1st April 1964, United managed to win the trophy by one point.

There were rumours in the national papers in December that Cambridge City and Cambridge United were planning to amalgamate, in order to strengthen their bid for Football League status. However, these rumours were strongly denied by the United Directors, who said that they had not even discussed the matter.

Although the home attendances were nearly a thousand down on the previous season's average of 3,976, the Club was doing well financially with its successful 'Daily Jackpot' tickets run by Dudley Arliss, and the fund-raising efforts of the Supporters Club. Another tireless worker for the Club was Mrs. Lily Harrison who ran the Christmas and Grand National Draws. She made such a success of them that the Christmas Draw in particular, with its vast array of prizes, was considered to be the biggest in East Anglia.

On 14th December the Club started a thirteen match unbeaten run which began with a 4-1 victory over Weymouth and ended with a 2-0 defeat at Guildford on 15th February 1964. During the run the forwards clicked into gear and scored 42 goals. Johnny Haasz started to score at quite a prolific rate, and moved into second place in the Southern League's goalscoring lists with 25 goals.

Cambridge United continued their dominance over Cambridge City for the season when they beat their local rivals 3-1 at the Abbey Stadium on Saturday 11th January in a Southern League match, but the game was marred by the collapse and subsequent death of a spectator, Mr. Edward Read of Reach, before first aid help arrived.

A competition was organized to find a more 'suitable' tune to replace "I've got a lovely bunch of coconuts" which was adopted as the Club's theme song, and for some years had been played at the end of all home matches whenever the Club either won or drew. However, no other song was found which was quite as popular.

As the season drew to a close United's league form wavered a little, and the Club finished in ninth place in the Southern League Premier Division, level on points with Cambridge City, but with a much better goal average. In the Second Leg of the Cambs Professional Cup Final, United took a five goal lead to Milton Road on Tuesday 7th April 1964, but although Cambridge City made a brave fight to pull back the deficit, United managed to regain the trophy with a 6-2 aggregate win. The season finished with two minor trophies being collected, the Wymondham Charity Cup and the Lakenheath British Legion Cup.

Generally fielding a young side, the reserve team finished in a creditable mid-table position in the Peterborough & District League Premier Division. The youth team did not have such a good season as the previous year, suffering defeat in the First Round Proper of the F.A.Youth Challenge Cup. After drawing 4-4 in the first match away to Peterborough United when 4-1 down at one stage, they then lost 5-2 at home in the replay after extra-time. For the first time in six years the youth team lost a match in the Cambs F.A. Youth Cup on Thursday 28th November 1963, losing 2-1 at home to Ely Youth in the Second Round, having beaten Impington V.C. Youth 14-0 in the First Round.

In an attempt to raise the standard of football in the youth team, the Club were prime movers in setting up a youth league for East Anglian clubs for the following season, as well as helping to form a floodlit competition for the first teams of senior clubs in East Anglia.

The Supporters' Player of the Year Award was won by Jackie Scurr. He took the trophy from Rodney Slack, who was injured on Boxing Day, and ably replaced in goal by his deputy, Andy Smith, for the remainder of the season.

F.A. Challenge Cup

Fourth Qualifying Round
Cambridge United 4 1 Hitchin Town

First Round Proper
Cambridge United 0 1 Chelmsford City

Southern League Cup

First Round First Leg
Cambridge United 2 0 King's Lynn

First Round Second Leg
King's Lynn 2 3 **Cambridge United**

Second Round
Cambridge United 2 4 Kettering Town

East Anglian Cup

Preliminary Round
Cambridge United 3 0 Histon

First Round
Cambridge United 11 4 Crittall Athletic

Second Round
Cambridge United 5 0 Cambridge City

Third Round
Cambridge United 2 3 Norwich City

Cambs Professional Cup

Final First Leg
Cambridge United 5 0 Cambridge City

Final Second Leg
Cambridge City 2 1 **Cambridge United**

Bancroft Cup

Final First Leg
Wisbech Town 5 1 **Cambridge United**

Final Second Leg
Cambridge United 2 1 Wisbech Town

Southern League Premier Division

	Pld	W	D	L	F	A	Pts
Yeovil Town	42	29	5	8	93	36	63
Chelmsford City	42	26	7	9	98	55	59
Bath City	42	24	9	9	87	52	57
Guildford City	42	21	9	12	90	55	51
Romford	42	20	9	13	71	58	49
Hastings United	42	20	8	14	75	61	48
Weymouth	42	20	7	15	65	53	47
Bedford Town	42	19	9	14	71	68	47
Cambridge United	42	17	9	16	92	77	43
Cambridge City	42	17	9	16	76	70	43
Wisbech Town	42	17	8	17	64	68	42
Bexley United	42	16	10	16	70	77	42
Dartford	42	16	8	18	56	71	40
Worcester City	42	12	15	15	70	74	39
Nuneaton Borough	42	15	8	19	58	60	38
Rugby Town	42	15	8	19	68	86	38
Margate	42	12	13	17	68	81	37
Wellington Town	42	12	9	21	73	85	33
Merthyr Tydfil	42	12	8	22	69	108	32
Hereford United	42	12	7	23	58	86	31
Kettering Town	42	10	5	27	49	89	25
Hinkley Athletic	42	7	6	29	51	104	20

Midland Floodlit League Cup

	Pld	W	D	L	F	A	Pts
Cambridge United	6	3	2	1	15	14	8
Worcester City	6	3	1	2	17	12	7
Peterborough United Res.	6	3	1	2	18	15	7
Corby Town	6	0	2	4	12	21	2

NOTE: Rugby Town withdrew from the competition and their record was expunged from the league table.

Lakenheath British Legion Cup

Final (at Lakenheath)
Cambridge United 2 0 Soham Town Rangers

Wymondham Charity Cup

Final
Wymondham Town 1 3 **Cambridge United**

Peterborough Senior Cup

First Round
Cambridge Utd Res 3 3 Chatteris Engineers

First Round Replay
Chatteris Engineers 0 1 **Cambridge Utd Res**

Second Round
Cambridge Utd Res 7 0 Newmarket Town Res.

Third Round
Haddenham Rovers 7 3 **Cambridge Utd Res**

First Team 1963-64 Season
Back Row: Jimmy Gibson, Billy Welsh, Graham Lawrence, Terence "Bill" Kelly, Jimmy Dunne, Geoff Sampson, Graham Atkinson, John Haasz, Willy Devine.
Front Row: Brian Adlam, Jackie Scurr, Jimmy James, Rodney Slack, Matt McVittie, Brian Boggis, Dai Jones.

First Team 1964-65 Season
Back Row: Roy Kirk (Manager), Derek Finch, Jimmy Gibson, Rodney Slack, Terence "Bill" Kelly, Andy Smith, Billy Welsh, Graham Lawrence, Brian Boggis, Dai Jones, Brian Doyle (Trainer).
Front Row: Jackie Scurr, Billy Day, John Haasz, Graham Atkinson, Dennis Randall, Peter Hobbs, Matt McVittie, Gerry Greene.

Peterborough & District League Premier Division

	Pld	W	D	L	F	A	Pts
Chatteris Town	32	30	1	1	171	47	61
Parson Drove United	32	22	3	7	121	57	47
Huntingdon Town	32	22	1	9	122	83	45
Warboys Town	32	18	9	5	102	51	45
Somersham Town	32	17	7	8	94	69	41
Downham Town	32	19	2	11	111	82	40
Soham United	32	18	1	13	95	95	37
Pinchbeck United	32	12	5	15	72	75	29
Newmarket Town Res.	32	11	6	15	87	92	28
Cambridge Utd Res	32	14	0	18	82	99	28
Haddenham Rovers	32	11	5	16	66	83	27
Perkins	32	10	5	17	56	79	25
Peterborough United 'A'	32	7	9	16	68	87	23
Sutton Bridge	32	9	4	19	58	113	22
Exning United	32	7	6	19	64	121	20
March Town Reserves	32	4	7	21	43	94	15
Ely City Reserves	32	4	3	25	50	135	11

F.A. Youth Challenge Cup

First Round Proper
Peterborough United Yth 4   4   **Cambridge Utd Yth**

First Round Proper Replay
Cambridge Utd Yth 2   5 Peterborough United Yth
(A.E.T., 2-2 at full-time)

Cambs F.A. Youth Cup

First Round
Impington V.C. Youth 0   14   **Cambridge Utd Yth**

Second Round
Cambridge Utd Yth 1   2   Ely City Youth

1964-65 SEASON

On 22nd August 1964 the Club embarked on the heaviest programme ever, which saw them play 91 first team games during the season, registering 46 wins and 18 draws. There was a bad start in the Southern League when only one point was gained from the first five fixtures, although the league position was improved when the team went unbeaten in the next seven matches.

Good progress was made in the Southern League Cup when Stevenage Town were overcome in the First Round, 5-1 on aggregate, followed by a 3-2 home win against King's Lynn and an excellent 4-2 away win against Nuneaton Borough in the Third Round.

Although exempt until the Fourth Qualifying Round of the F.A. Challenge Cup, the Club were given a difficult away match against Bedford Town, but a hat-trick by Peter Hobbs and a goal from Billy Day gave United a marvellous 4-1 victory before a crowd of 5,090 spectators at the Eyrie. In the First Round Proper, the Club again failed to draw a Football League club, and got another awkward match away to Barnet. Another large crowd of 5,565 people was attracted to Barnet's steeply sloping ground, but Billy Day's goal was not enough to stop the home side progressing into the Second Round with a 2-1 victory.

Despite moderate form in the Southern League, the Club had an amazing run of success in cup competitions, and lost only one of nineteen cup matches played during the season. In the East Anglian Cup three straight home wins against March Town United, Holbeach United and Wisbech Town, without conceding a goal, put the Club into the Semi-finals, but because of the congestion of fixtures the competition had to be held over to the following season.

Manager Roy Kirk suffered a disappointment early in December 1964 when the Club's leading goalscorer with 18 goals, Graham Atkinson, returned to Oxford United. The Club were a victim of his success, as his contract stipulated that Oxford could recall him at any time.

At the Supporters Club A.G.M., the Chairman, Wesley Nunn, reported on their most successful season to date. He said that important advances had been made with the purchase of the "Old Gardens", the property adjacent to the ground, which would eventually provide a magnificent "front door" to the Stadium. Despite extending the existing terracing, and installing a new floodlight system, which had been paid for, the Supporters Club were still left with a balance of nearly £3,000.

Improved form in the New Year saw the Club go six consecutive games without conceding a goal, and at the end of January the Club stood in second place in the league table. However, four defeats in the next five games dispelled any notions of winning the Championship.

The venture into the newly formed Eastern Professional Floodlit Competition was a great success with average home crowds of 2,750, the best in the competition. The Club finished second to Wimbledon out of seven teams.

In the other Midweek Floodlit League several promising youth team players were given a taste of first team football, and not surprisingly they were unable to retain the trophy, which was won by Worcester City at the Abbey Stadium on Monday 29th March with a 3-2 victory.

There was further talk of a merger between the two Cambridge clubs in early March, but United put an end to these rumours, stating quite clearly that they "wanted to go it alone". There was a merger for one night only on 8th April 1965 when players from both City and United joined forces in a Charity Match for the Winston Churchill Memorial Fund. Three weeks earlier a Benefit Match for Fred Howell and Andy Smith had seen United beat an International Club XI, including players of the calibre of Ted Ditchburn, Wally Barnes, Bill McGarry and Jimmy Hill, by 3 goals to 1.

The undoubted highlight of the season was the Club's progress once again into the Final of the Southern League Cup following victories over Folkestone (1-0) and Chelmsford City (2-0) in the Quarter and Semi-finals respectively. Top of the table Weymouth were the much fancied favourites, but in the First Leg of the Final in the west country on Saturday 3rd April 1965, United put up a superb rearguard action after Peter Hobbs scored an equalizing goal within 7 minutes of Weymouth taking the lead in the 36th minute. 4,200 people turned up at the Abbey Stadium a week later for the Second Leg of the Final, and the ground was electric with tension for the first time in several seasons. Weymouth had two first half 'goals' disallowed, then Billy Day edged United ahead in the second half, only for Weymouth to respond with some frantic pressure. However, when Dennis Randall scored a further goal, the match was decided, and United's captain, Gerry Graham, had the pleasure of holding aloft the Club's first cup of the season, much to the delight of the home supporters.

On Monday 26th April United went into the Second Leg of the Cambs Professional Cup Final with a 3-1 lead from the away match with Cambridge City earlier in the season. They duly made certain of winning the cup for another year with goals from Dennis Randall and Hugh Barr, although City had the pleasure of finishing two points and two places above United in the Southern League Premier Division. Even though United only finished in eleventh place with 41 points from 42 games, the home gates which averaged 3,020 per game were higher than any other team in the Southern League.

At the end of the season the Club retained two further minor trophies, the Lakenheath British Legion Cup and the Wymondham Charity Cup. The youth team also won the Cambs Youth Cup, beating St.Andrew's 5-0 in the Final, and they performed very creditably in the Mercia Youth League, finishing third in the League and the League Cup, both competitions being played on a league basis. The new youth league was a great success, and one match at Ipswich on 13th April 1965 was watched by 1,540 spectators.

F.A. Challenge Cup

Fourth Qualifying Round
Bedford Town 1 4 **Cambridge United**

First Round Proper
Barnet 2 1 **Cambridge United**

Southern League Cup

First Round First Leg
Stevenage Town 1 2 **Cambridge United**

First Round Second Leg
Cambridge United 3 0 Stevenage Town

Second Round
Cambridge United 3 2 King's Lynn

Third Round
Nuneaton Borough 2 4 **Cambridge United**

Fourth Round
Cambridge United 1 0 Folkestone

Semi-final
Cambridge United 2 0 Chelmsford

Final First Leg
Weymouth 1 1 **Cambridge United**

Final Second Leg
Cambridge United 2 0 Weymouth

Cambs Professional Cup

Final First Leg
Cambridge City 1 3 **Cambridge United**

Final Second Leg
Cambridge United 2 0 Cambridge City

East Anglian Cup

First Round
Cambridge United 3 0 March Town

Second Round
Cambridge United 6 0 Holbeach United

Third Round
Cambridge United 1 0 Wisbech Town

Semi-final
Cambridge United 5 2 Dagenham

Final
Cambridge City 2 1 **Cambridge United**

Lakenheath British Legion Cup

Cambridge United 2 1 Soham Town Rangers
Played at Lakenheath Nest

Wymondham Charity Cup

Wymondham Town 1 4 **Cambridge United**

Southern League Premier Division

	Pld	W	D	L	F	A	Pts
Weymouth	42	24	8	10	99	50	56
Guildford City	42	21	12	9	73	49	54
Worcester City	42	22	6	14	100	62	50
Yeovil Town	42	18	14	10	76	55	50
Chelmsford City	42	21	8	13	86	77	50
Margate	42	20	9	13	88	79	49
Dartford	42	17	11	14	74	64	45
Nuneaton Borough	42	19	7	16	57	65	45
Cambridge City	42	16	11	15	78	66	43
Bedford Town	42	17	9	16	66	70	43
Cambridge United	42	16	9	17	72	69	41
Folkestone Town	42	17	7	18	71	79	41
Romford	42	17	7	18	61	70	41
Cheltenham Town	42	14	12	16	70	78	40
King's Lynn	42	13	13	16	56	79	39
Tonbridge	42	10	16	16	60	75	36
Wellington Town	42	13	10	19	63	78	36
Rugby Town	42	15	6	21	71	98	36
Wisbech Town	42	14	6	22	75	91	34
Bexley United	42	14	5	23	67	73	33
Hastings United	42	9	14	19	58	86	32
Bath City	42	13	4	25	60	84	30

Eastern Professional Floodlit League

	Pld	W	D	L	F	A	Pts
Wimbledon	12	9	1	2	41	18	19
Cambridge United	12	6	3	3	23	20	15
Chelmsford City	12	5	4	3	30	23	14
Cambridge City	12	4	5	3	23	25	13
King's Lynn	12	5	2	5	26	22	12
Romford	12	2	4	6	17	25	8
Kettering	12	1	1	10	13	39	3

Midland Floodlit League Cup

	Pld	W	D	L	F	A	Pts
Worcester City	10	6	2	2	34	16	14
Corby Town	10	5	2	3	28	23	12
Kettering Town	10	5	0	5	15	24	10
Peterborough United Res	10	3	3	4	21	21	9
Cambridge United	10	2	4	4	18	21	8
Wisbech Town	10	3	1	6	17	28	7

Mithras Cup

First Round First Leg
Cambridge United 3 1 Hornchurch

First Round Second Leg (at the Abbey Stadium)
Hornchurch 1 4 **Cambridge United**

Second Round First Leg
Cambridge United 1 1 Dagenham

Second Round Second Leg
Dagenham 4 0 Cambridge United

F.A. Youth Challenge Cup

First Round Proper
Cambridge Utd Yth 2 2 Peterborough United Youth

First Round Proper Replay
Peterborough Utd Youth 5 1 **Cambridge Utd Yth**

Cambs F.A. Youth Cup

First Round Bye

Second Round
Cambridge Utd Yth 5 1 Littleport Town Youth

Semi-final
Cambridge City Youth 1 5 **Cambridge Utd Yth**

Final
St. Andrew's Youth 0 5 **Cambridge Utd Yth**

Mercia Youth League

	Pld	W	D	L	F	A	Pts
Ipswich Town Youth	12	10	2	0	47	19	38
Colchester United Youth	12	8	0	4	35	15	27
Cambridge Utd Yth	12	6	1	5	46	21	21
Cambridge City Youth	12	5	3	4	22	23	20
Bedford Town Youth	12	4	2	6	22	33	15
Chelmsford City Youth	12	2	1	9	19	32	8
Romford Youth	12	1	3	8	14	62	7

Mercia Youth League Cup

	Pld	W	D	L	F	A	Pts
Colchester United Youth	12	12	0	0	50	7	42
Ipswich Town Youth	12	8	0	4	52	21	27
Cambridge Utd Yth	12	6	1	5	31	27	22
Bedford Town Youth	12	6	0	6	28	29	20
Cambridge City Youth	12	4	1	7	21	32	14
Chelmsford City Youth	12	3	2	7	23	45	13
Romford Youth	12	1	0	11	17	61	3

NOTE: Points awarded: 4 Away win, 3 Home win, 2 Away draw, 1 Home draw.

1965-66 SEASON

Cambridge United's popular forward, Matt McVittie, was transferred to Cambridge City during the summer, and by coincidence he played against United in the first game of the season, a 1-0 Southern League win for his Chesterton colleagues. The second game of the season was another difficult away match against Weymouth in the annual Southern League Challenge match between the League Champions and the League Cup winners. Mainly because the Champions had home advantage the League Cup winners had never previously won the match, but thanks to a goal from new signing John Turley, and an own goal, then an outstanding performance from goalkeeper Rodney Slack, Cambridge United became the first League Cup winning side to carry away the trophy with a splendid 2-1 victory.

Roy Kirk strengthened his forward line at the start of the season with the signings of David Barrett and David Bennett, both of whom had played for Guildford City, and with ten wins and only three defeats in the first fifteen games, hopes were high for a successful season. At that stage the Club had already progressed through the First Round of the Southern League Cup with a 3-1 aggregate win over Corby Town. Holbeach United had been beaten 5-2 in the First Round of the East Anglian Cup, and in the First Leg of the Cambs Professional Cup Final a 33rd minute Gerry Graham goal gave United a slender lead over Cambridge City.

It was a great disappointment, therefore, when 5,582 people turned up at the Abbey Stadium only to watch United lose the F.A. Challenge Cup Fourth Qualifying Round match against Bedford Town. Northamptonshire County cricketer, Ray Bailey, put United out of the competition with two well-taken second half goals, the second one coming in the dying minutes of the game, after Gerry Graham had put the home team ahead in the 5th minute. Bedford went on to reach the Fourth Round Proper for the third time in four years, going out to the eventual Cup winners Everton, and were one of four Southern League teams to reach the Third Round Proper, highlighting the strength of the League which Cambridge United played in.

The Club's ambition of playing in the Football League was gathering momentum, and took a big step towards reality when construction of the steelwork frame for the new Main Grandstand on the Elfleda Road side of the ground commenced in October 1965.

In a carefully constructed campaign to attract support for their bid to attain Football League status, the Club arranged three pre-season friendlies against member clubs, narrowly losing 3-2 to Brentford, and improving their case with victories over Colchester United (3-0) and Barnsley (4-2). A gap in the Southern League fixtures in October was also filled with a friendly against Luton Town, and Cambridge United's cause was done no harm at all with another 3-1 victory. The reputation of the Club was further enhanced by their innovation of replacing the reserve team a year earlier with a first team squad of players, an idea which attracted the attention of several Football League clubs. They also put forward a proposal at the A.G.M. of the Football Association, which was carried by a large majority, that enabled non-league clubs to sign one apprentice professional for every five full-time professionals on their books. Graham Felton became the first apprentice professional to sign for Cambridge United, the first non-league apprentice in the country.

At the end of October the Club started a run of four consecutive drawn matches, nearly making it five matches when Worcester City won by the odd goal in nine scored on their ground in the Midland Floodlit League. United were building a reputation for being draw specialists, for their first five matches in the Eastern Professional Floodlit League were all drawn, but after losing the next game they recovered well and finished just one point behind the eventual winners, Cambridge City, and runners-up, Chelmsford City. In fact United would have won the trophy had they beaten Cambridge City in their home match on Monday 7th February 1966, instead of losing narrowly by 2 goals to 1.

In the Semi-final of the East Anglian Cup held over from the previous season, United had no difficulty in beating Dagenham 5-2 to earn a place in the Final against Cambridge City, which was staged at Milton Road on 19th January. Slightly aggrieved that the match should be staged on their neighbours' ground, United went ahead with a goal from leading goalscorer Peter Hobbs, but two goals from Eddie Bailham gave the trophy to City. Because of difficulty in squeezing the fixtures into their congested programme, Cambridge United decided to withdraw from the current season's East Anglian Cup competition, and proposed not to enter it the following year.

Seats in the new Main Stand were in use for the Southern League match against Romford on 21st February 1966, when United celebrated with a 4-1 win. However, disappointing results in the previous two months of the season had seen the Club lose any interest in winning the Championship, in addition to losing their hold on the Southern League Cup after suffering a 4-2 defeat against lowly Tonbridge.

A season of unfulfilled potential received a boost when the Cambs Professional Cup was won for a third successive year when a goal-less draw in the

Second Leg at Milton Road gave United the trophy 1-0 on aggregate.

The Mercia Youth League proved to be a great success once again with three new clubs in the competition and crowds of over 2,000 people turning up to see United's youth team's away matches at Ipswich and Colchester. In the Mercia League Cup table played before Christmas the Cambridge United youth team finished fifth, but improved performances after the New Year in the Mercia League saw them finish in third place. The youth team were knocked out of the F.A. Youth Challenge Cup at the First Round Proper stage once again, by 5 goals to 2 in a replay, after drawing 1-1 away to Norwich City Youth in the first match. The good name of Cambridge United was advanced by the youth team during an Easter International Youth Tournament in Liblar, West Germany, when they beat S.C.Euskirchin 3-0 in the Final, with a tournament record of: played 4 matches, won four, goals for 13, goals against 1.

At the Club's A.G.M. a balance of £14,220 was reported, and it was stated that in the last four years a total of £66,000 had been received in donations from the Supporters Club. Another popular and successful fund-raising idea was the introduction of several car competitions, in which the lucky number holder won a brand new car. The Club was certainly in a healthy position, despite finishing a disappointing tenth in the league, four places below Cambridge City. However, at the end of the season Cambridge United received an unexpected boost when they topped the non-league re-election vote with Wigan Athletic at the Football League's A.G.M. in June with 5 votes. Significantly, Cambridge City and Southern League runners-up Chelmsford City were eliminated from the poll because they signed Football League players without the League's consent, and in so doing seriously damaged their future chances.

F.A. Challenge Cup

Fourth Qualifying Round
Cambridge United 1 2 Bedford Town

East Anglian Cup

Preliminary Round
Cambridge United 5 2 Holbeach United
(Owing to fixture congestion Cambridge United withdrew from the competition)

Southern League Cup

First Round First Leg
Cambridge United 2 1 Corby Town

First Round Second Leg
Corby Town 0 1 **Cambridge United**

Second Round
Romford 0 2 **Cambridge United**

Third Round
Tonbridge 4 2 Cambridge United

Southern League Championship Match (1964-65 Season)

Weymouth 1 2 **Cambridge United**

Cambs Professional Cup

Final First Leg
Cambridge United 1 0 Cambridge City

Final Second Leg
Cambridge City 0 0 **Cambridge United**

Southern League Premier Division

	Pld	W	D	L	F	A	Pts
Weymouth	42	22	13	7	70	35	57
Chelmsford City	42	21	12	9	74	50	54
Hereford United	42	21	10	11	81	49	52
Bedford Town	42	23	6	13	80	57	52
Wimbledon	42	20	10	12	80	47	50
Cambridge City	42	19	11	12	67	52	49
Romford	42	21	7	14	87	72	49
Worcester City	42	20	8	14	69	54	48
Yeovil Town	42	17	11	14	91	70	45
Cambridge United	42	18	9	15	72	64	45
King's Lynn	42	18	7	17	75	72	43
Corby Town	42	16	9	17	66	73	41
Wellington Town	42	13	13	16	65	70	39
Nuneaton Borough	42	15	8	19	60	74	38
Folkestone	42	14	9	19	53	75	37
Guildford City	42	14	8	20	70	84	36
Poole Town	42	14	7	21	61	75	35
Cheltenham	42	13	9	20	69	99	35
Dartford	42	13	7	22	62	69	33
Rugby Town	42	11	10	21	67	95	32
Tonbridge	42	11	6	25	63	101	28
Margate	42	8	10	24	66	111	26

Eastern Professional Floodlit League

	Pld	W	D	L	F	A	Pts
Cambridge City	14	7	5	2	38	25	19
Chelmsford City	14	9	1	4	29	20	19
Cambridge United	14	6	6	2	23	18	18
Wimbledon	14	5	4	5	23	23	14
Bedford Town	14	5	3	6	27	25	13
Romford	14	5	3	6	27	27	13
King's Lynn	14	4	3	7	28	30	11
Kettering Town	14	2	1	11	9	36	5

First Team 1965-66 Season
Back Row: Bill Silk (Secretary), Jackie Scurr, Bill Tedds, Rodney Slack, Brian Foscolo, Gerry Graham, Andy Smith, Derek Finch, Brian Boggis, Brian Doyle (Coach).
Front Row: Billy Day, Alan Payne, Hugh Barr, Wesley Maughan, Roy Kirk (Manager), Peter Hobbs, David Barrett, David Bennett.
Holders of the Wymondham Charity Cup, Cambridgeshire F.A. Youth Cup, Southern League Challenge Cup, Lakenheath Charity Cup, Cambridgeshire F.A. Professional Cup. Photograph by courtesy of *Cambridge Evening News*.

First Team 1966-67 Season
Back Row: Graham Felton, John Harley, Colin Toon, John Turley, Gerry Baker, Peter Robinson, Bill Tedds, Derek Finch, Jackie Scurr.
Middle Row: Roy Kirk (Manager), Alan Payne, Rodney Slack, David Bennett, Gerry Graham, Bert Haggis, Mike Fairchild, Brian Doyle (Coach).
Front Row: David Barrett, Roy Poole, Alan O'Neill, John Fahy, Wesley Maughan, Peter Hobbs.
Photograph by courtesy of *Cambridge Evening News*.

Midland Floodlit League Cup

	Pld	W	D	L	F	A	Pts
Worcester City	14	8	4	2	30	23	20
Burton Albion	14	8	2	4	32	27	18
Wellington Town	14	7	4	3	22	19	18
Cambridge United	14	5	5	4	35	27	15
Corby Town	14	6	2	6	27	27	14
Lockheed Leamington	14	4	2	8	31	26	10
Kettering Town	14	4	2	8	21	25	10
Wisbech Town	14	4	1	9	23	35	9

F.A. Youth Challenge Cup

Preliminary Round
Cambridge Utd Yth 6 — 1 Histon Youth

First Round Proper
Norwich City Youth 1 — 1 **Cambridge Utd Yth**

First Round Proper Replay
Cambridge Utd Yth 2 — 5 Norwich City Youth

Mercia Youth League

	Pld	W	D	L	F	A	Pts
Ipswich Town Youth	18	15	3	0	67	11	57
Southend United Youth	18	11	1	6	44	24	40
Cambridge Utd Yth	18	10	3	5	51	32	38
Chelmsford City Youth	18	7	5	6	48	41	27
Stevenage Town Youth	18	7	3	8	25	35	27
Colchester United Youth	18	6	5	7	40	52	27
Cambridge City Youth	18	6	3	9	37	36	25
Romford Youth	18	6	2	10	33	44	25
Bedford Town Youth	18	6	2	10	37	43	23
Hitchin Town Youth	18	2	1	15	21	85	8

Mercia Youth League Cup

	Pld	W	D	L	F	A	Pts
Ipswich Town Youth	14	12	2	0	42	11	45
Southend United Youth	14	7	4	3	33	22	31
Stevenage Town Youth	14	7	3	4	20	20	28
Romford Town Youth	14	6	1	7	28	32	23
Cambridge Utd Yth	14	5	1	8	23	22	19
Colchester United Youth	14	5	1	8	28	34	19
Cambridge City Youth	14	4	1	9	29	37	15
Chelmsford City Youth	14	2	3	9	18	43	10

NOTE: Bedford Town Youth withdrew from the League Cup after 5 matches and their record was expunged from the league table.
Points awarded: 4 Away win, 3 Home win, 2 Away draw, 1 Home draw.

International Youth Tournament
(In Liblar, West Germany)

Group Matches
Cambridge Utd Yth 3 — 0 Erfa Guymich Youth
Cambridge Utd Yth 4 — 1 Frankfurt Hochst Youth
Cambridge Utd Yth 3 — 0 Tus Zulpich

Final
Cambridge Utd Yth 3 — 0 S.C. Euskirchin

1966-67 SEASON

Because of their elimination in the Fourth Qualifying Round of the F.A. Cup the previous season, Cambridge United had to play in the First Qualifying Round this time round for the first time in five years. However, the home tie against Biggleswade provided no real difficulties, and the forwards netted six goals without reply. The next round gave United a short trip across to Milton Road, but even against a struggling Cambridge City team, the "U's" were unable to score, and went out of the competition by a goal to nil before over 5,000 spectators. Wesley Maughan had the distinction of becoming the Club's first ever substitute to be used when he replaced the injured Dave Barrett on Saturday 20th August 1966 in the 2-2 home draw against Guildford in the Southern League.

For the second year running United met Corby Town in the First Round of the Southern League Cup, and this time went on a goalscoring spree to go through 9-6 on aggregate. John Fahy scored four times and won a penalty in the 5-2 win in the home leg. Although being drawn away to Kettering Town from Division One in the Second Round, United were expected to proceed further in the competition, but they lost 2-1 after Dave Bennett had put them ahead. That defeat plus a poor home record in the Southern League culminated in Roy Kirk handing in his resignation as Manager at the end of October. He continued at the Club, but Matt Wynn took over as temporary Manager while the Board of Directors advertised for a replacement.

The Cambs Professional Cup, which had previously only been competed for by Cambridgeshire clubs, was opened up to include Wisbech and Bedford. In the Semi-final on Monday 7th November United were drawn at home to Cambridge City, and reached the Final with goals from John Turley and John Fahy in a 2-1 win. Ten days later the youth team chalked up a notable achievement when they brought Ipswich Town's youth team's 55 match unbeaten run to an end, Barry Pawley scoring the only goal at the Abbey Stadium in a 1-0 Mercia Youth League win.

Rodney Slack, the Club's popular goalkeeper, who was voted the Supporters Club Player of the Year in 1963, 1965 and 1966, was honoured for more than five years' service with the Club with a Benefit Match on Sunday 20th November. His team, which included several players who had previously played with him in the "Amber and

Black", took on the stars of the B.B.C. Television series "United", and won a light-hearted game 4-3 before a crowd of over 4,000 people.

By the end of November the Club had moved into seventh place in the Southern League, five points behind the leaders with a game in hand, while neighbours Cambridge City were in an unaccustomed position at the bottom of the table. Following a couple of league defeats in the first half of December, United then started an unbeaten run of twelve Southern League matches which put them right back in contention for the Championship. It was unlucky thirteen for the trip to Yeovil on 18th March 1967 when the coach broke down on the way and the players had to take straight to the field on their arrival. Not surprisingly they lost 4-1. Three games in the west country in five days all ended in defeats and effectively ended United's challenge.

A month earlier, on 16th February 1967, Bill Leivers, a full back and regular member of the Manchester City team that won the 1956 F.A.Cup Final, was appointed as Manager. Just prior to his appointment, former Welsh International player Dai Ward was signed by United from Bath City to strengthen the forward line. Bill Leivers waited until May before making his first signing, Colin Booth, a prolific goalscorer with all his previous clubs.

One of the few occasions to raise the passions of the supporters during the season turned out to be the 15th A.G.M. of the Board of Directors. Promoter of the Club's lotteries, Dudley Arliss, and former Manager, Alan Moore, were proposed to fill two vacancies on the Board, but amid 'unforgettable' scenes, Stan Starr and Matt Wynn were re-elected to tumultuous applause - a tribute to their services to the Club and the general esteem with which they were held.

On Tuesday 11th April United lost 2-0 at Bedford in the First Leg of the Cambs Professional Cup Final, with the irony that John Fahy, United's leading goalscorer when transferred a couple of months earlier, scored Bedford's second goal.

Cambridge United were invited to represent the South in a North versus South Challenge match against South Shields, which they gratefully accepted as an important opportunity to further their claims for admittance into the Football League. United's claims were done no harm at all when they won the First Leg at the Abbey Stadium on Saturday 22nd April by 2 goals to 1, with both goals being scored by Gerry Baker. A week later United travelled to South Shields and held on to their lead, drawing 0-0 after an impressive performance. Unfortunately though United could only finish in eighth place in the Southern League, and with average home gates falling below 3,000 it was no surprise when the bottom four clubs were re-elected with ease at the Football League's A.G.M. in London. Cambridge United received just two votes.

There was talk once more early in May of an amalgamation of the two Cambridge clubs, but United were insistent that any combined team would have to play at the Abbey Stadium.

Former reserve team trainer, Ron Simpson, was granted a Benefit Match on Monday 15th May after falling ill, and teams of ex United and ex City players played out an entertaining 4-4 draw. The season finished with a rousing finale on Thursday 18th May 1967 when the Second Leg of the Cambs Professional Cup Final was staged at the Abbey Stadium. Bedford brought with them a two goal lead from the First Leg, and then scored an early goal to lead 3-0 on aggregate, but United staged a marvellous rally and fought back to draw 4-4 on aggregate in one of the most thrilling matches ever seen in Cambridge. Roy Kirk, who had become the coach under Bill Leivers, decided to leave the Club at the end of the season, ending a seven year association, and there was a public tribute before the start of the second half of that match, which brought the crowd to its feet to applaud the former manager and player. The replay of the Final was held over to the following season.

In two minor competitions, Cambridge United beat an Arsenal XI 2-0 to win the Playing Fields Association Cup, and drew 1-1 at Wymondham to retain the Wymondham Charity Cup.

The youth team did well to finish third in the Mercia Youth League, and successfully concluded their season on the 23rd May by beating St. Andrew's Youth 3-0 in the Final of the Cambs F.A. Youth Cup at Histon. Barry Pawley scored twice, and John Harley once from the penalty spot.

F.A. Challenge Cup

First Qualifying Round
Cambridge United 6 0 Biggleswade Town

Second Qualifying Round
Cambridge City 1 0 **Cambridge United**

Southern League Cup

First Round First Leg
Cambridge United 5 2 Corby Town

First Round Second Leg
Corby Town	4	4	**Cambridge United**

Second Round
Kettering Town	2	1	**Cambridge United**

Cambs Professional Cup

Semi-final
Cambridge United	2	1	Cambridge City

Final First Leg
Bedford Town	2	0	**Cambridge United**

Final Second Leg
Cambridge United	4	2	Bedford Town

Final Replay (at Cambridge City F.C.)
Cambridge United	3	1	Bedford Town
	(A.E.T.)		

North v South Challenge Match

First Leg
Cambridge United	2	1	South Shields

Second Leg
South Shields	0	0	**Cambridge United**

Southern League Premier Division

	Pld	W	D	L	F	A	Pts
Romford	42	22	8	12	80	60	52
Nuneaton Borough	42	21	9	12	82	54	51
Weymouth	42	18	14	10	64	40	50
Wimbledon	42	19	11	12	88	60	49
Barnet	42	18	13	11	86	66	49
Guildford City	42	19	10	13	65	51	48
Wellington Town	42	20	7	15	70	67	47
Cambridge United	42	16	13	13	75	67	45
Chelmsford City	42	15	15	12	66	59	45
Hereford United	42	16	12	14	79	61	44
King's Lynn	42	15	14	13	78	72	44
Cambridge City	42	15	13	14	66	70	43
Cheltenham	42	16	11	15	60	71	43
Yeovil Town	42	14	14	14	66	72	42
Burton Albion	42	17	5	20	63	71	39
Corby Town	42	15	9	18	60	75	39
Poole Town	42	14	11	17	52	65	39
Hillingdon Borough	42	11	13	18	49	70	35
Bath City	42	11	12	19	51	74	34
Worcester City	42	11	8	23	59	79	30
Bedford Town	42	8	13	21	54	72	29
Folkestone	42	6	15	21	44	81	27

Wymondham Charity Cup

Final
Wymondham Town	1	1	**Cambridge United**

Playing Fields Association Cup

Final
Cambridge United	2	0	Arsenal XI

Eastern Professional Floodlit Football League

	Pld	W	D	L	F	A	Pts
Chelmsford City	18	10	3	5	31	18	23
Romford	18	8	6	4	36	27	22
Bedford Town	18	7	7	4	33	26	21
Brentwood	18	8	5	5	28	29	21
King's Lynn	18	7	5	6	31	30	19
Barnet	18	5	7	6	38	28	17
Cambridge United	18	6	2	10	25	36	14
Stevenage Town	18	5	3	10	26	35	13
Wisbech Town	18	3	6	9	20	43	12

Midland Floodlit League Cup

	Pld	W	D	L	F	A	Pts
Wellington Town	16	10	1	5	30	17	21
Kettering Town	16	7	6	3	33	22	20
Worcester City	16	7	3	6	32	24	17
Cheltenham	16	5	7	4	26	32	17
Burton Albion	16	5	4	7	29	28	14
Nuneaton Borough	16	6	2	8	31	33	14
Corby Town	16	6	2	8	32	41	14
Lockheed Leamington	16	5	4	7	33	40	14
Cambridge United	16	4	5	7	25	34	12

F.A. Youth Challenge Cup

Preliminary Round
Cambridge Utd Yth	4	2	Newmarket Town Youth

First Round Proper
Cambridge Utd Yth	1	2	Stevenage Town Youth

Cambs F.A. Youth Cup

First Round
Willingham Youth	0	3	**Cambridge Utd Yth**

Semi-final (at Chatteris)
Cambridge Utd Yth	6	0	March Youth Centre

Final (at Histon)
Cambridge Utd Yth	3	0	St. Andrew's Youth

Mercia Youth League

	Pld	W	D	L	F	A	Pts
Ipswich Town Youth	24	19	2	3	69	16	68
Colchester United Youth	24	16	3	6	70	37	58
Cambridge Utd Yth	24	12	4	8	47	37	48
Romford Youth	24	11	2	11	46	38	41
Gillingham Youth	24	8	2	14	40	54	31
Chelmsford City Youth	24	4	4	16	28	63	18
Stevenage Town Youth	24	5	1	18	24	79	17

Mercia Youth League Cup

	Pld	W	D	L	F	A	Pts
Romford Youth	11	7	3	1	33	11	30
Ipswich Town Youth	8	7	0	1	23	2	27
Colchester United Youth	12	6	2	4	30	23	23
Cambridge Utd Yth	11	4	3	4	12	11	18
Gillingham Youth	11	4	2	5	15	15	17
Chelmsford City Youth	12	2	2	8	13	35	9
Stevenage Town Youth	11	1	2	8	8	37	6

1967-68 SEASON

The Main Grandstand was virtually complete for the start of the season and included new changing rooms and a lounge for entertaining visiting officials. A new car park was also created at the entrance to the ground, and facilities were improved further with another extension of the roof over the terracing on the Habbin Stand.

The season kicked-off with a local 'derby' at Milton Road, with both teams sharing the Southern League points in a 1-1 draw before 4,621 spectators. Four of the first five games were away from home, and in one of these United suffered a shock 3-0 defeat against Kettering Town in the First Round of the Southern League Cup. Kettering from the lower Division One, rushed them off their feet in the first match, but in the Second Leg at the Abbey Stadium, United made a brave attempt to retrieve the situation. In a thoroughly entertaining match they came within a whisker of doing so, eventually winning 3-1, but going out of the competition 4-3 on aggregate.

On Wednesday 13th September 1967, Cambridge United met Bedford Town at Milton Road, Cambridge, in the re-played Final of the Cambs Professional Cup, which was held over from the previous season. United were always superior in the match, which attracted 3,364 people, but they needed extra-time to eventually win the cup by 3 goals to 1, with two goals being scored by Dai Ward and one by Bud Houghton.

After eight league matches the Club were well placed, having lost only one game, but Manager Bill Leivers still wanted to strengthen his side and signed the following players: John Milne (ex-Bradford Park Avenue), Keith Lindsay (ex-Scunthorpe and Doncaster) and Brian Grant (ex-Nottingham Forest).

In the F.A. Challenge Cup the Club had to start in the First Qualifying Round again, but had no difficulty beating March Town United 6-0 and Ely City 3-1 to progress into the Third Qualifying Round. With home advantage once again, United avenged their Southern League Cup defeat with a polished 3-0 victory over Kettering Town, which attracted 3,918 people to the Abbey Stadium. United's support was increasing, and when they travelled to Lowestoft for the Fourth Qualifying Round tie on Saturday 28th October 1967, an estimated 1,500 supporters travelled from Cambridge to boost the crowd to 3,473. Bud Houghton and Dai Ward gave United a two goal lead, but the team which was dominating the Eastern Counties League fought back to level the match at 2-2. In the replay at the Abbey Stadium the following Wednesday another large crowd of 4,854 spectators turned up to see United again score first through Alan O'Neill, but it was Lowestoft who won the treasured prize of a home tie with Watford when they fought back again to win by 2 goals to 1.

The youth team found the going rather tough in the Mercia Youth League. Following the withdrawal of Stevenage Youth there were only four teams left in the competition, and to fill the season each team played the other teams six times. In the Mercia Youth League the Cambridge United youth team finished fourth, although they finished one place higher, above Colchester, in the League Cup competition. Two home victories over Corby Youth (3-1) and Eynesbury Rovers Youth (2-0) in the Qualifying Rounds of the F.A. Youth Challenge Cup gave United a trip to Northampton in the First Round Proper, but their more experienced opponents won comfortably by 6 goals to 0.

In the Semi-final of the Cambs Professional Cup Cambridge United produced an impressive 4-1 home victory over Wisbech Town. An equally impressive 3-1 home win against Wimbledon in the Southern League on Saturday 11th November 1967 started a run of seven unbeaten league matches which saw the Club move into second place in the league table. That run was ended on Boxing Day with a 2-0 defeat at King's Lynn, and over a disappointing Christmas period in which only one point was gained from three games, the Club slipped three places in the league table.

Despite that small hiccup, the turn of the year gave the Club the opportunity to reflect on the progress over the past twelve months. The home Southern League crowds had risen to an average of over 3,200 per game, and the highly successful fund-raising "United Pools" were now considered to be the best in Great Britain, making the future prospects bright.

A run of nine Southern League matches in which the Club only conceded two goals saw United go to the top of the table following a 1-0 win at Weymouth on 23rd March 1968. A week before the important Easter period, United were greatly encouraged when they drew 1-1 away to their main challengers, Wimbledon, with recent signing, Ian Hutchinson, scoring the vital goal. United's visit to Chelmsford on Good Friday attracted a crowd of

7,514 people, but the home team gained ground in their Championship bid with a 2-0 victory. The following day United recovered to beat Hastings United 3-1 at home, and this match whetted the appetite for the return game against Chelmsford City on Easter Monday. Another large crowd of 7,813 spectators crowded into the Abbey Stadium, but United's bogey team took the honours once more with a 1-0 win, although United hit the crossbar twice through Dai Ward and Alan O'Neill, and did everything but score. That effectively ended the title challenge, and the Club finished the season in third place.

The two-legged Final of the Cambs Professional Cup was left until the end of the season and was played on consecutive nights against Cambridge City. The First Leg on Tuesday 14th May 1968 was played at Milton Road, and resulted in a 1-1 draw, with City fighting hard to salvage some pride after getting relegated to Division One of the Southern League. The Second Leg at the Abbey Stadium, which attracted a crowd of 2,195 spectators, was a typical fast and furious local 'derby', but it was not until the 62nd minute that the deadlock appeared to have been broken when Ian Hutchinson planted the ball in the back of the Cambridge City net. Much to the annoyance of the home supporters and the United players, the referee disallowed the goal, and then sent off Dai Ward for disputing the decision. With tempers flared the game re-commenced, but eight minutes later fighting broke out amongst the players and spread to the spectators who ran on to the pitch and joined in. Faced with no alternative the referee, "Scotty" Denson, abandoned the match, and for the first time in the ten year history of the competition, there was no winner of the Cambs Professional Cup.

At the end of the season Dai Ward was appointed as Youth Team Manager, following the resignation of Peter Reeve, who left to join Soham Town Rangers F.C. as Manager, with Wally Warren as his assistant. Both had done a great deal in developing Cambridge United's youth team.

The Football League's A.G.M. was eagerly awaited, but the Club only received two votes, the same as the previous year, in its bid to get elected into the Football League. Bearing in mind the Club's improved playing record, the news was greeted with great disappointment by Cambridge United's ambitious members.

First Team 1967-68 Season
Back Row: Dai Ward, Colin Toon, John Harley, Jackie Scurr, Brian Grant, Alan Payne.
Middle Row: Geoff Hudson (Coach), Peter Robinson, Gerry Baker, Keith Barker, Rodney Slack, Harry "Bud" Houghton, Pat Quartermain, Bill Leivers (Manager).
Front Row: Richard Habbin, Billy Wall, David Chambers, Keith Lindsey, David Barrett, Alan O'Neill, Robin Hardy.

Cambridge United's new Main Grandstand was almost complete for the start of the 1967-68 Season. The project was considered to be a major part of the Club's plans for attaining Football League status. Photograph by courtesy of *Cambridge Evening News*.

Garden Machinery – talk to us first!

Always on the ball with grasscutting equipment for every application.

CONGRATULATIONS CAMBRIDGE F.C. ON YOUR 75th ANNIVERSARY!

Choppen

Thaxted Rd., Saffron Walden
Tel: (0799) 22407

Barnwell Rd., Cambridge
Tel: (0223) 212515

F.A. Challenge Cup

First Qualifying Round
Cambridge United 6 0 March Town United

Second Qualifying Round
Cambridge United 3 1 Ely City

Third Qualifying Round
Cambridge United 3 0 Kettering Town

Fourth Qualifying Round
Lowestoft Town 2 2 **Cambridge United**

Fourth Qualifying Round Replay
Cambridge United 1 2 Lowestoft Town

Southern League Cup

First Round First Leg
Kettering Town 3 0 **Cambridge United**

First Round Second Leg
Cambridge United 3 1 Kettering Town

Cambs Professional Cup

Semi-final
Cambridge United 4 1 Wisbech Town

Final First Leg
Cambridge City 1 1 **Cambridge United**

Final Second Leg
Cambridge United 0 0 Cambridge City
(Match abandoned after 70 minutes due to fighting)

Southern League Premier Division

	Pld	W	D	L	F	A	Pts
Chelmsford City	42	25	7	10	85	50	57
Wimbledon	42	24	7	11	85	47	55
Cambridge United	42	20	13	9	73	42	53
Cheltenham	42	23	7	12	97	67	53
Guildford City	42	18	13	11	56	43	49
Romford	42	20	8	14	72	60	48
Barnet	42	20	8	14	81	71	48
Margate	42	19	8	15	80	71	46
Wellington Town	42	16	13	13	70	66	45
Hillingdon Borough	42	18	9	15	53	54	45
King's Lynn	42	18	8	16	66	57	44
Yeovil Town	42	16	12	14	45	43	44
Weymouth	42	17	8	17	65	61	42
Hereford United	42	17	7	18	58	62	41
Nuneaton Borough	42	13	14	15	62	64	40
Dover	42	17	6	19	54	56	40
Poole Town	42	13	10	19	55	74	36
Stevenage Town	42	13	9	20	57	75	35
Burton Albion	42	14	6	22	52	73	34
Corby Town	42	7	13	22	40	77	27
Cambridge City	42	10	6	26	50	82	26
Hastings United	42	4	8	30	33	94	16

Professional Floodlit League

	Pld	W	D	L	F	A	Pts
Romford	16	8	6	2	27	20	22
Chelmsford City	16	9	4	3	38	19	22
King's Lynn	16	7	4	5	37	25	18
Barnet	16	6	5	5	29	25	17
Cambridge United	16	4	7	5	25	25	15
Cambridge City	16	6	2	8	31	29	14
Bedford Town	16	5	4	7	28	37	14
Stevenage Town	16	6	2	8	18	30	14
Brentwood Town	16	2	4	10	19	42	8

NOTE: Romford won the two-legged play-off 6-3 to decide the Championship.

F.A. Youth Challenge Cup

First Qualifying Round
Cambridge Utd Yth 3 1 Corby Town Youth

Second Qualifying Round
Cambridge Utd Yth 2 0 Eynesbury Rovers Yth

First Round Proper
Northampton Town Yth 6 0 **Cambridge Utd Yth**

Mercia Youth League

	Pld	W	D	L	F	A	Pts
Ipswich Town Youth	14	11	1	2	64	15	40
Colchester United Youth	13	6	3	4	33	32	24
Romford Youth	12	3	3	6	25	25	14
Cambridge Utd Yth	13	4	1	8	23	60	14

Mercia Youth League Cup

	Pld	W	D	L	F	A	Pts
Ipswich Town Youth	6	5	0	1	23	10	17
Romford Youth	6	3	1	2	9	13	12
Cambridge Utd Yth	6	2	1	3	9	11	9
Colchester United Youth	6	1	0	5	11	18	4

NOTE: Points awarded: 4 Away win, 3 Home win, 2 Away draw, 1 Home draw.

1968-69 SEASON

As a result of the crowd disturbances in the Cambs Professional Cup Final at the end of the previous season, the Football Association ordered the Club to post 'warning' notices around the ground, stating that the ground would be closed if there was a re-occurrence of misbehaviour from Cambridge United supporters. This was one of the first tasks for the new Club Secretary, Phil Baker, when he succeeded the highly respected Bill Silk, who had to resign from the position owing to ill health. The Club honoured Bill Silk for his nine years' service by inviting him to join the Board of Directors, which he accepted.

On the playing side the Club made a bad start in their bid for the Southern League Championship when they lost their first two games of the season and suffered four defeats in their first seven league matches. In the F.A. Challenge Cup the Club could only draw 1-1 away to March Town United in the Preliminary Round with the aid of an own goal, but a hat-trick from David Chambers at the Abbey Stadium enabled Cambridge United to comfortably beat the "Hares" 5-0 in the replay. Further disappointment was experienced in the First Qualifying Round when the Club lost 1-0 away to Kettering Town to end their hopes of a prestigious cup run to enhance their claim for Football League status.

Jackie Scurr, who had made over 300 first team appearances for the Club, was rewarded with a Testimonial Match against a Southern United XI on Monday 23rd September 1968, which resulted in a 4-4 draw, but at that stage the season appeared to be in tatters for the first team. The gloom was lifted in October when the Supporters Club reported on another very successful season at their A.G.M., although the biggest cheer of the evening came with the announcement that the Manager, Bill Leivers, had captured the signing of Bill Cassidy from Chelmsford City, shortly to be followed by his colleague Tony Butcher. The arrival of two renowned experts in the art of goalscoring aroused as much interest in local football circles as the appearance in the "Black and Amber" of such players as Wilf Mannion and Sam McCrory in the late fifties, and considerably improved Cambridge United's Southern League Championship prospects.

Because of the arrival of Cassidy and Butcher, David Chambers left to join Southend United, but he scored a goal in his last game for the Club, a 2-0 victory over King's Lynn in the Semi-final of the Cambs Professional Cup on Wednesday 16th October. This earned the Club a place in the two-legged Final against Cambridge City at the end of the season. The two Cambridge clubs met before that in the Semi-final of the Hunts Premier Cup on Wednesday 30th October, but with City now playing in a lower division the interest in the local 'derby' had declined, and only 2,769 people saw United win 3-1, with Tony Butcher getting off the mark with two goals.

The youth team, by virtue of their victories over Eynesbury Rovers and Soham Town Rangers youth teams, reached the First Round Proper of the F.A. Youth Challenge Cup and recorded an excellent 2-1 win against Reading's youth team with goals from Mike Circuit and John Peachey. However, in the next round they were drawn away to Orient Youth, and went out of the competition following a 4-0 defeat.

The first team, after gaining a 3-1 aggregate win against Wisbech Town in the First Round of the Southern League Cup, received a bye in the Second Round. The forward line then clicked into gear in the Third Round on Wednesday 11th December with a 6-1 victory over Brentwood. In the Fourth Round they won the hard way by drawing 0-0 at home to Chelmsford City, before travelling to New Writtle Street to register an excellent 3-1 win on a bitterly cold February night.

Twenty goals in six Southern League and Cup matches in December saw United move into second place in the league table, level with Wimbledon, but two points behind Hillingdon Borough, who also had two games in hand. Manager Bill Leivers made a surprise appearance at Margate in a Southern League match on Saturday 4th January 1969, and he helped the Championship cause by scoring a goal in the 5-0 victory. 4,536 spectators turned up to see Bill Cassidy score both goals as Cambridge United beat Hillingdon Borough 2-0 in an important Southern League match at the Abbey Stadium on Wednesday 8th January, which put Cambridge United on top of the table for the first time.

At the end of January the team was strengthened when Melvin Slack, a wing-half with Football League experience, was signed from Southend United. The first team remained unbeaten in February, conceding just one goal in six games, but everyone at the Club was saddened by the death of Bill Silk on 26th February. It was one of his most cherished hopes to see the Club gain Football League status, an aim for which he worked unceasingly. That bad news was followed by a further disappointment with two consecutive Southern League defeats, 3-1 away to main rivals Hillingdon Borough and 1-0 at home to Bedford Town.

Further additions were made to the first team squad of players with the signings of the former Grimsby Town full back Jimmy Thompson and centre-half Terry Eades from Chelmsford City, to provide extra competition for places and cover in the event of injuries. The Club recovered to beat Ashford Town 3-2 at home in the Southern League Cup Semi-final on Wednesday 12th March. Twice United fell behind in the match, but John Gregson equalized a second time and Rolley Horrey scored the winning goal near the end to earn a place in the

Final for the third time. There then followed a Club record run of nine consecutive Southern League and Cup first team matches without a goal being conceded. Included in this run were the two legs of the Southern League Challenge Cup Final against Cheltenham Town. Gerry Baker gave United a one goal lead in the First Leg at the Abbey Stadium on Saturday 5th April, and the defence were good enough to preserve that lead with a 0-0 draw in the Second Leg to win the trophy 1-0 on aggregate. A week later the two teams met for the third Saturday running when United won 2-1 in the league, to maintain their bid to become the first team to do the Southern League 'double' of winning the Championship and the Challenge Cup in the same season.

Further success was gained in the Cambs Professional Cup when United beat Cambridge City 2-0 at home in the First Leg of the Final on Monday 14th April. This time there was a three week gap before the return match, which United won again 1-0 thanks to a goal from Alan Doyle, to lift the trophy once more.

Three league wins in five days at the end of April put Cambridge United on top of the table on goal average with one game to go. That last game was at home to Kettering Town, who were just above halfway in the league table, and was watched by 6,390 spectators on Saturday 3rd May 1969. Tony Butcher delighted the home supporters by scoring a hat-trick as United won 3-0, and as Hillingdon Borough could only draw their last game, the Southern League Premier Division Championship was Cambridge United's by one point, and the much sought after 'double' was theirs. To achieve their finest hour the Club remained unbeaten in their last ten games.

Brimming with confidence the Club were keen to take on Peterborough United in the Final of the Hunts Premier Cup, but a date could not be agreed, and rather disappointingly the match had to be held over to the following season.

The youth team finished the season with a flourish by beating Colchester United and Norwich City youths to reach the Final of the Eastern Junior Cup. The Final of that competition, away to Ipswich Town youths, had to be held over to the next season, but when it was played United lost the match 10-0. At the end of the season the youth team went to West Germany to play in the Wessling Challenge Cup international youth tournament. Victories over Cologne, Frenchen 20 and S.C. Bruhl gave the young United team a place in the Final against V.F.L. Rheingold, and they produced their best form of the tournament to win by 4 goals to 0.

The season concluded with an anxious wait to see if the Club would be elected to the Football League. Boasting a Supporters' Club membership of 2,500 and an unchallenged claim to have the best fund-raising 'Pool' in the country, the Club felt more confident than ever that their ambitions could be realized, especially as the Football League had inspected United's ground, but not Cambridge City's, who had also applied. When the vote was announced, Cambridge United were disappointed not to be elected, but heartened that their total of 16 votes was just 6 behind Newport County, who were re-elected.

F.A. Challenge Cup

Preliminary Round
March Town United 1 1 **Cambridge United**

Preliminary Round Replay
Cambridge United 5 0 March Town United

First Qualifying Round
Kettering Town 1 0 **Cambridge United**

Southern League Cup

First Round First Leg
Wisbech Town 1 1 **Cambridge United**

First Round Second Leg
Cambridge United 2 0 Wisbech United

Second Round Bye

Third Round
Cambridge United 6 1 Brentwood Town

Fourth Round
Cambridge United 0 0 Chelmsford City

Fourth Round Replay
Chelmsford City 1 3 **Cambridge United**

Semi-final
Cambridge United 3 2 Ashford Town

Final First Leg
Cambridge United 1 0 Cheltenham

Final Second leg
Cheltenham 0 0 **Cambridge United**
(Cambridge United won 1-0 on aggregate)

Cambs Professional Cup

Semi-final
Cambridge United 2 0 King's Lynn

Final-First Leg
Cambridge United 2 0 Cambridge City

First Team 1968-69 Season
Back Row: Geoff Proctor (Director), Jack Woolley (Chairman), Mick Brown (Assistant Manager), John Gregson, Terry Eades, Keith Barker, Gerry Baker, Robin Hardy, Bill Leivers (Manager), Rodney Slack, Jackie Scurr, Peter Leggett, Phil Baker (Secretary), A.E. "Paddy" Harris (Vice-Chairman), Matt Wynn (Director).
Front Row: Brian Grant, Mel Slack, Roly Horrey, Bill Cassidy, Dennis Walker, Jimmy Thompson, Tony Butcher, John Saunders.

First Team 1969-70 Season
Back Row: Peter Watson, R.H. Smart, C. Heffer, S. Starr, G. Proctor, J. Woolley, M. Wynn, A.E. Harris, Bill leivers.
Middle Row: John Gregson, Colin Meldrum, Terry Eades, Keith Barker, Malcolm Lindsey, Rodney Slack, George Harris, John McKinven, Peter Leggett.
Front Row: Brian Grant, Mel Slack, Dennis Walker, Robin Hardy, Roland Horrey, Jim Thompson, Bill Cassidy.

Cambs Professional Cup (Cont)

Final-Second Leg
Cambridge City 0 1 **Cambridge United**

Hunts Premier Cup

Semi-final
Cambridge United 3 1 Cambridge City

Final
Cambridge United 1 2 Peterborough United
(A.E.T.)

Southern League Premier Division

	Pld	W	D	L	F	A	Pts
Cambridge United	42	27	5	10	72	39	59
Hillingdon Borough	42	24	10	8	68	47	58
Wimbledon	42	21	12	9	66	48	54
King's Lynn	42	20	9	13	68	60	49
Worcester City	42	19	11	12	53	47	49
Romford	42	18	12	12	58	52	48
Weymouth	42	16	15	11	52	41	47
Yeovil Town	42	16	13	13	52	50	45
Kettering Town	42	18	8	16	51	55	44
Dover	42	17	9	16	66	61	43
Nuneaton Borough	42	17	7	18	74	58	41
Barnet	42	15	10	17	72	66	40
Chelmsford City	42	17	6	19	56	58	40
Hereford United	42	15	9	18	66	62	39
Wellington Town	42	14	10	18	62	61	38
Poole Town	42	16	6	20	75	76	38
Burton Albion	42	16	5	21	55	71	37
Margate	42	14	7	21	79	90	35
Cheltenham Town	42	15	5	22	55	64	35
Bedford Town	42	11	12	19	46	63	34
Rugby Town	42	10	6	26	38	83	26
Guildford City	42	7	11	24	41	73	25

Eastern Professional Floodlit League

	Pld	W	D	L	F	A	Pts
King's Lynn	18	12	2	4	48	28	26
Chelmsford City	18	10	4	4	33	19	24
Bedford Town	18	9	3	6	33	39	21
Brentwood Town	18	7	6	5	30	22	20
Barnet	18	8	3	7	35	28	19
Romford	18	5	8	5	25	28	18
Cambridge City	18	6	5	7	27	31	17
Cambridge United	18	6	4	8	34	28	16
Boston United	18	6	2	10	30	41	14
Stevenage Athletic	18	2	1	15	20	51	5

F.A. Youth Challenge Cup

First Qualifying Round
Soham Town Rngrs Yth 1 3 **Cambridge Utd Yth**

Second Qualifying Round
Cambridge Utd Yth 3 0 Eynesbury Rovers Yth

First Round Proper
Cambridge Utd Yth 2 1 Reading Youth

Second Round Proper
Orient Youth 4 0 **Cambridge Utd Yth**

Eastern Junior Cup

First Round First Leg
Colchester United Youth 2 5 **Cambridge Utd Yth**

First Round Second Leg
Cambridge Utd Yth 2 1 Colchester United Youth

Semi-final
Cambridge Utd Yth 3 1 Norwich City Youth

Final
Ipswich Town Youth 10 0 **Cambridge Utd Yth**

Southern Junior Floodlit Cup

First Round
Colchester United Youth 2 0 **Cambridge Utd Yth**

Cambs F.A. Youth Cup

First Round
Cambridge Utd Yth 10 0 Girton Youth

Semi-final
Witchford Youth 0 8 **Cambridge Utd Yth**
(NOTE: Cambridge United Youth thrown out of competition for using an over-age player.)

Wessling Challenge Cup
(West Germany)

Group Matches
Cambridge Utd Yth 2 0 Cologne Select XI
Cambridge Utd Yth 3 2 Frenchen 20 Youth
Cambridge Utd Yth 3 0 S.C. Bruhl Youth

Final
Cambridge Utd Yth 4 0 V.F.L. Rheingold Youth

Mercia Youth League

	Pld	W	D	L	F	A	Pts
Ipswich Town Youth	8	7	0	1	37	6	24
Bedford Town Youth	7	2	1	4	14	22	8
Colchester United Youth	5	2	0	3	6	14	7
Cambridge Utd Yth	6	1	1	4	4	19	3

1969-70 SEASON

A new club was born with the formation of the Vice-President's Club at the start of the season, with members being given their own lounge, a seat in the grandstand, and a guaranteed car parking space as part of the membership package.

For the seventh year in succession though the season started badly with Cambridge United failing to win their first competitive match, losing 2-1 at home to Weymouth, who had not won at the Abbey Stadium before in their previous eight visits. As United had completed the Southern League 'double' the previous season, Hillingdon Borough as league runners-up were chosen as the opposition in the Championship Match, which United won 1-0 thanks to a goal from John Gregson.

After winning three and losing two of their first five league games, Bill Leivers decided to transfer-list three players, and warned four others for lack of effort after a 3-0 defeat at Hillingdon. The threat had the desired effect for the first team then produced a twelve match unbeaten run which saw them make progress in the F.A. Challenge Cup by beating Wellingborough Town (5-0), Potton United (10-0) and Newmarket Town (6-0), before losing 3-2 away to Chelmsford City in the Fourth Qualifying Round watched by 5,941 spectators. That defeat was followed by a 2-1 home defeat after extra-time against Peterborough United in the delayed 1968-69 season Final of the Hunts Premier Cup.

The youth team entered the Southern Junior Floodlit Cup, and were drawn to play away to Chelsea in the First Round, and although they made a favourable impression, they lost 4-0 to their more experienced counterparts. In the F.A.Youth Challenge Cup the youth team also went out of the competition at the First Round stage, when they lost disappointingly at home to Friern Barnet Boys by 3 goals to 2.

With membership at an all time high, the Supporters' Club decided to build another extension in September, to provide a new lounge for its members. A month later the first team squad was strengthened with the signing of two players from Third Division Reading, as the Club stepped up its bid to retain the league title. Colin Meldrum was a defender with considerable experience, while a Club record fee was paid for left winger George Harris who went on to be the first team's highest goalscorer, even after giving the other players a three month start. Another winger, John McKinven, was signed from Southend United in December to further boost the squad of players.

The introduction of the F.A.Trophy to replace the F.A. Amateur Cup, for which Cambridge United were not eligible, gave many Southern League clubs a realistic chance of playing at Wembley Stadium, and the Club's Officers were particularly keen that the team should perform well in the competition to reinforce their claim for Football League status. Cambridge United were the only fully professional team in the tournament, and were given exemption until the First Round Proper on Saturday 10th January 1970. They were drawn against Minehead and beat them 2-1, with goals from John McKinven and a George Harris penalty, after conceding an early goal.

Two days later the Club lost their first Eastern Professional Floodlit League match of the season by 3 goals to 1 at Chelmsford, having been unbeaten in the first seven matches. Paul Gilchrist was then signed from Charlton Athletic, initially on a month's loan, and he scored the winning goal in an important 2-1 league victory over Wimbledon, to avenge a defeat by the same scoreline two weeks earlier.

Having beaten Burton Albion 1-0 in a replay in the First Round of the Southern League Challenge Cup, after drawing 2-2 on aggregate in the first two legs, Cambridge United also required a replay to beat Corby Town in the Second Round after drawing 1-1 at home on Monday 29th December. They secured a place in the Third Round by winning 4-2 at Occupation Road three weeks later. The draw for the Third Round gave United a difficult match at Wimbledon, and so it proved as they lost their grip on the trophy following a 1-0 defeat.

That reverse only compounded the disappointment of losing away to Bromsgrove in the Second Round Proper of the F.A. Trophy on Saturday 31st January, especially as a large following of United supporters made the fruitless journey.

In February 1970 the Club took the decision to play in all white instead of the traditional amber and black, as the players felt that they were more fortunate in their white change strip. The change was immediately successful when United recorded their biggest win in the Southern League Premier Division, beating Crawley Town 8-0 at the Abbey Stadium on Saturday 7th February.

Bill Leveirs managed to sign Malcolm Lindsey from King's Lynn after several attempts. A much sought after centre-forward, he scored on his home debut against Cambridge City on 25th February as United won 2-0 to go top of the Eastern Professional Floodlit League for the first time.

After beating Bath City 1-0 at home on 21st March, the Club won nine consecutive Southern League matches and moved from sixth place to top of the league table with five games to go. Two of these games were against Yeovil Town, their main rivals, and it was against them on Thursday 16th April that 5,775 spectators were attracted to the Abbey Stadium hopeful of seeing Cambridge United virtually clinch the Championship. With a hastily re-arranged and injury-ridden team United lost 2-1, and the supporters' confidence that the

Championship would be won for a second time was badly shaken.

Amid a hectic and crucial end of season fixture list, Cambridge United and Cambridge City were ordered by the Cambs F.A. to play their previously abandoned Cambs Professional Cup Semi-final on Tuesday 21st April. Both clubs were furious at the decision, especially as they were top of their respective divisions, but although it meant playing two nights running United won 3-2 away from home before a poor crowd of 1,478 spectators. However, the Final against Wisbech Town was not played because of the congested fixture list.

The return league match at Yeovil on Saturday 25th April resulted in a heavy 4-1 defeat, which meant that United had to win both of their last two games to make sure of winning the Championship. Both games were not at home, against Worcester City on Thursday 30th April and two days later against Margate, but the matter was complicated by a potentially lucrative friendly match arranged against Chelsea on Friday 1st May, as part of Ian Hutchinson's transfer deal to Chelsea, which meant that three games would have to be played in three days.

Against Worcester City United calmed their nerves with a comfortable 3-0 victory to take them within two points of the title with a game to play. Despite the tension of the Championship race, it was the friendly against Chelsea which captured the imagination of the Cambridge public, and a ground record crowd of 14,000 people filled the Abbey Stadium to capacity to see the team that had just beaten Leeds United after a replay to win the F.A. Challenge Cup. Fielding nine of their Cup winning side, Chelsea built up a 1-0 half-time lead against United's first team. At half-time the United players were given a much needed rest. Chelsea Reserves took their place and proceeded to gain the upper hand over their 'seniors' to register a 4-3 victory.

The match whetted the appetite for the visit of Margate the following afternoon. Another big crowd of 5,298 spectators turned up to see Bill Cassidy and George Harris from the penalty spot score the goals which gave United a 2-0 win and the Championship by one point over Yeovil Town.

As if that was not enough for the season, United still had five Eastern Professional Floodlit League games to play in ten days, and they only needed one of these to win the competition for the first time, to add another trophy to the show-case in the Boardroom. The youth team also won a trophy by beating Ely Crusaders 1-0 in the Final of the Cambs F.A. Youth Cup, to win that trophy for the first time in three years.

Throughout the season the Club had worked hard canvassing chairmen and directors of Football League clubs for their support in electing Cambridge United into the Football League at their A.G.M. in London on Saturday 30th May. The players had done their bit, and a day before the meeting they were rewarded with a tour of Germany, having gone to Spain the season before.

The team won three of their four tour matches, but of greater importance was the re-election vote, which vindicated everyone's hard work and saw the Club's election to the Football League by a margin of fourteen votes. Cambridge United received 31 votes compared to Bradford Park Avenue's 17 votes, thereby extracting more than ample compensation for the F.A. Cup defeat against them sixteen years earlier. The news was greeted with overwhelming excitement by the Cambridge United supporters, many of whom travelled to Royston to meet the team on their return from Germany so that they could drive into Cambridge in a triumphant cavalcade of vehicles. Thousands greeted the team in the streets of Cambridge, and a reception was held at the Guildhall with a large crowd filling the Market Square to join the celebrations. For many this was the crowning moment of glory in a remarkable rise up the football ladder.

F.A. Challenge Cup

First Qualifying Round
Cambridge United 5 0 Wellingborough Town

Second Qualifying Round
Cambridge United 10 0 Potton United

Third Qualifying Round
Cambridge United 6 0 Newmarket Town

Fourth Qualifying Round
Chelmsford City 3 2 **Cambridge United**

Southern League Cup

First Round First Leg
Burton Albion 1 0 **Cambridge United**

First Round Second Leg
Cambridge United 2 1 Burton Albion

First Round Replay
Burton Albion 0 1 **Cambridge United**

Second Round
Cambridge United 1 1 Corby Town

Second Round Replay
Corby Town	2	4	**Cambridge United**

Third Round
Wimbledon	1	0	Cambridge United

F.A. Challenge Trophy

First Round Proper
Cambridge United	2	1	Minehead

Second Round Proper
Bromsgrove	2	1	Cambridge United

Cambs Professional Cup

Semi-final
Cambridge City	2	0	Cambridge United

(Match abandoned at half-time due to fog.)

Semi-final
Cambridge City	2	3	**Cambridge United**

Final
Cambridge United	v	Wisbech Town

(Match not played)

International Tournament
(In West Germany)

Group Matches
Cambridge United	2	1	S.C. Bonner
Cambridge United	3	0	Wessling District
Cambridge United	4	3	D.J.K. Gutersloh

Final
Bayer 04, Leverkusen	2	1	Cambridge United

Southern League Premier Division

	Pld	W	D	L	F	A	Pts
Cambridge United	42	26	6	10	84	50	58
Yeovil Town	42	25	7	10	78	48	57
Chelmsford City	42	20	11	11	76	58	51
Weymouth	42	18	14	10	59	37	50
Wimbledon	42	19	12	11	64	52	50
Hillingdon Borough	42	19	12	11	56	50	50
Barnet	42	16	15	11	71	54	47
Telford United	42	18	10	14	61	62	46
Brentwood Town	42	16	13	13	61	38	45
Hereford United	42	18	9	15	74	65	45
Bath City	42	18	8	16	63	55	44
King's Lynn	42	16	11	15	72	68	43
Margate	42	17	8	17	70	64	42
Dover	42	15	10	17	51	50	40
Kettering Town	42	18	3	21	64	75	39
Worcester City	42	14	10	18	35	44	38
Romford	43	13	11	18	50	62	37
Poole Town	42	8	19	15	48	57	35
Gloucester City	42	12	9	21	53	73	33
Nuneaton Borough	42	11	10	21	52	74	32
Crawley Town	42	6	15	21	53	101	27
Burton Albion	42	3	9	30	24	82	15

Southern League Championship Match
(1968-69 Season)

Cambridge United	1	0	Hillingdon Borough

Eastern Professional Floodlit League

	Pld	W	D	L	F	A	Pts
Cambridge United	18	10	6	2	41	21	26
Boston United	18	8	7	3	24	16	23
Brentwood Town	18	7	7	4	28	25	21
King's Lynn	18	6	8	4	33	29	20
Chelmsford City	18	7	4	7	31	25	18
Bedford Town	18	8	1	9	25	20	17
Romford	18	6	5	7	24	26	17
Barnet	18	5	3	10	25	42	13
Stevenage Athletic	18	5	3	10	18	34	13
Cambridge City	18	5	2	11	36	47	12

F.A. Youth Challenge Cup

First Round Proper
Cambridge Utd Yth	2	3	Friern Barnet Boys

Eastern Junior Cup

First Round First Leg
Clacton Town Youth	2	3	**Cambridge Utd Yth**

First Round Second Leg
Cambridge Utd Yth	2	0	Clacton Town Youth

Second Round First Leg
Cambridge Utd Yth	2	3	Harwick & Parkeston Youth

Second Round Second Leg
Harwich & Parkestone Youth	5	0	Cambridge Utd Yth

Southern Junior Floodlit Cup

First Round
Chelsea Youth	4	0	Cambridge Utd Yth

Cambs F.A. Youth Cup

First Round
Cambridge Utd Yth	8	1	Meridian Youth Club

Semi-final (at Pye's F.C.)
Cambridge Utd Yth	2	2	Soham Town Rngrs Yth

Semi-final Replay (at Histon F.C.)
Soham Town Rngrs Yth	0	2	**Cambridge Utd Yth**

Final (at Histon F.C.)
Cambridge Utd Yth	1	0	Ely Crusaders Youth

Mercia Youth League

	Pld	W	D	L	F	A	Pts
Ipswich Town Youth	12	10	1	1	60	7	36
Norwich City Youth	11	9	1	1	46	5	33
Harwich & Parkestone Yth	12	6	1	5	23	20	23
Brentwood Youth	11	5	2	4	23	29	20
Cambridge Utd Yth	12	4	0	8	18	36	13
Bury Town Youth	12	2	1	9	14	54	8
Clacton Town Youth	12	2	0	10	13	46	7

NOTE: Points awarded: 4 Away win, 3 Home win, 2 Away draw, 1 Home draw.

BEAT THE RUSH, TO THE SUN

From self-catering villas around the Mediterranean to skiing in the Alps.
A sports holiday in the sun.
Or simply a flight or even to buy a villa.
Call us for the best of everything.

BEACH VILLAS

Beach Villas Travel Ltd., 8 Market Passage, Cambridge CB2 3QR
Ring **(0223) 350777/353222** (24 hrs)
Bonded with ATOL 381B ABTA 1415X AITO IATA Access/Visa welcome

Friday 1st May 1970. Friendly. Cambridge United & Chelsea Reserves 4, Chelsea 3.
The night before their vital last home Southern League match against Margate, a club record home crowd of 14,000 spectators turned up to see United beat F.A. Cup winners Chelsea by 4 goals to 3 in a match arranged as part of the Ian Hutchinson transfer to Chelsea. United's first team played in the first half, and went in 1-0 down to a late goal, but the Chelsea "stiffs" turned that round to a victory in the second half. Chelsea fielded nine of the team that won the F.A. Cup, and displayed the trophy at the match. Photograph by courtesy of *Cambridge Evening News*.

Chapter Seven

THE SEVENTIES

1970-71 SEASON

As the Club embarked on its first season in the Football League, the moment was a particular one to savour for three members of the Board of Directors, A.E. "Paddy" Harris, Geoff Proctor and Stan Starr, who were all on the original Board of Directors formed over twenty years earlier.

The Club's first game in the Football League Fourth Division was at home to Lincoln City on Saturday 15th August 1970 and attracted a crowd of 6,843 spectators. Colin Meldrum had the honour of scoring the Club's first Football League goal as the team got off the mark with a 1-1 draw.

Four days later the Club travelled to Colchester for the First Round of the Football League Cup, but a large band of Cambridge United supporters were sent home unhappy after their team had suffered a heavy 5-0 defeat. The first win in the Football League was registered at the Abbey Stadium on Saturday 29th August against Oldham Athletic by 3 goals to 1. That match started a run of six games without defeat, which included a 4-2 home victory against Wimbledon on Wednesday 16th September in the Southern League Championship Match, enabling United to hold on to the trophy for one more year.

A setback was suffered when top goalscorer George Harris injured a knee against Oldham and was ruled out of the game for two months. This was followed by a mysterious chest illness to goalkeeper Trevor Roberts, which resulted in the Club signing Peter Vasper from Norwich City as a replacement.

The best home crowd of the season, 7,570, saw Cambridge United draw 1-1 against Peterborough United on Saturday 10th October. A week later, away to Lincoln City, a tough match ended with Peter Leggett and Colin Meldrum being sent off in injury time, although United won the game 1-0 thanks to a penalty scored by Dennis Walker. After that game the Club lost four Football League matches in succession, then made the signing of Ivan Hollett, a strong centre-forward from Crewe Alexandra, for a fee of £5,000. He made an immediate impact, scoring in three of his first four games, including the winning goal in an awkward F.A. Challenge Cup tie away to Enfield in the First Round Proper. Enfield were rated as the top amateur side in the country, but United won 1-0 to reach the Second Round Proper for only the second time in their history. However, they were given another difficult away match against Colchester United on 12th December. Cambridge United went into the match with the confidence of having beaten Colchester a week earlier by 2 goals to 1 in the league, but the Essex club upheld their cup reputation with an emphatic 3-0 victory.

The First Leg of the Cambs Professional Cup Final, after a couple of postponements, was played away to Cambridge City on Tuesday 1st December. It resulted in an embarrassing 3-1 defeat, despite United taking the lead in the 2nd minute through a goal from Rolley Horrey, before a modest crowd of 2,295 spectators. Some consolation for that defeat was obtained in the Eastern Professional Floodlit League, as United beat their close neighbours 6-1 at home and 4-1 away to help push themselves to the top of the league table.

Former first team full back Brian Boggis took over the running of the youth team at the start of the season, but they fared badly in their cup competitions, losing to Luton Town in the First Round of the Southern Junior Floodlit Cup (3-1), losing on aggregate (6-2) to Clacton Town in the First Round of the Eastern Junior Cup, and going down by a goal to nil at home to Soham Town Rangers in the First Round Proper of the F.A. Youth Cup. However, that defeat was avenged when after a replay the United youth team retained the Cambs F.A. Youth Cup with a 2-1 victory over Soham in the Final.

John McKinven received a broken leg in a 2-1 defeat at Barrow on the 28th November, to further deplete the 17 man squad of players, but shortly afterwards Jimmy White, who was formerly a player-coach with Bournemouth, joined the Club in the same capacity, taking over from Peter Watson.

On Boxing Day Cambridge United travelled to the league leaders, and eventual Champions, Notts County, and were watched by their biggest ever crowd of 15,722 spectators, in a 4-1 defeat. At the turn of the year home attendances averaged 5,314, which was virtually double the average of the previous season. Because of a poor record in the second half of the season, the average home attendance dropped to 4,921 people per game, but that was still as good as most clubs in the division, and proved that Football League soccer was popular in Cambridge.

John Collins was signed from Luton in February, an experienced player with over 350 Football League appearances to his credit, but despite his presence the team went through the month without a win and slipped dangerously close to the bottom four re-election places.

The Second Leg of the Cambs Professional Cup Final was played at the Abbey Stadium on Wednesday 24th March 1971 with United hopeful that they could pull back the two goal deficit. However, a solitary goal from Ivan Hollett was all they could muster, and Cambridge City won 3-2 on aggregate before 2,731 spectators.

Easter proved to be a profitable period, with the Club registering a 1-0 away win at Stockport on Good Friday, and then the following day the visit of Notts County attracted 6,935 people to the Abbey Stadium to see United achieve a notable 2-1 victory against the league leaders. Just one defeat in the last seven league games saw Cambridge United escape from the re-election zone by one place, although by a margin of four points. Had one more point been gained the Club would have moved up another four places and made the final position more respectable.

For much of the season the Club looked like winning the Eastern Professional Floodlit League for the second year in succession, but two defeats in the last three games, including a 3-0 defeat away to Boston United, enabled Bedford Town to take the title by two points. At the end of the season Cambridge United decided to withdraw from the competition, and instead enter the Midweek Football League.

F.A. Challenge Cup

First Round Proper
Enfield 0 1 Cambridge United

Second Round Proper
Colchester United 3 0 Cambridge United

Football League Cup

First Round
Colchester United 5 0 Cambridge United

Cambs Professional Cup

Final First Leg
Cambridge City 3 1 Cambridge United

Final Second Leg
Cambridge United 1 0 Cambridge City

Southern League Championship Match (1969-70 Season)

Cambridge United 4 2 Wimbledon

First Team 1970-71 Season

Back Row:
Bill Leivers (Manager), Bill Cassidy, Colin Meldrum, Terry Eades, Keith Barker, Trevor Roberts, Peter Leggett, Jimmy Thompson, John McKiven, Peter Watson (Coach).
Front Row:
Brian Grant, Roly Horrey, Mel Slack, Dennis Walker, George Harris, Malcolm Lindsay, John Gregson, Robin Hardy.
Photograph by courtesy of Press Association. Ref. No. 146776 - 1.

Football League Division Four

	Pld	W	D	L	F	A	Pts
Notts County	46	30	9	7	89	36	69
Bournemouth	46	24	12	10	81	46	60
Oldham Athletic	46	24	11	11	88	63	59
York City	46	23	10	13	78	54	56
Chester	46	24	7	15	69	55	55
Colchester United	46	21	12	13	70	54	54
Northampton Town	46	19	13	14	63	59	51
Southport	46	21	6	19	63	57	48
Exeter City	46	17	14	15	67	68	48
Workington	46	18	12	16	48	49	48
Stockport County	46	16	14	16	49	65	46
Darlington	46	17	11	18	58	57	45
Aldershot	46	14	17	15	66	71	45
Brentford	46	18	8	20	66	62	44
Crewe Alexandra	46	18	8	20	75	76	44
Peterborough United	46	18	7	21	70	71	43
Scunthorpe United	46	15	13	18	56	61	43
Southend United	46	14	15	17	53	66	43
Grimsby Town	46	18	7	21	57	71	43
Cambridge United	46	15	13	18	51	66	43
Lincoln City	46	13	13	20	70	71	39
Newport County	46	10	8	28	55	85	28
Hartlepool United	46	8	12	26	34	74	28
Barrow	46	7	8	31	51	90	22

Eastern Professional Floodlit League

	Pld	W	D	L	F	A	Pts
Bedford Town	16	9	4	3	36	19	22
King's Lynn	16	7	6	3	30	19	20
Boston United	16	7	6	3	28	19	20
Cambridge United	16	8	4	4	38	26	20
Southend United	16	7	2	7	26	24	16
Chelmsford City	16	6	3	7	24	25	15
Cambridge City	16	6	3	7	22	34	15
Romford	16	4	3	9	23	30	11
Stevenage Athletic	16	2	1	13	14	45	5

F.A. Youth Challenge Cup

First Round Proper
Cambridge Utd Yt 0 1 Soham Town Rangers

Southern Junior Floodlit Cup

First Round
Cambridge Utd Yth 1 3 Luton Town Youth

Eastern Junior Cup

First Round First Leg
Clacton Town Youth 5 1 **Cambridge Utd Yth**

First Round Second Leg
Cambridge Utd Yth 1 1 Clacton Town Youth

Cambs F.A. Youth Cup

First Round (result not known)
Semi-final (result not known)
Final (at University Press F.C.)
Cambridge Utd Yth 2 2 Soham Town Rngrs Yth

Final Replay (at Histon F.C.)
Soham Town Rngrs Yth 1 2 **Cambridge Utd Yth**

Mercia Youth League (Latest table available)

	Pld	W	D	L	F	A	Pts
Norwich City Youth	4	3	1	0	19	6	12
Ipswich Town Youth	3	3	0	0	10	2	11
Clacton Town Youth	7	3	0	4	10	22	11
Cambridge Utd Yth	6	1	1	4	8	13	4
Harwich & Parkeston Yth	3	1	0	2	3	6	4
Bury Town Youth	1	0	0	1	0	1	0

NOTE: Points awarded: 4 Away win, 3 Home win, Away draw, 1 Home draw

1971-72 SEASON

Seven players were signed on by Bill Leivers during the close-season in a bid to improve on the previous season's performance, and a new trainer, John Simpson, was added to the staff. Three players were signed from Luton Town F.C. for a joint fee of £15,000: Jack Bannister, Alan Guild and Peter Phillips, a University graduate who had previously played for the Club on loan.

The early season form was not encouraging, and the Club failed to win in the first five games. One of these games was in the First Round of the Football League Cup away to Fulham, but the London side won comfortably by 4 goals to 0 before 8,360 spectators. Three wins in succession early in September quickly revived the Club's fortunes, the third of these wins on Saturday 18th September 1971 being a Club record Football League victory over Darlington by 6 goals to 0. Brian Greenhalgh, another signing at the start of the season, scored four goals in the match.

The Club's first game in the Midweek Football League, at home to Charlton Athletic on Wednesday 25th August, drew a crowd of 1,688 spectators to see the first team win by 2 goals to 0, but the competition was generally used for giving the squad of players in reserve a competitive football match, and consequently the crowds declined. Initially the team struggled against the reserve teams of other Football League clubs, but eventually they managed to register 8 wins out of the 26 league and cup games.

Jimmy White took over the running of the youth team, who continued to play in the Mercia Youth League. In cup competitions they had little success, losing 8-0 on aggregate to Norwich City in the First Round of the Eastern Junior Cup, and losing 1-0 at home to Peterborough United in the Second Round Proper of the F.A. Youth Cup, having beaten Ely Crusaders in the First Round. Ely Crusaders did however gain their revenge when they beat United's youth team 2-1 in the Semi-final replay of the Cambs F.A. Youth Cup.

On Wednesday 3rd November 1971 the first team played at home to Cambridge City in the First Leg of the Cambs Professional Cup Final, and this time won 2-0 with goals from Brian Greenhalgh and Rolley Horrey. In the F.A. Challenge Cup the Club were successful in the First Round Proper, receiving a home draw against non-league Weymouth and winning by 2 goals to 1. A difficult away draw in the Second Round against Bristol Rovers saw United suffer a heavy 3-0 defeat, and left them with just the league to concentrate on.

Manager Bill Leivers was pleased with the signing of Ronnie Walton from Aldershot in November, after which the team went ten league games with just one defeat and moved into the fringe of the promotion race. On Boxing Day, Lawrie McMenemy's Grimsby Town, who went on to become Fourth Division League Champions, visited the Abbey Stadium and set a new Club record crowd for a home Football League match when 8,591 people turned up to see Cambridge United gain an exciting win by 3 goals to 1.

John Gregson was granted a Testimonial Match against Ipswich Town on Monday 24th January, just before a power crisis meant that all floodlit matches in February had to be postponed. Just two points gained from four games in the month upset the hopes for promotion, and an inconsistent set of results in March assured the Club that they would be playing Fourth Division football again the following season. At the request of the majority of Cambridge United's supporters, the Club decided that they would revert back to playing in their traditional colours of black and amber for the start of the 1972-73 season.

Three wins in the last three games enabled Cambridge United to finish in a satisfactory tenth place in the Fourth Division. The team scored 62 goals, eleven more than in the previous season, although the average home attendance was slightly down at 4,895 per game. Brian Greenhalgh was easily the highest goalscorer with 18 goals, although

1971-72 Season
Back Row: Alan Guild, Vic Akers, Peter Philips, John Peachey.
Middle Row: John Collins, Jimmy White, Ivan Hollett, Trevor Roberts, Terry Eades, Peter Vasper, Dennis Walker, Kevin Ormeroyd (Apprentice), Steve Haylock (Apprentice), John Simpson (Trainer/Physiotherapist).
Front Row: John Gregson, John Murray, Chris Foote, Roly Horrey, Jimmy Thompson, David Knight, Jack Bannister, George Harris, Brian Greenhalgh. Photograph by courtesy of *Cambridge Evening News*.

once again it was a defender who took the Player of the Year Award, Terry Eades winning the title for the second year in succession.

The last competitive game of the season was away to Cambridge City in the Second Leg of the Cambs Professional Cup Final at Milton Road on Tuesday 2nd May. This time United avoided any embarrassment, and increased their two goal lead from the First Leg, to regain the trophy by 4 goals to 1 on aggregate.

A Testimonial Match was arranged for Trevor Roberts on Monday 8th May 1972 between a Combined Cambridge United and Southend United XI and the West Ham United first team. Trevor had been seriously ill with cancer of the lung, but recovered bravely to play again for the first team. Tragically he then suffered a stroke, which forced him to quit the game of football prematurely.

F.A. Challenge Cup

First Round Proper
Cambridge United 2 1 Weymouth

Second Round Proper
Bristol Rovers 3 0 Cambridge United

Football League Cup

First Round
Fulham 4 0 Cambridge United

Cambs Professional Cup

Final First Leg
Cambridge United 2 0 Cambridge City

Final Second Leg
Cambridge City 1 2 **Cambridge United**

Football League Division Four

	Pld	W	D	L	F	A	Pts
Grimsby Town	46	28	7	11	88	56	63
Southend United	46	24	12	10	81	55	60
Brentford	46	24	11	11	76	44	59
Scunthorpe United	46	22	13	11	56	37	57
Lincoln City	46	21	14	11	77	59	56
Workington	46	16	19	11	50	34	51
Southport	46	18	14	14	66	46	50
Peterborough United	46	17	16	13	82	64	50
Bury Town	46	19	12	15	73	59	50
Cambridge United	46	17	14	15	62	60	48
Colchester United	46	19	10	17	70	69	48
Doncaster Rovers	46	16	14	16	56	63	46
Gillingham	46	16	13	17	61	67	45
Newport County	46	18	8	20	60	72	44
Exeter City	46	16	11	19	61	68	43
Reading	46	17	8	21	56	76	42
Aldershot	46	9	22	15	48	54	40
Hartlepool	46	17	6	23	58	69	40
Darlington	46	14	11	21	64	82	39
Chester	46	10	18	18	47	56	38
Northampton Town	46	12	13	21	66	79	37
Barrow	46	13	11	22	40	71	37
Stockport County	46	9	14	23	55	87	32
Crewe Alexandra	46	10	9	27	43	69	29

Midweek Football League

	Pld	W	D	L	F	A	Pts
Northampton Town Res.	22	16	0	6	52	34	32
Luton Town Reserves	22	13	2	7	41	18	28
Southend United Reserves	22	12	3	7	39	25	27
Watford Reserves	22	10	5	7	50	35	25
Charlton Athletic Reserves	22	10	4	8	47	31	24
Millwall Reserves	22	8	7	7	34	36	23
Peterborough United Res.	22	7	6	9	33	35	20
Orient Reserves	22	9	2	11	30	36	20
Brighton & Hve Albion Res	22	7	4	11	26	57	18
Aldershot Reserves	22	6	4	12	23	32	16
Cambridge United Res	22	7	2	13	24	36	16
Colchester United Reserves	22	7	1	14	21	45	15

MILLS & DOUGLAS (Builders) LTD

Directors: K. MILLS (Managing), R. MILLS, A.R. DOUGLAS, E.G. DOUGLAS, M.E. DOUGLAS, I.B. THOMPSON (Executive Director)

Office and Yard
BARRINGTON ROAD, ORWELL, NR ROYSTON, HERTS, SG8 5QP
Telephone: Cambridge (0223) 208123 / 207494

MILLS AND DOUGLAS (BUILDERS) LTD. would like to offer their congratulations to Cambridge United on reaching its 75th Anniversary and wish the Club every success in the future.

Midweek Football League Cup Section 'A'

	Pld	W	D	L	F	A	Pts
Peterborough United	4	3	0	1	11	1	6
Northampton Town	4	2	0	2	5	6	4
Cambridge United	4	1	0	3	1	10	2

F.A. Youth Challenge Cup

First Round Proper
Cambridge Utd Yth 3 1 Ely Crusaders Youth

Second Round Proper
Cambridge Utd Yth 0 1 Peterborough Utd Yth

Eastern Junior Cup

First Round First Leg
Norwich City Youth 2 0 **Cambridge Utd Yth**

First Round Second Leg
Cambridge Utd Yth 0 6 Norwich City Youth

Cambs F.A. Youth Cup

First Round
Cambridge Utd Yth 6 0 Chartfield Youth

Semi-final
Cambridge Utd Yth 2 2 Ely Crusaders Youth
(after extra-time)

Semi-final Replay
Cambridge Utd Yth 1 2 Ely Crusaders Youth

Mercia Football League
(Latest table available)

	Pld	W	D	L	F	A	Pts
Ipswich Town Youth	3	3	0	0	16	2	10
Norwich City Youth	2	2	0	0	6	1	7
Cambridge Utd Yth	3	2	0	1	7	7	7
Clacton Town Youth	6	0	0	6	5	24	0

NOTE: Points awarded: 4 Away win, 3 Home win, Away draw, 1 Home draw

1972-73 SEASON

For the tenth year running Cambridge United failed to win their first competitive game of the season, losing disastrously by 3 goals to 0 at home to Darlington. Once again the Club were unlucky to be drawn away from home in the First Round of the Football League Cup, and were unable to register their first goal in the competition, going down by a goal to nil against Brentford before 7,750 spectators.

A poor start to the season saw United in the danger zone at the bottom of the league after the first month, but in mid-September Graham Watson was signed from Doncaster Rovers for £5,000 to boost the midfield. In his first managerial job Bill Leivers had discovered Graham Watson as a local boy, and by his inclusion in the team he made an immediate impression as the Club struck form and rose rapidly up the table with a fifteen match unbeaten run which pushed them into third place in November.

The successful run came to an end on Saturday 18th November, coincidently with Graham Watson out of the side, when the First Round Proper draw in the F.A. Challenge Cup gave Cambridge United the hardest possible tie away from home against the Third Division leaders, Bournemouth. Not surprisingly United lost, but the size of their defeat, by 5 goals to 1, was a big disappointment to those favouring the black and amber amongst the 10,034 crowd.

Bobby Ross was signed from Brentford to help the Club's promotion bid, and he made his debut in the First Leg of the Cambs Professional Cup Final on Tuesday 17th October at the Abbey Stadium, but the game ended disappointingly for United in a 0-0 draw.

By entering a team in the Cambs Sunday Youth League, as well as the Mercia Youth League, the youth team had a very full programme. Victory by 4 goals to 2 against Luton Boys Club in the First Round Proper of the F.A. Youth Cup gave the Cambridge United youth team an attractive away match against Crystal Palace in the next round, but they were not up to the task and lost by 3 goals to 0. Thanks to a bye being received in the First Round of the Southern Junior Floodlit Cup, Cambridge United's youth team were given an even more glamorous cup tie in the Second Round when they were drawn to play Aston Villa at Villa Park. Unfortunately they did not do themselves justice, and lost heavily by 5 goals to 0.

From 16th December 1972 the first team drew five consecutive matches, all in Division Four, but the points gained kept the Club amongst the promotion places. Amidst the excitement of getting involved in the promotion race, the Club opened new administrative offices in the car park in front of the Supporters' Club during the first week of 1973.

Shortly afterwards a couple of defeats against promotion rivals Exeter and Hereford caused an upset to United's plans, but another run of seven games without defeat put the Club back in the frame once again. Hopes seemed to fade when with three games to go Cambridge United lost 2-1 at Lincoln, and then in midweek drew 1-1 away to third in the table Aldershot before an anxious crowd of 10,680 people.

The last match of the season was at home to Mansfield on Saturday 28th April 1973, and the situation was such that both sides needed a win to get promotion. A draw was no good as Newport County would have overtaken them if they had won. Not surprisingly the occasion set a new Football League attendance record for the Abbey Stadium when 10,542 people saw United win a thrilling game by 3 goals to 2. Ronnie Walton fired home the winning goal in the 62nd minute, his second goal of the match, with Bobby Ross scoring the other goal from the penalty spot. Cambridge United had to endure a 'nail-biting' last 28 minutes as they held onto their lead, after which the Abbey Stadium experienced scenes of wild delight as the supporters celebrated promotion. Despite having the most successful season since joining the Football League, the Club's average home attendances were down by over six hundred spectators per game on the two previous seasons; a statistic that must have confounded the Club's Directors.

Another disappointment was the Club's failure to retain the Cambs Professional Cup. With no goals being scored in the First Leg at the Abbey Stadium, United were outfought by Cambridge City in the Second Leg at Milton Road, and lost by 2 goals to 0.

After gaining promotion to Division Three, the team went on a tour of Cyprus to play in an international tournament, but they drew one and lost two of their three games, coming last in the four teams tournament.

The youth team just failed to win the Cambs Sunday Youth League, and at the end of the season the Board of Directors decided to scrap the youth team for the following season. The Club's Secretary, Phil Baker, also resigned at the end of the season after being in the position for five years, and Colin Benson was appointed as his successor.

F.A. Challenge Cup

First Round Proper
Bournemouth　　　　　5　1　Cambridge United

First Team 1972-73 Season
Back Row: Vic Akers, John Collins, Jimmy Thompson, Jack Bannister, Graham Watson.
Middle Row: Keith Pointer, Alan Guild, Peter Vasper, J.Marsh, Terry Eades, Chris Foote.
Front Row: Ron Walton, Brian Greenhalgh, Peter Philips, Bobby Ross, David Lill.

Saturday 28th April 1973. Football League Division Four.
Cambridge United 3, Mansfield Town 2.

In the last match of the season both Mansfield and Cambridge United needed a win to make sure of promotion. In a tense atmosphere at the Abbey Stadium, with the scores level at 2-2, Ronnie Walton burst through the Mansfield defence to hook home the winning goal, and the whole of Barnwell shook with the deafening roar.
Photograph by courtesy of *Cambridge Evening News*.

CASHMAN

Cashman Partitions & Ceilings

Unit 6
Dunmow Industrial Estate
Chelmsford Road
Dunmow
Essex CN6 1HD

Telephone: (0371) 4111
FAX: (0371) 5621

SUPPLIERS AND ERECTORS OF INDUSTRIAL AND OFFICE PARTITION SYSTEMS/CEILINGS/STORAGE AND SUNBLINDS

Castle Flooring

COMMERCIAL & INDUSTRIAL FLOORING SPECIALISTS IN

CARPET • CARPET TILES
VINYL • LINOLEUM
CORK • WOOD
• CERAMIC WALL/FLOOR FINISHES

CALL OR RING
CONTACT OFFICE
UNIT 2
BARNWELL ROAD

PROFESSIONAL ADVICE FREELY GIVEN

**CAMBRIDGE
(0223) 248054**

Football League Cup

First Round
Brentford 1 0 Cambridge United

Cambs Professional Cup

Final First Leg
Cambridge United 0 0 Cambridge City

Final Second Leg
Cambridge City 2 0 Cambridge United

International Tournament (In Cyprus)

Group Matches
Proionia (Romania) 3 0 Cambridge United
Brno-Marets (Bulgaria) 3 3 Cambridge United
Omionia-Nicosia (Cyprus) 2 1 Cambridge United

Football League Division Four

	Pld	W	D	L	F	A	Pts
Southport	46	26	10	10	71	48	62
Hereford United	46	23	12	11	56	38	58
Cambridge United	46	20	17	9	67	57	57
Aldershot	46	22	12	12	60	38	56
Newport County	46	22	12	12	64	44	56
Mansfield Town	46	20	14	12	78	51	54
Reading	46	17	18	11	51	38	52
Exeter City	46	18	14	14	57	51	50
Gillingham	46	19	11	16	63	58	49
Lincoln City	46	16	16	14	64	57	48
Stockport County	46	18	12	16	53	53	48
Bury	46	14	18	14	58	51	46
Workington	46	17	12	17	59	61	46
Barnsley	46	14	16	16	58	60	44
Chester	46	14	15	17	61	52	43
Bradford City	46	16	11	19	61	65	43
Doncaster Rovers	46	15	12	19	49	58	42
Torquay United	46	12	17	17	44	47	41
Peterborough United	46	14	13	19	71	76	41
Hartlepool	46	12	17	17	34	49	41
Crewe Alexandra	46	9	18	19	38	61	36
Colchester United	46	10	11	25	48	76	31
Northampton Town	46	10	11	25	40	73	31
Darlington	46	7	15	24	42	85	29

Midweek Football League

	Pld	W	D	L	F	A	Pts
Luton Town Reserves	20	12	6	2	49	17	30
Southend United Reserves	20	12	6	2	39	15	30
Northampton Town Res.	20	9	5	6	42	26	23
Orient Reserves	20	9	4	7	27	28	22
Brighton & Hove Alb. Res	20	7	7	6	31	33	21
Watford Reserves	20	9	3	8	25	28	21
Cambridge Utd Res	20	6	4	10	27	33	16
Millwall Reserves	20	6	4	10	35	41	16
Charlton Athletic Reserves	20	6	4	10	31	43	16
Gillingham Reserves	20	4	8	8	17	32	16
Colchester United Res.	20	3	3	14	14	41	9

Midweek Football League Cup
Section 'B'

	Pld	W	D	L	F	A	Pts
Southend United Res.	4	3	1	0	10	5	7
Colchester United Res.	4	1	1	2	8	9	3
Cambridge Utd Res	4	0	2	2	4	8	2

F.A. Youth Challenge Cup

First Round Proper
Luton Boys Club 2 4 Cambridge Utd Yth

Second Round Proper
Crystal Palace Youth 3 0 Cambridge Utd Yth

Southern Junior Floodlit Cup

First Round Bye

Second Round
Aston Villa Youth 5 0 Cambridge Utd Yth

Eastern Junior Cup

First Round First Leg
Norwich City Youth 5 1 Cambridge Utd Yth

First Round Second Leg
Cambridge Utd Yth 0 6 Norwich City Youth

Cambs F.A. Youth Cup

First Round
Cambridge Utd Yth 9 1 Guyhirn Youth

Second Round
Soham Town Rngrs Yth 2 3 Cambridge Utd Yth

Semi-final
Parson Drove Youth 2 4 Cambridge Utd Yth

Final (at Histon F.C.)
Cambridge Utd Yth 5 0 St. Andrew's Youth

Cambs Sunday Youth League Cup

First Round
Willingham Youth 0 3 Cambridge Utd Yth

Semi-final
St. Andrew's Youth 2 0 Cambridge Utd Yth

Mercia Youth League

	Pld	W	D	L	F	A	Pts
Ipswich Town Youth	6	5	0	1	25	4	17
Norwich City Youth	6	3	2	1	15	8	13
Clacton Town Youth	6	1	1	4	9	25	5
Cambridge Utd Yth	6	0	3	3	6	18	5

NOTE: Points awarded: 4 Away win, 3 Home win, Away draw, 1 Home draw

Cambridge & District Sunday Youth League

	Pld	W	D	L	F	A	Pts
Soham Town Rngrs Yth	16	14	1	1	89	19	29
Cambridge Utd Yth	16	11	2	3	60	11	24
Ely Crusaders Youth	14	10	2	2	70	18	22
St. Andrew's Youth	12	8	1	3	51	15	17
Iceni (Exning) Youth	12	5	0	7	40	37	10
Phoenix (Cottenham) Yth.	14	4	1	9	24	42	9
Chartfield Youth	12	3	2	7	25	36	8
Coleridge Youth Centre	14	1	1	12	13	98	3
Burwell Youth Centre	14	0	2	12	15	111	2

1973-74 SEASON

The season started on a sad note with the death of the Club's Chairman, John Woolley, before he could see his team play in Division Three. As Chairman for the past eleven years, and Board member for over twenty years, he had been a valued and loyal servant.

In preparation for the higher standard of football expected in the new division, Bill Leivers was busy in the transfer market looking for more skilful players, and he managed to capture the signings of experienced players such as Alan Harris, Mike Ferguson and Dave Lennard, a £10,000 transfer from Blackpool.

The first game in Division Three was at home to Southport on Saturday 25th August 1973, and for the first time in eleven years Cambridge United started the season with a victory, winning by 2 goals to 0 with Bobby Ross and John O'Donnell the scorers. The crowd of 4,565 spectators saw a champagne start to the season, with United playing their best football since joining the Football League.

Brian Greenhalgh scored the Club's first goal in the Football League Cup when United registered their seventh successive draw against Aldershot 1-1 away from home in the First Round. That sequence was broken a week later in the replay at the Abbey Stadium when Cambridge United reached the Second Round for the first time with a 3-0 win.

United's good form at home put them just above half-way in the league table by the end of September, but away form was poor. So it was with great disappointment that news of the draw for the Second Round of the Football League Cup was greeted when the Club were unluckily faced with an away tie against the unbeaten Fourth Division leaders, Bury. A crowd of 6,150 people watched United lose the match 2-0 in a spell of five games in which the Club failed to score a goal.

The first away win of the season was achieved against Cambridge City in the Final of the Cambs Professional Cup, which this time was being decided with just one match. Only 1,053 spectators turned up to see what turned out to be an exciting match. Cambridge City twice took the lead, but United scored twice in the last four minutes to win by 3 goals to 2.

Ray Freeman was appointed as the new Coach in November, at a time when two gloomy Government announcements were made affecting the Club. First the use of floodlights was banned because of an impending power crisis, and secondly, stadiums with a capacity of more than 10,000 would require a safety certificate based on the recommended standards set in the Wheatley Report, following the disaster at the Ibrox Stadium. Both announcements were likely to cost the Club money in the near future.

The Club were fortunate enough to get a home draw in the First Round Proper of the F.A. Challenge Cup, and thanks to a hat-trick from Dave Simmons they were able to beat Gillingham by 3 goals to 2. The same player scored both goals in the Second Round as United were drawn away to Aldershot, but were able to reach the Third Round Proper for the first time in the Club's history with a 2-1 victory. The Third Round tie proved to be an historic occasion in more ways than one. After being drawn at home to Oldham Athletic, the Club decided to play the game at the Abbey Stadium on Sunday 6th January 1974, owing to the State of Emergency which had resulted in petrol rationing, power restrictions, rail problems, and the three day working week. When Dave Simmons kicked-off at 10.45 a.m. he started the first ever F.A. Cup match, or for that matter the first ever senior professional competitive match, to be staged on a Sunday in this country. A crowd of 8,479 people, twice the average attendance, saw United fall a goal behind, but Dave Simmons pressurized Ian Woods into conceding an own goal for the equalizer, and although Oldham went ahead once more, Terry Eades rifled home a last minute equalizer to earn a profitable replay. A crowd of 10,250 people turned up for the replay to see United take a two goal lead with goals from Mike Ferguson and Dave Simmons, but Oldham fought back and eventually scored an equalizer eight minutes from time. During the extra period Graham Watson gave Cambridge United the lead once again, but Oldham equalized within three minutes to take the tie to a third match, on a neutral ground at Nottingham Forest. Only 3,563 people saw United play much the better football, with Dave Simmons scoring another cup goal, but eight minutes from time and against the run of play Oldham scored the goal which gave them a 2-1 win and clinched a home tie against Burnley in the next round.

The dejection experienced after losing in the F.A. Challenge Cup was compounded by the death of Geoffrey Proctor in January 1974, another loyal servant of Cambridge United. He was in his second term as Chairman, and as a driving force throughout the Club's development in professional football, he earned the title: "Mr. Cambridge United". David Ruston, an accountant, took over as Chairman after a short spell on the Board of Directors, while Charles Heffer continued as Vice-Chairman.

The good F.A. Challenge Cup run distracted everyone from the league, in which the Club had slipped in to the relegation zone and now had a fight on to stay in the Third Division. At the turn of the year Terry Eades relinquished the captaincy because the responsibility was affecting his form, and Mike Ferguson took over.

The first away win of the season at Rochdale on Tuesday 5th February 1974 had the dubious distinction of attracting the smallest crowd of any post-war Football League match of just 450 spectators. It was followed by another 2-0 win at home to Hereford United in the next game, giving the Club hope that it might pull clear of danger. However, a 6-1 defeat away to Oldham Athletic on 5th March, the heaviest since joining the League, prompted Bill Leivers to enter into the transfer market in a last ditch battle to stay up. By selling the popular Brian Greenhalgh to A.F.C. Bournemouth for a Club record fee of £40,000, he was able to buy Brendon Batson from Arsenal for £5,000, Nigel Cassidy from Oxford United for £25,000, and just before the transfer deadline he paid £30,000 to Walsall for Bobby Shinton.

Brendon Batson became the Club's third captain for the season when he took over the role at the end of March, but the impact of having new faces in the side was not immediate, and when bottom of the table Rochdale shared six goals at the Abbey Stadium on Saturday 6th April before the smallest home 'gate' since joining the Football League, relegation seemed virtually assured.

A 2-1 defeat at Wrexham on Good Friday 12th April, followed by a record 6-0 defeat at Aldershot the next day, confirmed that the Club would be playing Fourth Division football again the following season. United eventually finished fourth from bottom in the division, with 35 points from 46 games, 7 points adrift of Port Vale, the next club above them.

F.A. Challenge Cup

First Round Proper
Cambridge United 3 2 Gillingham

Second Round Proper
Aldershot 1 2 Cambridge United

Third Round Proper
Cambridge United 2 2 Oldham Athletic

Third Round Replay
Oldham Athletic 3 3 Cambridge United

Third Round Second Replay (at Nottingham Forest)
Oldham Athletic 2 1 Cambridge United

Football League Cup

First Round
Aldershot 1 1 Cambridge United

First Round Replay
Cambridge United 3 0 Aldershot

Second Round
Bury 2 0 Cambridge United

Cambs Professional Cup

Final
Cambridge City 2 3 Cambridge United

Football League Division Three

	Pld	W	D	L	F	A	Pts
Oldham Athletic	46	25	12	9	83	47	62
Bristol Rovers	46	22	17	7	65	33	61
York City	46	21	19	6	67	38	61
Wrexham	46	22	12	12	63	43	56
Chesterfield	46	21	14	11	55	42	56
Grimsby Town	46	18	15	13	67	50	51
Watford	46	19	12	15	64	56	50
Aldershot	46	19	11	16	65	52	49
Halifax Town	46	14	21	11	48	51	49
Huddersfield Town	46	17	13	16	56	55	47
A.F.C. Bournemouth	46	16	15	15	54	58	47
Southend United	46	16	14	16	62	62	46
Blackburn Rovers	46	18	10	18	62	64	46
Charlton Athletic	46	19	8	19	66	73	46
Walsall	46	16	13	17	57	48	45
Tranmere Rovers	46	15	15	16	50	44	45
Plymouth Argyle	46	17	10	19	59	54	44
Hereford United	46	14	15	17	53	57	43
Brighton & Hove Albion	46	16	11	19	52	58	43
Port Vale	46	14	14	18	52	58	42
Cambridge United	46	13	9	24	48	81	35
Shrewsbury Town	46	10	11	25	41	52	31
Southport	46	6	16	24	35	82	28
Rochdale	46	2	17	27	38	94	21

First Team 1973-74 Season
Back Row: Ray Freeman (Coach), Jack Bannister, Chris Foote, David Lill, Terry Eades, Alan Guild, Graham Rathbone, Mike Ferguson, John O'Donnell.
Front Row: Graham Smith, Brian Greenhalgh, Dave Simmons, Vic Akers, Alan Harris, Peter Vasper.

Sunday 6th January 1974. F.A. Challenge Cup. Third Round Proper.
Cambridge United 2, Oldham Athletic 2.
Much to the delight of the Abbey faithful, the ball screams into the roof of the Oldham net, as Terry Eades, partly hidden by the beaten keeper, Harry Dowd, hits Cambridge United's equalizer with the last kick of the game. The replay at Oldham attracted a crowd of 10,250 and United went into a two goal lead through Mike Ferguson and Dave Simmons, but this time Oldham fought back to equalize 8 minutes from the end. Graham Watson gave United the lead again in extra-time but once more Oldham levelled matters at 3-3 to take the game to a second replay at Nottingham Forest's ground. This time Oldham emerged victorious by the narrow margin of 2 goals to 1 to prevent United from reaching the Fourth Round for the first time. Photograph by courtesy of *Cambridge Evening News*.

Midweek Football League

	Pld	W	D	L	F	A	Pts
Portsmouth Reserves	24	14	7	3	57	26	35
Watford Reserves	24	14	5	5	44	25	33
Orient Reserves	24	10	9	5	39	27	29
Millwall Reserves	24	11	7	6	48	39	29
Peterborough United Res.	24	9	8	7	45	36	26
Southend United Reserves	24	9	6	9	39	33	24
Brighton & Hove Alb. Res.	24	8	7	9	40	32	23
Luton Town Reserves	24	8	5	11	37	54	21
Cambridge Utd Res	24	7	6	11	31	36	20
Gillingham Reserves	24	7	6	11	33	44	20
Colchester United Reserves	24	6	6	12	31	50	18
Northampton Town Res.	24	7	3	14	37	56	17
Charlton Athletic Reserves	24	5	7	12	26	49	17

Midweek Football League Cup (Section D)

	Pld	W	D	L	F	A	Pts
Peterborough United Res.	6	4	2	0	17	2	10
Luton Town Reserves	6	1	3	2	6	12	5
Cambridge Utd Res	6	2	1	3	4	11	5
Northampton Town	6	1	2	3	5	7	4

1974-75 SEASON

The bookmakers made Cambridge United joint favourites for the Fourth Division title, but they got off to a bad start with a 2-0 defeat at Reading in the League, and a 2-0 defeat away to Southend United in the First Round of the Football League Cup. The team were winning regularly at home, but also losing consistently away from home, as emphasized by the 5-0 home win against Lincoln City on Saturday 21st September, followed a week later by a 6-0 defeat away to lowly Darlington.

With gates down by an average of 1,600 people per game, and the team in the lower half of the league, the home supporters called for the dismissal of Bill Leivers as Manager after the 2-0 home defeat against Shrewsbury on Tuesday 15th October. A week later the Board of Directors did just that, prompting the players to consider a strike, but after a while they were persuaded to back Ray Freeman who temporarily took charge of the side, which then went on to draw six out of seven matches.

In the F.A. Challenge Cup the Club were drawn away in the First Round Proper against Isthmian League side Hitchin Town, and on a heavy pitch could only manage a 0-0 draw before a crowd of 4,200 spectators. Only 3,827 people turned up at the Abbey Stadium for the replay, but this time United won comfortably by 3 goals to 0, with two goals being scored by Nigel Cassidy and one by Bobby Shinton.

Ron Atkinson was appointed Manager, having formerly been with Kettering Town, at the beginning of December. His first game in charge was a disaster, with United losing 1-0 away to Stockport County, Brendon Batson being sent off, goalkeeper Graham Smith going off injured after half an hour and captain Nigel Cassidy requiring eight stitches in a gashed eyebrow. He had little time to prepare for the F.A. Challenge Cup Second Round match at home to Hereford United, but two goals from Graham Watson sealed a 2-0 victory, in the Club's first sponsored match (by Frank Holland Motors).

One of Ron Atkinson's first moves was to sign Stephen Fallon from Kettering Town before Christmas, from under the nose of Peterborough United. Two successive victories in December, including the first away win of the season at Doncaster, confirmed the Manager's belief that promotion in his first season was not an impossible task. His confidence building training methods certainly seemed to have an effect, especially with the reserves who scored ten goals in two games, including a 6-1 victory over the eventual Midweek League Champions Colchester United.

The New Year started with a tough draw in the Third Round of the F.A. Challenge Cup away to Fourth Division leaders Mansfield Town on Saturday 4th January. After falling behind to a ninth minute goal, on the balance of play United deserved at least a draw, but they went out of the competition with a 1-0 defeat. The only consolidation was the share of the receipts from a crowd of 10,486 spectators.

An unbeaten run of eight league games in January and February saw the Club close the gap on the promotion contenders and earned Ron Atkinson the Fourth Division's Bells Scotch Whisky Manager of the Month Award for February.

Early in February the Club played the Eire International XI in a practice match at the Abbey Stadium, and they registered a fine 3-1 win with Graham Watson scoring a hat-trick. Shortly afterwards Paddy Sowden was appointed as Assistant Manager, following Ray Freeman's move to manage Southern League Romford. Paddy Sowden came to the Club with a fine pedigree, and was regarded as one of the best talent spotters in the game. It was not long before he started making plans to re-form a youth team for the following season, and Peter Reeve was recruited to assist with giving trials to young players.

The Club's one chance of winning a trophy during the season was in the Cambs Professional Cup Final, in which United played at home to Cambridge City on Monday 10th March 1975. United were strongly fancied to win, as Cambridge City had just changed their manager and were struggling in their league, but it was not to be and the Southern League team won the cup with a notable 1-0 victory.

Two league defeats early in March spoiled the Club's promotion chances, but an eleven match unbeaten run to the end of the season allowed United to finish in sixth place, just three points away from a promotion place.

Bobby Shinton was the leading goalscorer with 16 goals, yet it was another forward, David Lyon, who received the Player of the Year Award. The season finished with high hopes that the team was good enough to achieve promotion next time around.

F.A. Challenge Cup

First Round Proper
Hitchin 0 0 **Cambridge United**

First Round Replay
Cambridge United 3 0 Hitchin

Second Round Proper
Cambridge United 2 0 Hereford United

Third Round Proper
Mansfield Town 1 0 **Cambridge United**

Football League Cup

First Round
Southend United 2 0 **Cambridge United**

Cambs Professional Cup

Final
Cambridge United 0 1 Cambridge City

First Team 1974-75 Season
Back Row: Pat Kane, David Lill, David Lyon, Mel Green, John O'Donnell.
Middle Row: Dave Smith, Bobby Shinton, Graham Smith, Brendon Batson, Peter Vasper, Terry Eades, Ray Seary.
Front Row: Kevin Tully, Dave Lennard, Graham Watson, Bobby Ross, Vic Akers, Graham Howell, Nigel Cassidy (Club Captain). Photograph by courtesy of *Cambridge Evening News*.

Football League Division Four

	Pld	W	D	L	F	A	Pts
Mansfield Town	46	25	12	6	90	40	68
Shrewsbury Town	46	26	10	10	80	43	62
Rotherham United	46	22	15	9	71	41	59
Chester	46	23	11	12	64	38	57
Lincoln City	46	21	15	10	79	48	57
Cambridge United	46	20	14	12	62	44	54
Reading	46	21	10	15	63	47	52
Brentford	46	18	13	15	53	45	49
Exeter City	46	19	11	16	60	63	49
Bradford City	46	17	13	16	56	51	47
Southport	46	15	17	14	56	56	47
Newport County	46	19	9	18	68	75	47
Hartlepool	46	16	11	19	52	62	43
Torquay	46	14	14	18	46	61	42
Barnsley	46	15	11	20	62	65	41
Northampton Town	46	15	11	20	67	73	41
Doncaster Rovers	46	14	12	20	65	79	40
Crewe Alexandra	46	11	18	17	34	47	40
Rochdale	46	13	13	20	59	75	39
Stockport County	46	12	14	20	43	70	38
Darlington	46	13	10	23	54	67	36
Swansea City	46	15	6	15	46	73	36
Workington	46	10	11	15	46	67	31
Scunthorpe	46	7	15	24	41	78	29

Midweek League Cup

First Round
Gillingham Reserves 3 4 **Cambridge Utd Res**

Second Round
Brighton & Hove Alb. Reserves 2 1 **Cambridge Utd Res**

Midweek Football League

	Pld	W	D	L	F	A	Pts
Colchester United Res.	26	16	6	4	63	35	38
Orient Reserves	26	15	7	4	60	23	37
Charlton Athletic Res.	26	14	6	6	43	33	34
Southend United Res.	26	13	6	7	46	37	32
Peterborough United Res.	26	12	7	7	53	37	31
Luton Town Reserves	26	12	7	7	55	40	31
Portsmouth Reserves	26	12	4	10	51	45	28
Brighton & Hove Alb. Res.	26	11	5	10	48	50	27
Watford Reserves	26	5	10	11	31	37	20
Gillingham Reserves	26	6	8	12	34	47	20
Cambridge Utd Res	26	6	6	14	29	44	18
Brentford Reserves	26	6	6	14	30	50	18
Northampton Town Res.	26	5	5	16	42	65	15
Millwall Reserves	26	6	3	17	29	70	15

1975-76 SEASON

The innovation of the Shipp Cup which added a competitive quality to the pre-season friendly matches, proved to be a great success. United were undefeated in their three matches following a 4-4 draw at Kettering, a 1-0 victory over Notts County and a final 3-3 draw against Peterborough United. Just one goal denied Cambridge United the trophy as Second Division Notts County won the tournament on goal average, 7-6 to United's 8-7.

With confidence high that the Club could gain promotion at the end of the season, the new campaign got off to a good start with a 2-0 win away to Doncaster Rovers. Two youngsters, Steve Spriggs and Alan Biley, both made their Football League debuts in the game, the latter marking the occasion with a goal.

It was quite ironic that the Club should be drawn at home in the First Round of the Football League Cup after the decision had been taken to stage the First Round over two legs, giving the advantage to the team drawn away first. In the first game Cambridge United gained a creditable draw against Second Division Charlton Athletic, with Alan Biley scoring another goal, but in the Second Leg at the Valley, the Club's unbeaten run of seventeen competitive matches, extending back to the previous season, came to an end with a 3-0 defeat. A crowd of 6,744 witnessed an unfortunate accident to Alan Biley which saw him break a leg and put him out of the game for half of the season. The defeat also spoiled Ron Atkinson's chance of meeting his old club Oxford United in the next round.

The team failed to score in four consecutive games, and an injury crisis caused a mix bag of results that saw the team hold a mid-table position in the league.

Young Charlton Gilder, coming on as substitute, scored a last minute goal as United beat Cambridge City 1-0 at Milton Road in the Cambs Professional Cup Final on Tuesday 28th October 1976 to regain the trophy, before a small crowd of only 844 spectators. Two days later he returned to the same ground to score in the youth team's 3-1 win over Cambridge City's youth team to maintain their unbeaten run in the Chiltern Premier Youth League.

The Supporters' Club bought the full first team squad of players a smart set of green blazers and flannels for their away matches. The players were able to wear them for their trip to Leatherhead in the First Round Proper of the F.A. Challenge Cup on Saturday 22nd November. The non-league team led by Chris Kelly created a name for themselves the previous season in the F.A. Cup before losing to Leicester City by the odd goal in five, and this time they gained another Football League scalp with a 2-0 victory over United in front of 2,500 spectators.

At the Club's A.G.M. in December Stanley Starr retired from the Board of Directors, having served as a founder member of the Board when the Company was formed on 26th April 1950. In recognition of his services he was made an Honorary Life-Member of the Club.

Despite the disappointing form of the first team, the reserve team were enjoying a successful season, and by Christmas had moved into second place in the Midweek Football League. With the youth team also enjoying success against good opposition, the foundations were being laid for future success.

Dave Simmons re-joined the Club in November to bolster the side, and he scored his fifth goal in nine games on 1st January 1976 in the 1-0 away win at Stockport County. It was the first time during the season that the Club had won two matches in succession, and a 3-1 win against Swansea nine days later made it three wins in a row to push United into seventh place in the league table, with an outside chance that promotion could be achieved. However, the team then went ten games without a win, which even a short break in Southern Spain in early February could not halt, after which any hopes of promotion were ruined for another season.

There was some concern when the Club was ordered to appear before an F.A. Disciplinary Commission following the misconduct of spectators at the Abbey Stadium for the game against Northampton Town in November. Fortunately the Club was exonerated from any blame, as it was evident that the trouble had been created by Northampton supporters.

Four consecutive wins by the reserve team up until the end of February consolidated their position in second place in the Midweek League. A home win against league leaders Watford on 9th March would have put United on top, but the North Londoners, reinforced with three experienced former Cambridge United first team players, won by 3 goals to 0. The Championship could have still been won, but youth team players were given valuable experience in the last few games, and by picking up five points in the last six matches United's reserve team were able to hold on to the runners-up spot, their best position since joining the competition.

Prior to most home Football League games, Peter Reeve ran a knock-out penalty competition for schools in the Cambridge area. The idea was very popular, and Comberton Village College were crowned the penalty kings when they beat Linton Village College 7-6 in the Final.

The first team, after remaining unbeaten in their last four league games, finished in 13th place with 43 points. Tommy Horsfall was top goalscorer with 18 goals, while the Player of the Year Award went to the industrious and promising midfield player, Steven Spriggs.

The youth team eventually finished fifth in the Chiltern Premier Youth League, fading somewhat in the latter part of the season.

F.A. Challenge Cup

First Round Proper
Leatherhead 2 0 Cambridge United

Football League Cup

First Round First Leg
Cambridge United 1 1 Charlton Athletic

First Round Second Leg
Charlton Athletic 3 0 **Cambridge United**
(Charlton won 4-1 on aggregate)

Shipp Cup

	Pld	W	D	L	F	A	Pts
Notts County	3	2	0	1	7	6	4
Cambridge United	3	1	2	0	8	7	4
Peterborough United	3	1	1	1	9	7	3
Kettering Town	3	0	1	2	8	12	1

Cambs Professional Cup

Final
Cambridge City 0 1 **Cambridge United**

Football League Division Four

	Pld	W	D	L	F	A	Pts
Lincoln City	46	32	10	4	111	39	74
Northampton Town	46	29	10	7	87	40	68
Reading	46	24	12	10	70	51	60
Tranmere Rovers	46	24	10	12	89	55	58
Huddersfield Town	46	21	14	11	56	41	56
Bournemouth	46	20	12	14	57	48	52
Exeter City	46	18	14	14	56	47	50
Watford	46	22	6	18	62	62	50
Torquay United	46	18	14	14	55	63	50
Doncaster Rovers	46	19	11	16	75	69	49
Swansea City	46	16	15	15	66	57	47
Barnsley	46	14	16	16	52	48	44
Cambridge United	46	14	15	17	58	62	43
Hartlepool	46	16	10	20	62	78	42
Rochdale	46	12	18	16	40	54	42
Crewe Alexandra	46	13	15	18	58	57	41
Bradford City	46	12	17	17	63	65	41
Brentford	46	14	13	19	56	60	41
Scunthorpe United	46	14	10	22	50	59	38
Darlington	46	14	10	22	48	57	38
Stockport County	46	13	12	21	43	76	38
Newport	46	13	9	24	57	90	35
Southport	46	8	10	28	41	77	26
Workington	46	7	7	32	63	87	21

1975-76 Season
Back Row: Graham Watson, David Lill, Stephen Fallon, David Lyon, Carlton Gilder, Brendon Batson.
Middle Row: Paddy Sowden (Assistant Manager), John Simpson (Trainer/Physiotherapist), Bobby Shinton, Tommy Horsfall, Phil Walker, Graham Smith, Ray Seary, Kevin Tully, Peter Reeve (Youth Team Officer).
Front Row: Graham Howell, Paul Smith, Steve Spriggs, David Ruston (Chairman), Ron Atkinson (Manager), Terry Eades (Captain), John O'Donnell, Alan Biley. Photograph by courtesy of *Cambridge Evening News*.

First Team 1976-77 Season
From Left to Right: Jim Hall, Steve Spriggs, Graham Watson, Colin Harper, Stephen Fallon, Terry Eades, Brendon Batson, David Stringer, Tom Finney, Malcolm Webster, Trevor Howard.
The Cambridge United players proudly display the Football League Division Four Championship trophy before their last home game of the season on Saturday 14th May 1977. However, the home supporters in the crowd of 7,795 went away disappointed when Swansea City spoiled the party with a 3-2 victory.
Photograph by courtesy of *Cambridge Evening News*.

Midweek Football League Cup

First Round
Charlton Athletic Res.   2   0   Cambridge Utd Res

Midweek Football League

	Pld	W	D	L	F	A	Pts
Watford Reserves	26	16	5	5	55	29	37
Cambridge Utd Res	26	13	8	5	42	32	34
Peterborough United Res.	26	14	5	7	59	34	33
Charlton Athletic Res.	26	15	3	8	65	42	33
Southend United Res.	26	13	4	9	37	28	30
Gillingham Reserves	26	11	7	8	54	33	29
Brighton & Hove Alb. Res.	26	10	7	9	48	44	27
Luton Town Reserves	26	9	8	9	35	39	26
Orient Reserves	26	10	4	12	36	37	24
Portsmouth Reserves	26	9	4	13	33	45	22
Millwall Reserves	26	7	5	14	43	59	19
Brentford Reserves	26	6	7	13	36	54	19
Colchester Reserves	26	7	4	15	34	63	18
Northampton Town Res.	26	6	1	19	39	75	13

F.A. Youth Challenge Cup

First Qualifying Round
Cambridge Utd Yth   2   6   Cambridge City Youth

Cambs F.A. Youth Cup

First Round
Cambridge Utd Yth   2   1   St. Andrew's Youth
(After extra-time)

Semi-final
Cambridge Utd Yth   1   4   Ely Crusaders Youth
(After extra-time)

Chiltern Premier League Cup

First Round
Cheshunt Youth   3   0   **Cambridge Utd Yth**

Chiltern Premier League

	Pld	W	D	L	F	A	Pts
Luton Town Youth	20	17	2	1	75	16	36
Dunstable Town Youth	20	15	1	4	50	23	31
Cambridge City Youth	20	12	2	6	65	39	26
Chelmsford City Youth	20	12	0	8	52	37	24
Cambridge Utd Yth	20	9	4	7	46	30	22
Hertford Town Youth	20	8	5	7	33	35	21
Wealdstone Youth	20	8	3	9	53	53	19
Cheshunt Youth	20	7	4	9	33	45	18
Stevenage Athletic	20	6	3	11	29	52	15
Hoddesdon Town Youth	20	2	1	17	17	63	5
Vauxhall Motors	20	0	3	17	17	77	3

Cambs & District Sunday Youth League

	Pld	W	D	L	F	A	Pts
Cambridge Utd Yth	8	4	2	2	24	18	10
Cambridge Hornets Youth	7	3	2	2	21	14	8
Ely Crusaders Youth	7	4	0	3	13	11	8
St. Andrew's Youth	7	3	2	2	19	20	8
Mildenhall Youth	7	0	2	5	7	21	2

Cambs & District Sunday Youth League Cup

	Pld	W	D	L	F	A	Pts
Ely Crusaders Youth	8	7	1	0	25	5	15
Cambridge Hornets Youth	8	6	1	1	29	6	13
Cambridge Utd Yth	8	2	1	5	12	16	5
St. Andrew's Youth	8	2	1	5	11	23	5
Mildenhall Youth	8	1	0	7	7	38	2

Ely Crusaders Youth Tournament

Group Matches
Cambridge Utd Yth   1   1   F.C. Aeolus Youth
Cambridge Utd Yth   2   0   St. Andrew's Youth
Soham Town Rngrs Yth   2   0   **Cambridge Utd Yth**

1976-77 SEASON

The Club's new £6,000 floodlighting system, which produced three times the light of the old system, was switched on for the pre-season friendly against Dutch Second Division side Dordrecht on Monday 2nd August, a game which United won 4-1. In the pre-season Shipp Cup Cambridge United only picked up one point from a draw with Lincoln City, and finished fourth in the four team tournament won by Sheffield Wednesday.

The season proper started with the two-legged Football League Cup First Round matches against Ron Atkinson's former club Oxford United. Cambridge lost the first match at Oxford 1-0, but in the Second Leg at the Abbey Stadium Alan Biley and Stephen Fallon scored the goals which gave the Club a 2-1 aggregate win and a Second Round match at Everton on Monday 30th August. It was Cambridge United's first ever competitive match against a First Division team, but a smaller crowd than expected at Goodison Park of 10,898 saw the Merseysiders show no mercy as they progressed through to the next round with a 3-0 victory.

In the league the Club made a good start by winning three and drawing two of the first five games, to move into the leading pack of clubs. The team was further strengthened with the scoop signing of Tom Finney, the Irish international forward, from Sunderland for £15,000. Prospects for promotion were improved further when the experienced defender, David Stringer, was signed on a free transfer from Norwich City on 29th September 1976.

Ron Atkinson was named the Bells Whisky Fourth Division Manager of the Month for October as the team went eight games without defeat to move to the top of the Fourth Division for the first time.

In the First Round Proper of the F.A. Challenge Cup on Saturday 20th November, the Club were favoured with a home tie against Colchester United, and an epic tussle ended all square at one goal apiece, thanks to an equalizing goal from Stephen Fallon. It was the fourth drawn match in succession. The replay attracted 6,041 spectators, but Colchester made home advantage pay, and won the match 2-0 to emphasize their superiority over Cambridge United in cup competitions.

The Club lost another long-serving member when Vice-Chairman Sam Tanner died following a heart attack, having been a Director for sixteen years. Tony Douglas succeeded him as Vice-Chairman.

Not only were the first team top of their division, but the youth team topped the league table in both the Chiltern Premier and Cambridge & District Sunday Youth Leagues. Following victories over Wisbech, Colchester and Letchworth, the youth team were drawn at home to the strong Ipswich Town youth team in the Second Round Proper of the F.A. Youth Cup, but they lost an exciting game 3-2 after twice equalizing through Floyd Streete and Paul Chapman. Later in the season the youth team gained revenge when they beat Ipswich 1-0 at Portman Road in the Semi-final of the Eastern Junior Cup, thanks to a penalty scored by Floyd Streete. In the Final they could not repeat that fine performance, and lost by 2 goals to 1 against Norwich City.

The first team went off the boil after Christmas, but Ron Atkinson was able to inject some new blood into the forward line with the signing of Jim Hall from Northampton Town, initially on a temporary basis. His presence had the desired effect and on New Year's Day he scored in the 2-1 victory over main rivals Bradford City, before the biggest crowd of the season at the Abbey Stadium of 6,965 spectators, to put United back on top of the table.

On Monday 3rd January 1977, Cambridge United entered the *Guinness Book of Records* when they scored after only six seconds of their match at Torquay. Ian Seddon sent over a high cross for Cambridge, and Torquay's Pat Kruse headed into his own net for the fastest ever Football League own goal.

From mid-February to early April, United won seven consecutive league games, conceding just one goal, to increase their lead at the top of the table to four points, and not surprisingly Ron Atkinson won the Manager of the Month Award for March, his second of the season. In the same month Club captain, Brendon Batson, received a gold medal as winner of the Fourth Division All-Star Award at the Annual Professional Footballer's Association Awards Dinner.

During the Easter period the youth team played abroad in the B.V.O. Osterfeld International Youth Tournament against the youth teams of Dutch and German First Division sides, and they did themselves full credit by winning all four games without conceding a goal, registering the biggest win by 5 goals to 0 against S.G. Osterfeld in the Final. Later in May they also played in the Eindhoven International Youth tournament, where they progressed into the Final before losing 2-1 to P.S.V. Eindhoven. The youth team won five competitions during the season, including the Cambridge & District Sunday Youth League Championship and League Cup, and the Chiltern Premier Youth League Cup.

Tom Finney scored twelve goals in twelve games, including two successive hat-tricks at home, to help the team preserve their lead at the top of the Fourth Division. Promotion was clinched on Tuesday 3rd May following the 3-0 victory over Doncaster Rovers at the Abbey Stadium, with three matches still remaining. Only 3,004 people witnessed the Club clinch the Fourth Division Championship away to Stockport County on Friday 6th May, with the point gained from a goal-less draw. Eight days later 7,795 spectators, the biggest home gate of the season, turned up at the Abbey Stadium to see Cambridge United parade the Championship trophy, but Swansea City spoiled the party by winning 3-2, as they fought desperately to clinch a promotion place. Alan Biley scored a penalty in that game to set a Club goalscoring record since joining the Football League of 19 goals in a season.

A 3-1 victory away to Aldershot in the last game meant that United finished on 65 points, three points ahead of Exeter City in second place. Home attendances were up by about 1,800 on the previous season to 4,437 per game, which was 180 per game up on the previous promotion season four years earlier.

Watford, who missed out on promotion by finishing in seventh place, made an approach to Ron Atkinson to be their manager, but he chose to stay with Cambridge United for their second campaign in the Third Division.

The Cambs Professional Cup was not played for as there had been a financial loss on the previous year's Final. The Cambs F.A. considered inviting Oxford United to play in the competition against Cambridge United, much to the annoyance of Cambridge City, but the idea did not materialize.

The first team's season was concluded with a Testimonial Match for Dave Simmons against Ipswich Town on Tuesday 24th May, as he had to retire from the game at the age of twenty-seven owing to a toe injury. However, the youth team continued their mammoth season until Wednesday 1st June when they won their fifth trophy of the season by beating Ely Crusaders 5-2 at Burwell in the Final of the Cambs F.A. Youth Cup. David Baker scored a hat-trick in the game, and in so doing scored the 300th goal of the season for the youth team.

F.A. Challenge Cup

First Round Proper
Cambridge United 1 1 Colchester United

First Round Proper Replay
Colchester United 2 0 **Cambridge United**

Football League Cup

First Round First Leg
Oxford United 1 0 Cambridge United

First Round Second Leg
Cambridge United 2 0 Oxford United

Second Round
Everton 3 0 Cambridge United

Football League Division Four

	Pld	W	D	L	F	A	Pts
Cambridge United	46	26	13	7	87	40	65
Exeter City	46	25	12	9	70	40	62
Colchester United	46	25	9	12	77	43	59
Bradford City	46	23	13	10	78	51	59
Swansea City	46	25	8	13	92	68	58
Barnsley	46	23	9	14	63	39	55
Watford	46	18	15	13	67	50	51
Doncaster Rovers	46	21	9	16	71	65	51
Huddersfield Town	46	19	12	15	60	49	50
Southend United	46	15	19	12	52	45	49
Darlington	46	18	13	15	59	64	49
Crewe Alexandra	46	19	11	16	47	60	49
Bournemouth	46	15	18	13	50	44	48
Stockport County	46	13	19	14	53	57	45
Brentford	46	18	7	21	77	76	43
Torquay United	46	17	9	20	59	67	43
Aldershot	46	16	11	19	49	59	43
Rochdale	46	13	12	21	50	59	38
Newport County	46	14	10	22	52	58	38
Scunthorpe	46	13	11	22	49	73	37
Halifax Town	46	11	14	21	47	58	36
Hartlepool	46	10	12	24	47	73	32
Southport	46	3	19	24	33	77	25
Workington	46	4	11	31	41	102	19

Shipp Cup

	Pld	W	D	L	F	A	Pts
Sheffield Wednesday	3	3	0	0	9	4	6
Peterborough United	3	2	0	1	5	4	4
Lincoln City	3	0	1	2	2	4	1
Cambridge United	3	0	1	2	3	7	1

Midweek Football League

	Pld	W	D	L	F	A	Pts
Portsmouth Reserves	20	12	2	6	48	29	26
Brighton & Hove Alb. Res.	20	10	3	7	38	26	23
Northampton Town Res.	20	8	7	5	41	37	23
Watford Reserves	20	9	4	7	35	37	22
Charlton Athletic Res.	20	8	5	7	37	24	21
Millwall Reserves	20	7	6	7	30	32	20
Peterborough United Res.	20	6	7	7	29	28	19
Cambridge Utd Res	20	8	2	10	33	39	18
Southend United Res.	20	8	1	11	29	32	17
Brentford Reserves	20	6	4	10	25	37	16
Gillingham Reserves	20	5	5	10	22	36	15

FLORSTOR

CARPET & VINYL CENTRE

3 ADKINS CORNER
PERNE ROAD
CAMBRIDGE
Tel: (0223) 213307

50 Rolls of Carpet } Always in stock
20 Rolls of Vinyl

Various patterns to Choose From

PERSONAL SERVICE
Fittings by Our Own Staff

Midweek Football League Cup Section A

	Pld	W	D	L	F	A	Pts
Watford Reserves	4	2	1	1	8	5	5
Cambridge Utd Res	4	2	0	2	5	4	4
Peterborough United Res.	4	1	1	2	5	9	3

F.A. Youth Challenge Cup

First Qualifying Round
Wisbech Town Youth 2 7 **Cambridge Utd Yth**

Second Qualifying Round
Cambridge Utd Yth 9 1 Colchester United Yth

First Round Proper
Letchworth Gdn Cty Yth 1 6 **Cambridge Utd Yth**

Second Round Proper
Cambridge Utd Yth 2 3 Ipswich Town Youth

Eastern Junior Cup

First Round
Cambridge Utd Yth 9 0 Hertford Town Youth

Second Round
Cambridge Utd Yth 2 2 Hitchin Town Youth

Second Round Replay
Hitchin Town Youth 1 3 **Cambridge Utd Yth**

Semi-final
Ipswich Town Youth 0 1 **Cambridge Utd Yth**

Final
Cambridge Utd Yth 1 2 Norwich City Youth

Cambs F.A. Youth Cup

First Round
Cambridge Utd Yth 7 0 St. Andrew's Youth

Semi-final
Cambridge Utd Yth 4 0 Romsey Town Youth

Final (at Burwell)
Cambridge Utd Yth 5 2 Ely Crusaders Youth

Chiltern Premier League Cup

First Round
Hertford Town Youth 0 4 **Cambridge Utd Yth**

Second Round
Hitchin Town Youth 1 4 **Cambridge Utd Yth**

Semi-final
Luton Town Youth 0 6 **Cambridge Utd Yth**

Final (at Letchworth)
Cambridge Utd Yth 3 0 Hoddesdon Town Youth

Cambs & District Sunday Youth League Cup

First Round
Manorians Youth 0 4 **Cambridge Utd Yth**

Semi-final
St. Andrew's Youth 0 7 **Cambridge Utd Yth**

Final (at Burwell)
Newmarket Valley Youth 3 1 **Cambridge Utd Yth**

Bicentennial Cup

Cambridge City Youthth 1 5 **Cambridge Utd Yth**

B.V.O. Osterfeld International Youth Tournament

Group Matches
Cambridge Utd Yth 4 0 B.W. Fuhlenbeck Youth
Cambridge Utd Yth 1 0 B.V.O. Osterfeld Youth
Cambridge Utd Yth 1 0 Sterkrade Youth

Final
Cambridge Utd Yth 5 0 S.G. Osterfeld Youth

Eindhoven International Youth Tournament

(In Holland)
Cambridge Utd Yth 0 0 E.V.V. Eindhoven Yth
Cambridge Utd Yth 1 0 Berchem Sports Youth
Cambridge Utd Yth 2 0 S.C. Fortuna Sittard Yth

Final
P.S.V. Eindhoven Youth 2 1 **Cambridge Utd Yth**
(After extra-time)

Chiltern Premier League

	Pld	W	D	L	F	A	Pts
Luton Town Youth	20	18	2	0	87	15	38
Cambridge Utd Yth	20	15	2	3	83	25	32
Wealdstone Youth	20	10	5	5	56	39	25
Hertford Town Youth	20	11	3	6	41	36	25
Hitchin Town Youth	20	10	2	8	51	43	22
Harlow Town Youth	20	7	2	11	38	40	16
Hoddesdon Town Youth	20	7	2	11	47	63	16
Letchworth G.C. Youth	20	6	4	10	27	43	16
Cambridge City Youth	20	6	3	11	27	47	15
Vauxhall Motors Youth	20	4	4	12	37	66	12
Stevenage Athletic Youth	20	1	1	18	15	90	3

Cambs & District Sunday Youth League

	Pld	W	D	L	F	A	Pts
Cambridge Utd Yth	18	15	2	1	114	20	32
Newmarket Valley Youth	18	13	2	3	66	27	28
Ely Crusaders Youth	17	13	0	4	87	22	26
Mildenhall Youth	18	6	2	10	48	88	14
Manorians Youth	18	6	1	11	39	73	13
St. Andrew's Youth	17	4	3	10	37	51	11
Papworth Youth	18	0	0	18	9	119	0

1977-78 SEASON

John Docherty was officially appointed as full-time Coach for the start of the season, having previously worked for the Club on a part-time basis in that capacity since September 1976. The Club now had a management team unequalled in experience and quality in the Third Division, giving them hope that the team could at least consolidate their position in the higher sphere of football.

The pre-season Shipp Cup tournament was entered again, and by beating Sheffield Wednesday for their only win in three games, the Club finished as joint runners-up to Huddersfield Town, who won all three games.

In the First Round of the Football League Cup the draw gave Cambridge United the 'plum' of the Round against Brighton and Hove Albion. The team performed heroically to get two 0-0 draws from the two matches, the Second Leg at Brighton attracting the largest crowd ever to watch Cambridge United, 18,281 people. The replay could have been held on a neutral ground, but United elected to play at Brighton a week later on Tuesday 23rd August and the crowd record was broken again when 18,976 people watched Brighton win by 3 goals to 1. The decision to play at Brighton was defended by the fact that the share of the receipts from the matches paid for the transfer fees of Peter Sylvester from the Washington Diplomats and Sammy Morgan from Brighton for £15,000, both of whom added competition for the positions in the forward line.

United lost their first two matches in Division Three, the first being a 4-0 thrashing away to Bradford City, but a run of six games without defeat pushed the team up the league table into a healthier position.

Central defender Lindsay Smith was signed from Colchester United for a bargain £12,000, and he made his debut in the 2-0 home win against his former club on Saturday 22nd October before 5,423 spectators, the best crowd so far that season. That attendance was bettered a week later for the 2-1 home win against Oxford United, but the game was marred by violence from the visiting supporters. This resulted in steel fences being erected at the Abbey Stadium to 'cage-in' visiting and home supporters behind each goal, costing the Club over £4,000.

The youth team were given exemption until the First Round Proper of the F.A. Youth Cup, and they nearly beat Norwich City at the Abbey Stadium, but the "Canaries" saved themselves with a last minute equalizer to make the score 2-2. Paul Chapman scored both of United's goals. In the replay, however, the young United players were overwhelmed by 6 goals to 1. An early exit was also made in the First Round of the Eastern Junior Cup, when the experienced Luton Town youth side won 4-1 at the Abbey Stadium.

Cambridge United's reserve team goalkeeper, Andy Beales, scored a remarkable goal in the 2-1 Midweek League Cup victory over Charlton Athletic on Tuesday 1st November 1977. With his team 1-0 down, Beales sent a tremendous kick from his hands into the Charlton penalty area, where the ball bounced over the stranded opposing goalkeeper and ended up in the net. A second goal from Tommy O'Neill sealed the victory.

In the F.A. Challenge Cup the First Round draw gave United an awkward trip to Eastern Counties League Champions Lowestoft Town on Saturday 26th November, but the part-timers were unable to repeat their shock win ten years earlier. United won 2-0 before 4,000 spectators as Alan Biley scored both goals in his first ever F.A. Cup match at a packed Crown Meadow. Hopes of a good cup run were dissipated in the next round with a 1-0 defeat away to Plymouth Argyle, a team United had beaten earlier in the season by a goal to nil at Home Park.

In December United made a surprise capture when John Cozens was transferred from fellow promotion candidates Peterborough United. Such was the rivalry between the two sides that when they met at the Abbey Stadium for an evening game on Monday 2nd January 1978 the ground was bulging to capacity, and a record crowd of 10,998 saw Alan Biley score the only goal of the game to give United another record of nine consecutive home wins.

Promotion was now a very real possibility, but two weeks later Ron Atkinson was appointed as Manager of West Bromwich Albion, and the chances of Division Two football looked to be severely jeopardized. The team gave Ron Atkinson a champagne send-off with a magnificent 4-1 victory over Bradford City at the Abbey Stadium on Saturday 14th January in his last game in charge of them. The match was the last in a sequence of ten successive home wins, and Alan Biley broke his own record by scoring his 20th goal of the season in that game, although by the end of the season he added only three more to that total.

No immediate successor was appointed to Ron Atkinson, and John Docherty partnered with Paddy Sowden were promoted to take over the joint management of the team until the end of the season. The turbulent period at the Abbey Stadium continued when the Club's Secretary, Colin

Benson, resigned and was replaced by Les Holloway.

For the first time on Saturday 11th February, John Courage Limited donated a trophy to be awarded at each home game to the "Cambridge United Man of the Match". Chairman David Ruston was chosen to select the first winner of the award, and he gave it to John Cozens, scorer in the 3-0 win over Plymouth Argyle. Under the new management team United had an unbeaten run of seven games, which took the Club into second place in the league table by mid-March, although they had played more games than their rivals. Supporters at the Abbey Stadium were encouraged to sing their team to promotion with a song devised by Mark Schofield to the tune of "My Darling Clementine", the words of which appeared in the match programmes.

Injuries to five players out of the eighteen man squad meant that there were seven players under 21 years of age in the 4-1 defeat at Lincoln on Saturday 8th April, but fortunately that proved to be the only defeat in the last nine games. The 'run-in' to the end of the season was incredibly tense, and with one game to go United needed just one point at home to lowly Exeter City to secure promotion. In front of a crowd of 8,741 spectators on Saturday 29th April 1977 United went a goal down, but fought back magnificently to win, and clinched promotion by finishing in the runners-up spot with 58 points from 46 games. The impossible dream had come true, and once again the champagne flowed in Cambridge.

For the first time since the competition's inception, Cambridge City were not invited to play Cambridge United for the Cambs Professional Cup, and the trophy went out of the County when Second Division Luton Town fought back from 2-0 down to level the scores, and then won a sudden-death penalty competition by 5 goals to 4.

The youth team also had another successful season by winning the Cambridge and District Sunday Youth League Cup and finishing second in the League. They lost 6-3 to Histon Youth in the Cambs F.A. Youth Cup Final, and finished third in the Chiltern Premier Youth League. In addition they failed to retain the B.V.O. International Youth Tournament trophy in Osterfeld, winning three games then losing 3-0 to N.A.C. Breda in the Final.

F.A. Challenge Cup

First Round Proper
Lowestoft Town 0 2 **Cambridge United**

Second Round Proper
Plymouth Argyle 1 0 **Cambridge United**

Football League Cup

First Round First Leg
Cambridge United 0 0 Brighton & Hove Alb.

First Round Second Leg
Brighton & Hove Alb. 0 0 **Cambridge United**

First Round Replay
Brighton & Hove Albion 3 1 **Cambridge United**

Cambs Professional Cup

Final
Cambridge United 2 2 Luton Town
(Luton won 5-4 on penalties)

Football League Division Three

	Pld	W	D	L	F	A	Pts
Wrexham	46	23	15	8	78	45	61
Cambridge United	46	23	12	11	72	51	58
Preston North End	46	20	16	10	63	38	56
Peterborough United	46	20	16	10	47	33	56
Chester	46	16	22	8	59	56	54
Walsall	46	18	17	11	61	50	53
Gillingham	46	15	20	11	66	59	50
Colchester United	46	15	18	13	55	44	48
Chesterfield	46	17	14	15	58	49	48
Swindon Town	46	16	16	14	67	60	48
Shrewsbury Town	46	16	15	15	63	57	47
Tranmere Rovers	46	16	15	15	57	52	47
Carlisle United	46	14	19	13	59	59	47
Sheffield Wednesday	46	15	16	15	50	52	46
Bury	46	13	19	14	62	56	45
Lincoln City	46	15	15	16	53	59	45
Exeter City	46	15	14	17	49	59	44
Oxford United	46	13	14	19	64	67	40
Plymouth Argyle	46	11	17	18	61	68	39
Rotherham United	46	13	13	20	51	68	39
Port Vale	46	8	20	18	46	67	36
Bradford City	46	12	10	24	56	87	34
Hereford United	46	9	14	23	34	60	32
Portsmouth	46	7	17	22	41	75	31

Shipp Cup

	Pld	W	D	L	F	A	Pts
Huddersfield Town	3	3	0	0	8	1	6
Cambridge United	3	1	0	2	4	5	2
Sheffield Wednesday	3	1	0	2	4	5	2
Peterborough United	3	1	0	2	3	8	2

Midweek Football League

	Pld	W	D	L	F	A	Pts
Brighton & Hove Alb. Res.	22	14	3	5	44	27	31
Peterborough United Res.	22	10	6	6	45	29	26
Brentford Reserves	22	10	5	7	45	35	25
Charlton Athletic Res.	22	11	3	8	45	41	25
Millwall Reserves	22	11	3	8	38	42	25
Gillingham Reserves	22	9	4	9	39	50	22
Cambridge Utd Res	22	9	6	7	39	28	21
Wimbledon Reserves	22	8	5	9	35	37	21
Portsmouth Reserves	22	7	5	10	36	36	19
Southend United Reserves	22	7	4	11	24	37	18
Watford Reserves	22	6	5	11	25	36	17
Northampton Town Res.	22	4	3	15	23	41	11

Cambridge United Reserves deducted 3 points for playing an unregistered player.

Midweek Football League Cup
Group C

	Pld	W	D	L	F	A	Pts
Charlton Athletic Reserves	4	2	1	1	10	3	5
Southend United Reserves	4	1	2	1	4	5	4
Cambridge Utd Res	4	1	1	2	4	10	1

Cambridge United Reserves deducted 2 points for playing an unregistered player.

F.A. Youth Challenge Cup

First Round Proper
Cambridge Utd Yth 2 2 Norwich City Youth

First Round Proper Replay
Norwich City Youth 6 1 **Cambridge Utd Yth**

Eastern Junior Cup

First Round
Cambridge Utd Yth 1 4 Luton Town Youth

Cambs F.A. Youth Cup

First Round Bye

Semi-final
Soham Town Rngrs Yth 1 6 **Cambridge Utd Yth**

Final (at Burwell)
Histon Youth 6 3 **Cambridge Utd Yth**

**Saturday 29th April 1978. Football League Division Three.
Cambridge United 2, Exeter City 1.**

Before their last game of the season Cambridge United knew that they had to win to make sure of promotion to the Second Division, but after 64 minutes Keith Bowker caused an upset when he put Exeter ahead. However, Tom Finney fired home an equalizer from a corner, and in the picture above Stephen Fallon clinched promotion with another goal from a John Cozens' corner when he climbed above Exeter defender Jimmy Giles to head Cambridge United's match winning goal.
Photograph by courtesy of *Cambridge Evening News*.

Chiltern Premier League Cup

First Round
Cheshunt Youth 1 3 **Cambridge Utd Yth**

Second Round
Cambridge Utd Yth 3 1 Harlow Town Youth

Semi-final
Cambridge Utd Yth 2 5 **Luton Town Youth**

Cambs & District Sunday Youth League Cup

First Round First Leg
Cambridge Utd Yth 10 2 Soham Town Rngrs Yth

First Round Second Leg
Soham Town Rngrs Yth 0 6 **Cambridge Utd Yth**

Semi-final First Leg
Newmarket Valley Youth 1 2 **Cambridge Utd Yth**

Semi-final Second Leg
Cambridge Utd Yth 3 1 Newmarket Valley Yth

Final (at Porson Road)
Cambridge Utd Yth 2 0 Ely Crusaders Youth

Chiltern Premier League

	Pld	W	D	L	F	A	Pts
Luton Town Youth	22	19	3	0	94	13	41
Bedford Town Youth	22	14	3	5	52	38	31
Cambridge Utd Yth	21	13	2	6	54	39	28
Letchworth Gdn City Yth	22	12	3	7	56	42	27
Barnet Youth	21	10	3	8	51	48	25
Harlow Town Youth	22	9	6	7	46	41	24
Cambridge City Youth	22	7	5	10	27	37	19
Ware Youth	22	9	1	12	43	59	19
Hertford Town Youth	22	6	5	11	35	50	17
Cheshunt Youth	22	6	3	13	40	53	13
Stevenage Borough Youth	22	4	4	14	38	70	12
Vauxhall Motors Youth	22	2	2	18	22	74	8

Barnet Youth awarded two points.
Vauxhall Motors Youth awarded two points.
Cheshunt Youth deducted two points.

Cambs & District Sunday Youth League

	Pld	W	D	L	F	A	Pts
Ely Crusaders Youth	12	9	2	1	63	16	20
Cambridge Utd Yth	12	8	2	2	44	10	18
Histon Youth	11	8	0	3	70	11	16
Newmarket Valley Youth	11	7	1	3	41	14	15
Cambridge Hornets Youth	12	4	1	7	33	51	9
Soham Town Rngrs Youth	12	2	0	10	15	53	4
Histon Imps Youth	12	0	0	12	12	123	0

B.V.O. Osterfeld International Youth Tournament

First Round Group Matches
Cambridge Utd Yth 7 0 Eintracht Duisburg Yth
Cambridge Utd Yth 1 0 S.G.O. Osterfeld Youth
Cambridge Utd Yth 2 0 V.S.B. Speldorf Youth

Final
N.A.C. Breda Youth 3 0 Cambridge Utd Yth

1978-79 SEASON

In preparation for life in the Second Division permanent new seats were constructed on the concourse in front of the Main Stand, considerably increasing the seating capacity. The seats were soon put to good use in the Willhire Cup, a pre-season tournament for East Anglian clubs, which proved to be very popular. All three of Cambridge United's matches were at home, attracting nearly 9,000 people in total, and the Club were able to beat Colchester United 2-1, although they lost 3-1 to both Norwich City and the eventual winners of the trophy, Ipswich Town.

The season officially started on Saturday 12th August 1978 but only 4,102 turned up at the Abbey Stadium for the First Round First Leg of the Football League Cup against Northampton Town, which resulted in a 2-2 draw. Defeat by 2 goals to 1 in the Second Leg ended hopes of a financially profitable cup run, and meant that once more the Club had failed to make its mark on the competition.

The Club's debut in the Second Division was a home match against Stoke City on Saturday 19th August which attracted 7,485 spectators. A tough match was anticipated, and so it turned out as Stoke took the points with a narrow 1-0 victory, but the stirring display by the Cambridge United players resulted in the supporters giving the team a standing ovation at the end of the game.

During the summer John Docherty had been appointed as Manager, with Paddy Sowden as his assistant, and they must have been pleased with the five star performance at Brighton the following Tuesday. A spectacular Floyd Streete header and an own goal silenced the 21,527 people in the crowd at the Goldstone Ground, to give Cambridge United a 2-0 win before the largest crowd ever to see them play. Five draws and a win in the next seven league games ensured that United were going to try and enjoy life in the Second Division and confounded fears that they would make an early return to the Third Division.

A home defeat by a goal to nil against bottom of the table Blackburn Rovers at the end of October prompted the Club to sign Derrick Christie from Northampton Town for a Club record fee of £50,000. Another forward, Bill Garner, was signed shortly afterwards from Chelsea, and United responded with a much needed 3-1 win over Orient, followed by their best Football League result up to that time, a 3-1 away win against Second Division leaders Stoke City before more than 19,000 spectators.

The youth team were withdrawn from the Cambridge & District Sunday Youth League before the start of the season, although a team was still entered in the Town & Country League (formerly Eastern Counties League) in addition to the Midweek Football League. This ambitious programme meant that over sixty games would have to be played at the Abbey Stadium throughout the season. Most of the youth team games were played at the *Cambridge Evening News* ground in Porson Road, although the F.A. Youth Cup First Round Proper match against Norwich City Youth was played at the Abbey Stadium, and resulted in a 3-1 win for the visitors. A week later the youth team had an opportunity for revenge when they travelled to Norwich for a First Round match in the Eastern Junior Cup, but the young "Canaries" won again by scoring the only goal of the match. For much of the season the youth team performed well in the Chiltern Premier League, at one time heading the table after Christmas, but a slump at the end of the season saw them slip to fourth place, although they recovered to win the Cambs F.A. Youth Cup by beating Manorians in the Final.

Unfortunately for Cambridge United fans, the trip to the historic Newcastle United ground was in midweek, which meant that only a few were able to be present in the crowd of over 20,000 which saw Newcastle win 1-0. There was a similar crowd of 21,379 people for the next away game against West Ham at Upton Park which the classy "Hammers" won by 5 goals to 0. For the third away match running a crowd of over 20,000 saw Cambridge United win 2-0 against Sunderland with Derrick Christie scoring both goals against the promotion contenders. Alan Biley scored a goal in the disappointing 3-1 defeat at Shrewsbury in the F.A. Challenge Cup Third Round Proper, a week before scoring a hat-trick in the 5-0 home win against Cardiff City on Saturday 13th January 1979 to take his total of league goals for the season to 18, one behind the Second Division's leading goalscorer, "Pop" Robson of West Ham United. The team then spent a short break in Benidorm as bad weather disrupted the fixtures for almost two months.

At a time when the Club were starting to establish themselves in the Second Division, there was something of a shock when the Assistant Manager, Paddy Sowden, resigned by mutual consent with the Board of Directors at the end of January, after having spent four successful years with the Club. However, no immediate successor was appointed, particularly as the experienced Ron Howard had joined the backroom staff as Chief Scout in the Autumn.

In February apprentice player Roger Avery, on his 18th birthday, became the first Cambridge born player to become a full professional with the Club since it joined the Football League.

The first team held a mid-table position largely due to a four month unbeaten home run which came to an end on 10th March with a 1-0 defeat against Notts County. West Ham United's visit on Saturday 7th April was keenly awaited, and the decision was taken to make it the Club's first ever 'all-ticket' match. The 'sell-out' crowd of 11,406, a new home record league attendance, watched United gain a creditable point in a goal-less draw.

Three days later United played another London side chasing promotion - Crystal Palace - and the record crowd watching them play was broken again when 21,795 spectators saw them gain another away point at Selhurst Park with Steve Spriggs scoring the goal in a 1-1 draw.

In the last game of the season Cambridge United sent Sheffield United down to the Third Division with a 1-0 win at the Abbey Stadium on Saturday 5th May. Over 7,000 spectators saw Steve Spriggs get the only goal of the match, but after the game over 500 supporters stayed for over half an hour to cheer their team, although amazingly they were from Sheffield and not from Cambridge!

The bad weather seriously affected the heavy reserve team programme, and they had to play 26 games in the last 52 days of the season, at one time playing 9 games in 11 days. Having to call upon a large number of youth team players in order to fulfil their fixtures, they did well to finish just below half-way in both the Midweek League and the Town & Country League. A special effort was made to win the Town & Country League Cup, and this the reserves did by beating Gorleston 2-1 in each leg of the Final. Understandably the decision was taken to withdraw from the Town & Country League at the end of the season.

F.A. Challenge Cup

Third Round Proper
Shrewsbury Town 3 1 **Cambridge United**

Football League Cup

First Round First Leg
Cambridge United 2 2 Northampton Town

First Round Second Leg
Northampton Town 2 1 **Cambridge United**
(Northampton Town won 4-3 on aggregate)

Football League Division Two

	Pld	W	D	L	F	A	Pts
Crystal Palace	42	19	19	4	51	24	57
Brighton & Hove Albion	42	23	10	9	72	39	56
Stoke City	42	20	16	6	58	31	56
Sunderland	42	22	11	9	70	44	55
West Ham United	42	18	14	10	70	39	50
Notts County	42	14	16	12	48	60	44
Newcastle United	42	17	8	17	51	55	42
Cardiff City	42	16	10	16	56	70	42
Preston North End	42	12	18	12	59	57	42
Fulham	42	13	15	14	50	47	41
Orient	42	15	10	17	51	51	40
Cambridge United	42	12	16	14	44	52	40
Burnley	42	14	12	16	51	62	40
Oldham Athletic	42	13	13	16	52	61	39
Wrexham	42	12	14	16	45	42	38
Bristol Rovers	42	14	10	18	48	60	38
Leicester City	42	10	17	15	43	52	37
Luton Town	42	13	10	19	60	57	36
Charlton Athletic	42	11	13	18	60	69	35
Sheffield United	42	11	12	19	52	69	34
Millwall	42	11	10	21	42	61	32
Blackburn Rovers	42	10	10	22	41	72	30

Willhire Cup

	Pld	W	D	L	F	A	Pts
Ipswich Town	3	2	1	0	5	2	5
Norwich City	3	2	0	1	6	4	4
Cambridge United	3	1	0	2	4	7	2
Colchester United	3	0	1	2	2	4	1

Town & Country (Eastern Counties) League Cup

First Round
Cambridge Utd Res 4 0 Histon

Second Round
Braintree & Crittall Ath. 1 4 **Cambridge Utd Res**

Third Round
Wisbech Town 0 0 **Cambridge Utd Res**

Third Round Replay
Cambridge Utd Res 3 2 Wisbech Town

Semi-final
Cambridge Utd Res 5 1 Soham Town Rangers

Final First Leg
Gorleston Town 1 2 **Cambridge Utd Res**

Final Second Leg
Cambridge Utd Res 2 1 Gorleston Town
(Cambridge United Reserves won 4-2 on aggregate)

Town & Country (Eastern Counties) League

	Pld	W	D	L	F	A	Pts
Haverhill Rovers	42	29	9	4	90	36	67
Great Yarmouth Town	42	28	10	4	112	44	66
Lowestoft Town	42	24	15	3	89	40	63
Bury Town	42	27	7	8	99	56	61
Sudbury Town	42	19	11	12	78	50	49
Ely City	42	18	11	13	50	57	47
Gorleston Town	42	21	4	17	74	67	46
Braintree & Crittall Ath.	42	18	9	15	78	72	45
Wisbech Town	42	17	11	14	68	69	45
Brantham Athletic	42	16	11	15	62	61	43
March Town United	42	16	9	17	65	69	41
Cambridge United Res	42	16	9	17	58	67	41
Soham Town Rangers	42	18	4	20	70	74	40
Thetford Town	42	14	9	19	73	78	37
Histon	42	15	6	21	61	73	36
Saffron Walden Town	42	13	9	20	64	68	35
Felixstowe Town	42	11	10	21	43	64	32
Colchester United Reserves	42	11	8	23	54	78	30
Stowmarket Town	42	10	9	23	62	84	29
Clacton Town	42	8	13	21	38	62	29
Chatteris Town	42	10	7	25	80	120	27
Newmarket Town	42	5	4	33	34	107	14

Midweek Football League

	Pld	W	D	L	F	A	Pts
Peterborough United Res.	22	13	6	3	37	21	32
Southend United Res.	22	13	5	4	45	20	31
Brighton & Hove Alb. Res	22	13	4	5	42	26	30
Charlton Athletic Res.	22	7	9	6	33	30	23
Watford Res.	22	8	6	8	30	29	22
Northampton Town Res.	22	9	3	10	36	30	21
Wimbledon Res.	22	9	2	11	29	42	20
Cambridge Utd Res	22	6	7	9	27	41	19
Brentford Res.	22	8	2	12	34	40	18
Gillingham Res.	22	6	6	10	23	31	18
Millwall Res.	22	5	5	12	27	33	15
Portsmouth Res.	22	7	1	14	30	51	15

Midweek Football League Cup Section 'D'

	Pld	W	D	L	F	A	Pts
Southend United Res.	4	4	0	0	13	4	8
Watford Reserves	4	1	1	2	8	9	3
Cambridge Utd Res	4	0	1	3	4	12	1

F.A. Youth Challenge Cup

First Round Proper
Cambridge Utd Yth 1 3 Norwich City Youth

Eastern Junior Cup
First Round
Norwich City Youth   1   0   **Cambridge Utd Yth**

Chiltern Premier Football League Cup
First Round   Bye

Second Round
Corby Town Youth   4   0   **Cambridge Utd Yth**

Cambs F.A. Youth Cup
Semi-final
Histon Youth   Walkover   **Cambridge Utd Yth**

Final (at Burwell)
Cambridge Utd Yth   4   0   Manorians Youth

Chiltern Premier Football League

	Pld	W	D	L	F	A	Pts
Luton Town Youth	20	13	6	1	53	13	32
Corby Town Youth	18	12	3	3	52	18	27
Bedford Town Youth	20	10	5	5	56	39	25
Cambridge Utd Yth	20	10	4	6	50	34	24
Letchworth G.C. Youth	20	10	2	8	45	32	22
Stevenage Borough Youth	20	10	2	8	32	37	22
Harlow Town Youth	18	7	3	8	43	47	17
Hitchin Town Youth	18	7	3	8	35	46	17
Ware Youth	20	5	3	12	36	51	13
Vauxhall Motors Youth	20	5	3	12	24	42	13
Rolenmil Youth	20	0	2	18	14	81	2

1979-80 SEASON

The pre-season programme was a heavy one, as the Club entered the Anglo-Scottish Cup as well as participating in the Willhire Cup, both of which involved three matches each in group matches. Two wins and two draws from the six matches saw United finish in second place in both of the four team groups. Sheffield United topped the Anglo-Scottish Cup group and Ipswich Town won the Willhire Cup by a point. A 2-0 home victory over Norwich City on Saturday 28th July was the most notable result of the pre-season matches.

The league programme started with three successive drawn matches, but defeat was tasted for the first time in the Second Round of the Football League Cup, away to Brighton & Hove Albion on Tuesday 28th August. United were unable to match the performance of two seasons earlier in the same competition, and lost 2-0 in the First Leg in front of a crowd of 15,193 people. The Second Leg at the Abbey Stadium attracted less than 5,000 spectators, and United lost the match 2-1.

A new bridge costing £4,000 in the Coldham's Common corner of the ground was completed for the visit of Chelsea on Saturday 29th September.

1978-79 Season
Back Row: Ian Buckley, Jamie Murray, John Clarke, Alan Biley, Derrick Christie, Steve Adams, Trevor Howard, Graham Watson, Tom Finney.
Middle Row: Peter Melville (Physiotherapist), Sammy Morgan, Floyd Streete, Richard Key, Stephen Fallon, Lindsay Smith, Malcolm Webster, Peter Sylvester, David Stringer, Peter Reeve (Youth Team Coach).
Front Row: Ron Howard (Chief Scout), Steve Spriggs, Peter Graham, John Cozens, John Docherty (Manager), Gordon Sweetzer, Tommy O'Neill, Roger Avery, Paddy Sowden (Assistant Manager).

The match resulted in a 1-0 defeat for United. Despite the recent signing of Chris Turner to strengthen the defence, that match was the first of three successive odd-goal defeats, the first time that had happened since John Docherty's arrival at the Club. Alan Biley, the Club's most prolific goalscorer since joining the Football League, was dropped for "not having his heart in the Club", although he was reinstated in the team after a week.

Two trips to the North-East both saw United's all-time attendance record broken, although both games ended in a 2-0 defeat. At Sunderland on Saturday 8th September, 22,898 turned up at Roker Park to see Cambridge fail to repeat their success of the previous season. Then at St. James' Park, Newcastle, on Saturday 27th October, 24,092 people witnessed the "Geordies" taking maximum points.

At the beginning of November, Cambridge United paid £140,000 for George Reilly, a tall centre-forward from Northampton Town, which not only smashed the Club's transfer record, but was a record fee for a Fourth Division player. His presence was much needed as the Club had slipped into the relegation zone, and he scored after four minutes of his home debut in the 2-0 win over Wrexham on the 17th November, which ended a sequence of nine games without a win.

Cambridge United's bad run of results had coincided with the Club's new flag being flown over the Supporters Club. Chief Scout Ron Howard suggested to the Secretary Les Holloway that the flag should be taken down for a change of luck, but before they could do so it disappeared one night later to be found in a Cambridge pub. By that time United had won for the first time in two months.

A quite sensational match took place at Burnley on 24th November when two United players, Derrick Christie and Jim Calderwood, were sent off in the first half, and a further five United players had their names taken. The scores were level at two goals each by the interval, and allowing for the setback the remaining nine players performed heroically to hold the score to 3-3 until the 87th minute when Burnley scored two late goals to snatch both points. A week later the team produced another outstanding performance when they beat Queen's Park Rangers 2-1 at the Abbey Stadium to knock them off the top of the Second Division.

It came as quite a surprise in November when the Chairman, David Ruston, announced that the Club had made a record profit of more than £100,000 in the previous financial year, even though the average home crowds were less than 7,000 in the Second Division. A month later work started on clearing the "Black and Amber" Shop and Police Box in preparation for the £210,000 extension of the Main Grandstand, which would create an extra 1,600 seats. The progress of the work was to depend on the Club's finances, as the Board of Directors considered that the retention of Division Two status was the top priority.

In the F.A. Challenge Cup the Club were exempt until the Third Round Proper and they were given an excellent opportunity of reaching the Fourth Round for the first time when they were dawn away to Isthmian League Division One side Chesham United on Saturday 5th January. Cambridge United were effectively five divisions higher than their non-league opponents, on a hiding-to-nothing, but before a capacity 5,000 crowd, and on a very muddy pitch, they eventually overcame their spirited opponents to score two second half goals from Roger Gibbins and George Reilly to win 2-0.

Cup fever gripped the city when the draw for the Fourth Round gave Cambridge United a home tie against Aston Villa on 26th January, making them the first Division One team to play at the Abbey Stadium in an F.A. Cup match. The clamour for tickets guaranteed a capacity 12,000 crowd and set a record for gate receipts of £21,985. Amid the excitement Derby County made a £450,000 bid for Alan Biley, who was striking up a formidable partnership with George Reilly, but the offer was too good to refuse, and was accepted by the Board.

United therefore went into the big match without their leading goalscorer, but after Aston Villa took the lead in the 16th minute, Chris Turner headed an equalizer in the 34th minute, and the classy Villa team then had to draw on all their reserves to withstand tremendous second half pressure from United to hang on for a 1-1 draw. The replay four days later created just as much interest, and thousands journeyed from Cambridge to Villa Park to boost the massive crowd to 36,835 spectators, a new record for Cambridge United. Steve Spriggs gave the United supporters hope that they could spring a surprise when he scored a 14th minute equalizer but Villa hit back to take the lead by half-time, and eventually won comfortably by 4 goals to 1. Never the less it was a great day for the supporters, and one of the most memorable landmarks in the history of the Club.

From the proceeds of the cup run, Manager John Docherty was able to buy David Donaldson from Millwall for £50,000. Thereafter the team extended their unbeaten league run to nine game before losing 2-0 away to Orient.

A fund raising committee calling itself "Abbey Action" was formed, consisting mainly of Vice-President Club members, with the intention of raising money for various items of equipment for the Club. Work also started on the construction of the new grandstand extension, and the Club were lucky to beat the steel strike, so that the erection of steelwork was able to take place before the end of the season.

On Saturday 22nd March promotion contenders Birmingham City were beaten 2-1 at the Abbey Stadium, thus extending the Club's unbeaten home run to eleven matches. The match also marked Stephen Fallon's 200th appearance, for which he received a presentation gift to mark the occasion.

A good run-in to the end of the season saw Cambridge United move into a final place of eighth, with 44 points from 42 games, but the average home league attendance of 6,126 spectators per game was disappointing.

The youth team joined the South East Counties League Division Two for under 17s at the start of the season, and performed very well by picking up 22 points from 22 games in a strong competition. They made early exits in their cup competitions, however, losing 3-1 at home twice to Colchester United's youth team at the first stage in the F.A. Youth Cup and Southern Junior Floodlit Cup.

Ron Atkinson returned to the Abbey Stadium on Monday 21st April when he brought his West Bromwich Albion team over for a Testimonial Match on behalf of Terry Eades, who had made a Club record 248 Football League appearances. Before 3,660 spectators West Bromwich Albion won 2-1 with goals from Peter Barnes and John Trewick, Lindsay Smith replying for United.

F.A. Challenge Cup

Third Round Proper
Chesham United 0 2 **Cambridge United**

Fourth Round Proper
Cambridge United 1 1 Aston Villa

Fourth Round Proper Replay
Aston Villa 4 1 **Cambridge United**

Football League Cup

Second Round First Leg
Brighton & Hove Alb. 2 0 **Cambridge United**

Second Round Second Leg
Cambridge United 1 2 Brighton & Hove Alb.
(Brighton won 4-1 on aggregate)

Football League Division Two

	Pld	W	D	L	F	A	Pts
Leicester City	42	21	13	8	58	38	55
Sunderland	42	21	12	9	69	42	54
Birmingham City	42	21	11	10	58	38	53
Chelsea	42	23	7	12	66	52	53
Queen's Park Rangers	42	18	13	11	75	53	49
Luton Town	42	16	17	9	66	45	49
West Ham United	42	20	7	15	54	43	47
Cambridge United	42	14	16	12	61	53	44
Newcastle United	42	15	14	13	53	49	44
Preston North End	42	12	19	11	56	52	43
Oldham Athletic	42	16	11	15	49	53	43
Swansea City	42	17	9	16	48	53	43
Shrewsbury Town	42	18	5	19	60	53	41
Orient	42	12	17	13	48	54	41
Cardiff City	42	16	8	18	41	48	40
Wrexham	42	16	6	20	40	49	38
Notts County	42	11	15	16	51	52	37
Watford	42	12	13	17	39	46	37
Bristol Rovers	42	11	13	18	50	64	35
Fulham	42	11	7	24	42	74	29
Burnley	42	6	15	21	39	73	27
Charlton Athletic	42	6	10	26	39	78	22

Willhire Cup

	Pld	W	D	L	F	A	Pts
Ipswich Town	3	2	0	1	4	3	4
Cambridge United	3	1	1	1	4	3	3
Norwich City	3	1	1	1	4	4	3
Colchester United	3	0	2	1	3	5	2

Anglo Scottish Cup

	Pld	W	D	L	F	A	Pts
Sheffield United	3	3	0	0	3	0	6
Cambridge United	3	1	1	1	4	3	4
Notts County	3	1	0	2	2	4	2
Mansfield Town	3	0	1	2	1	3	1

Midweek League Cup

First Round
Millwall Reserves 1 2 **Cambridge Utd Res**

Second Round
Cambridge Utd Res 0 1 Peterborough Utd Res.

Midweek Football League

	Pld	W	D	L	F	A	Pts
Watford Res.	24	16	6	2	63	25	38
Charlton Athletic Res.	24	14	5	5	59	41	33
Southend United Res.	24	14	5	5	53	38	33
Wimbledon Res.	24	10	8	6	44	37	28
Portsmouth Res.	24	9	6	9	39	35	24
Peterborough United Res.	24	9	5	10	42	37	23
Gillingham Res.	24	9	5	10	46	45	23
Millwall Res.	24	9	4	11	34	39	22
Northampton Town Res.	24	9	3	12	30	44	21
Brighton & Hove Alb. Res.	24	8	5	11	40	55	21
Cambridge Utd Res	24	6	5	13	31	49	17
Aldershot Res.	24	6	4	14	41	52	16
Brentford Res.	24	3	7	14	27	51	13

F.A. Youth Challenge Cup

Preliminary Round
Cambridge Utd Yth   1   3   Colchester Utd Youth

Southern Junior Floodlit Cup

First Round
Cambridge Utd Yth   1   3   Colchester Utd Youth

Eastern Junior Cup

First Round\
Corby Town Youth   1   3   **Cambridge Utd Yth**

Eastern Junior Cup (Cont)

Second Round
Ipswich Town Youth   1   0   Cambridge Utd Yth

South East Counties League Division Two

	Pld	W	D	L	F	A	Pts
Swindon Town Youth	22	16	2	4	52	18	34
Wimbledon Youth	22	13	4	5	56	28	30
Reading Youth	22	11	2	9	41	32	24
Tottenham Hotspurs Yth	22	9	6	7	43	39	24
Crystal Palace Youth	22	9	6	7	35	38	24
Oxford United Youth	22	11	2	9	46	51	24
West Ham United Youth	22	9	5	8	47	37	23
Cambridge Utd Yth	22	8	6	8	44	39	22
Peterborough United Yth	22	7	3	12	42	50	17
Bristol Rovers Youth	22	6	4	12	30	50	16
Chelsea Youth	22	3	8	11	28	47	14
Charlton Athletic Youth	22	5	2	15	36	71	14

South East Counties League Cup. Division Two Group C

	Pld	W	D	L	F	A	Pts
Tottenham Hotspur Youth	4	3	1	0	13	6	7
Cambridge Utd Yth	4	1	1	2	7	6	3
Peterborough United Youth	4	1	0	3	7	15	2

1979-80 Season
Back Row: Jamie Murray, Ian Buckley, Mel Brown, Tom Finney, Peter Graham, Nigel Smith.
Middle Row: John Clarke, Stephen Fallon, Lindsay Smith, Richard Key, John Cozens, Malcolm Webster, Floyd Streete, Bill Garner, Roger Avery.
Front Row: Derrick Christie, Tommy O'Neill, Gordon Sweetzer, Alan Biley, David Stringer, Steve Spriggs. Photograph by courtesy of Ray Clarke.

**Wednesday 30th January 1980. F.A. Challenge Cup Fourth Round Proper Replay.
Aston Villa 4   Cambridge United 1**

Cambridge United Captain Steve Spriggs darts behind the Aston Villa defence and goes airborne as he shoots left-footed past Jimmy Rimmer to score a 14th minute equalizer, to cancel out an early Villa goal. The crowd of 36,835 spectators was the largest to watch Cambridge United play, and the occasion proved to be too much for them as the famous Birmingham club eased to a 4-1 victory. Photograph by courtesy of *Cambridge Evening News*.

Air pollution control

We design, manufacture and install a complete range of systems and equipment for the extraction of dust and fumes at source. **We'll help you clean up!**

- AXIAL FLOW FANS
- SPRAY BOOTHS
- CENTRIFUGAL FANS
- WOODWASTE UNITS

BARJEK

J.E.K. Barnes Engineering Ltd., High Street, Fowlmere, Nr. Royston, Herts SG8 7SR. Tel: 0763 82 350/645 Telex: 817335

Target Litho

Lithographic Printers Unit A 299 High Street Cottenham Cambridge CB4 4TX

Superb printing at competitive prices

Four Colour Leaflets – Business Stationery – Instruction Manuals – Workshop Manuals – Brochures – Programmes – News Sheets – Price Lists

**Telephone:
Cottenham
(0954)
51189**

Please contact us for your printing needs

Chapter Eight

THE EIGHTIES

1980-81 SEASON

During the close-season Abbey Action held their "Family Fun Day" at the Abbey Stadium, in which the first "Miss Cambridge United" Gillian Theobold was chosen. The event was a big success and attracted over 4,000 people. Work on the Main Grandstand was almost complete by the start of the season, causing some minor inconveniences for the first few games of the season.

The Willhire Cup was entered again, and following 1-0 wins over Ipswich Town and Colchester United, the Club finished as runners-up to Norwich City, level on points but with an inferior goal average. The Final of the Cambs Professional Cup was also held pre-season on Wednesday 6th August, but a very poor crowd of only 896 people turned up at the Abbey Stadium to see Peterborough United beat Cambridge United by 4 goals to 2.

The 3-0 home win against Derby County on 16th August was the Club's best opening day result since joining the Football League, and temporarily put Cambridge United top of the table. The attendance of 9,558 was better than any home league game during the previous season, and helped fill the new stand.

Another good crowd saw United record their first ever win over a First Division team when they beat Wolverhampton Wanderers 3-1 at home in the Football League Cup Second Round First Leg at the Abbey Stadium on Tuesday 26th August with two goals from George Reilly and one from Tom Finney. A week later Cambridge United travelled to Molineux, and not only preserved their two goal advantage, but increased it when a Floyd Streete goal gave them a shock 1-0 win. They thereby earned a place in the Third Round for the first time, at home to Aston Villa, the team that were to become the First Division Champions at the end of the season.

The excitement of the Cup caused United to lose their three preceding league matches, and they seemed to be heading the same way in the match against Aston Villa when England international Tony Morley gave the visitors the lead in the 6th minute. Tom Finney quickly headed United level, and Steve Spriggs delighted the home contingent of the 7,608 crowd when he scored the winning goal for United with a superb 30 yard shot into the corner of the net after 18 minutes.

The team underwent several changes with John Lyons signed from Millwall for 100,000, followed by the signing of another forward, Alan Taylor, who had made a name for himself by scoring both goals for West Ham United in the 1975 F.A. Cup Final at Wembley. The loss of David Stringer, who returned to Norwich City to look after the youth team, was solved by the re-signing of Chris Turner after an eight month break in America. The team was altered further when Malcolm Webster was injured and had to be replaced by reserve goalkeeper Richard Key, but the team were able to string together four consecutive wins to lift them into the upper half of the table.

Alan Taylor was eligible for the Fourth Round League Cup match at Coventry, and he scored United's only goal in a 1-1 draw on his debut to earn a replay at the Abbey Stadium a week later on Tuesday 4th November. There was a big following of Cambridge United supporters amongst the 17,076 crowd to witness their team's marvellous display, and they must have been confident of victory in the return, but the 'Sky Blues' raised their game and won 1-0 to end United's best cup run since joining the Football League. However, the home supporters were left to ponder what might have happened had Steve Spriggs not missed a crucial penalty during the game.

In between the two cup matches with Coventry, the Club suffered a heavy Football League defeat when they went down by 6 goals to 1 away to Bolton Wanderers, but generally inconsistent form kept the team in a mid-table position in the league.

The youth team, which was being run by John Cozens, were having an improved season in the South East Counties League Junior Section, and eventually finished in third place. In the F.A. Youth Cup they overcame Tring Town (4-3), Northampton Town (3-2) and Corby Town (3-1) in the Qualifying Rounds, before losing 2-1 at home to Orient in the First Round Proper, a good achievement for a team consisting of under 17 year olds in an under 18 competition.

There was much delight when the first team were drawn away to Norwich City in the Third Round Proper of the F.A. Challenge Cup on Saturday 3rd January 1981, giving Cambridge United an excellent opportunity to justify their recently adopted title "The Pride of East Anglia". A crowd of 18,420 spectators saw United produce a good first half performance, but Norwich stole the honours with a narrow 1-0 victory.

A 3-1 home win against second in the table Swansea City, two weeks later, confirmed the belief that the Club could gain promotion after going five league games without a defeat, but the following Saturday Sheffield Wednesday won 2-0 at the Abbey Stadium to bring the United supporters back to earth. That game marked the opening of the new Sponsors' Lounge under the grandstand extension, which was inaugurated by Pye's Limited, and was such a success that they promised to sponsor another game.

On Saturday 21st February the Club played league leaders West Ham United before the biggest league crowd in their history, 36,002 spectators, at Upton Park, and although Steve Spriggs and George Reilly scored for United, the Hammers extended their lead at the top with a 4-2 victory.

A long list of injuries contributed to a dismal run which saw Cambridge United drop into the lower half of the table. In fact six of the last seven games were lost, although the last home game on Saturday 2nd May resulted in a surprise 5-1 win over Grimsby Town. Stephen Fallon broke Terry Eades' Club record number of Football League appearances by playing his 249th game, and celebrated the occasion by scoring a goal. A week prior to that United lost by 5 goals to 0 away to Queen's Park Rangers in the last game to be played on grass at Loftus Road, before the pitch was the first to be changed to the artificial astro-turf. Fans were invited to dig up pieces of turf after the match.

The youth team had a better finish to the season when they reached the Final of the South East Counties League Junior Cup by beating Peterborough United, Bristol Rovers and Wimbledon. However, after drawing 2-2 at home to Tottenham Hotspur in the First Leg of the Final, they had to be content with the runners-up medals, eventually losing 6-3 on aggregate. The Club were honoured when youth team player Andy Sinton, a product of Lew Nainby's scouting in the North East, represented the England under 15s on 28th March 1981, and scored the first goal in a 4-0 win.

F.A. Challenge Cup

Third Round Proper
Norwich City 1 0 **Cambridge United**

Football League Cup

Second Round First Leg
Cambridge United 3 1 Wolverhampton Wndrs

Second Round Second Leg
Wolverhampton Wndrs 0 1 **Cambridge United**
(Cambridge United won 4-1 on aggregate)

Third Round
Cambridge United 2 1 Aston Villa

Fourth Round
Coventry City 1 1 **Cambridge United**

Fourth Round Replay
Cambridge United 0 1 Coventry City

Cambs Professional Cup

Final
Cambridge United 2 4 Peterborough United

Football League Division Two

	Pld	W	D	L	F	A	Pts
West Ham United	42	28	10	4	79	29	66
Notts County	42	18	17	7	49	38	53
Swansea City	42	18	14	10	64	44	50
Blackburn Rovers	42	16	18	8	42	29	50
Luton Town	42	18	12	12	61	46	48
Derby County	42	15	15	12	57	52	45
Grimsby Town	42	15	15	12	44	42	45
Queen's Park Rangers	42	15	13	14	56	46	43
Watford	42	16	11	15	50	45	43
Sheffield Wednesday	42	17	8	17	53	51	42
Newcastle United	42	14	14	14	30	45	42
Chelsea	42	14	12	16	46	41	40
Cambridge United	42	17	6	19	53	65	40
Shrewsbury Town	42	11	17	14	46	47	39
Oldham Athletic	42	12	15	15	39	48	39
Wrexham	42	12	14	16	43	45	38
Orient	42	13	12	17	52	56	38
Bolton Wanderers	42	14	10	18	61	66	38
Cardiff City	42	12	12	18	44	60	36
Preston North End	42	11	14	17	41	62	36
Bristol City	42	7	16	19	29	51	30
Bristol Rovers	42	5	13	24	34	65	23

Willhire Cup

	Pld	W	D	L	F	A	Pts
Norwich City	3	1	2	0	7	3	4
Cambridge United	3	2	0	1	2	4	4
Ipswich Town	3	1	1	1	6	4	3
Colchester United	3	0	1	2	2	6	1

Midweek Football League Cup

First Round
Watford Res. 5 1 **Cambridge Utd Res**

Midweek Football League

	Pld	W	D	L	F	A	Pts
Brighton & Hove Alb. Res.	24	14	6	4	53	23	34
Watford Res.	24	12	7	5	46	25	31
Portsmouth Res.	24	12	5	7	30	26	29
Peterborough United Res.	24	9	8	7	41	38	26
Charlton Athletic Res.	24	10	5	9	46	45	25
Gillingham Res.	24	7	10	7	43	42	24
Southend United Res.	24	10	4	10	40	41	24
Millwall Res.	24	9	5	10	33	31	23
Brentford Res.	24	9	4	11	42	41	22
Northampton Town Res.	24	8	5	11	38	46	21
Cambridge Utd Res	24	8	3	13	28	45	19
Wimbledon Res.	24	7	4	13	36	51	18
Aldershot Res.	24	5	6	13	24	46	16

F.A. Youth Challenge Cup

Preliminary Round
Cambridge Utd Yth 4 3 Tring Town Youth

First Qualifying Round
Cambridge Utd Yth 3 2 Northampton Town Yth

Second Qualifying Round
Cambridge Utd Yth 3 1 Corby Town Youth

First Round Proper
Cambridge Utd Yth 1 2 Orient Youth

Southern Junior Floodlit Cup

First Round
Derby County Youth 3 2 **Cambridge Utd Yth**

South East Counties League Cup Division Two

First Round
Cambridge Utd Yth 3 2 Peterborough Utd Youth

Second Round
Bristol Rovers Youth 1 3 **Cambridge Utd Yth**

Semi-final
Wimbledon Youth 3 4 **Cambridge Utd Yth**

Final First Leg
Cambridge Utd Yth 2 4 Tottenham Hotspur Yth

Final Second Leg
Tottenham Hotspur Yth 2 1 **Cambridge Utd Yth**
(Tottenham Hotspur won 6-3 on aggregate)

1980-81 Season

Back Row: Dougie Evans, Jamie Murray, Roger Gibbins, Ian Buckley, Dave Donaldson, Graham Watson.
Middle Row: George Reilly, Floyd Streete, Richard Key, Steve Fallon, Malcolm Webster, Lindsay Smith, Martin Goldsmith.
Front Row: Steve Spriggs, Tommy O'Neill, Tom Finney, Dave Stringer, Graham Cox, Derrick Christie.

South East Counties League. Division Two

	Pld	W	D	L	F	A	Pts
West Ham United	28	19	6	3	77	33	44
Oxford United Youth	28	16	8	4	71	42	40
Cambridge Utd Yth	28	16	4	8	65	42	36
Swindon Town Youth	28	16	4	8	54	40	36
Tottenham Hotspur Youth	28	15	6	7	74	38	34
Charlton Athletic Youth	28	13	7	8	54	42	33
Wimbledon Youth	28	14	3	11	61	52	31
Luton Town Youth	28	12	5	11	57	42	28
Brentford Youth	28	8	9	11	50	49	25
Reading Youth	28	8	7	13	38	58	23
Chelsea Youth	28	7	9	12	38	58	23
Peterborough Utd. Youth	28	9	4	15	30	55	20
Millwall Youth	28	7	3	18	38	64	17
Orient Youth	28	6	4	18	33	65	16
Bristol Rovers Youth	28	3	3	22	32	92	9

Luton Town Youth had 1pt deducted
Tottenham Hotspur Youth and Peterborough United Youth had 2pts deducted

1981-82 SEASON

Several ground improvements were completed for the new season, including the provision of 374 seats in the Habbin Stand, the laying of a new car park with tarmac behind the Main Grandstand, and the provision of new box-section safety barriers as a requirement for the Club's ground safety certificate.

Another change was the introduction by the Football League of three points for a win, and one point for a draw. The playing staff was exactly the same as the previous season, although Stephen Pyle, scorer of over forty goals for the youth team in the past year, was signed as a full professional.

A bad start was made to the season as five defeats were suffered in the first seven Division Two matches, and consequently Joe Mayo was transferred from Orient to reinforce Cambridge United's attack. The move was particularly necessary as George Reilly was playing well in his emergency role as a central defender.

George Reilly scored in the welcome 1-0 home win against Chelsea on Saturday 3rd October, but the day was spoilt by scenes of violence and destruction in the city caused by followers of the Chelsea team. Although powerless to control the visiting supporters outside the area of the ground, the Club came under severe criticism from several quarters. Three days later Cambridge United suffered a crushing 3-1 defeat away to Fourth Division Colchester United in the Second Round First Leg of the Football League Cup. Colchester had beaten Cambridge in all four previous meetings in major cup competitions, and the jinx continued at the Abbey Stadium in the Second Leg when Cambridge United were reduced to ten men after 30 minutes play. A quite magnificent performance of courage and effort enabled Cambridge to level the aggregate scores at 4-4 after 90 minutes play, with Roger Gibbins scoring two goals and George Reilly getting the other one. Extra-time was then required, driving the Cambridge players to the point of exhaustion, and during that period Colchester grabbed the all important goal that put them into the next round. Between their two League Cup matches, United ended their run of nine successive away defeats with two away wins, 2-1 at Grimsby, and 4-3 at Bolton, to avenge the heavy defeat of the previous season.

A run of four wins on the trot pushed the Club into the upper half of the table, but a 2-1 reverse at Norwich on 14th November started a sequence of six defeats. A prolonged spell of bad weather allowed the Club to play only one game in seven weeks, that being in the Third Round of the F.A. Challenge Cup away to Doncaster Rovers on Saturday 2nd January 1982. United were expected to win through, having never lost to the "Dons" in eleven meetings, but an Alan Taylor goal was not enough to avert a disappointing defeat by 2 goals to 1.

In the F.A. Youth Cup, United's youth team had their best ever run in the competition by beating Banbury, Coventry Sporting, Southend United, Brighton and Millwall to reach the Fourth Round Proper. During the bad weather they managed to get their game in away to Birmingham City, who ran out as winners by a flattering 3-0 margin. Throughout the season the youth team headed their league, even though they were harshly deducted 3 points for a registration error, but they went on to win the South East Counties League Junior Championship by remaining unbeaten in 28 games, winning 21 and drawing 7 of the matches.

Youth team captain Ray Nicholls made his first team debut in the 0-0 draw at Watford on Saturday 6th March, and at the age of 16 years became the youngest player to have represented Cambridge United in a Football League match. The following week five goals were conceded in the first half away to Cardiff City, but a good fight back enabled United to salvage some pride as they pulled the final score back to 5-4. Unfortunately the crowd of 3,242 people was Cardiff's lowest post-war home attendance.

Many clubs were suffering from a loss of income caused by the postponement of many matches due to the bad weather, and by the poor economic climate, a result of which Cambridge United had to cut their playing staff by six, leaving themselves with little cover in the event of injuries. The Club began to slip dangerously close to the relegation zone, but they picked up a welcome point in a 1-1 draw against league leaders Luton Town on Easter Saturday before their largest home crowd of the season, 8,815 spectators. A 0-0 draw against Orient on Easter Monday followed by a 2-0 win against the same club a week later eased the situation, but relegation was only avoided when United managed to win their last two home games, 1-0 against Blackburn Rovers and 4-0 against Charlton Athletic. A 2-1 defeat away to Queen's Park Rangers in the last game did not matter, and the Club finished in 14th place, four points away from the relegation zone with 48 points under the new system.

The reserve team had an improved season in the Midweek Football League, finishing in sixth place, and they also reached the Semi-final of the Midweek League Cup, drawing 1-1 with Peterborough United Reserves before eventually losing the tie 5-4 on penalties, in a 'sudden-death' penalty decider.

On 31st May there was a "Classic Rock Evening" at the Abbey Stadium, an open-air concert featuring the London Symphony Orchestra and two choirs, with other personalities such as Ron Greenwood and the England squad of international footballers. The joint venture organized with Cambridge City Council and sponsored by Phillips attracted 3,500 people, and was a truly special evening a great success.

F.A. Challenge Cup

Third Round Proper
Doncaster Rovers   2   1   **Cambridge United**

Football League Cup

Second Round First Leg
Colchester United   3   1   **Cambridge United**

Second Round Second Leg
Cambridge United   3   2   Colchester United
(Colchester United won 5-4 on aggregate)

1981-82 Season
Back Row: John Lyons, David Donaldson, Roger Gibbins, Tom Finney, Graham Watson, Doug Evans, Jamie Murray.
Middle Row: John Cozens (Assistant Manager), George Reilly, Lindsay Smith, Martin Goldsmith, Richard Key, Malcolm Webster, Stephen Fallon (Club Captain), Floyd Streete, Chris Turner, Peter Graham (Coach).
Front Row: Tommy O'Neill, Derrick Christie, John Docherty (Manager), Stephen Pyle, Steve Spriggs (Team Captain), Peter Melville (Physiotherapist), Graham Cox, Andy Polycarpou. Photograph by courtesy of Ray Clarke.

Football League Division Two

	Pld	W	D	L	F	A	Pts
Luton Town	42	25	13	4	86	46	88
Watford	42	23	11	8	76	42	80
Norwich City	42	22	5	15	64	50	71
Sheffield Wednesday	42	20	10	12	55	51	70
Queen's Park Rangers	42	21	6	15	65	43	69
Barnsley	42	19	10	13	59	41	67
Rotherham	42	20	7	15	66	54	67
Leicester City	42	18	12	12	56	48	66
Newcastle United	42	18	8	16	52	50	62
Blackburn Rovers	42	16	11	15	47	43	59
Oldham Athletic	42	15	14	13	50	51	59
Chelsea	42	15	12	15	60	60	57
Charlton Athletic	42	13	12	17	50	65	51
Cambridge United	42	13	9	20	48	53	48
Crystal Palace	42	13	9	20	34	45	48
Derby County	42	12	12	18	53	68	48
Grimsby Town	42	11	13	18	53	65	46
Shrewsbury Town	42	11	13	18	37	57	46
Bolton Wanderers	42	13	7	22	39	61	46
Cardiff City	42	12	8	22	45	61	44
Wrexham	42	11	11	20	40	56	44
Orient	42	10	9	23	36	61	39

Midweek League Cup

First Round
Cambridge Utd Res 2 2 Aldershot Res.
(After extra-time: score 2-2 at 90 mins)

First Round Replay
Aldershot Res. 1 2 **Cambridge Utd Res**

Second Round
Gillingham Res. 2 3 **Cambridge Utd Res**

Semi-final
Cambridge Utd Res 1 1 Peterborough Utd Res.
(After extra-time: score at 90 minutes 1-1, Peterborough won 5-4 on penalties)

Midweek Football League

	Pld	W	D	L	F	A	Pts
Charlton Athletic Res.	26	18	4	4	52	25	58
Millwall Res.	26	11	12	3	40	29	45
Gillingham Res.	26	13	5	8	62	36	44
Portsmouth Res.	26	12	5	9	49	45	41
Brentford Res.	26	12	3	11	49	34	39
Cambridge Utd Res	26	10	8	8	47	45	38
Brighton & Hove Alb. Res.	26	11	4	11	31	36	37
Peterborough Utd. Res.	26	10	4	12	36	38	34
Wimbledon Res.	26	9	5	12	32	45	32
Bournemouth Res.	26	8	6	12	37	54	30
Exeter City Res.	26	8	5	13	37	47	29
Northampton Town Res.	26	8	4	14	31	47	28
Aldershot Res.	26	6	8	12	28	41	26
Southend Utd Res.	26	5	9	12	27	37	24

F.A. Challenge Youth Cup

First Qualifying Round
Banbury United Youth 0 1 **Cambridge Utd Yth**

Second Qualifying Round
Coventry Sporting Yth 1 8 **Cambridge Utd Yth**

First Round Proper
Southend United Youth 2 4 **Cambridge Utd Yth**

Second Round Proper
Cambridge Utd Yth 2 0 Brighton & Hove A. Yth

Third Round Proper
Cambridge Utd Yth 3 1 Millwall Youth

Fourth Round Proper
Birmingham City Youth 3 0 **Cambridge Utd Yth**

Southern Junior Floodlit Competition

First Round
Southampton Youth 4 2 **Cambridge Utd Yth**

South East Counties Junior League Cup Division Two

First Round
Cambridge Utd Yth 1 3 Luton Town Youth

South East Counties League. Division Two

	Pld	W	D	L	F	A	Pts
Cambridge Utd Yth	28	21	7	0	109	34	46
Brighton & Hove Alb. Yth	28	16	5	7	65	35	37
West Ham United	28	14	9	5	64	37	37
Charlton Athletic Youth	28	15	5	8	60	39	35
Chelsea Youth	28	13	5	10	47	42	31
Swindon Town Youth	28	11	10	7	52	49	28
Wimbledon Youth	28	12	4	12	58	60	28
Luton Town Youth	28	11	6	11	51	62	27
Oxford United Youth	28	9	7	12	65	60	25
Reading Youth	28	11	3	14	46	57	25
Brentford Youth	28	9	5	14	45	62	23
Tottenham Hotspur Yth	28	8	5	15	73	67	21
Millwall Youth	28	9	7	12	32	60	21
Bristol Rovers Youth	28	5	4	19	40	75	12
Southend United Youth	28	3	4	21	30	98	10

Luton Town Youth had 1 point deducted
Bristol Rovers Youth had 2 points deducted
Cambridge United Youth had 3 points deducted
Swindon Town Youth and Millwall Youth had 4 points deducted

1982-83 SEASON

Once again Manager John Docherty made little movement in the transfer market during the summer, releasing just one player, Roger Gibbins, and making no new signings, a situation dictated mainly by finance.

The league season got off to a bad start with three successive defeats, the worst start since joining the Football League. The first point was gained at home to Barnsley in the fourth game on Tuesday 7th September when Ray Nicholls headed his first Football League goal in a 1-1 draw. Four days later he scored again as United fought back from a 2-0 half-time deficit to win 3-2 at home to Charlton Athletic. He scored once more in the Final of the Cambs Professional Cup at the Abbey Stadium on Tuesday 14th September, as United beat their neighbours, Cambridge City, 4-0 after a goal-less first half. Gone though was the interest of past years, which was reflected in the paltry crowd of only 300 people.

Because of a sponsorship agreement, the Football League Cup was retitled the Milk Cup, and in the Second Round Cambridge United were drawn away to fellow Second Division side Barnsley. In impossible playing conditions the first match was abandoned after an hour with the score at one goal apiece. George Reilly scored United's goal, and the game was unfortunately stopped with his colleagues adapting better to the conditions than their opponents. The match was replayed a week later when an almost identical crowd of 8,794 spectators saw Barnsley take a two goal lead, before Tom Finney pulled back an important goal. Confident that they could overcome the one goal deficit in the home leg, United were overwhelmed by Barnsley who went on to win 3-1, a convincing 5-2 aggregate win.

With only one win in their first twelve league games Cambridge United found themselves at the bottom of the Second Division by the beginning of November, but two home wins in succession against well placed Wolverhampton Wanderers and Leicester City improved the situation. Over half of the team were products of the Club's youth team policy, including Keith Lockhart who marked the occasion by scoring a goal in each match. Sixteen year old Andy Sinton took over from Ray Nicholls as the youngest player to play in the Football League for Cambridge United.

Four players in the first team were still eligible for the youth team, and one of them, Kevin Smith, scored six goals in an astounding 19-0 home victory against Oxford City's youth team in the First Round Proper of the F.A. Youth Cup on Thursday 28th October 1982. In the next round, however, United lost 2-1 away to Luton Town's youth team, although in the South East Counties League they were making a strong bid to retain the Championship they had won the previous season.

Early in November there was tragic news of the death of John Lyons, just eight months after he was transferred from Cambridge United to Colchester. In the same month defender Lindsay Smith was transferred to Plymouth Argyle for £20,000, and to replace him Bobby Fisher was signed from Orient.

A 3-0 defeat away to Oldham Athletic on 11th December saw the Club slip to the bottom of the Second Division once more, but three home games without conceding a goal again improved matters. The Third Round draw for the F.A. Challenge Cup gave United a home tie against non-league Weymouth on 8th January, and although 5,019 turned up to see George Reilly score the only goal of the game, it was in fact the lowest attendance of the Round. A week later the Club equalled their heaviest Football League defeat, going down by 6 goals to 0 at Stamford Bridge against Chelsea.

Once again the draw was kind in the Fourth Round of the F.A. Challenge Cup when United were drawn at home to Barnsley, giving them an early opportunity to avenge their Milk Cup defeat. The attendance of 6,612 was also the lowest of the Round, but they saw United gain a tremendous 1-0 win thanks to a goal scored by Joe Mayo, and for the first time in their history the Club managed to progress into the Fifth Round. Having gone eight games without conceding a goal at home, Cambridge United had high hopes that they could progress even further in the competition when they were given another home tie against Sheffield Wednesday, a team they had drawn 2-2 against earlier in the season in the league. There was a marvellous atmosphere as a crowd of 10,834 people crammed into the Abbey Stadium, but United conceded their first home goal for a record 755 minutes when Gary Megson scored with an unstoppable shot. Although Chris Turner scored for United, Sheffield Wednesday won the match 2-1, and they rubbed salt into the wound with a 3-1 league win over United the following Saturday at Hillsborough.

At the Club's A.G.M. in January, "Paddy" Harris retired from the Board after 33 years as a Director. He was an original member of the Board when it was formed in 1950, and in recognition of his service, he was elected as the Club's first President since the change of name from Abbey United to Cambridge United.

Robbie Cooke was signed from Peterborough United in March to boost the forward line, and improved form during that month enabled United to edge away from the relegation zone. A 1-0 home victory on Tuesday 5th April 1983 extended Cambridge United's run of home league matches without conceding a goal to ten games, a feat that had only been achieved by two other Football League clubs. However, United's away form had been dreadful. The following Saturday changed matters when they came back from 2-0 down at half-time to beat promotion contenders Barnsley 3-2, ending their record run of 35 away games without a win.

Prior to the last game of the season the Club lost only one of the previous nine league games, giving them 51 points and a safe mid-table position. The second half of the season produced a fine defensive performance and the type of form which would have won promotion if it had lasted all season. In the last game on Saturday 14th May, United lost by 4 goals to 1 against Oldham Athletic, and conceded their first league goals at the Abbey Stadium since their 4-1 defeat against the Division Two Champions, Queen's Park Rangers, on 20th November. By so doing Cambridge United had set an all-time Football League record of twelve consecutive home games without conceding a goal.

Both the reserve and youth teams had a chance of winning honours at the end of the season when they reached their respective League Cup Finals. In the Midweek League Cup Final United's reserves lost 3-1 at home and 1-0 away against Gillingham's reserves, having finished one place below them in 5th place in the League. The youth team also lost both legs of their Final against Chelsea's youth team, 2-0 at home, and 5-1 away, having finished above them in the runners-up spot in the South East Counties Junior League.

Milk Cup (Football League Cup)

First Round First Leg
Barnsley 1 1 **Cambridge United**
(Match abandoned after 60 minutes)

First Round First Leg
Barnsley 2 1 **Cambridge United**

First Round Second Leg
Cambridge United 1 3 Barnsley
(Barnsley won 5-2 on aggregate)

F.A. Challenge Cup

Third Round Proper
Cambridge United 1 0 Weymouth

Fourth Round Proper
Cambridge United 1 0 Barnsley

Fifth Round Proper
Cambridge United 1 2 Sheffield Wednesday

1982-83 Season
Back Row: David Donaldson, Martin Goldsmith, Jamie Murray, Stephen Fallon (Club Captain), Keith Lockhart, Floyd Streete, Les Cartwright.
Middle Row: David Ruston (Chairman), Joe Mayo, Chris Turner, Lindsay Smith, Richard Key, Dean Greygoose, Malcolm Webster, Andy Beattie, George Reilly, Ron Howard (Chief Scout).
Front Row: Tom Finney, Tommy O'Neill, Steve Pyle, Steve Spriggs, John Cozens (Assistant Manager), Peter Melville (Physiotherapist), John Docherty (Manager), Graham Watson, Derrick Christie, Ray Nicholls. Photograph by courtesy of *Cambridge Evening News*.

Cambs Professional Cup

Final
Cambridge United 4 0 Cambridge City

Football League (Canon League) Division Two

	Pld	W	D	L	F	A	Pts
Queen's Park Rangers	42	26	7	9	77	36	85
Wolverhampton Wanderers	42	20	15	7	68	44	75
Leicester City	42	20	10	12	72	44	70
Fulham	42	20	9	13	64	47	69
Newcastle United	42	18	13	11	75	53	67
Sheffield Wednesday	42	16	15	11	60	47	63
Oldham Athletic	42	14	19	9	64	47	61
Leeds United	42	13	21	8	51	46	60
Shrewsbury Town	42	15	14	13	48	48	59
Barnsley	42	14	15	13	57	55	57
Blackburn Rovers	42	15	12	15	58	58	57
Cambridge United	42	13	12	17	42	60	51
Derby County	42	10	19	13	49	58	49
Carlisle United	42	12	12	18	68	70	48
Crystal Palace	42	12	12	18	43	52	48
Middlesborough	42	11	15	16	46	67	48
Charlton Athletic	42	13	9	20	63	86	48
Chelsea	42	11	14	17	51	61	47
Grimsby Town	42	12	11	19	45	70	47
Rotherham United	42	10	15	17	45	68	45
Burnley	42	12	8	22	56	66	44
Bolton Wanderers	42	11	11	20	42	61	44

Midweek League

	Pld	W	D	L	F	A	Pts
Portsmouth Res.	18	14	3	1	48	17	45
Brentford Res.	18	11	4	3	52	28	37
Bournemouth Res.	18	9	4	5	38	33	31
Gillingham Res.	18	7	5	6	38	36	26
Cambridge Utd Res	18	6	6	6	41	34	24
Southend United Res.	18	7	3	8	30	31	24
Peterborough Utd. Res.	18	7	2	9	38	48	23
Wimbledon Res.	18	3	6	9	29	42	15
Northampton Town Res.	18	4	1	13	35	57	13
Orient Res.	18	3	4	11	27	50	13

Midweek League Cup Section B

	Pld	W	D	L	F	A	Pts
Cambridge Utd Res	8	6	0	2	24	14	18
Peterborough Utd. Res.	8	4	1	3	16	10	13
Southend Utd. Res.	8	3	2	3	17	14	11
Orient Res.	8	2	2	4	14	13	8
Northampton Town Res.	8	2	1	5	11	32	7

Final First Leg
Cambridge Utd Res 1 3 Gillingham Res.

Final Second Leg
Gillingham Res. 1 0 **Cambridge Utd Res**

F.A. Youth Challenge Cup

First Round Proper
Cambridge Utd Yth 19 0 Oxford City Youth

Second Round Proper
Luton Town Youth 2 1 **Cambridge Utd Yth**

Southern Junior Floodlit Cup

First Round
Charlton Athletic Youth 4 1 **Cambridge Utd Yth**

South East Counties League Cup Division Two

First Round
Cambridge Utd Yth 3 0 Reading Youth

Second Round
Southend United Youth 2 2 **Cambridge Utd Yth**

Second Round Replay
Cambridge Utd Yth 8 2 Southend United Youth

Semi-final
Cambridge Utd Yth 3 1 Tottenham Hotspur Yth

Final First Leg
Cambridge Utd Yth 0 2 Chelsea Youth

Final Second Leg
Chelsea Youth 5 1 **Cambridge Utd Yth**

South East Counties League. Division Two

	Pld	W	D	L	F	A	Pts
Wimbledon Youth	24	15	5	4	59	30	35
Cambridge Utd Yth	24	14	5	5	65	35	33
West Ham United Youth	24	14	5	5	67	42	33
Chelsea Youth	24	13	5	6	52	42	31
Swindon Town Youth	24	11	8	5	55	51	30
Luton Town Youth	24	11	4	9	52	52	26
Tottenham Hotspur Youth	24	9	4	11	56	60	22
Brentford Youth	24	7	7	10	51	62	21
Oxford United Youth	24	7	6	11	57	78	20
Reading Youth	24	7	5	12	49	54	19
Brighton & Hove Alb. Yth.	24	7	2	15	45	59	16
Bristol Rovers Youth	24	6	3	15	51	57	15
Southend United Youth	24	3	5	16	36	73	11

1983-84 SEASON

Even before the season had started a note of pessimism had been struck regarding Cambridge United's ability to survive in the Second Division, when at the Football League's A.G.M. the decision was taken not to share the 'gate' money equally between the clubs' competing in a match. Clubs with smaller 'gates', like Cambridge United, were bound to suffer severe financial hardship as a result of the Football League's change in its traditional stance of sharing its wealth in order to provide a strong, healthy league.

The gloom was compounded when the Club's highest goalscorer in the previous season, George Reilly, effectively went on 'strike' by refusing to play for Cambridge United after a dispute. Placed in a dilemma, the decision was taken to sell the player to First Division Watford, at a bargain fee of £100,000, which meant that the Club lost money on a player they should have made a considerable profit from.

A goal-less draw at Carlisle, followed by a 2-0 win at home against Blackburn Rovers, was an encouraging start to the league season, but the lowest opening day crowd in the Club's Football League history of 2,636 confirmed that the Club would have a struggle for survival. After only one point had been picked up from the next four games, the slide down the league table seemed to be halted when Steve Spriggs scored a last minute winner in the 2-1 home victory against Oldham Athletic on Saturday 1st October. Few people amongst the meagre crowd of 2,696 could have envisaged that the Club were about to start the worst run of results in their history.

In the Milk Cup, First Division Sunderland were drawn to play at the Abbey Stadium in the Second Round First Leg, and they made their superior class tell as they eased into a three goal lead within an hour. A gutsy fight back by United enabled them to get back into the game with late goals from Robbie Cooke and Martin Goldsmith, although the chances of making up the deficit at Roker Park seemed remote. There was a three week gap between the two legs during which the Club suffered an injury crisis and lost three league games in a row, conceding three goals in each game. Matters were made worse when the previous season's Player of the Year, Chris Turner, was transferred to Southend United for £20,000 on 19th October 1983, at a time when the Club could least afford to lose an experienced defender. The decision appeared to have been taken on financial grounds, although the unanimity of the Board was not entirely convincing. Supporters expressed their disapproval as the Manager, John Docherty, was faced with losing his sixth senior professional player since the end of the previous season.

A virus, which reduced the Club to nine fit men, caused the postponement of the league match with Portsmouth on Saturday 22nd October, but four days later a team was scraped together for the Milk Cup Second Leg match at Sunderland, with everyone expecting a crushing defeat. Youth team players Graeme Heward and Stephen Clarke were drafted in for their first team debuts, but after a brave performance the team bowed out of the competition 7-5 on aggregate, having scored three away goals through Stephen Fallon, Kevin Smith and Robbie Cooke.

A last minute goal conceded against Brighton in the next home game resulted in another 4-3 defeat, and saw the Club slip into the relegation zone. David Moyes, a young Scottish youth international defender, was signed from Celtic for £15,000, but he was given a tough baptism against league leaders Portsmouth, as Mark Hateley scored a hat-trick in "Pompey's" 5-0 win. That victory on Tuesday 1st November gave Portsmouth the unique record of having beaten all 92 member clubs of the Football League.

For the next game at home to Derby County in the bottom of the table clash, there was a surprise inclusion in the team Graham Daniels, a philosophy graduate, who had previously played on the left wing for Cardiff Corinthians in the Welsh League. He nearly scored a spectacular equalizer in the 1-0 defeat, but there then followed a few anxious days as the Club had to fight off interest from Bristol Rovers and Cardiff City before he signed a contract for United. One of the main problems to be sorted out before signing was not the normal one of agreeing financial terms but overcoming his moral objections to using private medical facilities.

By coincidence the Club travelled to Cardiff for the next match, making the journey by train and walking for 20 minutes from the railway station to the ground. The match was a nightmare, and Cardiff stormed to a 5-0 victory, making it Cambridge United's ninth consecutive defeat, an unwanted all-time record.

News that prudent measures had reduced Cambridge United's losses from £220,000 to £56,000 could not lift the gloom, and the Club went two months without a win at either first, reserve or youth team level. Two days after the 1-0 defeat at Shrewsbury on Saturday 10th December, the Board announced that they had sacked John Docherty as Manager, severing his seven year association with the Club. The decision was taken with the Chairman out of the country on business on the other side of the world, although he was kept fully informed of the situation. Assistant Manager John Cozens was left temporarily in charge while the vacant position was advertised.

The youth team, which was also run by John Cozens, provided some cheer when after three 1-1 draws with Reading in the First Round Proper of the F.A. Youth Cup, they eventually won through by 4 goals to 1 having played a total of 420 minutes. The Second Round was postponed twice before they overcame Welling United 3-2 away on a heavy pitch, but the Third Round gave the United boys a tough match away to the cup holders, Norwich City. In that game United took a 2-1 lead before conceding a late penalty which was converted, but in the replay at the Abbey Stadium on Wednesday 11th January they stunned the "Canaries" with a jubilant 4-1 victory. That win over David Stringer's team greatly improved John Cozens' chances of being appointed as the Club's first team Manager, against one of the favourites for the post which was shortly to be announced. Six days later the youth team travelled to Highbury for the Fourth Round match, but the occasion proved to be too much for them, and they lost 1-0 to a 39th minute Arsenal goal, although giving a good account of themselves against a strong team.

In the F.A. Challenge Cup the first team were drawn at home to Derby County on Saturday 7th January, attracting the best home crowd of the season, 6,309 people, but the revitalized "Rams" won 3-0.

The new Manager was appointed on Friday 20th January, and the announcement came as quite a surprise when the Board gave the job to former Norwich City, Luton Town and Manchester City player John Ryan, who had no previous senior managerial experience. Taking the job on without a written contract, the new Manager faced a daunting task to change the fortunes of a team that had been bottom of the table since Christmas and had not won for twenty games.

His first league game in charge was against league leaders Chelsea, and attracted a large crowd of 10,602 spectators. Half of the ground was given over to Chelsea supporters, because of the large contingent expected to travel from London. Unfortunately though the day was marred by terrible violence before the game, caused by a group of hooligans from Cambridge, despite the presence of 450 policemen on duty in the city. Fortunately after lengthy investigation the guilty culprits were sent for trial and given lengthy custodial sentences. The game resulted in favour of Chelsea by a goal to nil, and started another run of seven consecutive defeats.

John Carter, a former commercial manager with Nottingham Forest F.C., joined the Club at the beginning of March to replace Dudley Arliss, who was retiring after doing a magnificent job for over 25 years. The Club's lottery had been one of the biggest in the country, and was a vital factor in the Club's rise to its current status. The turbulent times continued as Les Holloway resigned as Secretary after six years, to join Doncaster Rovers as their Chief Executive. John Cozens was retained as Assistant Manager, while goalkeeper Malcolm Webster was given the job of Youth Team Coach after injury ruled him out of the game.

Relegation was confirmed on Saturday 14th April after a 1-1 draw at Ayresome Park, Middlesbrough, the Club's third draw in succession. Crewe Alexandra's record run of thirty league games without a win was looming fast, and was broken at Grimsby on Monday 23rd April after a goal-less draw. A full house was anticipated at the Abbey Stadium the following Saturday when Newcastle United were expecting to pick up the points to help clinch promotion. Despite the presence of Kevin Keegan in the Newcastle line-up, the "all-ticket" match only attracted 7,720 spectators, but Geordie

BBC Radio Cambridgeshire

Wishes

Cambridge United Football Club
and all Supporters
A VERY HAPPY 75th BIRTHDAY

'U' TOO CAN SWITCH ON THE
BEST SPORTS COVERAGE

ON 96 FM

Kevin Smith scored the only goal of the game from the penalty spot to end the Club's longest run of games without a win, totalling 34 league and cup matches.

F.A. Challenge Cup

Third Round Proper
Cambridge United 0 3 Derby County

Milk Cup (Football League Cup)

Second Round First Leg
Cambridge United 2 3 Sunderland

Second Round Second Leg
Sunderland 4 3 **Cambridge United**
(Sunderland won 7-5 on aggregate)

Cambs Professional Cup

Final
Cambridge United 1 1 Norwich City
(Cambridge United won 4-3 on penalties)

Football League (Canon League) Division Two

	Pld	W	D	L	F	A	Pts
Chelsea	42	25	13	4	90	40	88
Sheffield Wednesday	42	26	10	6	72	34	88
Newcastle United	42	24	8	10	85	53	80
Manchester City	42	20	10	12	66	48	70
Grimsby Town	42	19	13	10	60	47	70
Blackburn Rovers	42	17	16	9	57	46	67
Carlisle United	42	16	16	10	48	41	64
Shrewsbury Town	42	17	10	15	49	53	61
Brighton & Hove Albion	42	17	9	16	69	60	60
Leeds United	42	15	13	14	53	56	58
Fulham	42	15	12	15	60	53	57
Huddersfield Town	42	14	15	13	56	49	57
Charlton Athletic	42	16	9	17	53	64	57
Barnsley	42	15	7	20	57	53	52
Cardiff City	42	15	6	21	53	66	51
Portsmouth	42	14	7	21	73	64	49
Middlesbrough	42	12	13	17	41	47	49
Oldham Athletic	42	13	9	20	47	71	48
Crystal Palace	42	12	11	19	42	52	47
Derby County	42	11	9	22	36	72	42
Swansea City	42	7	8	27	36	85	29
Cambridge United	42	4	12	26	28	77	24

1983-84 Season

Back Row: Bobby Fisher, Jamie Murray, Stephen Clarke, Tom Finney, Robbie Cooke, David Donaldson, Les Cartwright.
Middle Row: Andy Beattie, Chris Turner, Martin Goldsmith, Dean Greygoose, Malcolm Webster, Keith Lockhart, Stephen Fallon, George Reilly.
Front Row: Derrick Christie, Stephen Pyle, Andy Sinton, John Cozens, John Docherty (Manager), Peter Melville (Physiotherapist), Steve Spriggs, Kevin Smith, Ray Nicholls. Photograph by courtesy of *Cambridge Evening News*.

Bancroft Cup

Final
Wisbech Town 3 0 Cambridge Utd Res

Midweek League

	Pld	W	D	L	F	A	Pts
Portsmouth Res.	12	11	1	0	42	9	34
Cambridge Utd Res	12	5	4	3	24	20	19
Southend United Res.	12	5	2	5	15	18	17
Brentford Res.	12	4	3	5	20	15	15
Bournemouth Res.	12	3	4	5	21	13	13
Peterborough Utd. Res.	12	3	2	7	15	19	11
Northampton Town Res.	12	1	4	7	14	37	7

Midweek League Cup

	Pld	W	D	L	F	A	Pts
Portsmouth Res.	12	10	1	1	26	6	31
Peterborough Utd. Res.	12	6	2	4	23	19	20
Southend United Res.	12	5	3	4	16	15	18
Brentford Res.	12	6	0	6	15	17	18
Cambridge Utd Res	12	5	1	6	22	25	16
Northampton Town Res.	12	3	0	9	12	21	9
Bournemouth Res.	12	2	3	7	10	19	9

F.A. Youth Challenge Cup

First Round
Reading Youth 1 1 Cambridge United Youth

First Round Replay
Cambridge Utd Yth 1 1 Reading Youth
(After extra-time)

First Round Second Replay
Cambridge Utd Yth 1 1 Reading Youth
(After extra-time)

First Round Third Replay
Reading Youth 1 4 **Cambridge Utd Yth**

Second Round
Welling United Youth 2 3 **Cambridge Utd Yth**

Third Round
Norwich City Youth 2 2 **Cambridge Utd Yth**

Third Round Replay
Cambridge Utd Yth 4 1 Norwich City Youth

Fourth Round
Arsenal Youth 1 0 **Cambridge Utd Yth**

Southern Junior Floodlit Cup

First Round
Cambridge Utd Yth 0 3 Norwich City Youth

South East Counties League Cup Division One

First Round
Millwall Youth 1 0 **Cambridge Utd Yth**

South East Counties League. Division One

	Pld	W	D	L	F	A	Pts
Chelsea Youth	30	23	5	2	87	29	51
Norwich City Youth	30	19	6	5	66	44	44
Ipswich Town Youth	30	19	4	7	78	40	42
Millwall Youth	30	19	4	7	68	44	42
Arsenal Youth	30	17	4	9	84	54	38
Watford Youth	30	12	8	10	73	64	32
Queen's Park Rangers Yth	30	10	11	9	52	55	31
West Ham United Youth	30	12	6	12	65	52	30
Gillingham Youth	30	9	10	11	50	63	28
Orient Youth	30	8	9	13	40	54	25
Cambridge Utd Yth	30	7	8	15	48	65	22
Portsmouth Youth	30	7	7	16	29	58	21
Charlton Athletic Youth	30	7	6	17	38	68	20
Tottenham Hotspur Youth	30	5	9	16	43	82	19
Southend United Youth	30	6	6	18	45	62	18
Fulham Youth	30	8	1	21	48	80	17

1984-85 SEASON

As a cost cutting measure the Club pulled their reserve team out of the Midweek Football League, a move which meant that squad members out of the first team would not get a competitive game of football.

The Final of the Cambs Professional Cup was played pre-season against Norwich City at the Abbey Stadium on Saturday 18th August, but after a good first half performance which was goal-less, Norwich won comfortably by 3 goals to 0.

The first two games of the season resulted in 2-0 defeats away to Bradford City in the Third Division, and at Brentford in the Milk Cup First Round First Leg. The team bounced back to beat Millwall 1-0 at home in the league, and on Tuesday 4th September they staged one of their most heroic performances at home to Brentford in the Second Leg of the Milk Cup. After two players were carried off the pitch early in the game, Steve Spriggs in the 8th minute and Andy Sinton in the 20th minute, the remaining ten men responded magnificently, and completely outplayed the visitors with a heartwarming display of effort and fighting spirit. United were rewarded with a 70th minute penalty, which Robbie Cooke converted, but despite the brave efforts of Kevin Massey and Mark Cooper up front, they were unable to score a second goal, although the team was applauded to a man at the end of the game.

Following an injury crisis, Alan Comfort was signed from Queen's Park Rangers, and Danny Greaves, son of the legendary Jimmy Greaves, was signed as a non-contract player. He came on as substitute in the league match against Bristol City on

Saturday 15th September and scored a minute after coming on the field to put United 2-1 ahead. However, Bristol hit back with two goals to take the points.

Six successive defeats, four of which were at home, left the Club at the bottom of the league table, three points adrift of the nearest club. To add to the depression, the youth team lost all of their first eleven games to occupy the same position in the South East Counties League Senior Section. In the Southern Junior Floodlit Cup the youth team lost 3-0 away to Southend United, in addition to losing 6-0 away to Ipswich Town Youth in the First Round Proper of the F.A. Youth Cup.

In a bottom of the table clash on Saturday 27th October 1984 United's first team lost 2-0 at home to Swansea City, even though the "Swans" were down to ten men after half an hour, a defeat which left Cambridge United 6 points adrift at the foot of the table. The following Tuesday most of the first team appeared in the East Anglian Cup First Round tie at home to Cambridge City, in which they had a welcome 3-0 victory before 625 spectators.

Manager John Ryan played in the 2-1 away win against Newport County on Saturday 3rd November, the Club's first away win for 18 months. The revival seemed to continue a week later when United went 2-0 up at home to Burnley, then John Ryan was sent off for handball in the 63rd minute, and Burnley fought back to win 3-2. Such was his disappointment that John Ryan left the ground before the game had finished.

The Club's problems were added to when they lost 2-0 at home to Fourth Division Peterborough United in the First Round Proper of the F.A. Challenge Cup on Saturday 17th November before a crowd of 5,641 spectators, the best of the season.

On Wednesday 28th November John Ryan was sent off again for arguing with the referee in the first half of the match at Lincoln, but the team battled hard with ten men to earn a 1-1 draw. Tom Finney re-signed for the Club in mid-December on a free transfer from Brentford, and he helped the team achieve their first home win of the season on Boxing Day by a goal to nil over Bournemouth.

The innovation of the Freight Rover Trophy (the Associate Members Cup) offered Third and Fourth Division clubs the chance of playing at Wembley Stadium for the first time, and in the First Round First Leg, United lost 2-1 away to Peterborough United, with Tom Finney scoring a last minute lifeline goal.

Robbie Cooke was loaned to Brentford for a month, and while on loan he scored for the "Bees" in their 2-0 win over United on Saturday 2nd February, to add insult to injury. Three days later Peterborough United travelled to the Abbey Stadium for the Second Leg of the Freight Rover Trophy, and two second half goals from Alan Comfort and Andy Sinton gave the Club an encouraging 3-2 aggregate win.

A big effort was made to clear 6 inches of snow from the pitch the next Saturday for the home game against York City, but it hardly seemed worthwhile when the visitors adapted better to the conditions and romped to a 4-0 win, prompting one fan to publicly hand back to the Club his season ticket. When the Club conceded two late goals to lose 2-1 at home to ten men against Newport County on Saturday 23rd February, relegation became a foregone conclusion. Two days later John Ryan was sacked by the Board, having only signed a contract a month earlier in a vote of confidence.

John Cozens took over as Caretaker Manager while a successor was sought. Under his leadership the team achieved three impressive draws in the league, although in the Third Round of the East Anglian Cup, without any first team players, the Club lost 3-0 away to King's Lynn, having used the first team to win 4-0 at Histon in the Second Round. It was a period of considerable change, for as well as losing a Manager, two Directors, Tony Douglas and Jack Cooke, left the Board, while Commercial Consultant Keith Loring ended his six year association with the Club in that capacity.

Ken Shellito, a former Chelsea player and England international, was appointed as Manager, without a contract, in time for the home game with Orient on Saturday 16th March. His team appeared to be heading for a win when Roy McDonough put United two goals ahead, but they collapsed and allowed Orient to win the game 3-2. The following Wednesday Cambridge United travelled to Brentford for the Second Round tie in the Freight Rover Trophy, but once again Robbie Cooke, who had recently been transferred to Brentford, scored the only goal of the game in the 74th minute to end United's one chance of glory.

At the end of March Ken Shellito decided to dismiss John Cozens as his assistant, thereby ending his ties with the Club which stretched back to December 1977, and Malcolm Webster took over as his assistant. The Club failed to win in the first nine games under Ken Shellito's management despite the inclusion of Mark Farrington on loan from Norwich City, and relegation to the Fourth Division was confirmed after the 2-1 defeat at Millwall on Tuesday 16th April.

Support dwindled to such an extent that the Club's lowest ever Football League attendance was recorded against Lincoln City on Tuesday 30th April just 1,235 spectators for the 2-0 home defeat. The first win under Ken Shellito's management came in the last away game of the season against Rotherham United on Monday 6th May, when Roy McDonough scored a late penalty in a 1-0 win.

The Club broke four national and eight club records, for the wrong reasons, during the dismal season, by gaining just 21 points, and losing 33 league games in the season. The team finished 25 points adrift of the team above them, and scored only 37 goals, with the highest scorers being Robbie Cooke with 7 and Roy McDonough with 5, both of whom scored three penalties each.

The youth team also finished bottom of the South East Counties League Senior Section having only gained five points from 30 games.

The one chance of winning a trophy was in the Wallspan Cup, a competition entered to give the first team squad and promising youth team players a game. The Club reached the Final with victories over Barton Rovers, Oxford City, and Luton Town, but the Final against Berkhamsted Town had to be held over until the following season because it could not be fitted in at the end of the season. When the game was eventually played at Barton Rovers F.C.'s ground on Monday 25th November 1985 Cambridge United lost by a goal to nil.

F.A. Challenge Cup

First Round Proper
Cambridge United 0 2 Peterborough United

Milk Cup (Football League Cup)

First Round First Leg
Brentford 2 0 **Cambridge United**

First Round Second Leg
Cambridge United 1 0 Brentford
(Brentford won 2-1 on aggregate)

Freight Rover Trophy (Associate Members Cup)

First Round First Leg
Peterborough United 2 1 **Cambridge United**

First Round Second Leg
Cambridge United 2 0 Peterborough United

Second Round
Brentford 1 0 **Cambridge United**

Cambs Professional Cup

Final
Cambridge United 0 3 Norwich City

East Anglian Cup

First Round
Cambridge Utd Res 3 0 Cambridge City

Second Round
Histon 0 4 **Cambridge Utd Res**

Third Round
King's Lynn 3 0 **Cambridge Utd Res**

Football League (Canon League) Division Three

	Pld	W	D	L	F	A	Pts
Bradford City	46	28	10	8	77	45	94
Millwall	46	26	12	8	73	42	90
Hull City	46	25	12	9	78	49	87
Gillingham	46	25	8	13	80	62	83
Bristol City	46	24	9	13	74	47	81
Bristol Rovers	46	21	12	13	66	48	75
Derby County	46	19	13	14	65	54	70
York City	46	20	9	17	70	57	69
Reading	46	19	12	15	68	62	69
A.F.C. Bournemouth	45	19	11	16	57	46	68
Wallsall	46	18	13	15	58	52	67
Rotherham United	46	18	11	17	55	55	65
Brentford	46	16	14	16	62	64	62
Doncaster Rovers	46	17	8	21	72	74	59
Plymouth Argyle	46	15	14	17	62	65	59
Wigan Athletic	46	15	14	17	60	64	59
Bolton Wanderers	46	16	6	24	69	75	54
Newport County	46	13	13	20	55	67	52
Lincoln City	46	11	18	17	50	51	51
Swansea City	46	12	11	23	53	80	47
Burnley	46	11	13	22	60	73	46
Orient	46	11	13	22	51	76	46
Preston North End	46	13	7	26	51	100	46
Cambridge United	46	4	9	33	37	95	21

Wallspan Floodlit Cup

First Round
Barton Rovers 0 1 **Cambridge Utd Res**

Second Round
Oxford City 1 2 **Cambridge Utd Res**

Semi-final
Cambridge Utd Res 4 1 Luton Town Res.

Final (at Barton Rovers F.C.)
Berkhamsted Town 1 0 **Cambridge Utd Res**

1984-85 Season
Back Row: Kevin Smith, Dean Greygoose, Andy Higginbottom, Keith Branagan, Les Cartwright.
Third Row: Steve Fallon (Captain), Andy Beattie, Mark Cooper, David Moyes, Keith Lockhart, Stephen Clarke.
Second Row: Graham Daniels, Andy Sinton, Michael Bennett, Stephen Pyle, Steve Spriggs, Kevin Massey, Robbie Cooke.
Front Row: Karl Rutherford, Mark Chandler, Richard Anton, David Massingham, John Taylor.
Photograph by courtesy of Ray Clarke.

1985-86 Season
Back Row: Malcolm Webster (Assistant Manager), Stephen Clarke, Andy Beattie, Patrick Rayment, Mark Cooper, Keith Lockhart, Peter Melville (Physiotherapist).
Middle Row: David Moyes, Keith Osgood, Keith Branagan, Roger Hansbury, Dean Greygoose, Geoff Scott, Stephen Fallon.
Front Row: Michael Bennett, Stephen Pyle, Andy Sinton, Ken Shellito (Manager), Steve Spriggs, Kevin Massey, Alan Comfort, Tom Finney. Photograph by courtesy of *Cambridge Evening News*.

F.A. Youth Challenge Cup

First Round Proper
Ipswich Town Youth　6　0　Cambridge Utd Yth

Southern Junior Floodlit Cup

First Round
Southend United Youth　3　0　Cambridge Utd Yth

South East Counties League Cup Division One

First Round
Cambridge Utd Yth　0　4　Orient Youth

Eastern Junior Cup

First Round
Stevenage Borough Yth.　0　5　**Cambridge Utd Yth**

Second Round
Hitchin Town Youth　1　3　**Cambridge Utd Yth**
(After Extra-time)

Semi-final
Cambridge Utd Yth　0　4　Colchester United Youth

South East Counties League. Division One

	Pld	W	D	L	F	A	Pts
West Ham United Youth	30	24	3	3	120	27	51
Ipswich Town Youth	30	19	8	3	92	44	46
Tottenham Hotspur Youth	30	20	4	6	87	30	44
Chelsea Youth	30	17	8	5	76	40	42
Norwich City Youth	30	15	5	10	58	49	35
Arsenal Youth	30	16	1	13	59	45	33
Millwall Youth	30	12	6	12	59	51	30
Watford Youth	30	12	6	12	59	64	30
Portsmouth Youth	30	11	6	13	52	55	28
Gillingham Youth	30	10	8	12	39	57	28
Charlton Athletic Youth	30	9	8	13	60	73	26
Orient Youth	30	10	5	15	57	81	25
Southend United Youth	30	7	6	17	35	63	20
Fulham Youth	30	6	7	17	44	87	19
Queen's Park Rangers Yth.	30	6	6	18	45	71	18
Cambridge Utd Yth	30	2	1	27	32	137	5

1985-86 SEASON

Manager Ken Shellito made four major signings during the summer: Roger Hansbury (goalkeeper) from Burnley, Geoff Scott (defender) from Northampton Town, Stephen Massey (forward) from Hull City and David Crown (forward) from Reading. All four players were experienced, and were expected to considerably strengthen the backbone of the team.

The start of the season was eagerly anticipated by Cambridge United supporters, not so much for the impending Fourth Division campaign, but for the visit of Manchester United on Tuesday 30th July 1985 for a Testimonial Match on behalf of two long serving Cambridge United players, the two Stephens, Fallon and Spriggs. A crowd of 6,017 spectators maintained a full minute's absolute silence before the game in respect for the victims of the Bradford City F.C. fire disaster, and were rewarded with an excellent game. A Cambridge United team boosted by the inclusion of guest players Brendon Batson, Martin O'Neill and Alan Biley, competed on equal terms with their glamorous opponents, and went ahead with an Andy Sinton goal after 11 minutes. Manchester United hit back to take a 2-1 lead before Keith Osgood equalized ten minutes from time, only for Geoff Scott to concede an own goal shortly afterwards to give the visitors a 3-2 win.

On Wednesday 7th August Norwich City came to the Abbey Stadium to play Cambridge United for the Cambs Professional Cup, but there were only 700 people to witness them produce football of such pace and quality that they were 4-0 up at the interval. Norwich eased up in the second half, and an improved display from United saw them reduce the arrears before the end with a Stephen Massey penalty to make the score 4-1.

A few days before the official opening of the season the interim Popplewell Report on soccer hooliganism was published, with recommendations including the introduction of identity cards, banning visiting supporters, and stringent new fire and safety precautions, measures which seriously threatened the futures of Football League clubs in the lower Divisions if implemented hastily.

The first league game was at home to Hartlepool United on Saturday 17th August, a team Cambridge United had not lost to in their previous twelve meetings, and they continued that record with the help of a hat-trick from Stephen Pyle in a 4-2 victory.

Three days later the Club played at home in the First Round First Leg of the Milk Cup against Brentford for the second year in succession. After taking an early lead from an 11th minute penalty from Andy Sinton, United continued to play the better football, but were punished for not capitalizing on their dominance when Brentford scored a last minute equalizer from a corner. Two weeks later at Brentford, the "Bees" won the Second Leg 2-0 for a comfortable passage into the next round.

The Club's first away game of the season on Friday 23rd August was an unmitigated disaster, resulting in a 6-2 defeat against Tranmere Rovers. Former Spurs defender Keith Osgood received an injury to his back which eventually caused his retirement from the game. Captain Geoff Scott also had a nightmare of a match as the defence was ruthlessly exposed by the Merseysiders. That match started a run of seven successive defeats which saw the Club drift into the re-election zone, fuelling fears that the decline of the two previous seasons was going to continue.

Keith McPherson was signed from West Ham United on a month's loan to strengthen the defence, and he scored in the Club's first victory for eleven games, by 2 goals to 0 at home to Preston North End on Wednesday 2nd October. That was followed three days later with another home win against Mansfield Town by 4 goals to 2.

Centre-half David Moyes was then sold to Bristol City for £10,000, to be replaced by the more experienced Steve Dowman, who was transferred from Third Division Newport County. Before the 3-1 home league win against Peterborough United on Saturday 26th October the Club were presented with a cheque for £2,500 for winning the "Spell and Win" Competition organized by the Football League Sponsors "Canon" in the Third Division the previous season.

At the beginning of November Cambridge United suffered three successive league defeats prior to losing 2-1 away to non-league Dagenham in the First Round Proper of the F.A. Challenge Cup before only 1,351 spectators on Saturday 16th November. It was the final straw that broke the camel's back, and eventually led to the resignation of Ken Shellito as Manager. While at the Club he had not signed a contract, and had commuted to Cambridge for work each day from his South London home in Cheam.

Former Cambridge United favourite Chris Turner was appointed as the new Manager in time to take charge of the team for the away match at Torquay United on Saturday 14th December 1985, which resulted in a 1-1 draw. He would have been heartened by the recent return to the side of Stephen Fallon, after a year's absence through injury, but in his first game in charge captain Geoff Scott received an injury which ended his playing career.

The next three home games were all victories, producing ten goals for United, and the improvement was confirmed when United travelled to Aldershot for the Freight Rover Trophy First Round group match on Tuesday 14th January, and won 1-0, although the attendance of 826 was a paltry figure. A week later a much better crowd of 2,253 turned up to see Cambridge United beat Peterborough United 4-1 at the Abbey Stadium in their home group match to progress into the Second Round. That game was played away to Third Division Gillingham on Monday 24th February and resulted in a 2-0 defeat against an unquestionably stronger team.

Former Ipswich Town footballer Mick Lambert joined the Club's staff in mid-January as the youth team Coach at the same time that P.G.L. Limited agreed to sponsor the youth team in the South East Counties League. As in the previous season the youth team struggled in the Senior Section, finishing bottom of the table once again, but this time with a slightly improved record of 13 points from 30 games. In the F.A. Youth Cup they lost 3-1 away to Chesterfield after winning 3-2 away to Welling United in the First Round Proper.

The reserve team represented the Club in the Wallspan Cup, but after winning 1-0 away to Vauxhall Motors' first team, they were thrown out of the competition with Tring Town for failing to play their Second Round match by the stipulated date.

At the end of January, Peter Butler was signed on loan from Huddersfield Town for a period which lasted for three months, and his performances made him a firm favourite at the Abbey Stadium. With several other players signed before the transfer deadline the results improved in the last month of the season, as the Club were faced with quite a battle to get out of the re-election zone. David Crown scored six goals in four games to equal Alan Biley's Club scoring record of 21 goals in a season by Saturday 19th April in the 1-0 home win against Crewe Alexandra. He increased that total by three goals in the remaining three games to set a new record of scoring 24 goals in a season since the Club joined the Football League. Although the Club lost only once in the last eleven games, they just failed by one point to pull out of the re-election zone, finishing third from bottom with 54 points.

At the Football League's A.G.M., all four clubs seeking re-election were re-elected, only after it was decided that in future the top club from the G.M. Vauxhall Conference (formerly Gola League) would be promoted to the Football League, and the bottom club in Division Four would be relegated.

Following the failure of the Football League clubs' national "Top Score" lottery to get successfully off the ground, Cambridge United in conjunction with Ipswich Town, Norwich City and Peterborough United decided to set up their own lottery called "Lotto" for the East Anglia area. With first prizes of £4,000 in cash and a car, the venture was launched in March, in the hope that it would provide a major increase in the commercial revenue for the participating clubs.

F.A. Challenge Cup

First Round Proper
Dagenham 2 1 Cambridge United

Milk Cup (Football League Cup)

First Round First Leg
Cambridge United 1 1 Brentford

First Round Second Leg
Brentford 2 0 Cambridge United
(Brentford won 3-1 on aggregate)

Cambs Professional Cup

Final
Cambridge United 1 4 Norwich City

Football League (Canon League) Division Four

	Pld	W	D	L	F	A	Pts
Swindon Town	46	32	6	8	82	43	102
Chester City	46	23	15	8	83	50	84
Mansfield Town	46	23	12	11	74	47	81
Port Vale	46	21	16	9	67	37	79
Orient	46	20	12	14	79	64	72
Colchester United	46	19	13	14	88	63	70
Hartlepool United	46	20	10	16	68	67	70
Northampton Town	46	18	10	18	79	58	64
Southend United	46	18	10	18	69	67	64
Hereford United	46	18	10	18	74	73	64
Stockport County	46	17	13	16	63	71	64
Crewe Alexandra	46	18	9	19	54	61	63
Wrexham	46	17	9	20	68	80	60
Burnley	46	16	11	19	60	65	59
Scunthorpe United	46	15	14	17	50	55	59
Aldershot	46	17	7	22	66	74	58
Peterborough United	46	13	17	16	52	64	56
Rochdale	46	14	13	19	57	77	55
Tranmere Rovers	46	15	9	22	74	73	54
Halifax Town	46	14	12	20	60	71	54
Exeter City	46	13	15	18	47	59	54
Cambridge United	46	15	9	22	65	80	54
Preston North End	46	11	10	25	54	89	43
Torquay United	46	9	10	27	43	88	37

Freight Rover Trophy (Associate Members Cup)

First Round

	Pld	W	D	L	F	A	Pts
Cambridge United	2	2	0	0	5	1	6
Peterborough United	2	1	0	1	3	4	3
Aldershot	2	0	0	2	0	3	0

Second Round
Gillingham 2 0 Cambridge United

East Anglian Cup

First Round Bye

Second Round
Eynesbury Rovers 2 4 Cambridge Utd Res.

Third Round
King's Lynn v Cambridge Utd Res.
NOTE: Cambridge United Reserves were thrown out of the competition for failing to fulfil the fixture.

Bancroft Cup

Final
Wisbech Town 0 1 Cambridge Utd Res

Wallspan Floodlit Cup

First Round
Vauxhall Motors 0 1 Cambridge Utd Res

Second Round
Tring Town v Cambridge Utd Res
NOTE: Both Tring Town and Cambridge United Reserves were thrown out of the competition for failing to fulfil the fixture by a certain date.

F.A. Youth Challenge Cup

First Round Proper
Welling United Youth 2 3 Cambridge Utd Yth

Second Round Proper
Chesterfield Youth 3 1 Cambridge Utd Yth

Southern Junior Floodlit Cup

First Round
Cambridge Utd Yth 0 4 West Ham United Youth

South East Counties League Cup Division One

First Round
Cambridge Utd Yth 1 3 Arsenal Youth

Eastern Junior Cup

First Round
Cambridge Utd Yth 3 0 Royston Town Youth

Second Round
Colchester United Youth 4 1 **Cambridge Utd Yth**

Eastern Junior 'Plate'
(NOTE: Matches were played during 1986-87 season)

First Round Bye

Second Round
Cambridge Utd Yth 5 1 Stevenage Borough Yth

Semi-final
Norwich City Youth 0 1 **Cambridge Utd Yth**

Final
Rothwell Town Youth 2 2 **Cambridge Utd Yth**
(After extra-time. Cambridge United Youth won 6-4 on penalties).

South East Counties League. Division One

	Pld	W	D	L	F	A	Pts
Tottenham Hotspur Youth	30	23	2	5	94	21	48
Chelsea Youth	30	22	3	5	93	41	47
Norwich City Youth	30	18	6	6	65	35	42
Arsenal Youth	30	18	5	7	57	29	41
Watford Youth	30	18	2	10	69	52	38
Millwall Youth	30	15	5	10	53	44	35
West Ham United Youth	30	12	9	9	70	54	33
Charlton Athletic Youth	30	12	5	13	52	58	29
Gillingham Youth	30	8	8	14	46	52	24
Portsmouth Youth	30	11	2	17	40	80	24
Fulham Youth	30	7	8	15	44	67	22
Ipswich Town Youth	30	6	10	14	35	60	22
Southend United Youth	30	8	6	16	28	55	22
Orient Youth	30	8	4	18	42	62	20
Queen's Park Rangers Yth	30	6	8	16	35	65	20
Cambridge Utd Yth	30	2	9	19	26	74	13

1986-87 SEASON

Prior to the start of the season a new souvenir shop and catering outlet was constructed in the old changing rooms near the Cut-Throat Lane entrance. It was also decided to form a "Junior U's" Club offering benefits for children who became members as well as giving them their own reserved section on the terraces.

The Club's first game of the season was at Molineux on Saturday 23 August for Wolverhampton Wanderers' first game in the Fourth Division, just over two years after they had played in the First Division. Watched by a crowd of 6,000 spectators, Mark Cooper scored a last minute goal to give United a fine 2-1 away win.

In the Football League Cup, re-titled the Littlewoods Cup, the following Tuesday United played away to Orient in the First Round First Leg, and came away with a 2-2 draw, another good result. A solitary goal on his debut from John Beck in the 84th minute on Saturday 30th August at home to Halifax Town gave Cambridge United all three points, and put them briefly on top of the Fourth Division. The excellent start to the season was continued three days later when David Crown got the only goal of the match in the eighth minute at home to Orient in the Second Leg of the Littlewoods Cup and the team held out to earn an attractive two-legged tie against First Division leaders Wimbledon in the Second Round.

The Club called a surprise public meeting at the Guildhall on Wednesday 10th September where "Life-Line" was launched, a scheme designed to raise funds for buying new players. Having had such a good start to the season, it was a good time to launch such a scheme, and it received an enthusiastic initial response. The experienced Mike Flanagan made his first full appearance for the visit of Wimbledon to the Abbey Stadium on Tuesday 23rd September which attracted 5,290 spectators. Although United battled bravely to narrow the gap in class, Wimbledon seemed to be heading for a 1-0 First Leg win when Andy Beattie scored a dramatic equalizer with an 88th minute headed goal. The Second Leg at Plough Lane had a smaller attendance of only 3,359 spectators, and they saw Mark Cooper score an equalizing goal before John Beck went off injured. Substitute John Rigby won a penalty with his first touch of the ball in the game, but Lindsay Smith's spot kick was blocked. However, John Rigby scored two minutes after the interval to level the scores again at 2-2, and from then on United stood their ground courageously for an hour and a quarter, including extra-time, to win the tie on the "away-goals" rule; a quite magnificent achievement.

On Friday 3rd October Cambridge United ended a Club record run of seven consecutive draws with a 5-0 home win against Stockport County, their biggest victory for nine years. The match was also Peter Melville's last game as the Club's Physiotherapist, a position he had held for nine years, and he was replaced by Roy Johnson, a former Cambridge City Manager and Arsenal Physiotherapist.

With the Club fifth in the league, the first defeat of the season was suffered in the fourteenth game on Saturday 11th October, away to second in the table Preston North End, but that reverse triggered off an inexplicable run of five consecutive league defeats.

New improved floodlights were installed in time for the Littlewoods Cup Third Round home match against Second Division Ipswich Town on Tuesday 28th October, an eagerly anticipated match witnessed by 8,893 spectators. David Crown scored on the brink of half-time, and amid much excitement Cambridge United performed impressively to hold on for a 1-0 victory, which brought the loudest cheer at the Abbey Stadium since the victory over Aston Villa six years earlier.

Not to be outdone the youth team won the Final of the Eastern Junior Cup (1985-86) 'Plate' Competition, beating Rothwell Town 6-4 on penalties after a 2-2 draw, having previously disposed of Norwich City in the Semi-final. Under the management of Graham Scarff since the start of the season the youth team had once again struggled in the South East Counties League Senior Section, and had made First Round exits in the F.A. Youth Cup (losing 2-1 to Chester City) and the Southern Junior Floodlit Cup (losing 1-0 away to Northampton Town in the replay after a 2-2 draw).

News that the first team had been drawn at home to the mighty Tottenham Hotspur in the Fourth Round of the Littlewoods Cup raised the excitement in the city to fever pitch, guaranteeing an 'all-ticket' sell-out match. Before that, however, United had to play away to Exeter City in the F.A. Challenge Cup First Round Proper on Saturday 15th November, and thanks to a goal from David Crown drew the match 1-1. The replay at the Abbey Stadium the following Wednesday delayed the "Spurs" match for a week, but marked the return to the Club of folk hero Alan Biley on a month's loan from Brighton, playing his first full match for seven months. He pleased the crowd of 3,618 when he scored United's second goal in the 83rd minute to clinch a 2-0 victory.

Against Tottenham Hotspur the near capacity crowd of 10,033 people saw United have the worst possible start when Clive Allen put the visitors ahead after only five minutes. However, three minutes later Mark Cooper headed an impressive equalizer, and the score remained the same until half-time. The class of the "Spurs" team costing £3 million eventually told, and they won comfortably by 3 goals to 1, although the Club's Board of Directors were happy having taken record receipts from the game.

From a position of hope and excitement, Cambridge United's season was virtually destroyed in the space of less than two weeks. On Tuesday 2nd December interest in the Freight Rover Trophy was killed stone-dead when Fulham scored four times in nine minutes either side of half-time to win 4-0, and make the second First Round group match against Southend United irrelevant.

The following Sunday Cambridge United had to travel to Maidstone United for the Second Round of the F.A. Challenge Cup, fearful of suffering another embarrassing defeat against a non-league club. Their fears were well grounded, for in front of 4,087 spectators, Maidstone, with former Manager John Ryan on their staff, scored a late goal to win 1-0, to leave the Cambridge United players utterly dejected and shame-faced. Trouble on the pitch after the game, not helped by naive policing, resulted in the Club temporarily suspending coaches for away matches.

With all the interest centred on the cup competitions the Club had slipped to sixth from bottom in the league table. Attempts to rectify this position were made when Peter Butler was signed from Third Division Bury Town with proceeds from the "Life-line" scheme and the successful Littlewoods Cup run. There was an immediate improvement as the team produced three successive league victories, with Mark Cooper scoring a hat-trick in the 3-0 home win against Rochdale on Saturday 20th December.

Team captain Steve Spriggs was presented with a glass decanter to commemorate his 450th first team league and cup appearance before the 1-1 home draw against Tranmere Rovers on Saturday 14th February 1987. Before the same match a cheque for £11,500 was presented to the Club from the "Life-Line" scheme. One game later Steve Spriggs broke Stephen Fallon's Club record of 405 Football League appearances, scoring a goal in the 3-0 away win at Lincoln, which started a run of five games without conceding a goal.

With the Club moving into the top half of the table, hopes were high that the improvement could be maintained so that a final place in the "play-off" positions could be obtained, thereby offering a chance of promotion to Division Three. However, shortly after signing a new contract, leading goalscorer Mark Cooper was transferred to Tottenham Hotspur in a complicated deal which would give Cambridge United more money in staged payments depending on his progress.

Mark Cooper's departure, although in the best short term financial interests of the Club, seriously hindered the chances of getting among the "play-off" places, as did the absence of Chris Turner at a vital time with back trouble, which necessitated an operation. Four defeats in succession, without scoring a goal, meant that the Club finished in eleventh place with 62 points. David Crown was leading goalscorer again with 16 goals, and Ian Measham, who played in every first team game, won the Supporters Club Player of the Year Award.

At the beginning of May the Board of Directors decided to make Chris Turner General Manager of the Club, giving him overall responsibility for the day-to-day administration of the Club, as well as team matters.

F.A. Challenge Cup

First Round Proper
Exeter City 1 1 **Cambridge United**

First Round Proper Replay
Cambridge United 2 0 Exeter City

Second Round Proper
Maidstone United 1 0 **Cambridge United**

Littlewoods Cup (Football League Cup)

First Round First Leg
Orient 2 2 **Cambridge United**

First Round Second Leg
Cambridge United 1 0 Orient
(Cambridge United won 3-2 on aggregate)

Second Round First Leg
Cambridge United 1 1 Wimbledon

Second Round Second Leg
Wimbledon 2 2 **Cambridge United**
(After extra-time. Cambridge United won on the 'Away Goals' Rule).

Third Round
Cambridge United 1 0 Ipswich Town

Fourth Round
Cambridge United 1 3 Tottenham Hotspur

Cambs Professional Cup

Final
Cambridge United 0 3 Norwich City

1986-87 Season

Back Row: Mark Cooper, Andy Beattie, Keith Branagan, Steve Dowman, Lindsay Smith.
Third Row: David Headly, Farron Blackburn, Malcolm Webster (Assistant Manager), Patrick Rayment, John Beck, Graham Scarff (Youth Team Manager), Ian Measham, Stephen Fallon, Chris Turner (Manager), Patrick Conway, Mickey Woodhouse.
Second Row: Brian Mundee, Steve Spriggs, David Crown, David Tong, Tony Towner.
Front Row: Colin Littlejohns, Jason Cowling, Paul Casey, Aidan Dodson, Paul Holdgate.

Football League (Today League) Division Four

	Pld	W	D	L	F	A	Pts
Northampton Town	46	30	9	7	103	53	99
Preston North End	46	26	12	8	72	47	90
Southend United	46	25	5	16	68	55	80
Wolverhampton Wanderers	46	24	7	15	69	50	79
Colchester United	46	21	7	18	64	56	70
Aldershot	46	20	10	16	64	57	70
Orient	46	20	9	17	64	61	69
Scunthorpe United	46	18	12	16	73	57	66
Wrexham	46	15	20	11	70	51	65
Peterborough United	46	17	14	15	57	50	65
Cambridge United	46	17	11	18	60	62	62
Swansea City	46	17	11	18	56	61	62
Cardiff City	46	15	16	15	48	50	61
Exeter City	46	11	23	12	53	49	56
Halifax Town	46	15	10	21	59	74	55
Hereford United	46	14	11	21	60	61	53
Crewe Alexandra	46	13	14	19	70	72	53
Hartlepool United	46	11	18	17	44	65	51
Stockport County	46	13	12	21	40	69	51
Tranmere Rovers	46	11	17	18	54	72	50
Rochdale	46	11	17	18	54	73	50
Burnley	46	12	13	21	53	74	49
Torquay United	46	10	18	18	56	72	48
Lincoln City	46	12	12	22	45	65	48

Freight Rover Trophy First Round

First Round

	Pld	W	D	L	F	A	Pts
Southend United	2	2	0	0	7	5	6
Fulham	2	1	0	1	5	2	3
Cambridge United	2	0	0	2	4	9	0

Wallspan Floodlit Cup

First Round
Berkhamsted Town 2 2 Cambridge Utd Yth

First Round Replay
Berkhamsted Town 3 2 Cambridge Utd Yth

F.A. Youth Challenge Cup

First Round Proper
Chester City Youth 2 1 Cambridge Utd Yth

Southern Junior Floodlit Cup

First Round
Cambridge Utd Yth 2 2 Northampton Town Yth

First Round Replay
Northampton Town Yth 1 0 Cambridge Utd Yth

South East Counties League Cup Division One

First Round
Cambridge Utd Yth 0 1 Luton Town Youth

South East Counties League. Division One

	Pld	W	D	L	F	A	Pts
Tottenham Hotspur Youth	30	23	4	3	90	25	50
Watford Youth	30	21	6	3	92	32	48
Chelsea Youth	30	19	4	7	65	35	42
Arsenal Youth	30	16	7	7	73	41	39
West Ham United Youth	30	15	3	12	67	66	33
Millwall Youth	30	13	7	10	49	60	33
Portsmouth Youth	30	13	5	12	44	46	31
Norwich City Youth	30	11	9	10	41	45	31
Ipswich Town Youth	30	11	7	12	55	60	29
Charlton Athletic Youth	30	9	9	12	47	48	27
Gillingham Youth	30	8	9	13	51	62	25
Orient Youth	30	8	5	17	53	68	21
Southend United Youth	30	8	5	17	36	61	21
Queen's Park Rangers Yth	30	8	4	18	32	60	20
Cambridge Utd Yth	30	4	8	18	32	70	16
Fulham Youth	30	5	4	21	28	76	14

1987-88 SEASON

The Club played two Testimonial Matches in pre-season for Steve Dowman and Stephen Fallon. The former's Testimonial game at home to Ipswich Town on Friday 7th August resulted in a narrow 1-0 defeat, but Stephen Fallon's match at home to First Division Wimbledon three days later gave plenty of hope for the season when two goals from David Crown gave United a 2-1 victory.

Before the official start of the season, Club Secretary Phil Hough resigned after two years in the position to take over as Secretary of Second Division Oldham Athletic, and Kathy Robinson took over as Acting Secretary.

Having turned a £122,000 loss on the previous year into a small profit in the current year, and with several new players signed on, the season ahead was looked upon as having plenty of promise. However, that optimism was shattered with a shock opening day 3-0 defeat away to Exeter City on Saturday 15th August. The following Tuesday United could only draw 1-1 at home to Aldershot in the Littlewoods Cup First Round First Leg, but hopes were raised when David Crown scored a hat-trick in the 4-1 win in the next game, to be followed by an excellent 4-1 away win at Aldershot in the Second Leg of the Littlewoods Cup.

The Second Round draw gave Cambridge United attractive opposition in F.A. Cup holders, Coventry City, but the First Leg at the Abbey Stadium on Tuesday 22nd September attracted a crowd of only 5,166 spectators, over 600 less than the crowd that watched United gain an encouraging 2-0 away win at highly placed Burnley the previous Saturday.

Against First Division Coventry, United were unfortunate to concede an own goal early in the game, and thereafter deserved an equalizer which was not forthcoming. In the Second Leg in Coventry two weeks later David Crown managed to score a goal, but the "Sky Blues" registered two, to win the tie 3-1 on aggregate. Apart from the good experience for the players, the attendance of 10,096 brought in some welcome extra income.

In October the Club was granted a licence by the Football Association to run a Centre of Excellence at the Coldham's Common Sports Complex on Thursday evenings throughout the season. This provided the Club with the opportunity to train and develop the skills of the promising young players in the Cambridge area, at an age previously prohibited.

A reserve team was entered in the Essex & Herts Border Combination at the start of the season, a league consisting mainly of Vauxhall Opel League (formerly Isthmian League) sides. They managed to win their first six games in the competition before tasting their first defeat early in October, although they maintained a high place in the table throughout the season.

Following a comfortable 4-0 home win over bottom of the table Newport County on Saturday 10th October, Cambridge United's first team had an excellent 2-0 away victory against highly placed Leyton Orient a week later to push them into the top half of the table, just four points behind the leaders. The following Tuesday the Club had an excellent opportunity to close the gap further when they travelled to Molineux to play Wolverhampton Wanderers, but the promotion favourites satisfied their home crowd of 6,492 supporters with an emphatic 3-0 win.

The return to the Club of Jamie Murray from Brentford was added to when Ian Benjamin, a forward from Peterborough United, was signed for £25,000. However, on the debit side, leading goalscorer with twelve goals, David Crown, was transferred to Southend United for £45,000. It was a period of transition for the Club as Assistant Manager Malcolm Webster decided to sever his long association with the Club, leaving the game of football completely. Club Physiotherapist Roy Johnson was also appointed as the Club's Secretary in mid-November, while John Beck, an experienced player, was given extra coaching responsibilities for the first team.

On Monday 9th November 1987 the youth team produced a quite marvellous performance to beat Norwich City Youth 2-0 at the Abbey Stadium in the First Round Proper of the F.A. Youth Cup. To put the result in perspective, the youth team had lost all of their previous fourteen matches, and they had twice lost by 5 goals to 0 against Norwich City, once in the league, and again in the First Round of the South East Counties League Cup three days later. In the Second Round of the F.A. Youth Cup four weeks later they lost 4-2 away to Walsall Youth. Their only other cup game was away to Leyton Orient in the Southern Junior Floodlit Cup, but that resulted in another defeat by 3 goals to 2.

The first team were given a home draw in the First Round Proper of the F.A. Challenge Cup against Vauxhall Opel League side Farnborough Town. Andy Beattie and Ian Benjamin gave United a 2-0 lead after 17 minutes, but far from cruising to a comfortable victory, they allowed the non-league side to pull back a goal, and then had to hang on desperately to their narrow lead after Gary Clayton was sent off. The Second Round draw gave Cambridge United another home match against Yeovil Town, also from the Vauxhall Opel League, on Saturday 5th December. With a good following in the crowd of 2,588 spectators, Yeovil kept United at bay, and then scored in the 84th minute to win 1-0, to add a further chapter of embarrassment to the Club's dismal F.A. Cup record against non-league teams.

Four days before the F.A. Cup defeat, Cambridge United went out of another competition leading to Wembley Stadium, the newly named Sherpa Van Trophy (the Associate Members Cup). Not taking the competition seriously enough, several players were rested for the away match with Peterborough United, and not surprisingly they lost by 3 goals to 0. In the other group match at home to Colchester United, Cambridge United could only manage a 0-0 draw.

After some uncertainty first team captain Peter Butler was eventually sold to Southend United for a fee in the region of £60,000, which was virtually five times the sum paid for him. His last game was the 1-0 home win over Torquay United on Saturday 6th February, a match which saw Ron Hildersley and Les Lawrence make their debuts for the Club, while Andy Sayer, a forward from Wimbledon, also played his first game while one loan. Before that game a £15,000 cheque from "Life-line" was handed over to the Club, making a total of £46,000 in sixteen months.

A promising spell in February saw the Club move into contention for reaching the "play-off" places, but at the end of the month those hopes suffered a severe jolt with two successive 3-0 defeats, at home to Swansea City on 27th February, and three days later at Wrexham.

Cambridge United accepted an invitation to play Cambridge City for the Addenbrooke's Cup at Milton Road on Wednesday 9th March. A crowd of 825 people saw a thoroughly entertaining game finish level at two goals each, and in a penalty 'shoot-out' Cambridge City won the cup by 5 goals to 4.

As the transfer deadline approached at the end of March, first team goalkeeper Keith Branagan was sold to Millwall for a fee of £100,000. Former Cambridge United Manager John Docherty was leading Millwall towards the Second Division Championship, and was returning to his old club for the fifth time to buy a player. With the money received from the transfer, Chris Turner spend £11,000 of it in signing three promising young players: Gary Bull and Ian Hamilton from Southampton, and Phil Chapple from Norwich City.

The best home crowd of the season at Cambridge United - 5,106 spectators - was for the visit of league leaders Wolverhampton Wanderers on Sunday 10th April. United played well and deserved the point they got from a 1-1 draw when Gary Clayton scored with a superb shot from 25 yards.

When it was clear that United were not going to reach the "play-off" places, they were given permission by the Football League to play Laurie Ryan, a free scoring forward, who the Club signed from Dunstable after he had scored 46 goals for the Bedfordshire club during the season. In the couple of games he did play he was not able to get on the score sheet, and Cambridge United finished the season in fifteenth place with 61 points.

At the end of the season the decision was taken to withdraw the reserve team from the Essex & Herts Border Combination, in which United finished third, so that they could enter the new Capital League for Football League and top non-league reserve teams in the London area. Former Newmarket Town F.C. Manager Gary Johnson was appointed to take over the running of the reserve team for the new competition.

HOWLETT OFFICE EQUIPMENT LTD

WE SCORE with SALES, SERVICE and SATISFACTION

TECHNOPARK
645 NEWMARKET ROAD
CAMBRIDGE CB5 8PD
Telephone (0223) 242476

HOWLETT COMPUTER SYSTEMS

WE KEEP YOUR BUSINESS AT THE TOP OF THE LEAGUE

CHAPMAN HOW

FINANCIAL MANAGEMENT

Independent Financial and Insurance Advice
Services include:
Portfolio Management, Corporate and Personal Pensions, Life Assurance, Mortgage and all types of Insurance

197 High Street
Cottenham
Cambridge
CB4 4TB
Telephone (0954) 51453

A FIMBRA MEMBER

ALSO AT:
Cambridge, Burwell, Chesterton, Comberton, Littleport and Newmarket

The highlight of the season at the Abbey Stadium occurred on Wednesday 4th May 1988, when the Second Leg of the Gillette English Schools Trophy Final was staged there for the first time. The Cambridge and District Schoolboys had created considerable interest in Cambridge with their marvellous exploits in the national cup competition, which saw them win unexpectedly at Anfield against Liverpool Schoolboys in the Semi-final. In the First Leg of the Final, Cambridge Schoolboys performed well to draw 1-1 against West London at Fulham's Craven Cottage ground, and in anticipation of a good match, the biggest crowd of the season - 5,340 spectators, turned up at the Abbey Stadium for the Second Leg. A truly memorable game - a credit to both teams - resulted in a 2-2 draw, with the Cambridge goals coming from Steve Holden and John Ashdjian. The trophy was shared by both teams for six months each, with Cambridge a little disappointed that they had not won the competition outright. However, the quality of the football from the under fifteen year olds gave hope that some of those Cambridge players might some day win national honours once again with Cambridge United.

F.A. Challenge Cup

First Round Proper
Cambridge United 2 1 Farnborough Town

Second Round Proper
Cambridge United 0 1 Yeovil Town

Littlewoods Cup (Football League Cup)

First Round First Leg
Cambridge United 1 1 Aldershot

First Round Second Leg
Aldershot 1 4 **Cambridge United**
(Cambridge United won 5-2 on agregate)

Second Round First Leg
Cambridge United 0 1 Coventry City

Second Round Second Leg
Coventry City 2 1 **Cambridge United**
(Coventry won 3-1 on agregate)

Addenbrooke's Cup

Final
Cambridge City 2 2 **Cambridge United**
(Cambridge City won 5-4 on penalties)

Football League (Barclays League) Division Four

	Pld	W	D	L	F	A	Pts
Wolverhampton Wanderers	46	27	9	10	82	43	90
Cardiff City	46	24	13	9	66	41	85
Bolton Wanderers	46	22	12	12	66	42	78
Scunthorpe United	46	20	17	9	76	51	77
Torquay United	46	21	14	11	66	41	77
Swansea City	46	20	10	16	62	56	70
Peterborough United	46	20	10	16	52	53	70
Leyton Orient	46	19	12	15	85	63	69
Colchester United	46	19	10	17	47	51	67
Burnley	46	20	7	19	57	62	67
Wrexham	46	20	6	20	69	58	66
Scarborough	46	17	14	15	56	48	65
Darlington	46	18	11	17	71	69	65
Tranmere Rovers	46	19	9	18	61	53	64
Cambridge United	46	16	13	17	50	52	61
Hartlepool United	46	15	14	17	50	57	59
Crewe Alexandra	46	13	19	14	57	53	58
Halifax Town	46	14	14	18	54	59	55
Hereford United	46	14	12	20	41	59	54
Stockport County	46	12	15	19	44	58	51
Rochdale	46	11	15	20	47	76	48
Exeter City	46	11	13	22	53	68	46
Carlisle United	46	12	8	26	57	86	44
Newport County	46	6	7	33	35	105	25

Sherpa Van Trophy (Associate Members Cup)

First Round Group

	Pld	W	D	L	F	A	Pts
Colchester United	2	1	1	0	3	2	4
Peterborough United	2	1	0	1	5	3	3
Cambridge United	2	0	1	1	0	3	1

Bancroft Cup

Final
Wisbech Town 1 4 **Cambridge Utd Res.**

Essex & Herts Border Combination Cup

First Round
Cambridge Utd Res 2 0 Brimsdown Rovers Res.

Second Round
Leytonstone & Ilford Res. 2 1 **Cambridge Utd Res**

Fred Budden Trophy

First Round
Tilbury Res. 1 5 **Cambridge Utd Res**

Second Round
Wivenhoe Town Res. 3 0 **Cambridge Utd Res**

Kinsella Cup

Final
Wisbech Town 1 1 **Cambridge Utd Res**
(Wisbech Town won 2-1 on sudden-death penalties)

Essex & Herts Border Combination
Western Section

	Pld	W	D	L	F	A	Pts
Leyton-Wingate Res.	28	23	5	0	89	23	74
Leytonstone & Ilford Res.	28	19	3	6	95	31	58
Cambridge Utd Res	28	17	3	8	53	38	54
Enfield Res.	28	14	7	7	58	40	49
Kingsbury Town Res.	28	14	3	11	40	42	45
Cambridge City Res.	28	12	7	9	44	37	43
Barkingside Res.	28	11	4	13	36	40	37
Brimsdown Rovers Res.	28	10	4	14	36	47	34
Ware Res.	28	10	2	16	39	65	32
Bishop's Stortford Res.	28	8	6	14	32	59	30
Collier Row Res.	28	8	5	15	40	49	29
Walthamstow Avenue Res.	28	7	9	12	44	53	28
Harlow Town Res.	28	5	10	13	36	50	25
Hertford Town Res.	28	6	7	15	31	61	25
Clapton	28	7	3	18	28	66	24

NOTE: Leytonstone & Ilford Res. and Walthamstow Avenue Res. both had 2 points deduced for playing an ineligible player.

F.A. Youth Challenge Cup

First Round Proper
Cambridge Utd Yth 2 0 Norwich City Youth

Second Round Proper
Walsall Youth 4 2 **Cambridge Utd Yth**

Southern Junior Floodlit Cup

First Round
Leyton Orient Youth 3 2 **Cambridge Utd Yth**

South East Counties League Cup
Division One

First Round
Norwich City Youth 5 0 Cambridge Utd Yth

South East Counties League. Division One

	Pld	W	D	L	F	A	Pts
Tottenham Hotspur Youth	30	24	3	3	80	17	51
Watford Youth	30	22	5	3	75	30	49
Queen's Park Rangers Yth	30	18	6	6	48	25	42
Arsenal Youth	30	17	3	10	80	35	37
Chelsea Youth	30	16	5	9	65	42	37
West Ham United Youth	30	14	7	9	57	46	35
Charlton Athletic Youth	30	14	6	10	59	57	34
Ipswich Town Youth	30	15	1	14	50	55	31
Norwich City Youth	30	12	5	13	40	48	29
Southend United Youth	30	12	3	15	49	61	27
Gillingham Youth	30	9	7	14	41	58	25
Leyton Orient Youth	30	9	5	16	29	51	23
Millwall Youth	30	9	5	16	47	70	23
Portsmouth Youth	30	10	1	19	49	67	21
Cambridge Utd Yth	30	4	1	25	30	82	9
Fulham Youth	30	2	3	25	22	77	7

1987-88 Season

Back Row: Gary Poole, Neil Horwood, Paul Casey, Roy Johnson (Physiotherapist and Club Secretary), Keith Branagan, Gary Kimble, Alan Kimble.
Middle Row: Graham Scarff (Youth Team Manager), Gary Clayton, Ian Measham, Lil Fuccillo, Jason Cowling, Jon Rigby, Gary Bratton, Wayne Ewbanks, Malcolm Webster (Assistant Manager).
Front Row: Mark Crowe, Andy Beattie, Lindsay Smith, Chris Turner (Manager), Peter Butler (Captain), David Crown, John Beck. Photograph by courtesy of Cambridge United F.C.

Chapter Nine
STATISTICS

List of Honours

First Team
F.A. Challenge Cup. Fifth Round. 1982-83.
Football League Cup. Fourth Round. 1980-81, 1986-87.
Football League Division Three Promotion (2nd Place) 1977-78.
Football League Division Four Championship 1976-77.
Football League Division Four Promotion (3rd Place) 1972-73.
Southern League Premier Division. 1968-69, 1969-70.
Southern League Cup. 1961-62, 1964-65, 1968-69.
Southern League Championship Match. 1964-65, 1968-69, 1969-70.
Eastern Professional Floodlit Competition. 1969-70.
Midland Floodlit League Cup. 1963-64.
East Anglian Cup. 1961-62.
Cambs Professional Cup. 1958-59, 1959-60, 1963-64, 1964-65, 1965-66, 1966-67, 1968-69, 1971-72, 1973-74, 1975-76, 1982-83, 1983-84.
Cambs Invitation Cup. 1951-52, 1953-54, 1956-57.
North v South Challenge Match. 1966-67.
United Counties League Cup. 1950-51.
Cambs Challenge Cup. 1924-25, 1926-27 (Joint Winners) 1928-29.
Creake Charity Shield. 1924-25 (Joint Winners), 1925-26, 1928-29, 1929-30, 1933-34, 1935-36, 1938-39.
Cambs League Division One. 1925-26, 1928-29.
Cambs League Division Two. 1922-23.
Cambs League Division Three. 1921-22.
Bury & District Cup. 1928-29.
Culey Festival Cup. 1962-63.
Chatteris Engineering Works Cup. 1924-25, 1927-28.
Chatteris Nursing Cup. 1928-29, 1930-31.
Cottenham Nursing Cup. 1924-25.
Soham Nursing Cup. 1937-38.
Lakenheath British Legion Cup. 1963-64, 1964-65.
Wymondham Charity Cup. 1963-64, 1964-65, 1966-67 (Joint Winners).
Playing Fields Assocation Cup 1966-67.

Reserve Team
Town & County League (Eastern Counties) Cup. 1978-79.
Peterborough & District League Premier Division. 1951-52, 1952-53, 1954-55, 1958-59, 1960-61.
Peterborough Senior Cup. 1951-52, 1957-58, 1960-61
Peterborough Hospital Cup. 1950-51 (Joint Winners), 1951-52, 1952-53.
Isle of Ely Cup. 1953-54.
Cambs League Division Two. Section A. 1928-29.
Cambs League Division Three. Section B. 1926-27.
Chatteris Engineering Works Cup. 1957-58.
Doddington Hospital Cup. 1958-59 (Joint Winners).
Exning Charity Cup. 1960-61.
Bancroft Cup. 1985-86, 1987-88.

'A' Team
Cambs League Division Two. 1957-58.
Cambs League Division Three. 1955-56.
Cambs Lower Junior Cup. 1955-56.

Youth Team
South East Counties League Division Two. 1981-82.
Chiltern Premier League Cup. 1976-77.
Chiltern Youth League. 1959-60, 1960-61, 1961-62 (Under 18s).
Chiltern Youth League Cup. 1959-60 (Under 18s) 1960-61 (Under 16s) (Joint Winners).
Cambs F.A. Youth Cup. 1958-59, 1959-60, 1960-61, 1961-62, 1962-63, 1964-65, 1966-67, 1969-70 1970-71, 1972-73, 1976-77, 1978-79.
Cambs Youth League. 1958-59, 1959-60.
Cambs & District Sunday Youth League. 1976-77.
Cambs & District Sunday Youth League Cup. 1977-78.
Eastern Junior Cup 'Plate'. 1985-86.
Bicentennial Cup. 1976-77.
International Youth Tournament, Liblar, West Germany. 1965-66.
Wessling Challenge Cup, West Germany. 1968-69.
B.V.O. Osterfeld International Youth Tournament. 1976-77

Officers of the Club

President

1919-21	Rev. W. Warr
1921-39	H.C. Francis
1939-47	R.J. Wadsworth
1947-50	W. McLaren-Francis
1982-87	A.E. Harris

Chairman

1919-29	F. Mortlock
1929-39	T. Atkins
1939-45	F. Pettit
1945-48	W. Taverner
1948-51	W. McLaren-Francis
1951-54	R.J. Wadsworth
1954-61	G.C. Proctor
1961-62	J.B. Branch
1962-73	J. Woolley
1973-74	G.C. Proctor
1974-	D.A. Ruston

Vice-Chairman

1950-54	G.C. Proctor
1954-62	J. Woolley
1962-73	A.E. Harris
1973-74	C. Heffer
1974-77	S. Tanner
1977-83	A. Douglas
1983-87	C.R. Brett

1987-88	J.E.K. Barnes
1988-	R.H. Smart

Secretary

1919-22	S.J. Brown
1922-26	G. Chapman
1926-27	C.E. Elsden
1927-31	G. Chapman
1931-34	W. Taverner
1934-45	F. Pettit
1945-49	L.A. Sylvester
1949-55	F.T. Ward
1955-57	W.E.F. Silk
1957-61	V. Chapman
1961-68	W.E.F. Silk
1968-73	G. Baker
1973-78	J. Benson
1978-84	L. Holloway
1984-85	P.M. Daw
1985-87	P. Hough
1987-	R. Johnson

Treasurer/Accountant

1919-32	H. Bowman
1932-50	F. Pettit
1950-59	N.R. Barker
1959-71	J. Hallam
1971-74	R. Smith
1974-	D.A. Ruston

Directors

J.H. Brown (1950-56), A.E. Harris (1950-83), S.J. Starr (1950-75), C. Swainland (1950-60), R.W. Thulbourn (1950-60), J. Woolley (1952-73), K. Gilbert (1954-58), R. Duce (1956-68), B. Dosanjh (1958-62), S. Tanner (1960-74), J.B. Branch (1960-62), G.C. Proctor (1961-74), M. Wynn (1962-75), C. Heffer (1964-74), W.F. Silk (1968-69), R.H. Smart (1970-80, 1986), A. Douglas (1974-85), B. Moore (1974-80), J. Cooke (1975-85), J. Crook (1977-80), C.R. Brett (1980-87), S.W. Cutter (1980-83), B. Peacock (1980-84), N.R. Benton (1983-86), J.E.K. Barnes (1984-88), G.E. Taylor (1984-), S.G. Line (1984-87), R.J. Smith (1986-), R. Stops (1987-), J. Howard (1988-) C. Howlett (1988)

Managers

1948	A.E. Target
1949-50	Len Hartley
1951-55	Bill Whittaker
1955	Gerald Williams
1955-59	Bert Johnson
1959	Bill Craig
1960-63	Alan Moore (Player-coach 1959-60)
1963-66	Roy Kirk (Caretaker manager 1963-64)
1966-67	Matt Wynn (Caretaker manager)
1967-74	Bill Leivers
1974	Ray Freeman (Caretaker manager)
1974-78	Ron Atkinson
1978-83	John Docherty
1983-84	John Cozens (Caretaker manager)
1984-85	John Ryan
1985	John Cozens (Caretaker manager)
1985-86	Ken Shellito
1986-	Chris Turner

First Team Club Records

Record Transfer Fee Received: £350,000 from Derby County for Alan Biley, January 1980.

Record Transfer Fee Paid: £140,000 to Northampton Town for George Reilly, November 1979.

Best Performance in the Football League: 8th in Division Two 1979-80.

Most Football League points in a season: 65. Division Four. 1976-77. (Note: Total would be 91 points under new system of 3 points for a win).

Most Football League goals in a season: 87. Division Four. 1976-77.

Record Football League Victory and most goals scored in a match: 6-0 v Darlington HOME Division Four. 18th September 1971.

Record Football League defeat:

0-6	v	Aldershot AWAY Division Three. 13th April 1974.
0-6	v	Darlington AWAY Division Four. 28th September 1974.
0-6	v	Chelsea AWAY Division Two. 15th January 1983.

Largest Wins:

14-1	v	Godmanchester HOME Chatteris Engineering Cup 2nd Round. 11th February 1927.
14-3	v	Fakenham AWAY Friendly. 7th September 1954.
13-0	v	Gamlingay HOME Cambs League Premier Division. 14th September 1935.

Heaviest Defeats:

4-11	v	Wisbech Town AWAY F.A. Amateur Cup 2nd Round Replay. 22nd October 1932.
1-9	v	Cambridge Town AWAY F.A. Amateur Cup 1st Qual. Round. 7th October 1933.
0-8	v	Wisbech Town AWAY F.A. Challenge Cup Preliminary Round. 25th Sept. 1948.

Most Appearances for Club: Steve Spriggs -
Football League	411 (+) (5)
F.A. Cup	17
Football League Cup	30
TOTAL	458 (+) (5)

Record Goalscorer in a match:

5 Wally Wilson 12-0 v Chesterton Rovers. HOME. Cambs League Division Three. 10.9.21
5 Harvey Cornwell 8-1 v Warboys Town. HOME. Chatteris Nursing Cup 1st Round. 4.12.26
5 Brian Moore 6-1 v Sudbury Town. HOME. Eastern Counties League. 26.4.58
4 Brian Greenhalgh 6-0 v Darlington. HOME. Football League Division Four. 18.9.71

Record Football League Goalscorer in a season: 24 David Crown 1985-86.

Record Football League Goalscorer in a career: 74 Alan Biley.

Record Goalscorer in a season in all competitions: 68 Brian Moore 1957-58.

Record Goalscorer in career:
185	Harvey Cornwell	*
161	Russell Crane	*
117	Wally Wilson	*
115	Jimmy Gibson	
96	Phil Hayes	
87	Albert George	*
87	Alan Biley	

(* Denotes that total is incomplete)

Oldest player in Football League match: John Ryan 37 years 134 days v Derby County 1st December 1984.

Youngest player in Football League match: Andy Sinton 16 years 228 days v Wolverhampton Wanderers 2nd November 1982.

Most capped player: Tom Finney 7 appearances for Northern Ireland.

Record home gate receipts: £51,312.50 v Tottenham Hotspur, Littlewoods Cup 4th Round 25th November 1987.

First Team Sequences (In all competitions).

Consecutive undefeated matches: 23	26.12.28	to	4. 5.29
Longest run without a win: 34	4.10.83	to	28. 4.84
Most consecutive wins: 11	2.12.22	to	30. 3.23
Most consecutive defeats: 9	4.10.83	to	12.11.83
Most consecutive draws: 7	6. 9.86	to	30. 9.86
Longest run without conceding a goal: 8	26. 3.69	to	14. 4.69
Consecutive undefeated home matches: 23	10. 9.77	to	29. 4.78
Longest run of home matches without a win: 18	1.10.83	to	28. 4.84
Consecutive undefeated away matches: 15	10.11.28	to	21. 9.29
Longest run of away matches without a win: 35	14.11.81	to	2. 4.83
Consecutive home wins: 15	11. 2.22	to	16.10.24
Consecutive home defeats: 7	16. 3.85	to	30. 4.85
Consecutive away wins: 7	1. 4.29	to	21. 9.29
Consecutive away defeats: 12	6. 9.83	to	21. 1.84

First Team Sequences (Football League Only)

Consecutive undefeated matches: 14	9. 9.72	to	10.11.72
Longest run without a win: 31	8.10.83	to	28.4.84
Consecutive undefeated home matches: 22	10. 9.77	to	29.4.78
Consecutive undefeated away matches: 9	18. 3.86	to	11.10.86
Longest run without a home win: 16	8.10.83	to	28.4.84
Longest run without an away win: 32	24.10.81	to	9.4.83
Most consecutive wins: 7	19. 2.77	to	1.4.77
Most consecutive home wins: 10	27. 9.77	to	14.1.78
Most consecutive away wins: 3	9. 4.71	to	26.4.71
" " " " "	23. 4.75	to	16.8.75
" " " " "	26. 2.77	to	26.3.77

History of First Team Record Attendances

Attendance	Date	Venue	F-A	Opponents	Competition
3,000	3.9.27	AWAY	1-3	Great Yarmouth Town (F.A. Cup Extra Prelim. Round)
5,000	17.1.48	HOME	0-1	Cambridge Town (F.A. Amateur Cup 1st Round Proper)
6,879	5.9.51	AWAY	1-3	King's Lynn (East Anglian Cup 1st Round)
9,814	1.5.52	AWAY	2-0	Cambridge City (Cambs Invitation Cup Final)
7,344	25.10.52	HOME	0-0	King's Lynn (F.A. Cup 3rd Qualifying Round)
11,908	10.10.53	AWAY	3-1	Cambridge City (F.A. Cup 2nd Qualifying Round)
7,500	21.11.53	HOME	2-2	Newport County (F.A. Cup 1st Round Proper)
10,000	12.12.53	HOME	1-2	Bradford Park Avenue (F.A. Cup 2nd Round Proper)
14,000	1.5.70	HOME	4-3	Chelsea (Friendly)
15,722	26.12.70	AWAY	1-4	Notts County (Football League Division Four)
17,059	21.4.72	AWAY	2-1	Southend United (Football League Division Four)
10,542	28.4.73	HOME	3-2	Mansfield Town (Football League Division Four)
18,281	16.8.77	AWAY	0-0	Brighton & Hove Albion (Football League Cup 1st Round)
18,976	23.8.77	AWAY	1-3	Brighton & H. Alb. (Football League Cup 1st Rnd. Replay)
21,527	22.8.78	AWAY	2-0	Brighton & Hove Albion (Football League Division Two)
11,406	7.4.79	HOME	0-0	West Ham United (Football League Division Two)
21,795	10.4.79	AWAY	1-1	Crystal Palace (Football League Division Two)
22,898	8.9.79	AWAY	0-2	Sunderland (Football League Division Two)
24,092	27.10.79	AWAY	0-2	Newcastle United (Football League Division Two)
12,000	26.1.80	HOME	1-1	Aston Villa (F.A. Cup 4th Round Proper)
36,835	30.1.80	AWAY	1-4	Aston Villa (F.A. Cup 4th Round Proper Replay)
36,002	21.2.81	AWAY	2-4	West Ham United (Football League Division Two)

First Team League Attendance Records

Season	Number of Home Matches	Total Attendance	Average Home Attendance	League
1951-52	19 (3)	47,843	2,518	Eastern Counties League
1952-53	22 (1)	54,242	2,466	Eastern Counties League
1953-54	21	56,244	2,678	Eastern Counties League
1954-55	21	63,263	3,013	Eastern Counties League
1955-56	17 (5)	39,962	2,351	Eastern Counties League
1956-57	17 (2)	48,855	2,874	Eastern Counties League
1957-58	16 (2)	42,455	2,653	Eastern Counties League
1958-59	16	52,224	3,264	Southern League South East
1959-60	20 (1)	50,184	2,509	Southern League Division 1
1960-61	20	53,397	2,670	Southern League Division 1
1961-62	21	58,538	2,788	Southern League Premier
1962-63	20	78,961	3,948	Southern League Premier
1963-64	21	64,372	3,065	Southern League Premier
1964-65	21	63,414	3,020	Southern League Premier
1965-66	21	58,143	2,769	Southern League Premier
1966-67	21	57,309	2,729	Southern League Premier
1967-68	21	72,411	3,448	Southern League Premier
1968-69	21	63,063	3,003	Southern League Premier
1969-70	21	67,457	3,212	Southern League Premier
1970-71	23	113,192	4,921	Football League Division 4
1971-72	23	112,594	4,895	Football League Division 4
1972-73	23	97,229	4,227	Football League Division 4
1973-74	23	101,003	4,391	Football League Division 3
1974-75	23	69,485	3,021	Football League Division 4
1975-76	23	58,974	2,564	Football League Division 4
1976-77	23	102,052	4,437	Football League Division 4
1977-78	23	129,943	5,650	Football League Division 3
1978-79	21	144,854	6,898	Football League Division 2
1979-80	21	128,637	6,126	Football League Division 2
1980-81	21	121,711	5,796	Football League Division 2
1981-82	21	106,509	5,072	Football League Division 2
1982-83	21	94,711	4,513	Football League Division 2
1983-84	21	84,176	4,008	Football League Division 2
1984-85	23	48,357	2,102	Football League Division 3
1985-86	23	48,352	2,102	Football League Division 4
1986-87	23	64,090	2,787	Football League Division 4
1987-88	23	51,616	2,244	Football League Division 4

Note: Figures in brackets denote number of attendances missing that season.

Cambridge Evening News Player of the Year

Season	Player	Season	Player
1976-77	Stephen Fallon	1982-83	Chris Turner
1977-78	Stephen Fallon	1983-84	David Moyes
1978-79	David Stringer	1984-85	Steve Spriggs
1979-80	Steve Spriggs	1985-86	David Crown
1980-81	Steve Spriggs	1986-87	Keith Branagan
1981-82	Stephen Fallon	1987-88	Gary Clayton

NOTE: Cambridge Evening News Player of the Year based on points out of 10 awarded to each player in every League and Cup match, home and away.

Player of the Year

Season	Supporters Club Player of the Year	Season	Supporters Club Player of the Year
1962-63	Rodney Slack	1975-76	Steve Spriggs
1963-64	Jackie Scurr	1976-77	Malcolm Webster
1964-65	Rodney Slack	1977-78	Stephen Fallon
1965-66	Rodney Slack	1978-79	David Stringer
1966-67	Alan O'Neill	1979-80	Tom Finney
1967-68	Gerry Baker	1980-81	Lindsay Smith
1968-69	Robin Hardy	1981-82	Jamie Murray
1969-70	Dennis Walker	1982-83	Chris Turner
1970-71	Terry Eades	1983-84	Andrew Sinton
1971-72	Terry Eades	1984-85	Tom Finney
1972-73	Brian Greenhalgh	1985-86	David Crown
1973-74	Peter Vasper	1986-87	Ian Measham
1974-75	David Lyon	1987-88	Alan Kimble

V.M. DONNELLY
& SONS LIMITED
LANSDOWNE PROPERTY DEVELOPMENTS LIMITED

CIVIL ENGINEERING CONTRACTORS

GENERAL CIVIL ENGINEERING CONTRACTS
LARGE AND SMALL INCLUDING
BULK EXCAVATION - ROAD CONSTRUCTION - SEWER CONSTRUCTION
GENERAL SITE WORK - PLANT HIRE

**Osborne House, High Street
Cottenham, Cambridge**

Telephone: Cottenham (0954) 50297

First Team Goalscorers

(Note: Figures in brackets denote number of penalties scored)

1921-22 Season	League		
Wally Wilson	24 (1)		
Lennox Edwards	5		
Fred Stevens	4		
Joe Livermore	4		
Albert Dring	3		
Len Cash	3		
Bob Patman	3		
William Rouse	3		
Sid Brown	2		
George Alsop	1		
Edward Stubbs	1		
Stanley	1		
Unaccounted Goals	21		
TOTAL	**75**		

1922-23 Season	League	Cups	TOTAL
Albert Dring	14	5	19
Wally Wilson	10	3 (2)	13
Tom Langford	6	2	8
Lennox Edwards	5	1	6
Harvey Cornwell	2	1	3
Bert Langford	2	0	2
William Stearn	2	0	2
Fred Stevens	2	0	2
Bob Patman	1	0	1
Len Cash	1	0	1
Tom James	1	0	1
Sid Brown	1	0	1
Own Goal	1	0	1
Unaccounted Goals	32	3	35
TOTALS	**80**	**15**	**95**

1923-24 Season	League	Cups	TOTAL
Albert Dring	10	1	11
Edward Fuller	11	0	11
Wally Wilson	9	0	9
Tom Langford	2	0	2
William Walker	2	0	2
E. Jeffrey	1	0	1
Harvey Cornwell	1 (1)	0	1
Unaccounted Goals	9	0	9
TOTALS	**45**	**1**	**46**

1924-25 Season	League	Cups	TOTAL
Wally Wilson	9	13	22
Harvey Cornwell	3	14	17
George Alsop	5 (1)	5 (1)	10
W. "Fanny" Freeman	1	4	5
Fred Stevens	1	3	4
Harold Watson	2	2	4
Bert Langford	2	1	3
Bob Patman	1	0	1
Albert Dring	0	1 (1)	1
William Walker	0	1 (1)	1
Own Goals	2	0	2
Unaccounted Goals	9	16	25
TOTALS	**35**	**60**	**95**

1925-26 Season	League	Cups	TOTAL
Harvey Cornwell	22 (1)	4	26
Charlie Greaves	17	4	21
Edward Fuller	11 (2)	4	15
Joe Livermore	5	1	6
W. "Fanny" Freeman	6	0	6
Frank Luff	3	2	5
William Stearn	3 (1)	0	3
A. Haylock	3	0	3
George Alsop	0	2	2
Jim Self	1	0	1
Tommy Caldecoat	1	0	1
Unaccounted Goals	32	19	51
TOTALS	**104**	**36**	**140**

1926-27 Season	League	Cups	TOTAL
Harvey Cornwell	12	9	21
Albert Mickle	9	6	15
Harold Watson	7	3	10
Edward Fuller	9	0	9
Joe Livermore	6	3	9
George Alsop	6 (2)	1	7
R. "Dick" Harris	4	1	5
W. "Fanny" Freeman	3	2	5
Bob Patman	2	2	4
A. Haylock	1	2	3
C. Morley	0	2	2
Frank Luff	1	0	1
F. Archer	1	0	1
Tom Langford	1	0	1
Mathews	1	0	1
Unaccounted Goals	21	10	31
TOTALS	**84**	**41**	**125**

1927-28 Season	Cambs League	Bury League	Cups	TOTAL
Harvey Cornwell	14	3	6	23
Harold Watson	7	4	11 (1)	22
George Alsop	9 (1)	1	10 (1)	20
H.V. "Dick" Camps	8	2	6	16
Joe Livermore	0	2	9	11
George Chapman	0	0	8	8
Jack Raynerr	3	1	0	4
Wally Wilson	0	0	3	3
Charles Taverner	3	0	0	3
Albert Mickle	0	0	2	2
Fred Stevens	2	0	0	2
R. "Dick" Harris	1	0	0	1
Lennox Edwards	1	0	0	1
Own Goals	1	1	2	4
Unaccounted Goals	15	3	8	26
TOTALS	**64**	**17**	**65**	**146**

1928-29 Season	League	Cups	TOTAL
Harvey Cornwell	15	15	30
Harold Watson	15	13	28
Wally Wilson	10	11	21
George Alsop	7	3	10
Sid Hulyer	2	4	6
R. "Dick" Harris	3	3 (1)	6
Jack Rayner	2	1	3
Fred Taverner	2	0	2
B.F. Blayden	2	0	2
Harry Lucas	2	0	2
R. Ding	0	1	1
Cyril Haylock	1	0	1
Bob Patman	0	1	1
Lennox Edwards	1	0	1
Own Goals	3	2	5
Unaccounted Goals	17	35	52
TOTALS	**82**	**89**	**171**

1929-30 Season	League	Cups	TOTAL
Harold Watson	4	6	10
George Alsop	3	6	9
Harvey Cornwell	3	5	8
R. "Dick" Harris	4 (1)	3	7
Charlie Taverner	4 (1)	1	5
Sid Crooke	1	3	4
Joe Livermore	1	2	3
Lennox Edwards	0	2	2
Billings	0	2	2
Wally Wilson	0	1	1
Cyril Haylock	0	1	1
Sid Hulyer	1	0	1
William Walker	0	1 (1)	1
Ernie Caston	0	1	1
Harry Taylor	1	0	1
Tom James	0	1	1
W. "Fanny" Freeman	1	0	1
Own Goals	1	1	2
Unaccounted Goals	14	7	21
TOTALS	**38**	**43**	**81**

1930-31 Season	League	Cups	TOTAL
Fred Taverner	4	3	7
Harvey Cornwell	3	3	6
Roan	3	1	4
Harold Watson	2	1	3
William Walker	2 (2)	0	2
R."Dick" Harris	1	1	2
Wally Wilson	1	1	2
Ted Moule	0	1	1
Sid Hulyer	0	1	1
John Bradford	0	1	1
Ted Mathews	1	0	1
Own Goals	0	1	1
Unaccounted Goals	22	0	22
TOTALS	**39**	**14**	**53**

1931-32 Season	League	Cups	TOTAL
Harvey Cornwell	4	4	8
Jackie Bond	6	1	7
A. Edwards	3	1	4
Wally Wilson	2	1	3
Charlie Taverner	2	0	2
Fred Taverner	2	0	2
Tom James	2	0	2
Ablett	1	0	1
R. Ding	1	0	1
Whitehead	1	0	1
Reynolds	1	0	1
William Reeve	1	0	1
Own Goals	2	0	2
Unaccounted Goals	24	9	33
TOTALS	**52**	**16**	**68**

1932-33 Season	League	Cups	TOTAL
Jackie Bond	15	1	16
Ernie Collinge	8	2	10
Herbert Bailey	5	2	7
Harold Watson	5	1	6
Harvey Cornwell	3	2	5
R. "Dick" Harris	3	2	5
William Reeve	4	0	4
Cyril Haylock	3 (1)	0	3
Tom James	2	0	2
Wally Wilson	2	0	2
Butcher	2	0	2
Albert Flack	2	0	2
William Taverner	1	0	1
Own Goals	1	0	1
Unaccounted Goals	11	2	13
TOTALS	**67**	**12**	**79**

1933-34 Season	League	Cups	TOTAL
Jackie Bond	15	5	20
Harvey Cornwell	4	9	13
Harold Watson	5	7	12
Herbert Bailey	5	5	10
Albert Mickle	4	5	9
Fred Taverner	6	1	7
William Reeve	3	2	5
William Asplin	3	0	3
Wally Wilson	2	1	3
Tabor	2	0	2
S. "Fred" Johnson	2	0	2
Albert Flack	1	0	1
Williams	1	0	1
Cyril Haylock	1	0	1
A. Edwards	0	1	1
Own Goals	1	1	2
Unaccounted Goals	12	6	18
TOTALS	**67**	**43**	**110**

1934-35 Season	League	Cups	TOTAL
Jim Langford	7	4	11
Harvey Cornwell (Jun)	2	4	6
Fred Taverner	5	1	6
Wally Wilson	4 (1)	2	6
Ernie Amps	3	2	5
Harvey Cornwell (Sen)	3	2	5
Len Johnson	3	2	5
Basil Saunders	4	0	4
Monty Bull	3	0	3
Joe Richardson	1	1	2
Harold Watson	1	1	2
Sid Johnson	1	1	2
Albert Mickle	0	2	2
R. "Dick" Harris	1	0	1
Jackie Bond	1	0	1
Own Goals	1	0	1
Unaccounted Goals	22	2	24
TOTALS	**62**	**24**	**86**

1935-36 Season	League	Cups	TOTAL
S. "Fred" Sewell	18	15 (1)	33
Basil Saunders	9	8	17
Harvey Cornwell (Sen)	6	4	10
Fred Taverner	4	4	8
Wally Wilson	5 (1)	3	8
Len Johnson	4	4	8
Monty Bull	6	0	6
Mann	6	0	6
Ernie Wilsher	2	3	5
Jim Langford	3	1	4
William Asplin	1	2	3
Herbert Capper	2 (1)	0	2
William Whitmore	2	0	2
Herbert Bailey	1	1	2
Albert Flack	2	0	2
Sid Johnson	1	0	1
Ernie Humphries	1	0	1
Own Goals	1	0	1
Unaccounted Goals	10	15	25
TOTALS	**84**	**60**	**144**

1936-37 Season	League	Cups	TOTAL
Len Johnson	5	2	7
Fred Taverner	3	2 (1)	5
George Greenwood	3	2	5
A.S. Pink	3	0	3
William Asplin	1	2	3
Albert Flack	3	0	3
S. "Fred" Sewell	2	0	2
Monty Bull	2	0	2
Jim Langford	1	1	2
G. Parker	2	0	2
Harold Pink	2	0	2
Reg Kimberley	1	0	1
Lavender	1	0	1
Own Goals	1	1	2
Unaccounted Goals	16	1	17
TOTALS	**46**	**11**	**57**

1937-38 Season	League	Cups	TOTAL
Fred Mansfield	13	9	22
Herbert Smart	9	2	11
Harvey Cornwell (Sen)	7	2	9
Ernie Caston	4	1	5
Len Johnson	3	1	4
Monty Bull	1	3	4
Albert Flack	1	0	1
A.S. Pink	1	0	1
Ernie Wilsher	0	1 (1)	1
Robert Wilson	1	0	1
Jim Langford	1	0	1
Reg Kimberley	1 (1)	0	1
Own Goals	3	1	4
Unaccounted Goals	8	4	12
TOTALS	**53**	**24**	**77**

1938-39 Season	League	Cups	TOTAL
Fred Mansfield	14	4	18
Herbert Smart	12 (1)	5	17
Ron Sanderson	6	2	8
Jim Langford	6	1	7
Ernie Caston	3	1	4
Robert Brown	2	1	3
Joe Richardson	3 (2)	0	3
Smith	1	1	2
Joe Dye	1	0	1
Reg Wilson	0	1	1
Unaccounted Goals	23	1	24
TOTALS	**71**	**17**	**88**

1939-40 Season	League	Cups	TOTAL
Sid Hall	0	4	4
Fred Mansfield	2	0	2
Reg Wilson	2	0	2
Hutt	0	2	2
Burdett	0	2	2
Bob Bruce	0	1	1
Ernie Caston	0	1	1
Lawrence Miller	0	1	1
Unaccounted Goals	35	4	39
TOTALS	**39**	**15**	**54**

1947-48 Season	League	Cups	TOTAL
Russell Crane	7	3	10
Cyril Kirby	7	3	10
Roy Taylor	10	0	10
Reg Marsh	4	3	7
Albert George	5	0	5
Tommy Webb	3	2	5
Bill Bailey	3	1 (1)	4
John Gaunt	2	1	3
Bob Bishop	3	0	3
Brian Holmes	3	0	3
Reg Wilson	2	1	3
Jock Finlayson	0	2	2
Jim Smith	0	1	1
Ken Coates	1	0	1
Ernie Humphries	1	0	1
Own Goals	1	0	1
Unaccounted Goals	7	0	7
TOTALS	**59**	**17**	**76**

1948-49 Season	League	Cups	TOTAL
Russell Crane	40	3	43
Albert George	19 (4)	1	20
Roy Taylor	9	1	10
Derek King	7	0	7
Cyril Kirby	5	1	6
Ernie Humphries	3	1	4
Eric Brown	4	0	4
Terry McGrath	2	1	3
Gus Dasley	3	0	3
Ken Coates	2	0	2
David Robson	2	0	2
Neville Haylock	2	0	2
Keith Hudson	1	0	1
Wally Houston	1	0	1
Own Goals	2	0	2
Unaccounted Goals	1	0	1
TOTALS	**103**	**8**	**111**

1949-50 Season	League	Cups	TOTAL
Russell Crane	17	0	17
Albert George	14	2 (1)	16
Stan Thurston	14	1	15
Ken Coates	6	0	6
Maurice Hipkin	6	0	6
David Robson	4	0	4
Eric Brown	4	0	4
Len Hartley	4	0	4
Jimmy Summersgill	4	0	4
Derek King	1	0	1
Jack Lewis	0	1	1
Jim Connors	1	0	1
Neville Haylock	1	0	1
Dennis Smith	1	0	1
Ron Hilsden	1	0	1
Turner	1	0	1
Own Goals	1	0	1
Unaccounted Goals	3	0	3
TOTALS	**83***	**4**	**87**

*Note: Includes match abandoned v Stamford when leading 6-2.

1950-51 Season	League	Cups	TOTAL
Russell Crane	19	6	25
Ken Coates	18	5	23
Neville Rose	17	2	19
Stan Thurston	11	3	14
Albert George	7	1	8
Eddie Connelly	5	2	7
R. "Dolly" Pierson	2	3	5
Percy Anderson	0	2	2
Fred Mansfield	1	0	1
Roy Taylor	1	0	1
John Bell	1	0	1
Own Goals	0	1	1
Unaccounted Goals	5	2	7
TOTALS	**87**	**27**	**114**

1951-52 Season	League	Cups	TOTAL
Russell Crane	11	7	18
Joe Gallego	12	4	16
Albert George	8	4	12
Stan Thurston	8	2	10
Len Crowe	7	3	10
Bill Whittaker	10 (1)	0	10
Jack Bishop	4	1	5
Maurice Hipkin	4	0	4
Neville Rose	1	0	1
Sid High	1	0	1
Bob Bishop	1	0	1
Eric Brown	0	1	1
Unaccounted Goals	5	1	6
TOTALS	**72**	**23**	**95**

1952-53 Season	League	Cups	TOTAL
Jack Thomas	27	5	32
Russell Crane	12	4	16
Stan Thurston	11	3	14
Len Saward	10	1	11
Len Crowe	6	2	8
Bill Whittaker	5	2	7
Joe Gallego	3	1	4
Albert George	2	1	3
Ray Ruffett	2	1	3
Jack Bishop	2	0	2
Own Goals	2	0	2
TOTALS	**82**	**20**	**102**

1953-54 Season	League	Cups	TOTAL
Albert George	15	8	23
Jack Thomas	12	5	17
Joe Gallego	12	1	13
Stan Thurston	9	1	10
Len Saward	8	2	10
Teddy Bowd	5	4	9
Bill Whittaker	7 (4)	2 (2)	9
Les Stevens	5	3	8
Frank O'Hagan	5	0	5
Len Crowe	3	1	4
Russell Crane	2	0	2
Austin Egan	1	0	1
John Percival	1	0	1
Don Osborne	1	0	1
Own Goals	2	0	2
TOTALS	**88**	**27**	**115**

1954-55 Season	League	Cups	TOTAL
Peter Dobson	28	4	32
Les Stevens	11	0	11
Russell Crane	6	1	7
Teddy Bowd	5	2	7
Len Crowe	4	2	6
Jack Thomas	3	3	6
Percy Anderson	4	0	4
Jimmy King	4	0	4
Joe Gallego	3	0	3
Ian McPherson	3	0	3
Stan Thurston	3	0	3
Len Saward	2	1	3
Bob Bishop	1	0	1
Bill Whittaker	1	0	1
Own Goals	2	2	4
TOTALS	**80**	**15**	**95**

1955-56 Season	League	Cups	TOTAL
Peter Dobson	19	0	19
Jock Kyle	10	1	11
Len Saward	7	3	10
Jim King	4	3	7
Ron Murchinson	3	4 (1)	7
Russell Crane	5	0	5
Len Linturn	5	0	5
Bernard Butcher	2	2	4
Tony Copping	4	0	4
Edward Bernard	2	1	3
Bert Johnson	3	0	3
Harry Bullen	0	1	1
Len Crowe	1	0	1
Teddy Bowd	1	0	1
Ernie Hamper	1	0	1
Mike Renouf	1	0	1
Stan Thurston	1	0	1
Joe Gallego	1	1	2
Own Goals			
TOTALS	**71**	**16**	**87**

1956-57 Season	League	Cups	TOTAL
Kevin Barry	16	4	20
Bernard Moore	11	3	14
Brian Moore	10	3	13
Ron Murchinson	8 (1)	2	10
Wilf Mannion	9	1	10
Len Saward	5	3	8
Mike Renouf	4	2	6
Albert George	2	1	3
Jock Kyle	3	0	3
Les Stevens	2	1	3
Russell Crane	2	0	2
Keith Dunn	1	0	1
Ian McPherson	1	0	1
Neville Haylock	1	0	1
Keith Payne	1	0	1
Brain Iley	1	0	1
Own Goals	0	1	1
TOTALS	**76**	**22**	**98**

1957-58 Season	League	Cups	TOTAL
Brian Moore	49	19	68
Russell Crane	8	8	16
Kevin Barry	10	5	15
Bernard Moore	12	3	15
Wilf Mannion	7	5	12
Frank Lock	5	0	5
David Johnson	4	1	5
Vince Donnelly	3	1	4
Neville Brown	1	1	2
Len Saward	1	1	2
John McKinley	2	0	2
Vic Phillips	1	0	1
Jock Kyle	1	0	1
Ron Murchinson	1	0	1
Own Goals	3	0	3
TOTALS	**108**	**44**	**152**

1958-59 Season	Southern League	S.L. Zone	Cups	TOTAL
Brian Moore	10	4	6	20
Eddie Robinson	11	7	1	19
Kevin Barry	8	2	3	13
Allan Bull	7	1	3	11
Fred Howell	5	0	2	7
Jack Winter	4	1	0	5
Malcolm Handscombe	4 (1)	1 (1)	0	5
Ray Hamblett	1	2	1	4
Phil Hayes	0	0	4	4
Frank Lock	3 (1)	0	0	3
David Johnson	1	2	0	3
Gordon Quinn	0	3	0	3
Jim Campbell	0	1	0	1
Eric Farr	0	0	1	1
William Craig	0	0	1	1
Own Goals	0	1	0	1
TOTALS	**55**	**25**	**24**	**104**

1959-60 Season	League	Cups	TOTAL
Phil Hayes	30	4	34
Brian Moore	11	4	15
Fred Howell	4	5	9
Gordon Quinn	2	3	5
Alan Moore	4	1	5
Brian Basted	5	0	5
John Hancocks	1	4	5
Keith Payne	1	3	4
Eddie Robinson	3	0	3
Malcolm Handscombe	3	0	3
Tot Leverton	3	0	3
Tony Driver	2	0	2
Frank Allen	0	2	2
John Cutts	1	0	1
Dennis Woods	1	0	1
Own Goals	0	1	1
TOTALS	**71**	**27**	**98**

1960-61 Season	League	Cups	TOTAL
Phil Hayes	34	6	40
Brian Basted	13	6	19
Sam McCrory	8	8	16
Peter Rapley	11	5	16
Dennis Woods	9	5	14
Fred Howell	6	2	8
"Digger" Daley	7	1	8
Billy Welsh	5	2	7
Roy Kirk	3	2	5
Alan Moore	2	1	3
Alan Gammie	1	0	1
Own Goals	2	0	2
TOTALS	**101***	**38**	**139**

*Note: Includes Peter Rapley goal scored in abandoned match v Merthyr Tydfil.

1961-62 Season	League	Cups	TOTAL
Jimmy Gibson	19	16	35
Dennis Woods	12	6	18
Phil Hayes	6	12	18
Ray Colfar	9	5 (1)	14
Sam McCrory	6	5	11
Fred Howell	7	3	10
Graham Ward	3	3	6
Alan Moore	3	0	3
Harry Taylor	3	0	3
Mike Dixon	2	1	3
Roy Kirk	1	1	2
Brian Boggis	1	0	1
Alan Gammie	1	0	1
Tom Higgins	0	1	1
Tony Willson	0	1	1
Mick Granger	0	1	1
Peter Youngs	1	0	1
Billy Welsh	0	1	1
Own Goals	2	1	3
TOTALS	**76**	**57**	**133**

1962-63 Season	League	Cups	TOTAL
Jimmy Gibson	27	7	34
Matt McVittie	11	3	14
Norman Bleanch	13	0	13
Jim Sharkey	5 (1)	1	6
Dennis Woods	1	4	5
Fred Bunce	5	0	5
Fred Howell	1	3	4
Harry Taylor	2	1	3
Craig Bailey	3	0	3
Graham Ward	0	2	2
Roy Kirk	0	2	2
Billy Welsh	2	0	2
Graham Atkinson	2	0	2
Jackie Scurr	1	0	1
Graham Lawrence	1	0	1
Own Goals	0	1	1
TOTALS	**74**	**24**	**98**

1963-64 Season	League	Cups	TOTAL
Johnny Haasz	29	13	42
Jimmy Gibson	13	13	26
Colin Flatt	10	6	16
Graham Atkinson	9	4	13
Willy Devine	11 (2)	1 (1)	12
Graham Lawrence	7	3	10
Matt McVittie	5	3	8
Jimmy Dunne	2	4	6
Jackie Scurr	2	3	5
Brian Adlam	1	3	4
Billy Welsh	1	2	3
Norman Bleanch	1	0	1
Richard Ison	0	1	1
Own Goals	1	0	1
TOTALS	**92**	**56**	**148**

1964-65 Season	League	Cups	TOTAL
Peter Hobbs	11	14	25
Graham Atkinson	13	6	19
Dennis Randall	8	11	19
Johnny Haasz	4	15	19
Graham Lawrence	3	8	11
Matt McVittie	6	4	10
Jimmy Gibson	6 (2)	4 (1)	10
Billy Day	3	6	9
Jackie Scurr	5	4	9
Hugh Barr	6	1	7
Alan Payne	2	5 (1)	7
Billy Welsh	3	3	6
Derek Finch	0	4	4
Peter Hunt	0	3	3
Gerry Greene	0	2	2
Graham Felton	0	2	2
Brian Boggis	0	2	2
Lez Denzey	0	1	1
Gerry Graham	0	1	1
Brian Whitmore	0	1	1
Own Goals	2	2	4
TOTALS	**72**	**99**	**171**

1965-66 Season	League	Cups	TOTAL
Peter Hobbs	15 (1)	16 (4)	31
Philip Amato	8	9	17
Gerry Graham	7 (1)	9	16
Wesley Maughan	8	7	15
John Turley	10	4	14
John Fahy	7	5	12
David Barrett	6	5	11
David Bennett	1	7	8
Derek Finch	2	2	4
Brian Foscolo	0	4	4
Billy Day	1	2	3
Jackie Scurr	2	0	2
Gerry Baker	1	1	2
Brian Whitmore	0	2	2
Hugh Barr	0	2	2
Brian Boggis	1	0	1
Roy Poole	1	0	1
Alan O'Neill	1	0	1
Johnny Haasz	0	1	1
Alan Payne	0	1 (1)	1
Own Goals	0	3	3
TOTALS	**71**	**80**	**151**

1966-67 Season	League	Cups	TOTAL
David Bennett	13 (1)	7 (1)	20
John Fahy	3	17	20
Wesley Maughan	11	9	20
Alan O'Neill	11 (6)	8 (4)	19
David Barrett	12 (1)	3 (1)	15
Mike Fairchild	5	6	11
John Turley	2	7	9
Dai Ward	5	2	7
Jackie Scurr	3	2	5
Gerry Graham	3	1	4
Gerry Baker	2	2	4
Derek Finch	1	3	4
John Harley	1	2	3
Peter Hobbs	0	2	2
William Dickinson	0	2	2
Colin Booth	1	0	1
Billy Tedds	0	1	1
Own Goals	2	1	3
TOTALS	**75**	**75**	**150**

1967-68 Season	League	Cups	TOTAL
Harry "Bud" Houghton	15	13	28
Dai Ward	14	6	20
Alan O'Neill	10	5	15
David Barrett	7	5	12
John Harley	0	11	11
David Chambers	6	3	9
Bill Wall	6	2	8
Ian Hutchinson	6	1	7
Colin Booth	2	4	6
Jackie Scurr	2	2	4
Gerry Baker	3	0	3
Alan Payne	0	2 (1)	2
Pat Quartermain	1	0	1
Derek Finch	0	1	1
Own Goals	1	1	2
TOTALS	**73**	**49**	**122**

1968-69 Season	League	Cups	TOTAL
Bill Cassidy	18	8	26
Tony Butcher	13	4	17
Roly Horrey	7	7	14
John Saunders	7	3	10
John Gregson	4	6	10
Tony Nicholas	4	5	9
David Chambers	3	4	7
Gerry Baker	2	4	6
Dennis Walker	2	3	5
Jackie Scurr	2	2	4
Richard Habbin	1	3	4
Alan Doyle	0	4	4
Keith Lindsey	2	1 (1)	3
Terry Eades	2	1	3
Robin Hardy	1	1	2
Peter Robinson	0	2	2
Mick Brown	0	1	1
Bill Leivers	1	0	1
Alan Lord	0	1	1
Alan Payne	0	1	1
Own Goals	3	3	6
TOTALS	**72**	**64**	**136**

1969-70 Season	League	Cups	TOTAL
George Harris	23 (1)	12 (2)	35
Bill Cassidy	15 (2)	15	30
Tony Butcher	5	7	12
Malcolm Lindsey	8	3	11
Roly Horrey	4	6	10
John McKinven	3	6	9
John Gregson	3	5	8
Dennis Walker	4	4	8
Colin Meldrum	5	3	8
Robin Hardy	3	4	7
Paul Gilchrist	5	1	6
Alan Doyle	0	4	4
Terry Eades	0	4	4
Mel Slack	1	2	3
Peter Leggett	0	2	2
John Saunders	0	2	2
Brian Grant	1	1	2
Gerry Baker	1	0	1
Own Goals	3	0	3
TOTALS	**84**	**81**	**165**

1970-71 Season	League	Cups	TOTAL
Ivan Hollett	11	3	14
George Harris	7	4	11
Roly Horrey	3	8	11
Bill Cassidy	6	4	10
Dennis Walker	2	6 (3)	8
Peter Leggett	3	2	5
Malcolm Lindsey	1	4	5
Colin Meldrum	4	0	4
John Collins	4	0	4
John Peachey	0	4	4
Ron Howell	1	3	4
John McKinven	2	1	3
Jimmy White	2	0	2
Robin Hardy	1	1	2
Terry Eades	1	0	1
John Gregson	1	0	1
Chris Foote	1	0	1
Jim Thompson	0	1	1
David Knight	0	1	1
Peter Philips	0	1	1
Own Goals	1	0	1
TOTALS	**51**	**43**	**94**

1971-72 Season	League	Cups	TOTAL
Brian Greenhalgh	19	1	20
Peter Philips	8	2	10
David Lill	6	0	6
John Collins	4 (1)	1	5
Chris Foote	4	0	4
George Harris	4	0	4
Ron Walton	4	0	4
Brian Conlon	3	0	3
Ivan Hollett	2	1	3
Vic Akers	2	0	2
Roly Horrey	1	1	2
Terry Eades	1	0	1
Alan Guild	1 (1)	0	1
Keith Pointer	1	0	1
Dennis Walker	1	0	1
Own Goals	1	0	1
TOTALS	**62**	**6**	**68**

1972-73 Season	League	Cups	TOTAL
Brian Greenhalgh	18	0	18
David Lill	12	0	12
Bobby Ross	9 (2)	0	9
John Collins	8 (5)	1	9
Peter Philips	5	0	5
Ron Walton	5	0	5
Graham Watson	4	0	4
Terry Eades	1	0	1
Keith Pointer	1	0	1
Michael Robinson	1	0	1
Dennis Walker	1 (1)	0	1
Own Goals	2	0	2
TOTALS	**67**	**1**	**68**

1973-74 Season	League	Cups	TOTAL
Brian Greenhalgh	10	1	11
Dave Simmons	3	8	11
Dave Lennard	6	1	7
Bobby Ross	5 (4)	1 (1)	6
Bobby Shinton	5	0	5
Graham Watson	3	2	5
Mike Ferguson	4 (1)	1	5
Nigel Cassidy	4	0	4
Vic Akers	3	0	3
John O'Donnell	2	0	2
Chris Foote	1	1	2
Brendon Batson	1	0	1
David Lill	1	0	1
Terry Eades	0	1	1
Peter Philips	0	1	1
Own Goals	0	1	1
TOTALS	**48**	**18**	**66**

1974-75 Season	League	Cups	TOTAL
Bobby Shinton	15	1	16
Nigel Cassidy	7	2	9
Tommy Horsfall	7	0	7
Kevin Tully	7 (6)	0	7
Graham Watson	3	2	5
John O'Donnell	5 (1)	0	5
Brendon Batson	4	0	4
David Smith	3	0	3
David Lill	2	0	2
David Lyon	2	0	2
Graham Howell	2	0	2
Terry Eades	1	0	1
Paul Smith	1	0	1
Own Goals	3	0	3
TOTALS	**62**	**5**	**67**

1975-76 Season	League	Cups	TOTAL
Tommy Horsfall	15	3	18
David Lyon	9	1	10
Bobby Shinton	5	1	6
Dave Simmons	5	0	5
Alan Biley	3	2	5
Steve Spriggs	4	0	4
Nigel Cassidy	2	0	2
Ian Seddon	2	0	2
Paul Smith	2	0	2
Graham Watson	2 (1)	0	2
Brendon Batson	1	1	2
Stephen Fallon	1	1	2
Terry Eades	1	0	1
Kevin Griffin	1	0	1
Graham Howell	1	0	1
David Lill	1	0	1
John O'Donnell	1	0	1
Kevin Tully	1	0	1
Carlton Gilder	0	1	1
Own Goals	1	0	1
TOTALS	**58**	**10**	**68**

1976-77 Season	League	Cups	TOTAL
Alan Biley	19 (1)	1	20
Tom Finney	16 (1)	0	16
Jim Hall	15	0	15
Steve Spriggs	9	0	9
Tommy Horsfall	6	0	6
Graham Watson	6 (2)	0	6
Stephen Fallon	4	2	6
Trevor Howard	4	0	4
Keith Bowker	1	0	1
Tommy O'Neill	1	0	1
Ian Seddon	1	0	1
Floyd Streete	1	0	1
David Stringer	1	0	1
Own Goals	3	0	3
TOTALS	**87**	**3**	**90**

1977-78 Season	League	Cups	TOTAL
Alan Biley	21 (4)	3	24
Tom Finney	13	1	14
Stephen Fallon	8	0	8
Graham Watson	6	0	6
Steve Spriggs	5	0	5
Sammy Morgan	4	0	4
Floyd Streete	3	0	3
Gordon Sweetzer	3	0	3
John Cozens	2	0	2
Peter Silvester	1	0	1
Trevor Howard	1	0	1
Lindsay Smith	1	0	1
Jamie Murray	1	0	1
Kirk Corbin	0	1	1
Own Goals	3	0	3
TOTALS	**72**	**5**	**77**

1978-79 Season	League	Cups	TOTAL
Alan Biley	19	5 (1)	24
Tom Finney	8	1	9
Derrick Christie	3	0	3
Bill Garner	3	0	3
Steve Spriggs	2	0	2
John Cozens	2	0	2
Floyd Streete	1	0	1
Jamie Murray	1	0	1
Ian Buckley	1	0	1
Mick Leach	1	0	1
Sammy Morgan	0	1	1
Trevor Howard	0	1	1
Own Goals	3	0	3
TOTALS	**44**	**8**	**52**

1979-80 Season	League	Cups	TOTAL
Alan Biley	12	2 (1)	14
Tom Finney	13	0	13
George Reilly	11	1	12
Steve Spriggs	7	2	9
Derrick Christie	5	2	7
Roger Gibbins	4	1	5
Stephen Fallon	2	1	3
Lindsay Smith	2	0	2
Tommy O'Neill	2	0	2
Floyd Streete	1	0	1
Jamie Murray	1	0	1
Ian Buckley	1	0	1
John Cozens	0	1	1
Chris Turner	0	1	1
Bill Garner	0	1	1
Own Goals	0	1	1
TOTALS	**61**	**13**	**74**

1980-81 Season	League	Cups	TOTAL
George Reilly	8	3	11
Steve Spriggs	9	1	10
John Lyons	6	0	6
Tom Finney	3	3	6
Derrick Christie	5	0	5
Floyd Streete	4	1	5
Roger Gibbins	4	0	4
Tommy O'Neill	3	1	4
Stephen Fallon	3	1	4
Alan Taylor	2	1	3
Lindsay Smith	2	0	2
Martin Goldsmith	1	0	1
Own Goals	1	0	1
TOTALS	**53**	**11**	**64**

1981-82 Season	League	Cups	TOTAL
Joe Mayo	8	0	8
George Reilly	7	1	8
Steve Spriggs	7 (1)	0	7
Roger Gibbins	4	3	7
Stephen Fallon	5	0	5
Floyd Streete	5	0	5
Alan Taylor	2	1	3
Tom Finney	2	0	2
Lindsay Smith	2	0	2
Tommy O'Neill	2	0	2
Martin Goldsmith	2	0	2
Chris Turner	1	0	1
Derrick Christie	1	0	1
TOTALS	**48**	**5**	**53**

1982-83 Season	League	Cups	TOTAL
George Reilly	10	2	12
Joe Mayo	6	1	7
Andy Sinton	5 (1)	0	5
Floyd Streete	4	0	4
Chris Turner	2	2	4
Derrick Christie	2	1	3
Kevin Smith	2	1	3
Robbie Cooke	2	0	2
Keith Lockhart	2	0	2
Tom Finney	1	1	2
Ray Nicholls	1	1	2
Les Cartwright	1	0	1
Stephen Fallon	1	0	1
Martin Goldsmith	1	0	1
Steve Spriggs	1	0	1
Jamie Murray	0	1	1
Own Goals	1	0	1
TOTALS	**42**	**10**	**52**

1983-84 Season	League	Cups	TOTAL
Robbie Cooke	6	2	8
Andy Sinton	6 (4)	1 (1)	7
Derrick Christie	3	0	3
Keith Lockhart	3	0	3
Kevin Smith	2 (1)	1	3
Steve Spriggs	2	0	2
Stephen Pyle	2	0	2
Graham Daniels	2	0	2
Stephen Fallon	1	1	2
Martin Goldsmith	1	1	2
TOTALS	**28**	**6**	**34**

1984-85 Season	League	Cups	TOTAL
Robbie Cooke	6 (2)	1 (1)	7
Roy McDonough	5 (3)	0	5
Tom Finney	3	1	4
Mark Cooper	3	0	3
Alan Comfort	2	1	3
Andy Sinton	2	1	3
Steve Spriggs	2	0	2
Stephen Pyle	2	0	2
Graham Daniels	2	0	2
Stephen Fallon	1	0	1
Keith Lockhart	1	0	1
Patrick Rayment	1	0	1
Mark Farrington	1	0	1
Danny Greaves	1	0	1
David Moyes	1	0	1
Keith Osgood	1	0	1
Own Goals	3	0	3
TOTALS	**37**	**4**	**41**

1985-86 Season	League	Cups	TOTAL
David Crown	24 (1)	3	27
Stephen Massey	11 (3)	1	12
Steve Spriggs	5	0	5
Stephen Pyle	4	0	4
Alan Comfort	3	1	4
Steve Dowman	2	1	3
Tom Finney	2	0	2
Keith Lockhart	2	0	2
Patrick Rayment	1	1	2
Steve Richards	2	0	2
Peter Butler	1	0	1
Mark Cooper	1	0	1
Stephen Fallon	1	0	1
Kevin Massey	1	0	1
Keith McPherson	1	0	1
Brian Mundee	1	0	1
Andy Sinton	0	1	1
Clive Walker	1	0	1
Own Goals	2	0	2
TOTALS	**65**	**8**	**73**

1986-87 Season	League	Cups	TOTAL
David Crown	12	4	15
Mark Cooper	13	2	15
Lindsay Smith	7	1	8
John Beck	6	0	6
Steve Spriggs	4	0	4
Peter Butler	4	0	4
Mike Flanagan	3	0	3
Gary Kimble	2	0	2
Mark Schiavi	2	0	2
Colin Littlejohns	0	2	2
Jon Rigby	1	1	2
Steve Dowman	1	1	2
Andy Beattie	1	1	2
Jason Cowling	1	0	1
Aidan Dodson	0	1	1
Roy McEvoy	1	0	1
Alan Biley	0	1	1
Own Goals	2	0	2
TOTALS	**60**	**14**	**74**

1987-88 Season	League	Cups	TOTAL
David Crown	8	2	10
Jon Rigby	4	2	6
Gary Clayton	5	0	5
Peter Butler	5	0	5
Lindsay Smith	5 (2)	0	5
Alan Kimble	3	0	3
Ian Benjamin	2	1	3
Ron Hildersley	3	0	3
Gary Bull	3	0	3
Neil Horwood	2	0	2
Andy Beattie	1	1	2
Jon Purdie	2	0	2
Lil Fuccillo	2	0	2
Daral Pugh	1	0	1
Ian Hamilton	1	0	1
Phillip Chapple	1	0	1
Andy Hollis	0	1	1
Gary Poole	0	1	1
TOTALS	**50**	**10**	**60**

Football League Appearances 1970-1988

Name	Full	Sub	Name	Full	Sub	Name	Full	Sub
Spriggs, Steve	411	5	Rayment, Paddy	42	6	Farrington, Mark	10	0
Fallon, Stephen	405	5	Fisher, Bobby	42	0	Sweetzer, Gordon	9	0
Finney, Tom	323	9	Poole, Gary	41	2	Hildersley, Ron	9	0
Smith, Lindsay	257	1	Philips, Peter	40	13	Bull, Gary	9	0
Webster, Malcolm	256	0	Tully, Kevin	40	4	Hamilton, Ian	9	0
Eades, Terry	248	0	Kimble, Gary	39	2	Massey, Kevin	8	8
Murray, Jamie	226	16	Lennard, Dave	39	1	Lee, Andy	8	1
Watson, Graham	206	4	Ferguson, Mike	39	0	Calderwood, Jimmy	8	0
Lill, David	166	6	Horrey, Roly	37	2	Towner, Tony	8	0
Batson, Brendon	162	1	Daniels, Graham	37	2	Horn, Bobby	8	0
Biley, Alan	160	8	Meldrum, Colin	37	1	Richards, Gary	8	0
Stringer, Dave	153	4	Hollett, Ivan	37	1	Turner, Paul	7	7
Reilly, George	136	2	Roberts, Trevor	36	0	Flanagan, Mike	7	2
Vasper, Peter	136	0	Simmons, Dave	35	6	Griffin, Kevin	7	1
Christie, Derrick	132	6	Graham, Peter	35	3	Purdie, Jon	7	0
Donaldson, Dave	130	2	Smith, Paul	35	3	Pointer, Keith	6	2
Akers, Victor	122	7	Harris, George	35	3	Brattan, Gary	6	1
Guild, Alan	117	10	Rathbone, Graham	35	1	Pugh, Daryl	6	0
Thompson, Jimmy	116	1	Mayo, Joe	35	1	Robinson, Terry	6	0
Greenhalgh, Brian	116	0	Seddon, Ian	34	3	Lindsay, Malcolm	6	0
Streete, Floyd	111	14	Morgan, Sammy	34	3	Mardenborough, Steve	6	0
Branagan, Keith	110	0	Osgood, Keith	34	1	Harris, Allan	6	0
Crown, David	106	0	Slack, Mel	33	2	Philiben, John	6	0
Howard, Trevor	105	0	Smith, Kevin	30	8	Cleary, George	5	3
Shinton, Bobby	99	0	McDonough, Roy	30	2	Ryan, John	5	0
Gibbins, Roger	97	3	Gregson, John	30	0	Davies, Ian	5	0
O'Neill, Tommy	96	20	Goldsmith, Martin	28	7	Horwood, Neil	4	10
Beattie, Andy	94	3	Bannister, Jack	28	4	Tong, David	4	2
Collins, John	93	4	Massey, Steve	28	3	Chapple, Phil	4	2
Sinton, Andy	90	3	Rigby, Jon	28	3	Neal, Dean	4	0
Smith, Graham	85	0	White, Jimmy	28	2	Waugh, Keith	4	0
Lyon, Dave	84	1	Cassidy, Bill	27	6	Measures, George	4	0
Turner, Chris	83	7	Baldry, Bill	27	0	Richards, Steve	4	0
Horsfall, Tommy	79	4	Greygoose, Dean	26	0	Ewbanks, Wayne	3	1
Moyes, David	79	0	Schiavi, Mark	24	6	Hollis, Andy	3	1
O'Donnell, John	79	0	Hall, Jim	24	0	Moncur, John	3	1
Foote, Chris	76	10	Leggett, Peter	21	0	Green, Mel	3	0
Bennett, Mike	76	0	Benjamin, Ian	20	4	Walker, Colin	3	0
Kimble, Alan	72	4	Lyons, John	20	1	Murray, John	3	0
Butler, Peter	70	0	Walker, Phil	19	0	Corbin, Kirk	3	0
Howell, Graham	68	3	Scott, Geoff	19	0	Sayer, Andy	2	3
Beck, John	68	2	Nicholls, Ray	18	5	Silvester, Peter	2	2
Key, Richard	65	0	Fuccillo, Lil	18	1	Greaves, Danny	2	2
Clark, Steve	63	1	Leach, Mick	18	1	Ryan, Laurie	2	0
Cooper, Mark	62	8	McKinven, John	18	0	Conway, Paddy	2	0
Cooke, Robbie	62	3	Garner, Bill	17	7	Polycarpou, Andy	1	4
Walton, Ronnie	62	0	Taylor, Alan	17	1	Adams, Steve	1	2
Comfort, Alan	61	2	Conlon, Bryan	17	1	Goble, Steve	1	1
Ross, Bobby	57	8	Mundee, Brian	16	0	Evans, Ian	1	0
Pyle, Steve	56	13	Hardy, Robin	15	2	Casey, Paul	1	0
Lockhart, Keith	55	3	Smith, Dave	15	2	Wainwright, Robin	1	0
Seary, Ray	55	2	Harper, Colin	15	0	Heward, Graeme	1	0
Cozens, John	52	9	Grant, Brian	14	1	Rushbury, Dave	1	0
Cartwright, Les	52	8	Bowker, Keith	12	5	Williams, Dean	1	0
Cassidy, Nigel	52	2	Lawrence, Les	11	2	Binks, Martin	1	0
Buckley, Ian	51	6	Tuddenham, Tony	11	1	Owen, Terry	1	0
Crowe, Mark	51	0	Evans, Doug	11	1	Higginbottom, Andy	1	0
Walker, Dennis	48	8	McPherson, Keith	11	0	Cowling, Jason	0	2
Hansbury, Roger	48	0	Littlejohns, Colin	10	2	Gilder, Carl	0	2
Measham, Ian	46	0	Howell, Ronnie	10	2	Avery Roger	0	1
Clayton, Gary	45	0	McCevoy, Ricky	10	1	Smith, Nigel	0	1
Dowman, Steve	45	0	Bastock, Paul	10	0	Galloway, Steve	0	1

NOTE: Football League statistical information by courtesy of Colin Faiers.

Cambridge United Football League Goalscorers

Name	Goals	Name	Goals
Biley A	74	Walker D	4
Finney T	61	Bull G	3
Spriggs S	57	Conlon B	3
Greenhalgh B	47	Dowman S	3
Crown D	45	Flanagan M	3
Reilly G	36	Garner B	3
Horsfall T	28	Hildersley R	3
Fallon S	27	Howell G	3
Own Goal	26	Leggett P	3
Shinton B	25	Murray J	3
Watson G	24	Seddon I	3
Lill D	22	Smith D	3
Christie D	19	Smith P	3
Smith L	19	Sweetzer G	3
Streete F	19	Turner C	3
Cooper M	17	Beattie A	2
Collins J	16	Benjamin I	2
Hall J	15	Buckley I	2
Cooke R	14	Evans D	2
Mayo J	14	Fuccillo L	2
Ross B	14	Horwood N	2
Cassidy N	13	Kimble A	2
Hollett I	13	Kimble G	2
Philips P	13	McKinven J	2
Sinton A	13	Pointer K	2
Gibbins R	12	Purdie J	2
Harris G	11	Rayment P	2
Lyon D	11	Richards S	2
Massey S	11	Schiavi M	2
Butler P	10	White J	2
Walton R	9	Bowker K	1
Beck J	8	Cartwright L	1
Lockhart K	8	Chapple P	1
O'Donnell J	8	Cowling J	1
O'Neill T	8	Farrington M	1
Pyle S	8	Greaves D	1
Simmons D	8	Gregson J	1
Tully K	8	Griffin K	1
Batson B	6	Guild A	1
Cassidy B	6	Hamilton G	1
Foote C	6	Hardy R	1
Lennard D	6	Howell R	1
Lyons J	6	Leach M	1
Akers V	5	Lindsay M	1
Clayton G	5	Massey K	1
Comfort A	5	Moyes D	1
Eades T	5	Mundee B	1
Goldsmith M	5	McCevoy R	1
Howard T	5	McPherson K	1
McDonough R	5	Nichols R	1
Rigby J	5	Osgood K	1
Cozens J	4	Pugh D	1
Daniels G	4	Robinson M	1
Ferguson M	4	Silvester P	1
Horrey R	4	Stringer D	1
Meldrum C	4	Walker C	1
Morgan S	4	Total	995
Smith K	4	Games	804
Taylor A	4	Average	1.23

NOTE: Football League statistical information by courtesy of Colin Faiers

Autographs/Notes